DAPHNE DE MARNEFFE

Daphne de Marneffe is a psychologist and the author of *Maternal Desire: On Children, Love, and the Inner Life.* In her clinical practice, she offers psychotherapy to couples and individuals. She teaches and lectures widely on marriage, couple therapy, adult development and parenthood. She and her husband have three children and live in the San Francisco Bay Area.

ALSO BY DAPHNE DE MARNEFFE

Maternal Desire: On Children, Love, and the Inner Life

DAPHNE DE MARNEFFE

The Rough Patch

The Art of Living Together

VINTAGE

1 3 5 7 9 10 8 6 4 2

Vintage
20 Vauxhall Bridge Road,
London SW1V 2SA

Vintage is part of the Penguin Random House group of companies whose
addresses can be found at global.penguinrandomhouse.com.

Penguin
Random House
UK

First published by Vintage in 2019
First published in hardback by Harvill Secker in 2018

penguin.co.uk/vintage

A CIP catalogue record for this book is available
from the British Library

ISBN 9781784702632

Printed and bound in Great Britain by Clays Ltd, Elcograf S.p.A.

Penguin Random House is committed to a sustainable future
for our business, our readers and our planet. This book is
made from Forest Stewardship Council® certified paper.

For Terry

Contents

Author's Note

In this book, I illustrate ideas with stories drawn from my experiences as a therapist, teacher, and interviewer. I've changed all names and identifying information to protect the confidentiality of the people who have sought my help and the privacy of those I have interviewed. I hope that readers recognize themselves in these pages, but any resemblance to actual persons is coincidental.

The ideas in the book represent my synthesis of an enormous body of research on couples, emotion, and human development. For the sake of readability, I rarely cite specific studies and authors in the text, but I encourage readers to consult the notes for sources and further information.

The

ROUGH PATCH

1

The Rough Patch: An Introduction

You are forty-three. You have been married twelve years. You didn't marry too young. You had your adventures and your choices. You now have two little girls (ten and seven), or two little boys, or one of each. You were in love when you married. That's what you've always believed, at least, although now sometimes you wonder. You knew you were different from each other, but at the beginning that was fine—it helped you feel stable, or it helped you grow, and it was even exciting, as you noticed how much you wanted to reach out and understand and even indulge each other's differences. Yet now you feel *too* different. Sometimes you drive each other crazy. Or leave each other feeling deeply hurt. Or kind of neutral. Or each of these, at different times.

A lot of advice is out there to help you deal with the problem. Social scientists tell you that people are happier at sixty-five than forty-five, so if you wait it out another twenty years, you might feel better. The couple specialists, the work-family balance people, the sex and intimacy experts, all have something to say that almost fits. But somehow they don't get at the crux of the problem. The crux is that you feel lost, or lonely, or at times almost blindingly miserable. Sometimes you feel you can't breathe. It's true that you're exhausted at work, or your mother's ill, or your hormones are out of whack. But it's hard to believe that that's the whole story. You didn't always feel this stuck in your relationship. There was a time when the marriage made sense.

What changed? And why? Perhaps you felt fine about your marriage, until you surprised yourself by becoming infatuated with someone else. Or maybe you were absorbed by the care of your kids when they were small and didn't give much thought to your personal satisfaction. But now your older daughter/son spends time texting her/his friends (how did that happen so quickly?) and doesn't seem interested in being around you on the weekends. Even if the child-centered marriage didn't foster much passion, at least it provided a meaningful framework. Now things are shifting. What felt tolerable before doesn't anymore. You are left wondering, where am I in all this? Who have I become?

It's not quite fair, but you can't help blaming your partner for how dissatisfied you sometimes feel. It's hard to imagine putting up with her/his workaholism/drama/withdrawal/insensitivity for another few decades. Yet you know feeling this way is wrong somehow. Marriage takes work. Immature people think relationships should be easy or fun; selfish people leave when the going gets rough. You've always been a good worker; you're great at work. But it's not clear what you are working for. Deep down, you aren't sure things can change. And the truth (shameful and hard to utter) is that sometimes you feel you're not sure you *want* things to change anymore. You don't want to have to work so hard for whatever incremental satisfactions you might gain. Occasionally you feel a whiff of freedom, and it is shockingly exhilarating. You feel guilty about it, but on the other hand, you are still youngish. You deserve to have some intimacy and passion and real connection in your life. You won't have your energy or looks forever. How long is it reasonable to go on like this?

But you don't want to make any destructive decisions. That's the path your sister/uncle/best friend took, and look where it left them. The kids, let's face it, suffered. Shuttling back and forth between houses, forced to witness their parents' heartaches at way too close a range, and no money saved for college. And the adults imported their same old problems into the next relationship. Lately, though, you find yourself calling to mind the success stories: the kids who seem to have emerged unscathed, and the parents who seem so much happier, like new people. Still, you don't want to divorce. It would be easier, better, if you could find a way not to be so unhappy in your marriage. Or maybe not to be so unhappy, period.

THE ROUGH PATCH. "Lonely." "Confused." "Stuck." "Stirred up." "Going through the motions." "Falling apart." I see a hitting-the-wall unhappiness in the middle slice of life, when people struggle, alone or in pairs, to figure out why their marriages don't feel right. In my work as a therapist, I am reminded every day of people's conundrums:

- Is my problem that I need to find a way to resuscitate some loving feeling toward my partner? Or is it my own harsh insistence that I shouldn't give up?
- I know I should *think* about my predicament, but I'm so sick of thinking. I just want to *feel* for a change.
- I know my infatuation with my coworker is a "fantasy," but why does it feel like the most real thing in my life?
- Reminding myself how grateful I should be for what I have just makes me feel worse.
- Can I, or should I, spend the rest of my life with minimal affection or sex?
- Can I, or should I, keep living with my partner's substance use/ spending habit/mental illness?
- My partner is withdrawing from me but I don't know if I can, or want to, change in the ways (s)he wants me to.
- If my greatest goal is to give my children a happy childhood, how can I do that if I am unhappy in my marriage? Yet what if trying to find more happiness for myself comes at the expense of theirs?

People who seek my help often feel they are caught between what they *should do* and what they *feel*. When I spoke with Lisa, a professional, she had just turned forty-seven, and she struggled with the sound of it. "I never felt middle-aged. Then I turned forty-seven. It's a number that sticks in my mind. Forty-seven is a big deal. Fifty is a big deal." Why? "I feel like I should have figured it out by fifty."

She hadn't figured it out; she felt more confused than ever. Feeling exhausted from work, parenthood, and family life, and alienated from her husband of fifteen years, she found herself acting entirely against her values, embarking on an affair with a younger man. "I was shocked to be with someone I was excited about—texting and calling someone I can communicate with, without the burden of all the family stuff. My physical relationship with my husband is dismal, and I sort of chalked it up to the inevitable effect of aging. What's funny is this guy reminds me of my husband—smart, professional—but ten years younger. Now I've really become a middle-aged cliché: almost fifty, in a rut in my marriage, finding someone young and exciting . . ."

I am struck by how often people try to dismiss their marital distress as "cliché," embarrassed to have fallen prey to the "midlife crisis," a construct toward which they felt, until recently, comfortably disparaging. We're voyeuristically critical toward middle-age flameouts—"She's divorcing him and marrying their tenant!" "He ran off with a lap dancer and now he's bringing her to the kids' soccer games!"—partly to protect ourselves. We feel vulnerable to life's surprises and attempt to fortify ourselves through the communal conviction that people should be more grown-up. Finding ourselves susceptible to feelings that we so recently judged as selfish or immature in others is a rude awakening, especially destabilizing when we felt, not so long ago, pretty confident and successful about our choices.

But humbled as we are by our lack of originality, we may privately feel something momentous is happening. We feel we are waking out of a stupor, and that we can't bear to go back and re-anesthetize ourselves. Perhaps we had a strange sort of relief in plunging into the childrearing years, when our own desires were back-burnered. Serving our children's needs allowed us to take a break from wanting things for ourselves, and all the complicated dilemmas it engendered. But somewhere inside we knew this wasn't a tenable long-term solution. Kids grow up. Statistically, we may be looking at another forty years of life. Unlike in the 1950s, it's no longer realistic to wait for our two-pack-a-day habit to kill us at sixty-two. It's obvious we can't keep swallowing the vague adage that "marriage is compromise," if compromise means suppressing whole swaths of our personalities. Life is too long, and too short. We have to find some way to stay vital, engaged, desiring, and *ourselves* while being married, if married is what we want to be.

When we trivialize the rough patch as a "middle-aged cliché," we are actually trying to find a way to disarm the intensity of the forces we are grappling with. We hope that if we can distance ourselves from others' crises or minimize our own, we might escape their disruptiveness. But something important and meaningful is occurring in the rough patch—even if we don't yet know exactly *what* that meaningful or important thing *is*. We don't call it a cliché when a two-year-old starts saying no, or when a teenager starts experimenting with sex; we consider these to be common expressions of what it *means* to be a two-year-old or a teenager. Both the toddler and the teenager are trying to grow, to become more complex and whole—the toddler's task is striving for autonomy, the teenager's is figuring out how to be a sexual person. Though the tasks are different, the challenges of the rough patch are in some sense the same. Like the toddler and the teenager, we are looking to discover and fully express who we are, while staying connected to others. We want to take risks and feel secure. We want autonomy and connectedness in optimal balance. These are *completely valid goals* at any age. We have every right, and even a responsibility, to pursue them. So what makes the rough patch so *rough*?

THE MIDPOINT OF life represents the moment of *maximal conflict* between our drive to seek external solutions to our emotional dilemmas and our recognition that, ultimately, they don't work. In the rough patch we are forced to realize, often against our will, that the life-building activities of youth—job, relationship, children, house—have not taken care of what's unresolved within. We still yearn—for what we're not sure—and what we've achieved doesn't entirely fill us.

But it's not only that external achievements have not taken care of internal problems. It's that we've begun to take a more complicated view of ourselves. By virtue of experience, we *know* more, and this unsettles us from three directions.

First, we know more now about time and loss. Our own eventual mortality is becoming less of an abstraction and more of a fact. We've almost inevitably suffered some disappointments and setbacks along the way. The spiritual wisdom of the ages is starting to make visceral sense. No person, job, or acquisition, no matter how wonderful, can ever entirely fill our sense of incompleteness. We even begin to sense that those who "have everything" are in exactly the same boat.

Second, the passage of time gives a new urgency and poignancy to the state of our intimate relationships. This is our *life*. Can this relationship last for the next four decades? Is now the time to reckon with that question? We may begin to feel tendrils of doubt, the upwelling of inconvenient longings and needs, an uneasy sense that suppression or chronic discord will not be sustainable. We may encounter dread, fear, and a desire to escape through work, or screens, or drink. We're dimly aware we may have to lose in order to gain, that painful upheavals may be the cost of emotional growth or inner peace. Oscillating between what is and what could be, between reality and possibility, between embracing and relinquishing, we feel disoriented and confused.

When things feel bad, two options may loom up in our minds: *endure* (for the children, the shared history, the finances, the stability, the vow) or *strive* (for something more, another chance, a better relationship). Surrender or escape. Give in or start over. Depressive resignation or manic flight. These occur to us largely because it's not at all clear where else to go. But the thought that soon follows is that we want to be honest, and we ask ourselves, what is the line between seizing vitality and manically defending against decline? What's the difference between "settling" and acceptance? How might the effort to have more in our lives unwittingly result in less? When does accepting limits help us to make the most of what we have, and when does it signal premature resignation? Our dawning awareness of life's limits means we know that we've reached the point where dismantling what we have and starting something new does not come cheap. We know there's really no such thing as "starting over," only starting something different and trailing the inevitable complications in our wake. The acting out we see around us, which till now we've casually dismissed, begins to looks like one way that people try to combat the stasis of depression with the action of escape, attempting to transcend (at least temporarily) the "hitting a wall" feeling that this life stage can induce.

Finally, as time presses in, we inevitably confront questions of value. What are our values about marriage? What might it mean to stay or to go? "An open secret in our world is that we do not know what legitimizes either divorce or marriage," wrote the philosopher Stanley Cavell. Deep down, many of us don't know where we stand on marriage. Sociologists find that people absorb highly contradictory cultural messages and hold stunningly inconsistent romantic narratives within themselves. We believe, for example, *both* that couples should stay together for the children *and* be free to pursue their own happiness. We maintain that relationships that begin with exciting strong attraction are simultaneously highly desirable and likely to be "unrealistic." We espouse the romantic worldview that marriage derives meaning from the unique specialness of our mates, their status as "one and only." Yet we endorse the more functionalist ethos that life is long and people "grow apart," and that different people may be better partners at different stages of life. We're constantly trying to strike a psychic balance between the ideals of freedom and domestic life. If we are even moderately self-aware, we know enough to be suspicious of the ways our longed-for romantic and sexual experiences conform so predictably to scripts handed to us by Hollywood and advertising. But unless we can nest a sexually or romantically compelling element within our long-term relationship, we fear we won't make it through the decades that yawn before us.

Trying to ground our marital values in universal principles seems next to impossible. Not many rules are left. The rules that remain are all pretty much self-assigned, and this seems true even among those who strain to obey a higher law. Studies indicate that people on the religious right divorce *more* often than other people, not less. Orthodox communities that insist on the sanctity of marriage vows often have benighted views of women's rights and purvey an oppressive model of marriage. Instead of shared social values or universal principles, the most robust determinants of whether people get married and stay married are money and education. Demographic research over the past two decades demonstrates that people who command more economic resources and education marry and stay married at higher rates than do people with fewer resources. Greater resources not only correlate with fewer divorces; they allow for more choices in living arrangements. But regardless of their position on the economic spectrum, increasing numbers of people view the goal of long-term monogamy as separate from the goal of being a good parent.

Still, for many of us, our qualms about divorce relate directly to our children—their feelings and their growth into loved and loving adults. Couples often feel that children are the most compelling reason to revitalize a marital bond. The psychoanalyst Wilfred Bion wrote, "There is absolutely no substitute for parents who have a loving relation with each other. No amount of talk or theory is going to take the place of parents who love each other." Where children are concerned, parents sharing a loving bond comes close to an absolute good. But parents sometimes feel they don't have a loving bond. People want to stay married for the children, but *also* because they have a loving relationship.

On the values questions about marriage and divorce, the culture at large doesn't offer much guidance. For one thing, it keeps throwing us back on youthful preoccupations and sows panic about "giving up" on "our potential." The market's desire-stoking engines promote the mirage that there's nothing about our dispiriting situation that we can't buy, or trade in, or surgically alter our way out of. For another, the culture continues to play the seductive refrain that romantic passion is the preeminent conduit to personal renewal. Even if you entertain the idea that long-term monogamy *could* be an enduring vessel for romantic love, you will face countless reminders that new love is essential to life, and its monomaniacal focus is a state to be prolonged and nurtured. Its attenuation signals not the bittersweet end of an era, but a sign that a relationship is static, dead, and in need of correction. At minimum, it demands the purchase of candles, massages, and getaway hotel packages.

I am an enthusiastic proponent of psychotherapy, but aspects of therapy culture can encourage the tendency to scrutinize our love relationships and find they come up short. To get through the rough patch you may have to enlarge your perspective and expand your focus beyond your marriage's minute emotional ebb and flow, but such outward focus arouses therapeutic suspicion that you are "not taking care of your marriage" or "not being emotionally present." Consumerism urges us to look at the small details and slice them as thin as possible (how else are we going to be convinced we need the next iPhone?), and this mentality can seep into our view of relationships, encouraging us to focus on tiny details and amplify pockets of discontent. Where does an admirable attention to personal growth end and a "more-different-better" mind-set begin? It's a fine line we can't always detect, and the cultural surround encourages us to blur it.

Glowing youth. Passionate sex. Romantic love. All great things. I'd say they are among some of the very best things. But that's different from saying that the only way through the rough patch, to a sense of renewed vitality or purpose, is to somehow double down on our preoccupation with them. With that kind of striving, people too often end up in misdirected solutions, relational or otherwise, that can only temporarily relieve their desolation. The reality that life is lived in one direction means that things we might have had in concrete form at earlier points in life—youthful beauty, our high school sweetheart, Herculean sexual stamina—become increasingly costly and delusional to pursue. As time passes, the stakes of not squarely facing the reality of loss, of relinquishing what you can't actually have, *get higher*. We have to develop and refine other capacities, *inner* capacities, if we want the second half of life to go well.

Of course, living in America at this cultural moment means not always knowing what constitutes a realistic acceptance of limits. Our cultural heroes are guys who hang out in their dorm rooms fooling around on their computers, until, at twenty-six, they become internet billionaires. Teenagers inhale the daily doings of suddenly world-renowned YouTube personalities, aspiring to their instantaneous and magical reach, while their parents look on with mystified boredom. We all now live with prosthetic minds called smartphones that extend our communication and knowledge exponentially, while colonizing our consciousness in as-yet incomprehensible ways. Seventy-year-olds can look fifty, through good health or body modification, and the "longevity dividend"—the twenty to thirty more years than our grandparents had—means that a whole life phase is only now being truly charted.

Yet even as we extend the boundaries of the possible to previously unimaginable limits, we live in bodies that die, and most of us believe we have only one life on this earth. If this leads some of us toward a "seize the day" impulse to escape marital malaise, it leads many others back toward their marriages in hopes of making them more fulfilling. If these people turn to self-help, they may encounter the secular religion of health, where research findings suggest that it's worth staying married as protection against heart-attack risk. When in doubt, these writings seem to imply, we should think of marriage as part of a fitness routine, even if couching it as a good workout rather than the marriage of true minds lacks for a bit of inspirational grandeur. More psychologically oriented are the studies of happiness, which document that changing some key habits—setting goals, practicing gratitude, cultivating optimism—can improve our relationships to a surprising degree. Working in the spiritual genre is the raft of latter-day sages who counsel that the ego is a delusion, and detachment holds the key to personal transformation. When we're unhappy in our personal relationships, they suggest, it derives from our limited view of love, namely our attachment to form (i.e., the personal) over formlessness (i.e., infinity and transcendence).

Certainly it's a relief to breathe in the practical, empowering spirit of positive psychology, which pinpoints the aspects of happiness we can attain through effort and healthy routines. Ironically, though, the well-intentioned messages about the health benefits of long-term relationships, as well as the New Age–inflected spiritual formulas, carry with them an astonishingly simplistic view of the one thing that lies at the beating heart of marriage: our *emotions.*

Our emotions form the core of our sense of meaning. They define and create our central love relationships. It's fine to intone about detaching from the ego, until you admit that the ego is part of the self, and self is grounded in emotions, and emotions happen within a body. Marriage, like parenthood, inevitably and necessarily involves the stubborn reality of the flesh. That's one reason why marriage and parenthood are so hard. When we move from airy abstraction to actual human relationships, we quickly realize that the only route toward wisdom, love, and a sense of aliveness is *through* the sensitive and skillful management of emotion. As the philosopher Immanuel Kant put it, the dove may wish that the air had no resistance so that it could fly higher, yet resistance is the very thing that allows the dove to fly. Likewise, we can't escape our bodies or emotions; we can only discover who we are and how to love from *within* our fleshly human medium.

What most people want from marriage is affection, trust, safety, fun, soothing, encouragement, excitement, and comfort. They want to have companionship and be left alone in all the right ways, neither intruded upon nor abandoned. They want to be seen, accepted, valued, and understood for who they are. *All* of this stands or falls on the quality of emotional sharing and communication. That's why the rough patch inescapably calls us to struggle with our emotions on a whole new level of awareness, and to figure out what they mean for our relationships. This is a profound personal and relational journey. There aren't any shortcuts. Relationships are messy and complicated. No wonder the deceptive simplicity of all the checklists and tweets and seemingly endless reminders that our happiness is under our own control can come to intimidate rather than reassure us.

From the last three decades of psychological research, we know that our minds are formed in relationships. This means not simply that our minds are *concerned* with relationships (which they are), but that relationships shape the ways we process and experience reality. Psychology has made huge strides in mapping the connections between early attachment, emotional development, and adult intimate relationships. Throughout life, our emotions signal what's important, and what's important—at any age—is satisfying relationships. In a real sense, then, marriage picks up where childhood left off. As a close relationship that engages body, heart, and mind, marriage offers a powerful lifelong vehicle for knowing another, being known, and developing our deep emotional life.

Overall, research finds that the most important factors in whether our relationships are satisfying all have to do with emotions: how we tune into our emotions, experience them, manage them, communicate about them, calm them enough to respond to others, and align them with our behavior and goals. Throughout this book, I will sum up the key capacities of healthy emotional relating as *curiosity, compassion*, and *control*. When we're curious, we are open to trying to understand our own and the other's truth. When we're compassionate, we feel empathy for our own and the other's struggles. When we exert self-control, we contain and communicate our emotional responses to others in ways that are accurate, sensitive, and likely to get heard. The triad of curiosity, compassion, and (self-)control takes us toward a sense of personal agency, and away from holding our partner responsible for our own feelings. It helps us build the inner capacities we need to reckon well with the rough patch.

Finding a way to be happy in marriage depends on our ability to exercise emotional skill, flexibility, and resilience. But it also depends on something else: our ability to value both the needs of the individual partners and the needs of the marriage. Rough-patch breakdown often occurs when people lose track of one side or the other. Sometimes, they've conceptualized marriage as demanding a suppression of individuality, and they reach a point when that solution is no longer sustainable. Or, they find themselves only able to advocate for their own needs, in a sort of zero-sum survival strategy, without being able to hold on to a vision of the marriage as a resource for comfort and excitement, stability and growth. Throughout life, we continually learn about ourselves through pressing up against the personalities of others. Ideally, we don't simply react, but use our interactions with others to increase our self-awareness. The result is greater self-definition, which leads to the possibility of more authentic connection. This recurrent back-and-forth of relating to self and other is the engine of adult development, as well as the engine of growth in marriage. If the emotional interactions are basically healthy, we gradually become more self-realized as individuals and more deeply relational as partners.

But marriage itself, not to mention the romantic ideology that surrounds it, so easily tends to produce misunderstanding about who's responsible for whose emotions. It's almost as if the ideal of passionate fusion that we welcomed so blissfully at the outset returns, like a swamp monster, in the form of chronic confusion about who's doing what to whom. As time goes on, if people don't step up to the challenge of communicating in an emotionally healthy way, they fall into the trap of thinking that individual and couple needs are doomed to conflict. They now imagine there's no way around the unshakable reality of competing agendas. In both cases, people overlook that their way of handling their *own* emotions powerfully influences the very ways they conceive of, and participate in, marriage. Throughout these pages, we will be looking closely at the individual—not only because it receives short shrift in writings on couples, but because, paradoxically, individual development represents one of the most potent paths to marital happiness.

Since marriage presents one challenge after another, we need to bring our best resources, as individuals and as a couple, to solve them. Three of the biggest challenges—children, sex, and work—pervade the emotional climate of marriage, and accordingly, they thread through every chapter of this book. More specific challenges, such as money or aging, are addressed in individual chapters. I hope that couples will read this book together, or at least sequentially. I also hope that each reader will embrace the opportunity to focus on three questions: Who do I want to be as an individual? Who do I want to be as a partner? And how do the two fit together?

My goal is to create more breathing room around these questions. In a broad sense, I believe that the vast and troubling energies of the rough patch will have been harnessed for good if they contribute to personal progress on the following fronts:

- Becoming a more loving person. Really. By this I don't mean going on loving-kindness retreats that are stealth missions to indulge a crush on your meditation teacher, but rather engaging full heartedly in becoming more kind and compassionate, toward others *and* yourself.
- Seeing your partner's perspectives and experience as equal in importance to your own. This means recognizing narcissism for what it is (it's not just you, we *all* have it). Relating to others as genuine people, rather than need satisfiers or projections of your own psyche, is a lifelong effort, never complete.
- Expressing emotion skillfully rather than simply emoting. Marriage offers a ready-made dumping ground for our bad moods and tendency to blame and judge. Taking responsibility for how you express yourself, and repairing after negative interactions, pave the way for closeness.
- Developing a nuanced relationship to your fantasy life. That means cultivating awareness that actions and thoughts aren't the same thing, building confidence in the difference between them, and using your imagination and fantasy life as a source of creativity rather than for numbing out and escapism.
- Discovering the need for committed living, where a value higher that your own emotional weather prevails. In adulthood, a sense of purpose and meaning derives from the dual psychological movements toward *deepening inward* and *expanding outward*. We in the rough patch need to use the fuel of waning youth and the whisper of mortality to vitalize and intensify our self-awareness, love for others, and our engagement with the world.

ONE OF MY guiding assumptions as a therapist is that you shouldn't stay in a marriage if there's no hope for it to become a secure, loving relationship. Another guiding assumption is that staying in a marriage, even if it is difficult, can be one of the most effective ways of developing a secure, loving relationship. Anyone can decide that being married to one's partner is not the way one wants to pursue an intimate life. But people can undertake that decision under pressures that they don't understand. They feel pushed, pulled, and not free to flexibly choose. For many of the people who seek my help, I believe that working through the problems in their marriage is a more direct and ultimately satisfying route to a secure, loving bond than leaving.

In all my talk of the responsibility of the individual in marriage, I might be mistaken for endorsing two common ideas. The first is that the duty of a mature adult (especially one with children) is to *suck it up*. So what if you are unhappy? Distract yourself. The second is that *marriage takes work*, a position that consigns me, in some people's minds, to the camp of puritanical libido-killers who advocate a work ethic for everything from sex to fine dining ("Are you still *working* on your prime rib?").

As to the first, I believe that the things we feel are lacking in the rough patch are all good things to want and to strive for: a sense of aliveness, the flexibility to change, the desire to feel, to love and be loved. We should not give up on the goal of having them in our intimate relationship. But we should also think about those goals more broadly—not only in terms of our marriage, but also in terms of the opportunity the rough patch presents for taking responsibility for, and recommitting to, who one is. The challenge of the rough patch is not only to discover whether it is possible to find a way to be happy with one's partner, but is to reckon—yet again—with our relationship to ourselves and to the world.

As to the second, the idea that marriage takes work: if you ask older married people, they'll sometimes say one of their proudest accomplishments is their marriage. They say this because it wasn't always easy, God knows, and because they recognize the marriage for the creative project that it is. But people generally abhor the idea of marriage as work, not only because it reinforces the message that somehow marriage is the death knell for spontaneity, excitement, fun, but also because it depressingly pits our current experi marriage against the very hopes and pleasures that gave rise to it in the first place.

But this interpretation entirely misnames the activity at the center of the enterprise. The "work" involved is not the drudgery of cleaning the bathroom or the mind-numbing repetition of the assembly line. The work is in facing authentic emotion and vulnerability. The work is in the challenge of *opening up*—to being present, to listening, to learning about feelings, to having hard conversations, to facing reality. The work is in having the courage to take risks, and to speak one's truth and listen to the other, in the effort to create an intimate relationship.

When people don't take those risks, they shut down and disengage, and then marriage can't possibly feel like anything but boring and static. They start telling themselves, "I shouldn't have to work this hard." But if it's too depressing to think about working on your relationship, think about working on yourself. Not only is it true that the less you work on yourself, the more effort other people put in to deal with you (have you ever noticed how often people stepping forth to renew themselves leave wreckage for others?). It is also true that making the effort to look within, and to struggle with your own demons, repays you in more fulfilling relationships.

The rough patch offers the possibility to become a more integrated person. I don't think there's any way around the fact that wrestling with the conflicts that arise is a psychological journey of self-understanding that can take every ounce of your fortitude. It entails holding in tension both the intense reality of what you are going through, and the ability to take some distance from it. The challenge is to arrive at an understanding of your life that is self-compassionate but not self-serving, satisfying but also true.

People are so often caught feeling that their situation is both impossibly complicated and insufferably trite. Simply *knowing more* about the titanic forces with which we all grapple, in midlife and marriage, can help us apply more compassion and less judgment toward ourselves and others, and to exercise more patience and wisdom in discerning our individual path. As will be obvious, I am not in the business of keeping fatally flawed marriages together. Certain marriages should end. Rather, I am interested in the states of mind that beset people in the rough patch, and what they can teach us about living the rest of our lives with verve, creativity, and commitment. The rough patch, for all its pain and bewilderment, presents an opportunity—to know ourselves, to expand our scope, to grow, and to grow up.

A Brief History of the Midlife Crisis

Once upon a time, people didn't have midlife crises. But by the 1960s, a combination of demographic trends, cultural messages, and academic research conspired to create the idea. Just as social conditions fostered the invention of "childhood" in the 1600s and "adolescence" in the early 1900s, it is no coincidence that the stage of "midlife" began to capture the public imagination in the mid-twentieth century. White men's life expectancy in 1900 hovered around forty-six; by 1970 it was sixty-seven. "Lifespan development" began to make sense as a field because people had more of a life span to study. The psychologist Erik Erikson, whose classic opus, *Childhood and Society*, appeared in 1950, demarcated a series of adult stages that formed the guiding popular framework for decades. Young adults grappled with "intimacy versus isolation." People in midlife faced the challenge of "generativity versus stagnation." Old people's acceptance of a life well lived, or disappointment at having failed, was captured by "integrity versus despair."

In a 1965 article cheerfully entitled "Death and the Midlife Crisis," the psychoanalyst Elliott Jaques coined a term for the malaise of middle age. Midlife development germinated in Erikson's model, but it reached full flower in the big longitudinal studies of the 1960s and 1970s based at Harvard, UCLA, and Yale. George Vaillant, Roger Gould, and Daniel Levinson—the latter's work would be popularized by Gail Sheehy's *Passages*—each set out a theory of the tasks of a successful (male) adulthood. Two interwoven social shifts lent urgency to the 1960s model of the midlife crisis as a crucial opportunity for new beginnings. First, there was the birth control pill, which revolutionized adult sexual life. Second, there was the sexually experimental youth culture of the baby boom generation, which made some who had contracted a pre-1967 marriage feel that they had missed the boat. Between 1966 and 1979, the American divorce rate doubled. The view of the midlife crisis that emerged bore the massive imprint of a 1960s liberationist sexual ethos and an optimistic faith that the existential "crisis" of midlife could be addressed and solved through a renewed quest for sexual passion and romantic fulfillment.

The pioneers of lifespan development contributed the crucial insight that we keep *developing* throughout adulthood. But true to their time, their writings skewed both individualistic and male. Not only were the effects of late twentieth-century feminism yet to be fully felt, but the prevailing models of psychological health were unenlightened about the emotional processes *between* people that enhance or damage intimate relationships. The marriages represented in these writings rarely feel as if they involve two actual people navigating a relationship. Rather, the genre typically called for a "hero," the protagonist at the center of the drama, whose journey was paramount. Perhaps one reason that the notion of the midlife crisis has lent itself to so much derision over the years ("red sports cars," "younger wives") is that at its very genesis the concept failed to disentangle authentic soul-searching from narcissistic self-justification.

In his influential 1978 account of male adult development, *The Seasons of a Man's Life*, Daniel Levinson tracks the life of "Jim Tracy," whose story unwittingly offers as good an example as any of the self-absorption that came to be baked into the developmental theory itself. After graduating from the Naval Academy, we are told, Jim marries Victoria because he's "lonely as hell," but he quickly concludes she is "kind of cold, semifrigid, a slob, and a poor housekeeper." Years of casual affairs and career building ensue, followed by an affair with Joan, "a special woman who would help him pull his life together, enrich it, and give expression to his hopes and dreams." Scarcely five years into his divorce and new marriage, however, Jim bemoans Joan's drastic change from an "attractive twenty-eight-year-old newlywed" to a dependent and self-restricted "hausfrau," who evokes "his concern about her growth as a person." Jim Tracy, Levinson solemnly reports, is "learning to accept her limitations."

Reading the account of Jim's trajectory, it's hard not to infer that Joan's deterioration relates to Jim's expectation, proofed in the yeast of his egotism and leavened by sexist culture, that Joan's life should utterly revolve around his. After his daughter's unplanned pregnancy and his son's suicide attempt, Joan's distress over his chaotic family situation almost tears the marriage apart. But far from catalyzing a painful confrontation with his own woeful distraction as a father, Jim instead reassesses Joan and finds her even more limited than he thought; indeed, "her withdrawal" from his children "undermine[s] his formerly idealized view of her."

Perhaps we might expect a 1960s munitions executive such as Jim Tracy to be myopic and culture-bound about his own part in turning his womenfolk into depressed, diminished people. But we don't expect as erudite and humanistic a guide as Levinson to agree with Jim's assessment. Yet here is how Levinson ruefully concludes:

> Tracy began doing things [Joan's] way, restricting his life to please her. He turned down invitations to be with other men and gave up activities that meant much to him. He sold his boat, built a swimming pool, worked in the garden and fixed up their house. . . . To please Joan, he chose to restrict his vision and his existence. He tried in his own way, to have as "peaceful" and "stable" a family life as possible. But the costs were great.

The blame for Joan's frustrated dreams, Levinson seems to suggest, rested squarely on her own "problems and frailties." By contrast, he treats Jim's "choice to restrict his vision and his existence" to "please Joan" as a weighty imposition. We might wonder whether *it was about time* that Jim reined in his sense of entitlement. Maybe he finally realized that relationships include caring about another person's desires and goals. Joan may have become more contented not only because Jim "sold his boat" or "built a swimming pool," but because she felt that Jim had, in some recess of his being, stopped feeling fine about designing his life solely around himself.

Today, despite Levinson's gravitas as a scholar of adult development, his account of Jim Tracy reads as a form of outrageous prefeminist benightedness, a *Mad Men*–style relic from a time when men thoughtlessly claimed center stage. Yet at the start of the twenty-first century, remarkably similar ideas were repackaged, this time by women for women. And far from critiquing the self-absorption that clung to the male account, these writers co-opted it, hailing women's midlife crises as "feminist" acts.

When Gail Sheehy launched the romantic genre of adult development in her 1976 book *Passages*, she intended to inspire hope in a brighter future and a world of possibilities. Midlife development meant slaying our dragons, the most formidable of which was "the inner custodian," a "nasty tyrant" first personified by our demanding parents. Sheehy starkly divided our dreams, passions, and impulses from our inhibitions, conscience, and inner taskmaster. This division cast the midlife crisis as a clear-cut fight between Good (the desires and dreams of our "true self") and Evil (the rules and inhibitions of the "inner custodian"). Difficult as it may be, "whatever counterfeit safety we hold from overinvestments in people and institutions must be given up." Indeed, we are heroic when we let go of attachments that we've outgrown. In *Sex and the Seasoned Woman*, Sheehy's "other," the one from whom we need to wrest our freedom, is often as not portrayed as a demanding husband or time-intensive children.

Sue Shellenbarger took these same precepts to even greater extremes in her midlife manifesto, *The Breaking Point*. There we meet Anna, seemingly plucked from a bad romance novel: "Alone with a man twenty years younger, relaxing by a lake under a starlit summer sky . . . she never expected to hear again what she is hearing from the virile, muscular man across from her—that she is sexually attractive. She did not expect to feel what she is feeling—romantic, excited, eager." Anna's midlife trials begin with mundane burdens anyone might relate to: the repetitive job, the false ingratiation with her boss, the husband on the couch "clicking the remote" (the quintessential signifier of deathly marital boredom). Plotting Anna's tale as a romantic adventure, Shellenbarger's first order of business is for Anna to rescue her true self from beneath a pile of meaningless crap.

What happens next incites our sympathy for the imagined person of Anna, if not her slapdash fictionalized character. She shows signs of an emotional and spiritual crisis, careening "from euphoria to black despair." We worry she might be clinically depressed, even taking self-destructive risks. Shellenbarger appears intent on penning a tale of liberation, yet even she seems confused about her mission. Observing that midlife crises are often preceded by months of "an emotional deadness that set[s] in like smog," she follows up with this ambiguous pronouncement: "With the darkness came the growing conviction that suppressing deep dreams and desires was no longer worth the sacrifice. Old values and standards of behavior began falling away."

"Suppressing deep dreams and desires" sounds bad, for sure. Midlife is supposed to be about reclaiming these dreams, right? But, if Anna's "growing conviction" comes out of "the darkness," doesn't that suggest that the mood of despair is messing with her judgment? If you find your energy waning and your hope fading and your self-esteem plummeting, you may well also be prone to thinking, "I don't care anymore about my old values and standards of behavior." *You're depressed*. This may lead you to stay in bed and not wash your hair. Or it may lead you to look for any available source of energy to keep your connection to life, even some that your nondepressed self wouldn't approve of. In the face of breakdown, we grasp at anything as a survival strategy.

But Shellenbarger wants to turn this desperate move into a form of healthy self-assertion, a woman-power refusal to put up with anyone or anything that frustrates us. Indeed, she goes so far as to install "frustrations" as the prime mover and intuitive guide as to whether your life needs a complete overhaul. "The frustrations that erupt," she declares, "are as diverse as the women themselves. A look, a passing touch, a solitary sexual dream reignite a passion for intimacy. A forgotten yen to see the Himalayas at sunset bursts forth into a full-blown resolve. A thirst to do new, more meaningful work takes center stage, causing a woman to jettison her hard-won career of thirty years."

We are not talking about *frustrations* here. We are talking about a full-blown taxonomy of manic flight. Yet the term *frustrations*, we come to realize, doesn't refer to frustrations per se. It's an elastic term for any noxious emotion that a midlife woman can't or doesn't want to try to think about or evaluate. Noting that midlife crises are more common among affluent and educated people, Shellenbarger approvingly suggests that money and education "create a sense of entitlement and a more activist stance in expressing personal frustration." Judging from this statement, it would seem that money and a sense of entitlement also expose us to the serious, and delusional, risk of believing that "expressing personal frustration" is a form of activism.

We've come full circle to Jim Tracy, and his problems decentering from his own experience long enough to recognize another person. In 1978, Tracy's behavior was justified as a man's need to follow his dream. By the turn of the century, a midlife woman's putting herself first was celebrated and affirmed as an act of liberation. In both scenarios, midlife disgruntlement in the ordinary world gives way to a call to adventure, and the hero sets out, crossing the threshold and facing trials. The structure of the story guarantees that the "little people" remain secondary. The individualistic tilt of the heroic genre of midlife development utterly erases the dynamic nature of relationships, the cycle of interaction that Jim and Joan Tracy, or Anna and her husband, undoubtedly created together.

This individualistic tilt obviously minimizes the dynamic effect of two people on each other. But it also casts the individual's feelings in overly simplistic terms. "To continue to grow as a human being," Shellenbarger writes, "a woman has no choice but to make whatever journey is necessary to rekindle her inner passions." Worlds of meaning and complexity lie within the phrases "no choice" and "whatever journey." Figuring out *why* we feel we have "no choice," or *why* we feel driven to take "whatever journey," or *how* we are conceptualizing "to grow as a human being" are the starting points, not the end points, for making meaning of midlife emotional turbulence.

If we accept that midlife development involves the dual psychological challenges of *deepening inward* and *expanding outward*, then the personae of Jim Tracy and Anna don't work, even as narrative devices. Deepening inward is not solely about excavating suppressed feelings and expressing them. It's not simply about throwing off the shackles of outward roles or the "inner custodian." It is about coming to a new, more satisfying relationship between conflicting desires and goals. Our desires, our conscience, and everything in between—they are all *our own*. We each struggle to reconcile our own conflicts in a livable way. Stories that off-load responsibility—Jim's first wife is a semifrigid slob, after all, and Anna's husband is a couch potato—encourage a self-serving tendency to attribute the "problem" to others and reserve the "solution" for ourselves.

Especially for women, it's appealing and inspirational to hear a clarion voice calling for our right to self-actualization, given the millennia of female oppression. Until shockingly recently, and even still today, the relation of the sexes has reliably meant the silencing of female identity, desire, and goals. Even in the precincts of enlightenment and privilege, women often feel that we've handed over our entire minds to caring for others. We understandably feel put-upon, deprived, and resentful. Scholars provide ample evidence of the costs of workplace bias, and the corrosive effects on relationships of gendered divisions of labor. Getting in touch with our anger is a first step to positive change. But our challenge is to work toward solving the problems in the actual relationships in front of us. We reclaim genuine space for our identities not by rushing headlong into simplistic remedies, but by engaging in the less glamorous spadework of paying attention to our feelings, clarifying what matters to us, asserting our point of view, and negotiating for change. There are valid and healthy reasons women leave their marriages; a quarter of women cite drugs and alcohol, and over a third cite emotional abuse. But the decision to divorce takes all our faculties, and is not best achieved in the keyed-up mind-set that the "prophets of personal invention" tend to adopt.

Fortunately, adult development researchers provide a more complex picture of our midlife drive to deepen inward, to move beyond the conventional and conforming roles we took on in early adulthood. The psychologist Gisela Labouvie-Vief studies the life course and has identified a midlife tendency she calls the "de-repression of emotions." As young adults, we may be eager to adopt the standards and customs we associate with adulthood, but as life progresses, we become less interested in conformity, and more interested in change and transformation. Still, "de-repression" isn't all about cutting loose. It's a much more complex process, in which people begin to revisit their emotional life and history in new ways. Through self-reflection, people become more fully aware of the "self and others as truly complex beings" who are "combining, if not reconciling, in themselves many opposing affects in sometimes tragic fashion." Midlife brings on a greater awareness of our *"inner states, in which conflicting feelings may war with one another."* We may feel disturbed and disoriented by the conflict. But dealing with our feelings through a frantic transformation negates the need to come to a new and fuller sense of integration.

Expanding outward, the second aspect of midlife development, is about reaching out for connection in the world. It may include tackling new adventures or pursuing new goals, but it also relates to the idea of generativity that Erikson devised. Sheehy counsels in *Pathfinders* that the midlife journey should cause "a minimum of human damage," but frankly, that's a pretty low bar. The psychologist Dan McAdams conceptualizes generativity as the core of midlife growth, defined as being able to see others as the center of their own worlds, and to care for them as separate beings whose interests and concerns matter as much as our own. Generativity is also rooted in a deepening appreciation of limits and mortality. When we allow the reality of finiteness to penetrate our consciousness, it helps us think about what matters. A generative person imagines a world in which she is no more and strives to create good things that will outlast her.

In this sense, a generative mind-set contrasts with the make-believe realm of "endless possibilities" that characterizes the romantic narrative of midlife.

By these measures, Jim Tracy and Anna are remarkable for their level of self-absorption. We all tend to be self-absorbed in a personal crisis, and self-absorption can be the starting point for an unflinching inventory that leads to meaningful change. But if your "forgotten yen to see the Himalayas" trumps attending to the reality of the people around you, you've pretty much jettisoned the pressing midlife question of how to reconcile your own desires and needs with concern for others. This reconciliation can be a hugely complicated challenge in midlife. Stories that oversimplify the genuine dilemmas we face fail to provide a useful path forward.

IF MIDLIFE DEVELOPMENT involves the de-repression of emotions, it will mean we're sometimes playing with fire, or at least trying to orchestrate a controlled blaze. In the popular imagination, the midlife crisis includes a sense of eruption, of impulsiveness, and of passion overwhelming structure. When we witness such awakenings in real life and at close range, we see them shake people to the core, sometimes leading them to break with their pasts and strike out in new directions. Outside observers have mixed reactions to such moments. They're intrigued, suspicious, jealous, annoyed, anxious, and stirred up by their friends' and acquaintances' immersion in these forms of ecstatic experience. They simultaneously wonder, "What's wrong with her/him?" and "What's wrong with me?"

We may need to open up new parts of ourselves to thrive and grow. But how do we harness the emotional forces involved for good rather than ill? That was the question in my mind when I met Ariel through a mutual acquaintance. She'd heard about my writing and was eager to talk to me about having recently "gone through a transformation." A forty-two-year-old married mother of two elementary-school children, and a clothing designer, Ariel exuded an effortless beauty and calm that momentarily made me want to crawl into her life and take up residence there. Maybe it was because we met on a sparkling day at San Francisco's Alta Plaza Park overlooking the whitewashed city, and she was wearing a gorgeous violet boiled-wool coat. Be that as it may, I soon learned that there was more to her story than initially met the eye.

"My husband, Richard, and I both had struggles growing up," she began. "I had a very critical mother. I was pretty lost in my early twenties. He was constantly striving against his dad's bad opinion, and dealing with addictions in his family and verbal abuse. I'd even say we both went through periods of depression. We both learned the huge importance of working on yourself, and we have a shared passion for staying on top of that.

"When he and I met, we adored each other unconditionally. And we've always believed that shared values are the foundation of a strong marriage. We agree that people always need to develop and grow. What I've always admired about him is that he's always working on himself. We always try to be intentional, especially since we had kids. Having kids has been an amazing opportunity to reflect on who we are, where we came from, and who we want to be. And even though we've had the usual stresses, we both felt it awakened us to a whole new process of growth. It's very healing, trying to do something different with your own kids. We've always seen eye to eye on that."

Ariel conveyed genuine warmth and curiosity, yet I kept noticing how she peppered her speech with "always," as if propelled to express fullness and enthusiasm at every moment. I wondered whether I was detecting a recognizable Bay Area blend of high-strung perfectionism and amplified positivity, or whether it reflected something deeper about her personal struggles.

"About a year ago, I realized it was time to invest in a fuller way in my professional life, since I'd really pulled back when the kids were little." Her tone turned less ebullient. "It caused some stress between Richard and me because I was less available, and I was trying to launch a line of clothing, which is financially risky and required his support. I suggested we start meditating together to deal with the stress, and that helped a lot. Around that time, I became interested in more serious meditation, and in the summer I went on a four-day meditation retreat. I wanted Richard to go too, but he couldn't take the time from work. I totally understood; he's a super-responsible worker, and really good at what he does."

She gazed into the middle distance. "I can't explain what happened at the retreat. But it's fair to say I had a spiritual-awakening experience. I remember I was sitting, meditating, and my body started shaking uncontrollably. Tears literally gushed from my eyes. Then, I started to feel extremely light. I had an enveloping sense of love and compassion. I remember looking around and thinking, 'Is everyone experiencing this? Have you all already been here?'

"When I got home, I felt as if a huge weight had lifted. A lot of baggage just dropped away. I felt extraordinarily clear and grounded. My body felt like a conduit or a vessel. I understood the world beyond my own ego, and its attachments, anxieties, and fears. I had a profound sense of confidence, and a complete lack of self-critical censorship. Everything was flowing in me—I had a sense of calm, perspective, and ease, without getting entangled."

"Wow," I said.

"Yeah, it was amazing." She laughed. "I had a totally newfound sense of life. My mood was revved up, but I had laser focus. For about a month, I was up late into the night writing. Richard thought I was going crazy, and it terrified him. I was more scared that the feeling would go away; and it did, after about a month. I no longer have that same enveloping sense of bliss. But, you know, the insights continue to this day."

"Why do you think your husband was so worried?"

"I think he worried it meant some kind of breakdown, or rift between us. I think he felt that I was talking in abstractions about accepting and embracing him, but that I was going away from him somehow. And I think he worried our paths would get out of sync. I worried a bit about that too, but I was also exhilarated."

"Did *you* feel you were going away from him?"

"I had a huge amount of compassion for him, and for my parents, and for my entire family. I loved his essence and who he was. But he would also try to argue and reason with me about what I was describing, and he'd think I was telling him he was unenlightened or flawed. Those were very painful and difficult conversations. I so wanted him to see that what I was going through was attainable by anyone."

As I walked toward my car after our conversation, two feelings intermingled inside me. I felt drawn into Ariel's compelling world, and momentarily, outside the beam of her radiant light, my life appeared a bit uninspired, a bit charmless. Maybe it was the slant of afternoon light in the trees, but I felt a strange longing to stay within her charismatic orbit and drink in her special insight. Yet I also felt off center, not quite myself, as if I'd temporarily joined her cult of one. Was she describing a purely progressive journey, or was she spinning out? She seemed so sure of the value of what she'd experienced, yet she didn't know what had happened to her. Even her certainty of its benefits vaguely alarmed me. I wondered if maybe I was feeling something like what her husband had felt.

In an individualistic hero narrative of her midlife crisis, Ariel might have realized her husband had become an impediment, traded her boiled-wool coat for some love beads, and ended up living with her meditation teacher in a yurt. Her expansive language carried a trace of the midlife hero's sense of destiny, and there was a note of self-certainty when she said that her husband "needed to grow on a spiritual and emotional level." But I was also struck, in this and our subsequent conversations, by how hard Ariel was trying to use her newfound insights to connect more fully to her husband, children, and community. She genuinely yearned for her husband to share in what she was going through, both to experience it himself and to strengthen their bond.

We come into a marriage at a given point in our development, but like rivers we keep on moving. Unexpected events unfold, we change, and it's not always clear how to adapt. Ariel and Richard were each fearful of what recent events meant for their relationship. They'd both had difficult backgrounds, but were devoted to creating a family more loving than the ones they'd come from. Now, it seemed, Ariel was trying to use her sense of cosmic acceptance to dispel the atmosphere of negativity and criticism she'd experienced as a child. While this was a productive aspiration, in translating it into actionable change with her husband, things got sticky. Ariel was engendering in Richard a feeling of insecurity about their implicit emotional contracts, and even about who she was becoming. Though I wasn't hearing his perspective firsthand, I could imagine that, to him, her strategies felt unmodulated and even a bit grandiose.

In an email after our first talk, Ariel put me in touch with a number of people who had played some role in her recent spiritual search. Before our next conversation, I spoke with her meditation teacher. He was welcoming, thoughtful, and low-key, but I came away more confused than enlightened. He spoke of helpful psychological concepts such as boundaries and self-awareness and choice. But he also talked about past lives and reading auras and energy fields, and the idea that we choose our parents in order to learn certain things in this lifetime. "In a past life," he explained, "maybe something was happening that helps us understand why we chose this life. Maybe we chose these parents to learn x, or y, or z, which we had to learn. The question is, I've had this experience. Why did I create that? I am the creator of the world."

All this made me wonder if Ariel was on the razor's edge between inspiration and unbalanced thinking. I could see that she was trying to be open-minded and flexible, struggling to use her awakening to work against the rigidities and certainties of her perfectionism and internalized critic. People who grow up at the whim of other people's craziness certainly benefit from a practice that reminds them that they have control over their own boundaries and choices. Yet neither I nor Ariel nor her meditation teacher is "the creator of the world."

In ways that science may eventually be able to explain, Ariel's physical release in meditation seemed to trigger a psychological response that put her in contact with a state of profound security and safety—

perhaps a "primitive" state derived from an early developmental period, yet one that translated in the present to feeling connected to the fundamental ground of humanity. Whatever its origins, the experience spurred Ariel to practical action in her current life. She was, for example, applying what she was learning about compassion and mindfulness to being a more patient and contented parent, working to undo the harsh-disciplinarian models she'd been brought up with. She was trying to understand the scientific research that might account for her subjective sense of old emotions and thought patterns being "released." She was also trying to put her sense of interconnectedness to work by giving to her larger community. Through her church, she had spearheaded a citywide clothing-donation drive, and through her fashion-industry connections, she had become part of an active network lobbying for fair-trade, sweatshop-free clothing-manufacture practices. This, all while she was mothering two active children and launching her own line of clothing. (The list was exhausting; I couldn't entirely rule mania out.)

When we met again, I asked more about her marriage: "I am so curious about how you and your husband have worked through the period when you two seemed so out of sync. It sounds as if you've spent a lot of time trying to talk, and yet it still can be so hard to understand each other."

"When he first expressed skepticism about what I was going through, I felt disappointed and sad. It felt like a lost opportunity. I wanted him to share my new reality. We've always had this tension; he's very logical and scientific. He's one of the most disciplined people I know. I've tried to help him see that joy comes from within."

"Did he feel you were pressing too hard?"

"Yes. Everything came to a head around October. I was having headaches, and I was trying a bunch of different therapies. I went to an alternative healer, and when I told Richard, he blew up. He said it was pseudoscience, and there were no data to support it. He even said he was sick of paying for all this stuff, that we should be saving for the kids' college. It shook us up. I was hurt that he brought up the money, it made me feel ashamed and indebted. I remember thinking, 'I feel so full, I don't need to rely on him to fill me up.' But at the same time, I was afraid we might be falling apart. We agreed to give each other space and not discuss our different viewpoints for a while. We both spent more time reaching out to friends."

This period was truly a struggle. They both had to grapple with feeling they hadn't married whom they thought they married. The alignments they'd counted on—their commitment to the children, to self-improvement, to their shared values—now felt stretched and misshapen. They could no longer draw the same automatic pride in their almost-too-perfectly-shared worldview. Both felt a sense of loss that their partner could not fully understand them. There were several months of détente and loneliness.

"We'd leave each other alone for a while, and then we'd try to talk. He said I was irrational, I said he was narrow-minded. He'd get exasperated, and I'd get superior. During that time, I cried and cried, like I haven't cried since I was a kid." She looked sad telling me this, and I felt relieved at the groundedness of it. For the first time in our conversations, I felt that she was fully grappling with the unsettling gains *and* losses of this extraordinary experience. Whatever its meaning, which she would probably never entirely know, it now felt more connected to the full range of her emotions, and to the hard reality of actual relationships.

"What helped the most, I think, is that Richard and I never stopped respecting each other. We felt misunderstood, but we respected each other enough to grant that what the other person was saying mattered. We both tried to see our part. And seeing each other try also made a difference." A strength in Ariel and Richard's relationship was that ultimately they had enough trust to tolerate their separateness, and loneliness, as they sorted out their own feelings. Just as important, they had the capacity to reflect on themselves.

As Ariel gradually integrated her experience into the fabric of her life, she made more room for Richard's. "We see each other more clearly now, not as much through projection. I was acting as if there was a path of growth that he should get on. I can see my hypocrisy now. He rightly pushed back. That's not something you should do to another person. You need to give other people space and not foist your own agenda onto them. You need to embrace your partner, including his flaws, and not be so arrogant to think you don't have flaws yourself. In hindsight, I think maybe we had to grow apart to grow together. My experience was groundbreaking for me personally, but our experience together illuminated where we lacked compassion for each other. I was all wrapped up in compassion, but I wasn't being entirely compassionate with him. Loving the essence of the other person allowed us to pull through this."

PARADOXICAL AS IT might sound, we can learn a great deal about midlife marital difficulty if we backtrack to the phase of marriage when a couple is expecting their first child. For couples, it is a moment filled with both promise and risk. In my clinical practice, it's not unusual for couples to say that their problems began when they had children, and research is unequivocal that the transition to parenthood is a vulnerable time. I teach a class to expectant couples at a local hospital, aimed at helping them stay close as they become first-time parents. Most of the couples sitting in front of me visibly seek closeness with each other. Partners huddle together, the men rub their pregnant wives' feet. They are open, dewy, and tender. They murmur and joke, as if weaving protective cocoons around themselves. Some report hearing friends' cautionary tales about postbaby spousal alienation, looking on in semihorror as their friends' marriages unravel. When I ask them, "What are you most concerned about?," their answers all revolve around the same concerns: "How can we stay connected? How can we communicate so that we stay close? How can we make sure the baby doesn't replace our bond?"

I tell couples that the single most important thing they can do to stay connected is to hold on to the feeling of *wanting* to stay connected. Viewing the sweep from first pregnancy to middle age, I've concluded that the most significant risk of new parenthood is that couples will stop taking their own emotional needs seriously *enough*. They'll let their needs slide, out of the best of intentions, only to realize in midlife that their fuel tanks are empty.

A baby's arrival is a miracle, but it's also an organizing mission, and a couple's allocation of time and resources necessarily shifts. New parents take on the role of caretakers and adjust their couple expectations for the good of the whole. But emotionally, it's a complicated upheaval. Up until now, partners have treated each other as their primary emotional source; they've been *each other's* "baby." Now, they begin to prioritize "necessities" such as parenthood and work over "luxuries," such as tending to themselves and their relationship. It's not simply a matter of more demands on energy and time. It's also about the emotions aroused in coping with limited resources. New parents are still full of their own emotional and physical needs, but they try to take the "adult" approach and "accept" that their feelings should take a backseat. For many couples, this is precisely where the slippery slope to midlife marital disaffection begins. There's little time to process or repair the inevitable miscommunications because the baby must be taken care of, and after all, *we need our sleep*.

Sleep, one of the most coveted resources of this life phase, is also one of the high-stakes battlegrounds for new parents. Beyond having no more lazy Saturday mornings for cuddling and sex, people feel their entire lives have been hijacked by dire levels of sleep deprivation. Like starving people fighting over scraps, couples get down and dirty about who's getting more. In a research study entitled "The Rested Relationship: Sleep Benefits Marital Evaluations," the authors found, unsurprisingly, that "spouses were more satisfied" with their relationship "on days after which they had slept for longer periods of time." In my clinical work with parents of young children, it's clear that a non-negligible portion of hair-trigger reactivity and blame could be alleviated if people got more sleep.

But sadly, it's hard for people to stay clear about how thoroughly their physical depletion is seeping into their emotional discontent.

Physical deprivation merges with the sense of emotional deprivation, creating a negative filter through which partners view each other's actions. People start to feel justified in refusing to do things they know could bring back a sense of warmth and harmony ("I shouldn't have to make the first move"). They focus on their children, their jobs, the laundry. They default to prioritizing their children even when it's at the price of ignoring their spouse.

If both people could *catch* themselves at these critical moments, turn toward their spouse, and seek the closeness they long for, the descent into marital disillusionment could be interrupted. If they could accept and tune into their own and their partner's vulnerable needs and wants, without covering them over with bossing or blaming, the public health impact could be huge. Turning toward each other, no matter how fumbling, draws people closer, especially if they manage to recognize and admit their own role in whatever the problem was and genuinely apologize for causing pain. If they turn toward each other, couples stay in touch with their desire to be close, rather than insidiously start to treat distance as the "new normal" and organize their emotional lives accordingly.

Couples turn away from each other for any number of apparent reasons, but underneath it all, it's usually because they feel misunderstood, unheard, or unable to agree. What are the essential ingredients in satisfying emotional communication? I will spend the next two chapters exploring this question. But to set the stage, a metaphor may help. Perhaps you've heard the adage about marriage "Would you rather be right or happy?" It rings true because we all struggle between two competing mind-sets in relating to our partner. The first I call the seesaw view. In this mind-set, only one person's truth can be valid. In states of high emotion, each person tries to get rid of their bad feelings by attributing them to the other, making themselves "all" right and the other "all" wrong. The second image is that of a ring—and since we're talking about marriage, let's call it a golden ring. Here, partners figuratively stand alongside each other and look together at their shared problem, collaborating rather than competing.

Let's take a minute to imagine how this might work in action. In the seesaw scenario, one partner feels she needs or wants, and she anxiously presses her partner to respond or agree. In the grip of her own emotions, she can't think about him as a separate person, with needs and constraints of his own. If he doesn't respond as she hopes, it's hard for her to imagine a nuanced or exonerating reason (for example, that he didn't understand what she was asking for or has a different point of view). Instead, she's likely to chalk it up to rejection or neglect. Instead of coming to her aid, her partner is deciding to stay "up" and leave her "down." Each partner must vie to be heard, seen, or responded to. The two individuals each fear that one's gain is the other's loss; there's not enough to go around. The atmosphere can quickly deteriorate to one of blame, defensiveness, taking things personally, and feeling wronged.

In the golden-ring mind-set, a partner may feel the same intense need as in the seesaw example, but she has the emotional where-withal not to panic, to withstand frustration, and to trust in her partner's good intentions. Rather than propel her experience of need "into" her partner, she's able to "place" her need in a ring that we'll call "the relationship." Her partner does the same. The relationship then becomes a shared space for expression. Each partner brings his or her individual feelings into the "ring," and they think together about the problem at hand. Both implicitly recognize that there are *two people*, each with a complex mind and body, which means that they can't expect their communication to be magically, telepathically received. Even between intimates the distance between minds can be great, and it will take time to come to an understanding.

When you are stuck in the seesaw mind-set, it's easy to mistake the golden-ring approach as capitulating or "not getting heard." But taking the golden-ring approach to marriage does *not* require suppressing our emotions. In fact, it helps us communicate our feelings and advocate for our own needs. We hold on to ourselves as individuals and, as a result, we can more productively collaborate. I tell the expectant couples in my class that their relationship, like their soon-to-be child, is a creation between them. Many of the high-anxiety moments of parenthood will draw them into seesaw states of mind, breaking down their thinking into who's "right" and who's "wrong." But if they keep trying to apply the golden-ring approach, both their relationship and their child can flourish. I tell them that the trying *is* the loving.

TODAY, SCHOLARS OF adult development collectively scratch their heads at the curious durability of the "midlife crisis" as an organizing idea, since their research turns up little actual evidence for it. I think the midlife crisis doesn't show up today as a psychological phenomenon in life-span research because the issues it targets have migrated out of our discussion of life phase and into our discussion of marriage. The idea that a marriage may well interfere with your personal development—and may need to be terminated for that reason—has become widespread and normative. We don't need to claim a "crisis" in order to espouse this idea, or to act on it. Gone are the days when we felt the pressure to invoke a majestic psychological theory to explain the obvious, now-acceptable desire to find something better for ourselves when we feel our marriage has run its course.

In his book *The Marriage-Go-Round*, the sociologist Andrew Cherlin depicts an American worldview in which "marriage" and "individual satisfaction" are treated as clearly defined and neatly divided. He locates its roots in a cultural model of individualism that began in the 1960s with experiments in marriage and "expressive divorce." Describing the way this model of individual development functions as an ideal, Cherlin says:

> As a twenty-first-century individual, you must choose your style of personal life. You are allowed to—in fact, you [are] almost required to—continually monitor your sense of self to look inward to see how well your inner life fits with your married (or cohabiting) life. If the fit deteriorates, you are almost required to leave. For according to

the cultural model of individualism, a relationship that no longer fits your needs is inauthentic and hollow. It limits the personal rewards that you, and perhaps your partner, can achieve. In this event, a breakup is unfortunate, but you will, and must, move on.

To write a phrase such as "a relationship that no longer fits your needs is inauthentic and hollow" as a straight-ahead factual statement on the order of "the sky is blue" is to gently ridicule the false certainty with which people declare their individual satisfaction to be frustrated by marriage. As if we can ever be completely sure what "our needs" are, or will be, or at what point a relationship can be deemed unequivocally "inauthentic and hollow." As if "the fit" simply "deteriorates" without agency or will. These are hardly straightforward facts.

Cherlin's dry pronouncement gestures toward the self-certainty of both the individualistic narratives of midlife and the ensuing cultural backlash. Clearly, the "midlife crisis" genre draped a veil of narcissism over the entire enterprise of individual development. In the era of Levinson's Jim Tracy, an individual problem, "I'm unhappy with my wife," gave rise to an individualistic solution, "I need a divorce." But the resulting critiques leveled against "individualistic marriage," "consumer marriage," and "expressive divorce" were also problematic; in their effort to protect children from their parents' misguided seeking, they shortchanged people's authentic emotional longings. The "heroic" midlife crisis genre wrongly characterized the connection of individuality and intimacy, by suggesting that we develop ourselves by casting off relationships we've done little to change. But if we've learned anything from the profusion of research on marriage and emotions, it's that emotions are not best managed by simple suppression. Staying married by stifling individual needs isn't a solution either.

Happily, today, we've gained a subtler understanding of couples' actual *processes* of relating, and how these enhance or inhibit the emotional experience of satisfaction for the individuals involved. The growing research on intimate relationships deepens our understanding of "needs" in marriage, and casts doubt on the clean categories to which Cherlin alludes. In reality, the rhetoric of "needs" conceals a teeming mass of complex emotional miscommunications, poorly managed disappointments, and dysfunctional bids for attention. We insist on our "needs" in marriage as an ante-upping way to communicate frustration, a self-assertive rebranding of our pain at disconnection. When the emotional processes are working in our marriage, we tend to be able to disentangle what is a want and what is a need. The deft and gentle *handling* of our needs is what enables us to satisfy both our individual desires and our loving marital intentions.

Today, even the longest-running study of men's adult development has come around to the view that how we handle our emotions is central to our individual well-being and the health of our relationships. When the Grant Study was started at Harvard in the 1930s, the researchers believed that life satisfaction would come about through superior achievement. That view still had currency when the study participants hit middle age in the individualistic 1960s. But over time, the study showed that life satisfaction hinges on good relationships. High-conflict marriage, alcoholism, and loneliness are negatives; family, friends, and community connection are positives. Quality, not quantity, is key. Recent data analyses show that it's our ability to deal with challenging emotions without distortions or suppression that allows us to authentically engage with others. Entering into the other person's experience while holding on to ourselves; listening and sharing differences directly and nondefensively; expressing difficult emotions without becoming overreactive or withdrawn—these prove to be the essentials of fulfilling intimate relationships.

In adulthood, we hopefully begin to see that changing our internal perspective is at least as important as changing our outward circumstances when it comes to improving our emotional connections with others. We look within and realize some of the ways that our own emotional style affects our behavior with our partner. In the best case, we perceive that being happy *is* better than being right, that the golden ring beats the seesaw every time. We begin to feel secure enough, in ourselves and our relationships, to relinquish a need for certainty. "The older I get, the less I know" is one way people express a growing comfort with complexity. When Ariel makes room for her husband's perspective, or when I tell my childbirth students that the trying is the loving, it's about recognizing that "who's right" and "who's wrong" is a destructive simplicity that doesn't reflect real life. Real life, it turns out, is what emotional maturity allows us to see.

Feeling Close, in Love and Sex

When Stephen first called me, he said that he and his wife, Diana, were at the end of their rope. "We don't have sex," he said in a tone that mingled anger and pain. As he told it, their way of relating—icy silence punctuated by lacerating argument—was just the latest, worst version of their long-standing lack of warmth. Diana was hard to reach at first. When we finally spoke by phone, I detected in her voice a mix of annoyance and anxiety and apology: "I haven't had a chance to call you back. Stephen has no clue what it's like to be in charge of the daily kid stuff and my own work responsibilities. I'm doing the best I can."

I could tell that Stephen felt victimized by an untenable situation, and Diana felt both put-upon and blamed. A familiar anxiety welled up in me, akin to the dread you feel in a dream where you face a daunting task and lack the necessary tools. I was urgently being asked to repair a rift and not given the resources to do it. In our first interchanges, they gave me a taste of their own experience—overwhelmed, confused, and unequipped to respond. I could predict there'd be plenty of anger and accusations to go around.

When they first arrived at my office, Diana and Stephen's turmoil was belied by their put-together, professional appearance. I marveled, yet again, at how rarely inner confusion bears a discernible relationship to career success or outer cool. They both looked, well, sexy: fit, attractive, he (I learned) devoted to biking, and she to yoga. Apparently, unlike many other couples, their regimens of self-care had not been derailed by parenthood; it was their "couple care" that was in shambles. Both in their early forties, they each let me know how hard they were working to balance demanding corporate jobs with being attentive parents. In the absence of comfort from each other, I sensed that their physical regimens were their main vehicle for managing emotional duress.

Turning to the state of their relationship, Stephen said, with resentful matter-of-factness, "At the moment I'd say we're cordial, but there's no connection." This, I learned, was when things were good. When things were bad, Diana said, "I don't want to be around him." She itemized her complaints on manicured fingertips—Stephen was disengaged, he didn't care about her feelings, and he had no idea how to apologize.

If either Diana or Stephen had confided the state of things to a friend over coffee, their relationship would have seemed like an excellent candidate for divorce. Today, no one has to keep tormenting himself in an unloving, actively hostile, virtually sexless relationship, and arguably no one should. It is unhealthy to be in such a relationship. Stress levels soar. Kids don't thrive. Theirs looked to be exactly the kind of conflictual marriage that our social acceptance of divorce was meant to humanely dissolve.

For me, it was not so simple. I felt under enormous pressure to be as hopeless as they were. But my job is to keep open a space for exploring and thinking, something that can be hard for couples to do for themselves. The first thing that struck me was that ever since Diana and Stephen had gotten together, they had been coming apart. Before they married, they'd broken up twice. Passionate sex had given way to physical disconnection, but they were still exquisitely vigilant about each other's emotional state. They claimed not to see eye to eye on much of anything, though they were both besotted by their children. Despite their avowed lack of romance, they were planning a special anniversary trip for the next year. By the time I saw them, they had known each other for eleven years and had been married for nine. In our first few weeks of meeting, Stephen blurted out four times that he was "done," though he kept their appointments. Diana would say she didn't "feel much," then express loneliness at his lack of attention. They were continually criticizing each other, but they kept trying to get something from each other.

When I thought about what Diana and Stephen had been able to build, I saw in their persistence an ineffective but real attempt to make something good happen between them. "You've been together a long time," I said. "Bad feelings always threaten to tear you apart. But there's glue there. Something keeps bringing you back. We can use that." Diana teared up. Stephen visibly relaxed. Both were relieved to be seen as loving and good.

Though they momentarily softened, they quickly reverted to mutual faultfinding. Watching them, it struck me how incredibly difficult it is for people to see the closing down of warmth and excitement as something they are doing to *themselves*, rather than something solely perpetrated by their partner. Stephen was convinced that he was the well-meaning victim of Diana's misunderstanding and neglect; Diana was convinced of the same with Stephen. Both were blind to their own participation. Each scanned the environment for moments when the *other* one was hypocritical, went back on his own rules, or applied a double standard. There was precious little room for honest mistakes, inadequacy, or weakness. Each disparaged the other's "oversensitivity." "Grow up" was a common refrain. They called each other "babyish," but were also dismissive toward their own wish for care.

Sex and physical closeness were particularly hard to navigate. Stephen and Diana dutifully read the popular sex experts and tried to follow their advice to spice things up by injecting a bit of risk, even anxiety, into sex. Unsurprisingly, this effort became just one more source of contention. Once, stung by Diana's sexual rejection, Stephen called her a "prude," and Diana indignantly headed off to the local sex shop to prove him wrong. When they tried to incorporate the paraphernalia she'd purchased, it ended up in the trash because he was such an "asshole." Their problem with sex wasn't that they generated *too little* anxiety or sense of risk. They couldn't *stop* generating anxiety, and taking it out on each other.

"It makes sense that sex is difficult," I said. "Sex is play, and to play you have to relax. When you're scared, you can't relax. You are both so fearful about the other's emotional impact on you." They both nodded blankly, as if in assent, but in their relationship now, words such as *play* and *relax* had no traction. They couldn't even begin to *imagine* playing together in sex. Sexual roles such as "doer" and "done to" were entirely out of the question, precisely because "who was doing what to whom" was such a deadly serious emotional struggle between them.

The field of couple therapy debates whether couples like Stephen and Diana should be cajoled into sexual interactions to kindle an emotional spark, or whether developing their sense of security will free up their libidos. The debate can mimic the polarization of the stereotypical couple's standoff ("he isn't tender," "she isn't desiring"). Sex and attachment are *both* expressed in relationships, and *both* take place in our bodies. In long-term relationships, their common pathway is a trusting, pleasurable emotional flow. Whether couples can create that flow hinges not only on what goes on *between* partners, but also what goes on *within* each person. Feeling close with your partner, in love or in sex, has more to do with your own psychology than you might initially think.

HENRY V. DICKS, a British psychiatrist working with couples in the middle of the last century, is widely credited with having originated couple therapy. In his book *Marital Tensions*, he observed:

> A great number of both men and women in our clinical marital practice have stressed, in monotonously identical terms, that their greatest deficit in the marriage has been the spouse's lack of tender-ness. . . . I think one can begin to get a fairly consistent specification of the foundations of marriage as a mutual affirmation of the other's identity as a *lovable person*, not as a coitus machine for tension relief. The failure to fulfill this mutual need, its denial through secret fear, hate and rigidity, or its belittlement as "sloppy," "babyish," and so on *is* the heart of our topic. Childlike, unashamed dependence and its gratification by caressing words and actions, both immediate

and in the sense of continual thoughtfulness and cherishing in daily relations is, paradoxically, what makes "mature" unions.

Dicks described Diana and Stephen's essential struggle. He also identified what makes contemporary marriage both an ingenious psychological creation and a demanding emotional balancing act. Marriage is a *mature* relationship in which we affirm each other as lovable people through accepting each other's childlike—read *human*—dependence. In fact, a marriage is a "mature union" *insofar* as it creates an atmosphere where partners can gratify each other's "unashamed dependence." When Dicks alludes to "childlike" needs, "caressing words and actions," and "cherishing," he's talking about the desires for tenderness, shared pleasure, and excitement that are at the core of emotional and sexual closeness. Troubled relationships can often be recognized by the ways their members treat dependence as a problem, relegating sexual and emotional longings to the territory of shameful need.

When we express our body-based needs and desires with our partner, we take a risk. We want to be treated as lovable, to feel understood and valued, yet we also risk being ignored, rejected, or simply misread. These risks come up in any marriage, any day. It's in the nature of being human that we never get over wanting to be affirmed as lovable and never stop feeling hurt when we aren't. The astonishing yet normal reality of marriage is that we never feel cared for once and for all. The reservoir of goodwill needs to be replenished through loving words and actions. And if emotional communication works well, it *can* be replenished. This is the peculiar, hopeful truth at the heart of every meaningful human attachment, including marriage.

How we handle these inherent risks determines whether we end up protecting or damaging the marital atmosphere. Our personal and cultural paradigm of marriage so often seems to insist that if we aren't happy, it's because our partner isn't meeting or responding to our needs. We jump prematurely to the question "Is my *partner* taking care of *my* emotions?" We can hardly keep from jumping there. But in the process, we can lose track of a prior step: the need to engage our caretaking capacities on our own behalf. We need to use our developed capacities for thought, sustained attention, patience, sensitivity, and tact in the service of expressing our own deep, tender, and body-based emotions. It's *both* staying in touch with our vulnerable emotions *and* acting as a caretaker and communicator of these emotions that I consider to be the hallmark of emotional maturity.

If we can't take care of our own emotions, it'll be harder for our partner to take care of us. It will be hard to communicate a plea for our partner's help or comfort that is unsullied by projection, pressure, or blame. Our partner won't have a prayer of delivering the response we desire if we can't find an effective way to express our feelings. And, think how painful it is when your partner doesn't take responsibility for his own emotions. Facing our own emotions and expressing them skillfully permits us to take better care of our partner and to give him the same experience of comfort that we'd like him to give to us.

The hope in marriage is that both people manage to take care of their own *and* their partner's emotions. We move in a flexible and balanced way between caretaking ourselves and caretaking each other. Each of us imagines what it feels like to be the other person and tries to communicate in ways that our partner can understand and constructively respond to. If all goes well, when we can't recruit our mature capacities—when we react poorly or blame for no reason—then our partner steps in and helps "co-regulate" us. Our partner accesses his or her own mature capacities and provides enough support and containment to save us both from going down a death spiral of over-reaction or withdrawal. However, if we do plunge down that spiral, maturity allows partners to repair the breach relatively quickly by avoiding undue blame of themselves or each other.

This marital balancing act is hard, especially under the pressures of life and kids. Our children need a lot, but we'd feel terrible blaming them for their "childish" needs. As good parents, we eagerly tend to them—getting another glass of milk, reading another bedtime story—and willingly expend energy for their benefit. Yet when our inner reserves are depleted and we want the demands to stop, we can find ourselves redirecting our resentment toward our spouse. While we know it's entirely unfair to get angry at our children's needs, it can seem almost reasonable to get angry at our spouse's.

It's also hard because entering the forcefield of our own dependency heightens our sense of vulnerability. By sidestepping—and fighting about—sex, Stephen and Diana avoided being in the position of *needing* anything from each other. Hunger made each of them feel "babyish," out of control, and a target for humiliation. In an oddly stable arrangement, they both turned against the other's vulnerability from a perch of pseudomature superiority. Neither could see that their difficulties accepting and caring for their *own* emotions lay at the heart of their bitter blame of their spouse for not doing so. Diana's criticism of Stephen for being "oversensitive" expresses a criticism she continuously, if unconsciously, levels against herself. If she felt less critical toward her own dependency, she might be less judgmental toward his. If she didn't feel such acute shame at her own wish to be indulged, she would spend less time shaming Stephen. So we arrive at still another turn of complexity: Diana's recoil from affirming Stephen's lovableness mirrors an internal move directed toward herself. Little is more anti-erotic than shame, so Diana's criticism doubtless inhibits her own capacity for excitement, as well as Stephen's. Escaping such patterns is as much a matter of self-acceptance as accepting the other. "Mutual affirmation" includes reinstating both our partner and *ourselves* as lovable people.

"Grow up," directed at oneself or one's spouse, isn't going to do the trick. That's because a healthy emotional life doesn't spring fully formed from the cognitive, "just do it" part of our psyches. It develops within loving and responsive relationships. Our childhoods took us so far in this regard, and our hope is that our marriages can take us further. To zero in on the core experiences that enable us to feel close, we'll take a brief detour into the dynamics of early parent-child relationships.

WHEN WE'RE VERY young, we're all about expressing needs, and we can't modulate our own emotions; they're raw, powerful, and sometimes hard to read. We depend on a parent to read them, respond to them, and help us make sense of them. A loving parent tolerates the intensity of our emotions and tries to "sit with" them until she's deciphered them enough to respond in a sensitive and effective way. She stays present to our emotional experience and thinks about what we might need. For a child to feel comforted and understood, his parent must communicate both that she knows what he feels ("feels with" him) *and* takes her own perspective on his experience ("thinks about" him). These two facets of her response—*feeling with* and *thinking about*—are the fundamental aspects of the responsiveness that lead to our feeling loved and understood.

Consider instances where this process between parent and child breaks down. When a parent can only *feel with* her child's emotions, her child's fear, sadness, or anger arouses an identical feeling in her. She becomes overwhelmed or "lost" in the experience, and her child starts to feel *more* distress, not less. Conversely, when a parent can only *think about* her child, she may respond with too little empathy, and her child will feel misunderstood. He'll experience a basic gap between what he feels and what his parent can accept, and he starts to lose track of what his feelings really are. The relationship suffers when the parent is either too *absorbed* in the child's emotional experience, or too *distant* from it.

In good relationships, loving parents find the right balance. Take the childhood example of needing comfort when you were hurt. When you fell off your bike, for instance, you wanted your mom or dad to *both* empathize (feel with) *and* try to fix (think about) the problem. First, you wanted him to hug you and say, "Oh, ouch, I know how much that must hurt." Then you wanted him to say, "Hey, let's go clean up that cut and get a Band-Aid." If your parent only reacted to the emotional and physical pain ("Oh, gosh, oh, jeez, that must hurt so much, your poor thing!"), you might feel overwhelmed and panicky, with no soothing or effective solution in sight. If your parent only reacted by giving a solution ("Okay, let's get cleaned up, come on"), you might feel that your need for comfort went ignored and was perhaps even seen as a bother.

Having a benign and thoughtful adult who strives to understand our thoughts, desires, and intentions is an essential ingredient for developing trust in intimate relationships. In psychology, this parental activity goes by the name of *reflective functioning*. The underlying attitude, in the words of one prominent researcher, is "the non-defensive willingness to engage emotionally, to make meaning of feelings and internal experiences without becoming overwhelmed or shutting down." The "good enough" relationship includes occasional miscommunications and failures of empathy, but if, on balance, our parents are attuned and responsive in this way, it leads us to develop the same capacity within *ourselves*. We learn to identify our own emotions, organize our experience, and distinguish whose feelings are whose. Internalizing the *feeling-with-and-thinking-about* process enables us to know and respond to our *own* emotions and forms the basis of relating to ourselves and others in a loving way.

Let's keep these crucial capacities in mind as we consider a familiar shape that couples' conflicts take: "I shouldn't have to do x or y until/unless you do x or y." This general form can be expressed by any number of variations:

- "I shouldn't have to stop interrupting you until you stop interrupting me."
- "I'll stop getting mad at you when you start being more responsible."
- "I'll start being sensitive to your needs when you start being sensitive to mine."
- "I had a hard day." "No, I had a hard day."

It's important to notice here that the shape of these statements would constitute a completely fair approach if applied to the relationship of a small child to a parent. As a *child*, I shouldn't have to be able to calm myself down without you (my *parent*) trying to calm me. I shouldn't be expected to manage my own emotions without having your help in managing them. I shouldn't have to be sensitive to your needs before you've been sensitive to mine. It's in the very definition of a loving parent that *the parent does these things first* and thus helps her child internalize these capacities. As one of my patients said, "A mother is supposed to know that a crying child *needs something*. That's what a mother is supposed to *be*."

The difficult truth is that even if our early caregivers let us down in this regard, we're not entitled to demand it from our partners in the present. As adults who are presumably emotionally and cognitively on par with each other, we reasonably expect our partners to be able to communicate their emotions, rather than expect us to magically know them (though we all have unreasonable fantasies sometimes that they *will* magically know them). We request that our partner channel his thoughts and feelings through an articulation apparatus such as speech, rather than through emotional contagion or mind reading.

Yet, the more our caregivers *did* let us down in this regard, the more vulnerable we *are* to demanding it from our partners. It's not as if this is conscious or intentional. If you grew up in a family, say, where your father left and your mother was depressed or anxious or preoccupied, and she wasn't able to kneel down and look you in the eye and hold you and help you manage your own anxiety, is it any wonder that you look to your mate now to *finally* help you contain your anxiety? And is it any surprise that when your mate doesn't contain your anxiety—when, for example, he doesn't follow your specific instructions on tending to the children in your absence, or fails to understand what you are trying to tell him—that you feel uncared for and abandoned? From the perspective of emotional development, there is no reason why you *wouldn't* feel these things. And there are also plenty of reasons why you might feel unwilling, or frankly unable, to self-reflect or calm yourself down enough to notice and take responsibility for the unfairness of your demand.

If our parents fell short in soothing our emotions and thinking about what we needed, we're more likely to regard our partner's failure of responsiveness as an emergency. Say you are trying to talk to your wife and she appears bored or critical. If you grew up in a family where people responded to your needs and emotions, and misattunements were generally followed by repair, you will likely apply a nondire lens to this situation. Uncomfortable and frustrating, yes; desperate, no.

But what if the adults you depended on were dismissive toward your emotions or so easily overwhelmed that they couldn't offer a calming perspective? What if they were so depressed or self-absorbed or even, frankly, crazy that you had the repeated experience of being left alone with your fear or anger or sadness without any reassurance that comfort would be reliably offered? Perhaps you were even blamed or punished for having your feelings at all. In that case, when your wife fails to tune in empathically, you will likely be sent right back into the soup of your troubling childhood emotions. No one helped you make sense of your emotions back then, after all; no one received your signals in a way that helped you integrate them into an understanding of what they meant, or how to manage them. Now, beset with strong feelings in the moment, you lack a clearly marked mental path to self-reflection that can help you self-soothe or communicate effectively.

A common difficulty in intimate relationships is not feeling seen and loved in our *difference*. As a child, if the people you depended upon either got lost in your distress and couldn't maintain a separate point of view, or required you to suppress your feelings and take their point of view, it taught you that being a separate individual with a different perspective was somehow a problem. If my experience taught me that separate points of view create ruptures in empathy, it's no wonder I might fight with my partner tooth and nail to enforce agreement. By passionately insisting that you should see things as I do, I both echo and warp the original protest, at the heart of every human, that I should be loved as *myself*.

The breakdown of *feeling with* and *thinking about* is one of the most pervasive sources of couple pain. Person A feels something and Person B doesn't respond adequately. Person A escalates, no longer able to see Person B as a separate person with thoughts and feelings of his/her own. Duly threatened, Person B either counterattacks or withdraws into self-protection, now unable to think about why Person A behaves or feels the way (s)he does. The couple may head into a self-reinforcing "pursuer" and "distancer" dynamic, with one escalating emotion to get a response, and the other retreating to find some space to think. But notice, this breakdown doesn't only play out *between* people, but also *within* people. We can work with it on both fronts. If we can find our "inner caregiver" in the heat of the moment or soon after, we can pause and notice what is happening inside, and deliver a message that had more chance of eliciting a sensitive response.

THE ABILITY TO *feel with* and *think about* oneself and one's partner underlies closeness, whether emotional or physical. Looking inside, sitting with feelings, tolerating confusion, not leaping to blame—these are aspects of intimate relating that, ideally, we experienced in our early relationships with loving others. Not all of us had such good fortune while young, however, yet somehow we're supposed to manage to be the mature advocate and mouthpiece for our "unashamed dependence" with our partner, even at those moments when our emotions are most intense. This can be a huge challenge. We can't help but sometimes fail, no matter how knowledgeable or therapized or well slept we are.

How can we move more smoothly between mature and "child-like" positions without grinding the gears excessively, or busting the gearshift altogether? How do we endure when strong emotions breed accusations and irrational statements, then repair and really listen to each other's point of view? How can I think while staying connected to my feelings, and feel while staying connected to my thoughts? How can I struggle with all these things and simultaneously give you the opportunity to do so too?

One useful starting point is to stop *dumping on* our "childlike" emotions. They are the wellspring of our desire to connect and our need to be close. The problem is that we spend energy judging and blaming ourselves and each other for these emotions, instead of becoming as skilled as possible in expressing them. We can actually cultivate the needed capacities and skills. Mainstream psychology refers to these capacities as "emotional regulation," broadly defined as the strategies people use to "influence which emotions they have, when they have them, and how they experience and express these emotions." We regulate emotions through a variety of different methods, but two of the most adaptive ones—metacognition and mindfulness—rely on reflective functioning, or what I've called the *feeling-with-and-thinking-about* process.

Metacognition is the ability to recognize that our thoughts *are* thoughts, and not a direct representation of reality. When faced with an angry mother, a child who has achieved metacognition can replace the idea "I am a bad person" with the idea "Mommy is treating me like I am a bad person, but sometimes she's been wrong about things in the past." When a wife employs metacognition, she can move from the thought "My husband is a son of a bitch" to "My husband can say mean things sometimes and it's not okay, but I also know he's extremely anxious in this moment." Through metacognition, we understand that subjective reality is not objective reality; that our perception of reality, and other people's perception of reality, are colored by our respective desires, beliefs, and goals.

By now, the term *mindfulness* is so overused that it's at risk of becoming background noise. Put off by its commercialized aura of pseudo-enlightenment, we may tune it out before we're even "mindful" of doing so. But in principle, mindfulness is a useful technique for cultivating nonjudgmental awareness of our moment-to-moment perceptions, feelings, and thoughts. Mindfulness helps us notice our judgments, emotions, and bodily responses and let them be without becoming caught up in them. Like metacognition, it creates breathing room for reflection and more attuned responsiveness.

Many contemporary practices—meditation, yoga, exercise—offer methods of self-regulation. Often described in the idiom of *stress relief*, they help us by creating a subjective sense of spaciousness and acceptance, and delinking our feelings and thoughts from the impulse to react. Though many of us engage in these practices to foster more emotional balance, we can also find that in the heat of the moment with our partner, it all goes out the window. Of course you can't reflect during a fight; that's what a fight *is*. When your passionate and vulnerable emotions are engaged, you are not always going to be on your best behavior. Here, it's good to remember that *feeling with* and *thinking about* do not have to be, and often *aren't*, simultaneous operations. A responsive partner isn't someone who never loses perspective in the grip of emotion; it's someone who circles back and thinks about what happened. People who understand this can get over bad moments and re-attune with each other much faster than people who don't.

Being able to circle back and think about our feelings helps us put them in the context of our larger goals. And the larger goal in couples, if you think about it, is maintaining a sense of closeness and friendship. When we act as friends, we respond to each other's bids for attention, try to learn what's important to each other, and express fondness and gratitude. Acting as friends also means being able to disengage when things get hot, and giving each other the needed space in a loving and nonpunitive way. When we do these things, we feel attuned to and want to attune to each other. When we attune to each other, give each other the benefit of the doubt, and trust in each other's good intentions, then we continue to act as friends. It's a virtuous circle.

The people who can't circle back and think about what happened tend to get stuck in their negative emotional reactions. They become lost in absorbing negative states that feed on themselves. They don't behave with each other's best interests at heart. They don't behave in their *own* best interests, either. They self-destructively redefine their own best interests as not letting the other person off the hook. In that state of mind, they are incapable of accessing the thought "Is my partner my friend or my enemy? Overall, (s)he's my friend, and if I treat him/her nicely, I am likely to repair this painful moment and restore good feeling."

When you can't feel or act in a way that connects you to your bigger-picture goal of warmth and harmony, it's worth attempting a "bottom-up" rather than a "top-down" strategy, focusing on the in-the-moment possibilities for awareness, kindness, and responsiveness. A finer-grained attention to what you are each *doing* to cause bad interactions can enable you to notice what each of you could do differently and gently lead you away from dwelling in a miasma of emotional negativity that toxifies the whole relational atmosphere. Attention to process, not outcome; awareness in the moment; tuning in to your own emotional weather—these are valuable mindfulness techniques under *any* circumstances, but they are particularly important to creating the moments of repair or attunement that can then promote a more positive big picture.

As a couple therapist, I am moved, and even stunned, to witness the hope and closeness that couples generate, even when they've changed *nothing else*, by trying to access the big picture. A whole world of difference exists between these two statements:

- "I'd stop yelling if you were more helpful."
- "I know I'm a piece of work, but I'm trying to control my yelling."

I'd go so far as to say that, even when the offending behaviors don't seem to be budging, what makes the biggest difference between hope and hopelessness is whether partners demonstrate *self-awareness* and *self-responsibility*—acknowledging their impact on each other, and taking responsibility for trying to do something different. When we're self-aware, we reflect on the source and effect of our emotions. When we're self-responsible, we face our impact on the other person and commit to adjusting our behavior. People who want to stay married can live with a lot—a lot of limits, a lot of annoyances, even a lot of deprivations. But feeling they are being heard is one of the basic requirements for feeling loved. And the flip side is also true: *not* feeling heard is what people find most corrosive to their sense of trust and potential in marriage. Self-awareness means we're listening to ourselves. Self-responsibility means we're listening and responding to the other.

Self-awareness and self-responsibility are highly relevant to a repetitive issue couples face, namely who owes whom an apology. Insisting one's partner apologize is often an attempt to find evidence of these attributes. Although it's a blunt instrument, trying to get an apology is a way of saying, "I don't yet have faith that you're fully aware of your own behavior in this bad interaction. Until I feel you are taking some responsibility for your part in it, I can't trust you." In practice, the problem with such communications is how often their stealth message seems to be "I won't even talk to you until you admit that *my* bad feelings are all *your* fault." Over time, it becomes unbearable to the other partner to feel that the only way back to peace and tranquillity is to take all the blame. Any time you demand (or, better, request) an apology, it's hugely important to take responsibility for your own part first. And if you believe you had *no* part? That's your clue that some self-reflection is in order.

Heartfelt apologies are enormously meaningful to people. They are an essential aspect of repair. But when they work, it's because they are based on something even more fundamental: *understanding*. Returning to Diana and Stephen, if either could have said to the other, "I can see why you feel bad when I say things like that, I get it," it would have changed their conversation. Not immediately perhaps. If Diana said it, for instance, Stephen might be caught off guard and use it to get a couple digs in. But if she could stick with the attitude and not retaliate immediately, Stephen's trust in her would increase as he saw that she could think about her own behavior and its impact on him. He might then adjust his behavior and reflect on his *own* part, which could then help her feel more hopeful that they could understand each other and become closer.

WORDS SUCH AS *maturity* and *responsibility* can't help but elicit a groan from anyone who feels his marriage is already a slog. Marriage's constant need for maintenance, restraint, self-control, tact, and discipline can make us bridle and rebel inside. In this of all places, we can't help protesting, "I shouldn't have to *work so hard.*" We fantasize about letting desires overtake us that are, for once, not the product of conscience or duty. We sometimes feel these give us clues to who we "really are." When feeling unsatisfied, we might alight on the view that the "real, natural me" has been squelched, hidden, and suppressed by the more "superficial, dutiful me." We feel frustrated that we are enduring rather than living. Maybe it is my spouse's fault, (s)he's so controlling. Or maybe it's society's fault; long-term monogamous marriage is essentially unnatural, as sociobiologists are quick to point out.

In his book *Can Love Last?* the psychoanalyst Stephen Mitchell gave an intriguing alternative: "Becoming a person entails self-organization. . . . Loss of richness, immersion, and density is an inevitable feature of development, of becoming *a* person. . . . Both pathological *and* healthy self-development generate loss and, perhaps, a longing for return, expansion, *relief from the strain of psychic structure itself* [italics mine]." The problem, he suggests, is not only the constraints a long-term relationship puts on the self, but rather the constraints inherent in *having* a self. Keeping ourselves together, forging dependability and consistency in our personalities, causes strain. A wish to escape that maintenance effort is universal. Given the effort, it's natural that we look to our intimate partner to soothe us, replenish us, and help us relax. Yet we repeatedly confront the reality that it takes effort to be a skillful and sensitive partner who can collaborate in the creation of a soothing and replenishing relationship.

I've said we're more likely to fulfill our desires for emotional closeness with our partner if we're compassionate and caretaking toward our *own* emotions. A similar approach helps when it comes to sex. There may be no aspect of marriage that people feel is more dispiriting to "work on" than sex. I'll turn to other aspects of sex in marriage later in the book, but here I want to get clear on exactly what "working on" sex might mean within the framework we've been discussing.

One thing we seek and hunger for in partner sex is the experience of affecting another person, and being affected by them, mentally and physically, in pleasurable, immediate, and involuntary ways. A core feature of erotic excitement is seeing how excited someone becomes with us—seeing him lose control, seeing that she "can't get enough," or is "going after what (s)he wants." We feel least sexy when we can't persuade ourselves that we could be sexy in someone else's eyes. New mothers can feel this way, as can new fathers. The unfortunate combination of youth-focused culture and the steady drumbeat of time provide an all-purpose wet blanket. Sexual performance preoccupies people because they want physical release, but also because performance problems provoke fears, in both parties, of not being sexually compelling.

Good sex, then, depends to some extent on having the experience of being found attractive. That sounds obvious, but here I want to emphasize the word *found*. We want the experience of being "discovered" as attractive. This can be a challenge in long-term relationships. A sense of discovery *can* happen, it should be said, in sexual routines. A couple already know what works, they feel comfortable with the basic themes, and they can improvise when the spirit moves them. But a sense of discovery can also be hard to come by with a long-term partner. Routines become ruts, and ruts are defined by a lack of imagination and exploration. When people lament the predictability of married sex, they aren't primarily talking about a dearth of new positions or sex toys or places in the house. These matters are easy enough to solve if there's the will and desire to solve them. People are after a more elusive experience of seeing themselves and their partner in a different, more erotic light. To make use of novel experiences—vacations, venues, playacting—the emotional atmosphere has to allow for discovery and play.

As a therapist, I see marriages where the "(s)he wants sex, (s)he doesn't" dynamic is in full swing. Like all cultural scripts, this one obscures a slew of specific complexities, but the emotional atmosphere in such situations tends to be airless and inflexible. The couple is locked into a pattern. Perhaps one perceives the other as relentless and grasping, and feels more like an instrument than an enigma. A woman might complain that the version of herself she sees her husband seeing (hey, in old pj's, but perfectly serviceable) is not one that she experiences as sexually arousing. Yet without her taking steps to guide him, he may not know how to discover her most erotically alluring self. In these situations, neither partner takes the risks that would lead to discovery, and they both retreat to their own lonely, disempowered corners.

From my perspective, "working on" sex in marriage means *taking an active role in creating the conditions under which you can have the experience of discovery*. Like other areas of relating, it's about using our mature capacities for thinking and planning to create situations where we can feel creative or surprised or out of control. Conceived in that way, it's not actually the "work" that is the stumbling block; the work is at least as fun as planning our kid's birthday party, and arguably more so. No, the problem is the *inhibition* we feel in undertaking the work, in acting intentionally to fulfill our own and our partner's desires and needs. Our inhibitions can take surprising forms; even the insistence on spontaneity can be an avoidance ploy. The challenge in sex, as in *every other* sphere of marriage, is to find a way to activate and express our mature, caretaking capacities so that we can satisfy our primal needs and wants, whether carnal or comfort seeking or both.

People can be ambivalent about actively participating in engineering the conditions for good sex, and I think it partly relates to the challenges of moving fluidly between aspects of ourselves. Having a personality of many parts psychologically housed under one roof—that's an achievement. Being able, for instance, to talk about problems of sexual desire or technique when we have to (i.e., analyze, problem-solve) and also to *not talk* about sex when needed (i.e., feel, experience) requires flexibility of personality. So does allowing tender sex, physical-release sex, makeup sex, and every other kind of sex to coexist without needing to reconcile them all. We express our desire to escape "the strain of psychic structure" in all sorts of ways. Perhaps romance novels and porn are ways people take vacations from this strain and indulge the pleasure of relating to body parts and familiar formulas, rather than to the taxing, complicated personalities of the real world. In our actual sex life with our actual partner in our actual long-term relationships, we have to find a way to move between psychological positions. We have to be able to use one part of ourselves to create the context for good sex, and another part to have it.

Our impatience with having "to work" at sex, our insistence that it be spontaneous or effortless in order to be good—doesn't this attitude limit our sexuality in all the same ways we limit our relationship generally? The same assumptions operate: the relationship (or sex) is better if you can read my mind and I don't have to actively tell you what I want; the relationship (or sex) is too disappointing unless I get just the response I want from you; something's wrong with the relationship (or sex) if we have moments of awkwardness, inadequacy, or misunderstanding. In all these scenarios, we forget that to connect well, sexually or emotionally, we feel with *and* think about. We use our mature capacities to create space for excitement, fun, and emotional pleasure.

We need look no further than the widely prescribed "date night" to observe how runaway anxieties and their destructive forms of expression—reactivity, blame, and projection—wreak havoc on what is in principle a fine vehicle for the spontaneous emergence of warm feeling and sexual attraction. Why do so many marital date nights go awry? Because as a magnet for hope and fear, they attract to themselves a heightened version of the very conflicts we're talking about. A wife becomes angry that her husband, who has *finally* bestirred himself to plan something, doesn't "know her well enough" (aka hasn't read her mind) to have chosen something she would like to do. A husband dreads the prospect of getting it wrong and fears the cold shoulder or having to hear about it for the next week. Both partners bog themselves down in a high-stakes vision of having a "successful" date night, instead of rolling with whatever happens and embracing the "failures" as well as the "successes," or being able to talk nondefensively afterward about what worked and what didn't, as part of the collaborative project of enjoying each other more.

In any creative endeavor, it's always a problem when we believe there's only one right way for events to unfold. If we're curious and open, we can't guarantee outcome. It's in the nature of creativity to risk, and in the nature of risk to fail. The essence of eroticism is openness to emotional and sexual creativity, discovery, and surprise. If you're not willing to open yourself, you're less likely to feel excited. Any person who is creatively engaged in her sex life, who's trying to push the envelope, is going to have "failures"—that is, times when things felt silly, or stupid, or just not fun. The sex therapist Barry McCarthy says something important: it's not performance but attitude that's key. *It's okay. It's great to try.* Nurture a playful attitude toward sex and laugh about it once in a while. You always have more chances. People may bemoan the downsides of married sex, but that is one of its virtues.

Marriage is, as Dicks wrote, a mature relationship in which we mutually affirm each other through accepting dependence and the need for affection and care. But Dicks offers a further point to consider: "Perhaps the key to the secret of *all* human relations is the ability to 'contain hate in the framework of love.'" We can't sustain any relationship for long without finding a way to manage our hate. People both gratify and frustrate us. Some of us even consider leaving because our partner has become "hateful" to us. Yet Dicks suggests that whether we find our partner hateful will have something to do with our *own* capacity to "contain hate in the framework of love."

Sex is one arena in marriage where we actually have the opportunity to express our hate constructively. In one important respect, it would help people to think about sex in "childlike" terms: refusing to have sex with a "hated" partner is not that different from how we felt when we had a tantrum as a child. *Nothing* is good, *everything* stinks; *"I hate you!"* was our passionate response when offered comfort or a distraction. Eventually, our caregiver would swoop in and hold us as we flailed, and then, through her presence and physical contact, somehow we were soothed. The world changed, it got brighter.

Adult life doesn't give us the same opportunities as childhood does for cathartic physical tussles, the kind where you were mad as hell one minute and giggling the next. But sometimes touch helps more than talking, and sometimes sex stands a better chance of defusing our irritation than talk does. When couples are locked in a competition of defensive apathy, or one is gaining power from not gratifying the other's need, they lose that opportunity. Some of the most regretful divorced people I know are those that eroded their marriage by using sex as reward or punishment. Everyone loses. I think women are especially susceptible to the mistake of using sex as a method of control, because they spend their youths absorbing so many objectifying, confusing messages about their sexuality as a currency of power and worth. The more people treat sex as a favor to be doled out, or as something they refuse so as not to relinquish their "principles," the more they deprive themselves of sex as a useful form of catharsis. Such "principles" aren't useful. The most useful principle is that you get to be a paradoxical, complicated human being who doesn't have to have a consistent, airtight point of view. People who stop having sex have closed off an avenue for working off their resentment constructively. They act out their hate by forgoing sex, but they lose a mechanism for transforming it.

Am I a loving person, and how could I be more so? This is a shocking question, especially given that so many of us first encounter it in middle age. We assume we are loving: we got married after all, we were in love, and of course we love our children. But development forces us to take the next step, to enlarge the question. Midlife's press to deepen inward can't help but mobilize reflection about our own role in creating the relationships we have. If we're honest, we begin to take the measure of our own mundane forms of destructiveness. The midlife push to expand outward encourages us to consider how we might transcend the vigilant quid pro quo that defines our arrangement and come to care for our partner as a separate person whose concerns matter as much as our own.

If by love we mean affirming the other's identity as a lovable person, neither Stephen nor Diana had yet arrived at loving the other. But they were trying. After the pursuit and the passionate romance; after the proposal, the engagement, and the marriage; after the house and the kids—one, two—and the overspending and in-law problems and job problems, there remains the question "Will you set yourself on the path of discovering how to love a genuinely separate person, not in the person's capacity to give you children, or a structure, or a dumping ground, but as a distinct being whose contours and interior you have yet to truly know?" Marriage, for all its complexities and frustrations, presents us with that opportunity and that question. By its persistent one-on-oneness, its sheer ongoing linearity, it keeps asking whether we will choose to pursue a continuing conversation, of body, heart, and mind, with this other human who is known to us in some ways but still mysterious to us in others.

4

Marriage as a Story

At a dinner party a couple years ago, I was seated next to an attractive man of about forty who was in the midst of a major upheaval. Explaining his solo status, he mentioned that he and his wife had recently separated. As the wine flowed, he confessed that he'd had an affair. By dessert, I learned that he and his wife had a two-month-old baby, and two older children. Being a therapist, I sometimes attract these sorts of confessions, and I try to lend a sympathetic ear. But this time I was challenged. First, he offered a familiar brand of self-regard that never fails to irritate me with its coupling of an impassioned claim that his children were the beating heart of his existence with a breezy detachment in handling their actual fates. He seemed quite content to dispatch me with an emotional shorthand he was accustomed to using on people ("I need more," "She doesn't accept me," "I'm sick of playing by her rules"), and given the norms of dinner-party conversation, I could do little but nod politely, quietly galled that he was using the etiquette of the situation to engineer my passive endorsement of his platitudes. He seemed confident that his talk would convince me of everything that his evident behavior didn't. How did he get this far in life mouthing such words and still having people believe them?

Later on, I softened somewhat, imagining that perhaps he'd had a desolate childhood, when he'd learned early to paper over any wisps of authentic sadness or anger or fear with a smooth, indifferent exterior.

Perhaps he'd learned, wisely, that being unflappable and coolly seductive, and having a ready explanation for everything, got him further in life than behaving like the anxious, bereft child. If it was true that he hadn't been in touch with his genuine feelings since roughly the age of six, when those feelings had been roundly neglected, was it any surprise that a strong-willed woman had scooped him up and then, frustrated by his unreachability, railed at him for being so uninvolved? Further, was it any surprise that a handsome, fit fortyish man with an angry wife and flirtatious air, himself deeply but unknowingly aggrieved by all the people in his life who demanded much but gave little, would find himself having an affair while his wife was home with a newborn?

On some level it made complete emotional sense. But privately I couldn't help but feel it would be a terrible decision for him to leave his family. He was a perfect candidate for the kind of messy affairs and ugly divorces that embroil the kids and enrage the ex-wives. He was in grave danger of making a complete hash of his life. And the reason, I concluded, was primarily his self-absorption: he couldn't think beyond himself. He told himself that he wasn't getting what he deeply needed from his wife, but he also had no apparent interest in the ways he was the co-architect of their problems. He had a litany of complaints about her attitude, but was myopic about his own role. One of the many paradoxes of human psychology is that the more you pin the blame for your emotions on someone else, the more stifling and claustrophobic the world you've created starts to feel, and the more you feel you have to "get out." But from how he presented himself to me, all this was inaccessible to him.

A few weeks later, I saw him on the street with his wife, who was struggling with a double stroller and baby carrier strapped to her chest, while he trailed behind. Her posture announced an extravagant sense of beleaguerment, while he ambled along, as if in passive-aggressive retort, savoring the sun and the air, immersed in his poetic love of the world. Despite his affectation, he looked to me like a lost and lonely boy. I was suddenly struck with a stab of surprising grief. Their family scene looked at once so fragile, and poignant, and even strangely valiant. His facile claims at dinner had presented only one angle. My just-so version had presented another. The scene on the street complicated both our stories.

AS A THERAPIST, my days are filled with people's compelling stories. I am interested in their stories, but I am at least as interested in how they tell their stories. Does a person understand his own story as *one* version of reality, or as the *right* version? Is he flexible about it? Can he imagine that his feelings could fit more than one story, and that one story might be more conducive to producing certain feelings than another? In a couple, can each partner be interested in, or curious about, the other one's story?

The man at the dinner party was telling me a story about himself. And I was telling myself a story about him. Neither of us could help it. We humans simply can't help telling stories; it's how we understand who we are, and how we figure out what to do next. We are always actively creating our story about the past in the present. What makes each of us unique is not only what happened to us, but the story we tell about what happened to us. As the critic Jonathan Gottschall writes in *The Storytelling Animal*, "The human mind was shaped *for* story, so that it could be shaped *by* story." Personal identity *itself* takes the form of a story. In adolescence, we start to weave our tastes, interests, and talents into a set of identifications and values and link them to larger social purposes. Creating an identity—relational, occupational, sexual, spiritual, political—is a primary goal of young adulthood in our culture. We see the self as a project we work on, improve, and craft to reflect who we "truly" are.

In our love stories, like our life stories, we choose which elements to emphasize and which to obscure. We get into marriage with an incomplete story, not least because life is lived in one direction. The deep education we received in our families about what emotions were safe to express, which desires were permissible, and what was possible to expect from relationships creates subliminal master narratives. Driven by our wish to bond, we begin by mentally amplifying compatibility and minimizing incompatibility. At the initial phase of romance when we notice things that bother us, we make semiconscious assessments of the threat they pose to our overall choice. Often these hang in liminal awareness, consigned to vague categories such as "No one's perfect" or "She'll change." These are "narrative choices," fitting our feelings to the story we want to tell about them.

As the years pass, problems that we initially ignored or brushed aside demand to be acknowledged. This relates to how having a good story relates to having a good life. Life satisfaction relates to telling a meaningful story about where we are and where we're headed. In mid-life more than ever, we need a story that has coherence and meaning. The questions we ask ourselves—Am I progressing or standing still? Am I excited or just going through the motions?—concern our story *and* our relationships. Identity, as one writer put it, is "the capacity to keep a particular narrative going." When our story isn't working, our identity feels as if it's in crisis. Marriage invites particular scrutiny. It's the emotional centerpiece of many adult lives, and a freighted arena for determining whether we perceive our lives to make sense, and whether they are moving forward or "stuck."

That we didn't entirely understand or choose consciously the story we were telling when we launched into marriage is one reason why rough-patch marital reckoning can feel like a *return to oneself*—a moment of remembering who we really are, distinct from the illusions we accepted in order to be married. We may start feeling that our real life story is elsewhere, that somehow we got on the wrong track. The continual thrum of *time passing* is our silent partner in this uncertainty. Stories, like songs, help us experience time; they give us a way to grasp time and mark its passage. When our story starts to break down, we start wondering if life is passing us by. We feel mounting desperation that if a change must be made, the time is *now*.

In adulthood, wrote the psychologist Ernest Schachtel, "experience increasingly assumes the form of the cliché under which it will be recalled." Many of us have found ourselves talked at by a distressed divorcing friend, where loyalty demands we ask no questions, but we feel increasingly uncomfortable and trapped. We try to nod supportively as our friend seeks affirmation for his or her ex's awfulness.

But the tale doesn't fulfill its cathartic promise because we can't in good conscience identify a perpetrator and a victim. We can't turn a complicated story into a self-exonerating cliché, much as we feel pressured to do so.

Our conflicted response may spring from the intuition, borne out by research, that people forming relationships pay selective attention to the positive aspects of their partner, just as people leaving relationships pay selective attention to negative ones. Both craft a story to fit their feelings. When dissatisfied partners disengage, they reconceptualize the relationship as flawed from the start and call up vivid supporting evidence from the past. Even when, as is often the case, people don't understand why they got together or broke up, they still need a story that makes sense of it.

Cultural stories are also clichés. Without the frameworks they provide, people find it hard to know how to live life. We're barraged with competing messages, and in constant danger of mistaking slogans for personal experience. As the psychologist Dan McAdams observes, "people pick and choose and plagiarize selectively from the many stories and images they find in culture to formulate a narrative identity." American culture espouses contradictory story lines in which marriage is forever—until it isn't. Even the devoutly religious struggle to mesh the time frame of eternity with here-and-now emotional satisfaction. Is authentic love to be found, as Søren Kierkegaard argued, in transcending our personal preferences, or is the fulfillment of our personal preferences the wellspring of love? Ideally, our marital devotion emanates from both our feelings of love and our values about marital commitment. But at those times when commitment and feelings diverge, when the marriage no longer feels eternal and destined, but endless and deadened, it can be hard to find the overarching narrative that reunites them.

The contemporary frame of mind about love, says the sociologist Eva Illouz, is characterized by a "persistent sisyphian attempt to conjure up the local and fleeting intensity of the love affair within long-term global narratives of love (such as marriage)." At times we focus on the fleeting intensity, at other times the long-term love. But if we're not alert to our mixing and matching of discordant romantic time frames, we can end up blaming our relationship or partner for our not managing to reconcile them. When we ask ourselves whether we're happy in our marriages, we're implicitly asking whether the relationship can propagate into the future in a loving way. We wonder, is this relationship a lifelong love, or a more contingent pairing? We actually have some control over the answer. Yet our vacillation about whether to conceive of the relationship as a lifelong or a more temporary narrative can play a stealth role in how much control we choose to believe we have. One couple I met with had gotten together after an unplanned pregnancy, and they both felt they had no firm emotional foundation. The wife spent the sessions blaming her husband for all his failures, but it seemed to me that a far more basic problem was her lack of interest in being married at all, and her wish to be a free agent back on the dating scene. In this case, it would have been more constructive for the woman to bring forward her genuine questions about her commitment to, or desire for, a long-term monogamous marriage.

In America, we're particularly enamored of the "hero's quest" narrative, where we're called to a special destiny from an early age. We speak in terms of "epiphanies," discoveries, and "turning points" and reiterate a common theme of progress versus decline. But our cultural stories rarely conceive of "turning points" and "epiphanies" as part of a happy marital journey. Those terms are more readily applied to the realization that we have to "get out." In the narrative of progress, marriage tends to be a hard sell. It's more likely to be cast as "static" and "boring," and the study of narrative helps us understand why. Stories tend to take three basic shapes: those where progress toward a goal is enhanced, those where it is impeded, and those where no change occurs. In tragedy, a progressive narrative rapidly gives way to a downfall narrative. A comedy reverses that order, and an impediment is followed by progress. In the "happily ever after" narrative, progress is followed by stability. Happily-ever-after stories end just at the moment when progress gives way to stability, for the obvious reason that stability lacks dramatic engagement.

Happily-ever-after stories distort our expectations of marriage by suggesting we will, or should, always be happy. But "ever after" may be the more problematic distortion. What drives stories forward is alternating periods of adventure and repose. Repose has to give way to adventure or there is no story. If the cultural story about marriage is boring stability, it is easy to lump marriage in with repose. Indeed, the discourse of marital leave-taking often lays claim to the adventure narrative—"I needed more," "I couldn't grow"—and deposits repose in the "static" partner or the marriage itself.

In reality, marriages are *rarely* stable or boring. People feel *enormously affected* by their marital partners. When people freeze over, they do so for many dramatic and meaningful reasons. When they invoke the word *boring*, it's often because they've stopped listening or paying attention. The "boring and static" narrative obscures the more complicated reality in two directions. Not only are distressed couples rarely bored by their predicament, but happy couples rarely feel they are in repose. Some sizable subset of long-term couples report ongoing feelings of intensity, sexual interest, and engagement with each other, though there's one aspect of early-stage love they *don't* report: obsessive, uncertain, intrusive anxiety about the bond. This high anxiety figures so prominently in our cultural scripts about the nature of passionate love, we forget that for many couples trust and security *fuel* the "adventure" of long-term marriage.

"I DON'T KNOW if I love my husband anymore," Emily said. She came to see me on a gray Monday morning, her energy as electric as the day was bleak. I felt drawn into the middle of things by her confiding intensity. "I don't know if I ever really loved him. I think I married him because he knew what he wanted, and he wanted me. Then suddenly I was pregnant and he convinced me to move here. Now we have our girls, we have a house. We have a *life*, and I'm thinking, 'How did I *get* here? I want *so badly* to move back to be near my family.' And he says, 'Forget it.' I think, 'What am I *doing* with this man?' "

Emily shifted in her seat and looked down, perhaps thinking about how she sounded. "Bill's really a good person. He'd do anything for the family. He works hard." She revved up again. "But he can't talk about his feelings to save his life. Whenever I try to talk about mine, he won't listen to me. I feel like I'm living the wrong life." Her eyes welled up, from frustration as much as grief. "Sometimes I feel so stuck, it's like I want to back the truck out of the mud and take another road."

I saw Emily several times over the next few weeks, and at each meeting she revisited the question of whether her marriage was a mistake. But I found myself equally riveted by what an engaging storyteller she was. Her descriptions of pained miscommunications were darkly funny and damning. She dramatized her husband's lack of perceptiveness and her sister-in-law's subtle condescension with entertaining set pieces. Sometimes I felt her stories took on a life of their own. I imagined two Emilys—the flesh-and-blood person who actually interacted with Bill, and the storyteller who fashioned those interactions into a convincing narrative. I also imagined what it felt like to be Bill, retreating into disengaged, slightly contemptuous rationality as protection against Emily's dramatic presentations. She took the floor so forcefully that it was hard to find any room to weigh in. As time went on, I felt a mounting pressure to convey that therapy could only help her if we used it to question her stories.

Then, one day, Emily surprised me. In a moment of reflection she said, "If Bill and I were getting along better now, I probably wouldn't be saying that I never really felt much for him. I'd tell the story differently. I'd say something like 'The relationship took a while to jell.' Or, 'We've grown closer over time.' Or, 'He's not the most emotional guy in the world, but I really appreciate how solid he is.'" I strained to detect if her utterance was a sop to fair-mindedness, or a perfunctory wave toward life's theoretical possibilities. It seemed that it was neither. Instead, Emily knew that the narrator's perspective is always part of the story itself. I felt an outsize burst of hope as I realized that Emily, unlike many of the people who cross my office threshold, was not entirely wedded to her story.

The couples that feel most connected and hopeful in their relationship are those that can tell a story of their relationship—psychologists call it a "we story"—that emphasizes loving elements such as empathy, respect, pleasure, and acceptance. The question is, how do people *do* it? How do they get from warring marital stories and standoffs to a meaningful shared narrative they can use as an aspirational, inspirational vision of the relationship? What exactly is involved in getting from one to the other?

To understand our relationship stories, it helps to continue the exploration of emotional development that we began in chapter 3. The stories we tell about our current relationship aren't simply about what's happening now. They draw upon our early experience of relationships in specific and systematic ways. If we want more freedom to review and change our current marital stories, we need to understand how our memories of our earliest relationships form, and how they continue to affect us.

Babies learn an enormous amount in the first year of life, but they process experiences in a whole-body, *feeling* way. They don't yet have the cortical development or cognitive ability to "recall" or "perceive" experience the way we do. Emotions, bodily sensations, visual images, perceptions, and response patterns between baby and caregiver are all laid down as "implicit" memories, which do not involve conscious attention or focus, either during the encoding of the memory or its retrieval. From our very beginnings, our brains are "anticipation machines," in the psychiatrist Daniel Siegel's words, and the mental models we construct have critical survival value, since identifying what's *likely* to happen enables rapid processing of potential threats as well as situations of safety and pleasure. These mental models, saturated with nonverbal, emotion-laden interaction patterns, become our first "memories" of relationships, well before we have any conscious sense of an "I." Two important implications follow. First, our implicit memories color our relationship experiences later in life, yet we have no conscious awareness of their origins. Second, when our implicit memories are reactivated in our relationships, we don't *experience* them as memories we are *recalling*. As Siegel puts it, "We simply enter these engrained states and experience them as the reality of our present experience." The very *nature* of early memory fuels our tendency to experience current interactions (with our partners, for instance) through the emotional lens of the past.

Around eighteen months of age, we begin to develop conscious or "explicit" memory. The development of the prefrontal cortex and neural networks ushers in the form of memory we equate with consciousness and allows for the experience "I am remembering." This is the beginning of autobiographical memory and a conscious sense of self. With the explosion of language development in the second year, children begin to understand and tell stories, which involve new levels of social understanding and reflective thought. The self that can tell a story about itself, the "narrative self," is born, and it develops and deepens over time.

Both implicit and explicit forms of memory are central to our experiences of who we are, and the tone of our emotional lives. Healthy emotional development involves weaving our body-based, experiential memories into a meaningful narrative conception of self. An integration, or fluid "conversation," between preverbal emotional memory and the conscious "self" story gives us a felt sense of authenticity. These two aspects of self and memory become integrated through our relationships with loved others, via the development of human attachment.

Human attachment unfolds in the first fifteen months of life, during the period of embodied, nonconscious, "implicit" memory we've been discussing. As is now commonly known, all infant-caregiver pairs display one of four distinct patterns of secure or insecure attachment, and these arise from specific and observable features of the caregiver's style of responsiveness. These widely validated patterns of infant attachment—secure, avoidant, resistant/ambivalent, and disorganized—reflect the *impact* of the parent's *responses* to the child's attachment-seeking behavior. A parent's responses to attachment-seeking behaviors teach a child, in effect, how to behave in order to continue to elicit care from this particular parent. These responses form the early basis for our expectations in intimate relationships.

When a caregiver is sensitive and responsive to the child's attachment-seeking behavior, it fosters a secure attachment bond. When a parent ignores or exaggerates the child's communication, the child responds by distorting his own attachment behavior accordingly. Children whose caregivers reject their attachment bids become avoidantly attached;

they avoid seeking proximity and turn their attention to other activities. Children with resistant/ambivalent attachment respond to the caregiver's oscillating insensitivity and unpredictability by failing to be soothed. Children whose caregivers display simultaneously frightened and frightening behavior develop a disorganized attachment style because they lack a clear strategy for seeking safety.

Children develop attachment security when their parents can *feel with* and *think about* their experience. When a parent is responsive, the child's developing story of self can fluidly incorporate and make use of his preverbal, embodied feelings. Defensive adaptations are at a minimum. Communication *within oneself* and communication *with another* can emerge in concert. In secure relating, parents and children share a world where feelings, perceptions, and intentions are deemed centrally important. Children are free to reflect on, review, and explore situations and thoughts in the present and construct a personal narrative of self with access to their full range of experience. The parent's behavior is benign and trustworthy enough to allow the child to explore his own and her mind without fear. The parent elicits and scaffolds her child's stories, and they work together to piece together "what happened," making meaning together. We can anticipate the value of such collaboration in fostering the child's future ability to construct a we story with his adult partner.

In contrast to securely attached children, those with insecure attachment develop problematic models of the attachment figure and the self. Attachment figures prone to unpredictable behavior give children disturbingly disjunctive images of the person they rely on for comfort and thereby decrease the child's experience of safety and trust. If a parent is intrusive one minute and neglectful the next or veers between comfort and anger, the child is left with confusing questions and painful feelings: Am I bad or good? Is Daddy mean or nice? If children have parents who deny, distort, or offer verbal accounts of events and emotions that conflict with the children's own witnessed and felt experience ("That wasn't scary!" "Grandpa's taken a long trip [when he's died]," "That didn't hurt [when insulted]"), the children cannot square their felt *experience* with the inaccurate

story that they absorb from interactions with their attachment figures. Conversely, dismissive parents influence their children to ignore
attachment-oriented emotions, which results in simplistic, minimal,
and emotionally depleted stories of self and other.

All this goes to show that we emerge from childhood with central
attachment stories, master narratives about who it is possible to *be* in a
relationship, and what it is possible to expect from others. These stories tell
us where dangers lurk (e.g., "Don't need too much, don't scare Mom")
and where we are likely to find a safe harbor (e.g., "Dad will comfort
me if I'm sad"). But just as impressive as the deep, organizing power of
these central narratives is that they can *change*. The ability to change our
story is another of the stunning discoveries from attachment research.

To see how stories can change, consider that attachment security
in adulthood does not simply relate to what happened to you as a
child. It relates to the *story* you can tell about what happened to you
as a child. Using an instrument called the Adult Attachment Interview
(AAI), researchers find that an adult's ability to tell *a coherent story*
about her own attachment history is what predicts the attachment
security of her child. In other words, if a woman, now a mother, can
reflect upon and coherently describe her relationship with her own
parent, *however insecure it may have been*, that becomes a decisive factor
in whether the attachment between her child and herself is secure.

When describing their childhoods on the AAI, adults who are rated
as "secure-autonomous" can simultaneously access emotional memories of their childhood relationships, reflect on their meaning, and
convey them clearly and collaboratively to another person. Adults rated
"dismissive-avoidant" speak in cognitively organized but emotionally
impoverished ways about their early attachments. Those rated "anxious-
preoccupied" get flooded with their attachment-related emotion, and
their memory, thinking, and speech become distorted. These categories
of parents' narrative discourse map onto their children's attachment
security status. Thus, the parents of secure children tend to talk in
coherent, self-reflective ways about their own childhoods. Parents of
avoidant children describe their relationships with their own parents in
non-introspective and oversimplified ways, and give global descriptions

("happy childhood," "wonderful mother") that are unsupported by specific memories. Parents of ambivalent/resistant children tend to describe their own attachment histories in ways that are confusing, vague, and lacking awareness of the interviewer's perspective.

The crucial point is that a parent who can now tell a coherent story about her own past attachment relationships, and whose own child is securely attached, *didn't necessarily have a secure childhood attachment herself.* That's what attachment researchers call "earned" or "evolved" security. An "evolved secure" parent arrives at a perspective on her past experience that enables her to feel, behave, and speak *differently* in her current relationships. The evidence is strong that a supportive, trusting relationship is what helps us heal from the attachment insecurity that arises from early insensitivity, trauma, or loss. Emotional support from a therapist, or some other important figure who came through in moments of need, contributes to earned security in new mothers. A study of children reared in institutions showed that many became good parents "following warm and confiding marital experience." Mothers who were abused in childhood are less likely to abuse their own children if they have therapy or an emotionally satisfying relationship with a partner. Marriage and parenthood both tend to move people toward greater attachment security. And a secure attachment between romantic partners appears to contribute more to the emotional quality of their relationship than does their attachment patterns with early caregivers.

The brilliance of the AAI is that it requires people to *both* remember formative emotional experiences with caregivers *and* think coherently and maintain self-awareness in the present. This is harder than it sounds. Our attachment relationships naturally arouse our passionate emotions. Securely attached adults are distinctive in their ability to think and speak coherently about their early attachment relationships *in the context* of powerful attachment emotions. This is the essence of reflective function, the *feeling-with-and-thinking-about* process that we explored in chapter 3. "The capacity to think about feeling and feel about thinking," in the words of one attachment researcher, is the heart of both reflective functioning and attachment security. Secure adults can *feel with* and *think about* the child they were, and about the child they now have.

Marriages are also attachment relationships, engaging our deepest hopes and fears about safety, comfort, and care. And because attachment bonds activate our most primal emotional needs, it's not always easy to apply our thinking—our contact with the big picture, our we story—to modulate, moderate, and shape our responses within them. Close relationships suffer when people habitually override feelings with thoughts or overwhelm thoughts with feelings. A dismissive-avoidant spouse, for instance, might give an official story of his own past ("no problems," "loving family") that is spectacularly negated by the particulars ("Oh yeah, my dad was an alcoholic, but he didn't beat us that much"). His idealized image of his childhood will cover over his early emotional experience and block access to feelings of vulnerability with his partner. In reality, such a person likely felt that his needs for comfort and responsiveness were neglected by his parents. As a result, he became prematurely self-sufficient, and now he sparks fights with his wife by ridiculing her emotionality. To truly soften toward his wife (and himself), he would have to begin to see the ways his story was an attempt to survive his childhood situation, and the ways his story unwittingly turns his wife into the "whiny" child he was once blamed for being, and which his entire identity has organized itself around forgetting. If the couple were in therapy, we would try to open up his painful past in order to understand the emotions of the present and try to create a new experience between the couple in the present to better integrate and heal the past.

The possibility of changing our story in response to new emotional experience means that a secure, loving marriage is a potentially "therapeutic" relationship. In a loving relationship where we trust in our partner's care, we can begin to reevaluate our own stories, reopening the channel between our early emotional memories and our conscious story of self and relationships. We can expand our awareness of how earlier attachment patterns contribute to current behavior, reviewing tendencies that may once have been a means of survival, but now create barriers. We might notice, for example, that when we feel needy and dependent, we quickly become vigilant or defensive. Or we might try, in those moments when our partner doesn't overreact, to overcome our fear and risk seeking more closeness. By reflecting on our tendencies, we are more able to talk about them and gradually move toward a more loving and responsive we story.

Even minor experiences, if we reflect on them, can open the way to changing our story. Imagine a young woman who is torn about whether she wants to have a child. She goes to her friend's house one day, and they chat, as her friend feeds her thirteen-month-old sitting in his high chair. The child—perhaps to get attention—flings his bowl of cereal onto the floor. The young woman observes her friend say in a friendly way, "Oh, whoops! That's a big mess, isn't it?" and calmly clean it up. The young woman is surprised, even a bit shocked. She expected anger. She becomes aware of a gap between her expectation and reality, which prompts her to reflect. She realizes she has a mental model of a mother-child relationship in which exuberant acts of self-assertion are met with harshness. Witnessing her friend's different "story" shakes loose the inevitability of her own. She can now begin to imagine a different story about her potential experience as a mother, and her potential interaction with a child. Her story of her relationship with her mother also starts to make sense in new ways.

When Emily questioned her own story that day early in her therapy, it evoked in me a burst of hope because it signaled that she was open to other viewpoints. It was hard for her to reflect on her powerful emotions, and to stop believing so wholeheartedly in their ability to tell the whole story. But one of her strengths was that she wanted to try. As Emily and I worked together over the months, our therapy relationship gave her the emotional support and mental space to think about her experience, to seek understanding rather than simply react. By my listening and responding to her, she came to listen and respond more to herself. She also became more able to listen to her husband, and more interested in knowing what *he* felt and thought. She gradually quieted her reflex to have the last word and supply the ruling narrative. As she tempered her rush to interpretation, she discovered that what she most craved was a sense of sharing. Years into their marriage, it seemed, she and Bill were beginning to find a "we story."

*   *   *

RESEARCH FINDINGS ON attachment, emotion regulation, meta-cognition, and mindfulness all demonstrate that being able to narrate our inner experience is one of the most powerful ways we can change how we *feel*. Telling a coherent, accurate story about our experience directly relates to our ability to modulate and modify our emotions. Each helps the other: a coherent story helps organize emotion, and modulating our emotions helps us tell a coherent story. When we can calm our emotions, we are more able to reflect. The sheer act of becoming aware, not only of the particular story we are telling, but also of our telling a story at all, is *itself* a powerful instrument of emotion regulation.

The breakdown of emotion regulation contributes to both bad marriages and bad divorces. Who among us hasn't watched someone hurtling into a marital train wreck who is unable, or unwilling, to fore-see the consequences? As a therapist, I might try to slow things down and help someone think about his decisions from the perspective of his future self. But people are sometimes unable or unwilling to do so. If I try to explore the big picture and the likely losses and gains he will encounter, he may blow past me and see me as a moralizer or someone who doesn't get it. He may even reject the notion that losses and gains *are* inevitable in every potential outcome. In states of high emotion, people lose the ability to disentangle feelings, interpretation, and reality. It takes *effort* to keep in mind that our experience and our story about it differ; that we are often motivated by factors we do not understand to tell the story we do; and that the story we are telling is not complete. It's an effort that people are not always willing or able to expend.

Yet once the marriage is dismantled or the affair has run its course, a new but not very different kind of pain often sets in. The person who was unable to look at the big picture is now shocked and angry at what has come to pass. She feels wronged, yet she doesn't know where to place the blame.

These issues were at the forefront when I spoke with Britta, who had initiated divorce but was now distraught that her ex-husband planned to remarry. Her reaction surprised her. She had not been attracted to her husband for years and had always found his meticulous approach to life suffocating. She was much happier around her artist friends and had several imagined future lovers among them. When we met, she delivered her account to me matter-of-factly—she didn't want to be in therapy, but her friends told her she should be—and she spoke as if her own actions had little relevance to the unfolding of events. Listening to her talk, I was struck that her narrative completely lacked any foreshadowing of the state she was now in. In her telling, she was utterly blindsided that her fifty-two-year-old ex-husband, who had wanted to stay married to her, had found someone else to love. With her husband starting a new life and her own recent romance having crashed and burned, she felt angry and blaming, as if she had been victimized by events that she had had no hand in choosing.

Feeling alone, worried, strapped financially, and deprived, Britta began, without realizing it, to cast about for a target of reproach. When she was married, her husband had filled that role; but now she felt that her two preadolescent children's demands and needs were depleting her. She told the children, who were bewildered by all the recent changes, that they "shouldn't act so entitled" and that "money doesn't grow on trees." Such fixtures of their former lives as vacations and music lessons were luxuries Britta could no longer afford. But rather than sympathize with her children's feelings of loss, or experience her own guilt or grief, she criticized them for expecting too much. She seemed unaware that she had changed the terms and saw it as a problem within *them* that they clung to old expectations. Her in-the-moment emotional experience completely drowned out the larger story across time.

Britta was seeking a meaningful path forward, but lacking an internal conversation that could link her thoughts and feelings, she fluctuated between chaos and rigidity. She was chaotic when her feelings of anxiety and deprivation felt so powerful that she couldn't reflect on her choices and learn from them. She was rigid when she repetitively turned to her unsuccessful strategy of looking for external fixes for her internal unhappiness. The psychiatrist Daniel Siegel suggests that chaos and rigidity are signposts of emotional dysregulation. Britta's problems, by her report, "were over" when she became involved with a new man. But just as quickly, they flooded back when the new man disappeared. Unable to use metacognition to manage her emotions,

Britta was incapable of referencing an overarching story that could help her organize her thoughts, feelings, and actions. She was both overly convinced of her story and not sure what it was.

From Britta's description of her growing up, I sensed that she hadn't received the loving parental interest that might have helped her integrate her emotions with a stable sense of self. The term *narcissism* is bandied about as an all-purpose condemnation, but it's more usefully understood as a deep sense of lack that makes it hard to see other people as *real people*, with agendas and feelings on a par with one's own. Insensitive parents present children with an unmet craving for love, tenderness, and affection. The children pursue the consolation prize of admiration, seeking attention for being special in some way their self-absorbed parents might reward. The children take care of themselves in this way, but it leaves them feeling empty. Eventually, they discount other people in the same way they themselves were discounted. This is the tragedy of narcissism. Britta's sense of deprivation led her to behave in self-absorbed ways that put other people off, leaving her feeling more alone and deprived than ever.

Despite my hope that people will revise the narratives that bring them pain, I have been listening to people for long enough to have a healthy respect for the unconscious forces that give our stories their stubborn power. Just as not all attachments are wholesome, neither are all we stories. Our stories are nourished by deep streams of primal, conflicting emotions—aggression, envy, guilt, fear, and jealousy, to name a few. Our early experiences and the feelings they engender coalesce to form lasting, buried beliefs that govern the way we see ourselves and the stories we tell about life. One reason we get stuck in our stories is because they so economically and effectively express the complex mixture of wishes, fears, and fantasies that structure our unconscious lives.

This was the case with Geoff and Tanya, a couple in their early fifties. When they came to see me, the first thing that struck me was the loftiness of Geoff's speech. His pretentious diction seemed a bit crazy to me, not because of anything he said, but because he seemed to be acting out a fantasy about his effect on his audience (me) that seemed private and self-referential. His wife, Tanya, on the other hand, seemed practical and down-to-earth, pretty and neat, more Talbots than Anthropologie. In looks, they could have emerged from different movie casts—he was a sort of Harvard-bred John Cleese, she a more prim, upscale version of Skyler White from *Breaking Bad*. The "performance" of their marriage seemed, within my first moments of meeting them, scripted, contrived, and oddly enchanting to them both. I almost felt they were enacting some quasi-erotic scenario that was utterly opaque to me.

When I asked them why they were seeking couple therapy, they genially mentioned several normal things. They aspired to grow old together. They had a rich history, sharing laughs and warmth and children, which they wanted to preserve. But they had drastically different ideas about the kind of life they wanted now. His work was centered in the city. Her life revolved around their suburban neighborhood. In a year, their last child would be leaving for college. Geoff looked ahead to his son's departure with trepidation and mournfulness, but he also eagerly anticipated more freedom and flexibility to pursue his city life more fully. Images of their soon-to-be-emptied house gave Geoff's craving for stimulation a slightly desperate edge. Tanya, on the other hand, looked forward to their last child's departure as an opportunity to reconnect with her husband and find the close coupledom they had enjoyed in their twenties. Her vision was simple. He would return from work every day and they would enjoy a dinner together, followed by a movie, followed by bed. To her, it seemed a pleasurable and deserved reward for their many years in the harness of childrearing.

As I began to grasp the basic contours of their situation, I found myself thinking that two people who had raised a family while continuing to laugh together and profess love certainly had enough on the ball to find a workable compromise between their priorities. I asked all the obvious questions. Had they tried to meld their two worlds by including her in his activities? Yes, they had, but she found his work events boring and the people pompous. Had they experimented with designating certain nights of the week for independent activities? No, for the simple reason that they argued on any night he chose to stay out rather than come home. Had he tried to involve himself fully in the domestic activities she wanted to share? Yes, he enjoyed them, but he became restless and didn't feel that always doing things her way should be the price of harmony.

The puzzle, so common in marriages, was how seemingly straightforward and yet frankly impossible their dilemma was. Their story contained a striking juxtaposition: they loved each other and wanted to remain married, yet neither could bear compromising in a way that allowed the other to fulfill important desires. As we talked about their pasts, Geoff spoke of his inflexible mother, who left him in the cold when he didn't comply with her wishes. By his account she was demanding and superior. He'd spent a lot of energy trying to get her approval, feeling that only a narrow band of behavior would win it. When he wandered into this territory in subsequent meetings, I never knew which version I would get from him. Sometimes he spoke of his mother in almost reverential tones. At other times I could feel his fury at her radiating from him like a hot blast. At still other times, he gave off an almost aggressively childlike belief that he should be free to express himself and be accepted and celebrated for who he was. All these feelings found expression in his core problem with Tanya. He saw Tanya as inflexible and narrow in her definition of "good" behavior, just like his mother, and yet part of him wanted to please her. Another part was furious at not feeling understood, and he took it out on her by insisting on his right to freedom. He could vent his anger and satisfy his love in one fell swoop by simultaneously punishing her by his unavailability while earnestly trying to respond to her needs. He protested Tanya's rejection of his independent interests, yet he also subtly excluded her from them. He was both acting out something old and trying to do something new.

Tanya had grown up in a family where rigidity meant safety. Her mother's rules and routines were like a retaining wall against anxiety and dread. The well-manicured lives of her family, where everyone behaved well and did things together, established norms that kept people "safe." When we explored the extraordinary pressures to behave correctly, she divulged that just beyond the generational limits were a horde of drunks and abusers. One of her own siblings had been exiled for his bad behavior, and no one talked about him anymore. "He's living in the street now, for all I know," she said. Tanya expressed both aggression and anxiety through her black-and-white view of safety and danger, much as her mother, by invoking the traumatic specter of her own alcoholic father, had kept Tanya's fun-loving father in line. Tanya's outward justification was dependency—the desire for closeness and anxiety at being alone— which made Geoff feel valued and needed, a feeling he had longed for from his own mother. But it also amounted to a steely effort at control, partly to deal with Tanya's feelings of envy and jealousy about the good things in Geoff's life that had nothing to do with her.

The problem Geoff and Tanya came to get help with was, in a deep sense, the very thing that made the relationship meaningful to both of them. They were enacting a pattern of relating with each other that gave expression to their conflictual wishes. Tanya could be the controlling mother, Geoff the placating child. Geoff could be the rebellious child, and Tanya the angry or scared mother. Geoff could punish Tanya for her control by leaving (acting on his "right to be himself"), then come back into her good graces by submitting to her wishes. A painful arrangement for sure, but painful in a way that their early lives had taught them to expect. They chose each other because the story they could act out together felt so *right*.

Sitting with Geoff and Tanya, I felt a knotted stuckness, yet they had admirably collaborated in creating a marriage and a family for almost twenty-five years. The same themes had been there all along, so why were they creating more of a problem now? The utterly normal and expectable life task of confronting the empty nest and reconfiguring their priorities was creating a challenging disruption. With their children gone, they would be forced to figure out how, or whether, they wanted to change and grow, as individuals and as a couple.

A signature element of growth in marriage is the shift from blaming one's spouse for the state of one's world ("I am an innocent victim of your faults") to bearing responsibility for the impact of one's own conflicted and destructive feelings. If I am able to see, and to own, that I am doing something negative to you, it helps me both to stop doing it, and to reinstate you as a good person toward whom I feel love. Even if I am ending the relationship, it is crucial for me to move from blaming you for not being the wife/husband you *should* be, to bearing the guilt of no longer wanting to be with the husband/wife that you *are*. Bearing guilt and responsibility for one's own feelings is a huge part of what it means to be an adult.

A marriage carries the potential for growth and antigrowth. Couples can choose to develop individually and in their relationship, or they can treat marriage as a bulwark against change, keeping them safe from effort or thought. A significant source of rough-patch distress is when partners differ on whether they even want to try to grow or have different ideas of the direction that might take. Couples can also have tacit agreements to stay put and to play out their projections forever. As time wore on, I wondered if this was what Geoff and Tanya were doing. It wasn't just that their core dilemma didn't seem to budge, but also something about their attitude in the face of change. When I tried to hold one of them to account, things would get slippery; the other would step in with excuses, or they would laugh conspiratorially, as if they were teammates and I was their opponent in some imagined game. I felt sometimes that they were acting out their secretly satisfying scenario—me as the exacting mother, them as naughty partners in crime?—and it situated them together in an oddly safe, childlike position. They had a deep agreement to stay in a holding pattern, even though they had ostensibly come to therapy in order to change.

Outwardly, Geoff and Tanya expressed in extreme form the two drives of midlife, deepening inward and expanding outward. Tanya stood for a version of deepening inward that cocooned her and her husband in a stifling dyad. Geoff carried the banner of engagement with the world, though with a stealth dose of Peter Panism that goaded Tanya's insecurity. Divergent as these aims appeared, they existed in a perverse equipoise. In the best case, marriage in midlife expands the middle space between the cozy dyad and the huge impersonal world. Rather than becoming increasingly polarized and sequestered, the partners make room for both an expanding web of connection, and a deepening sense of intimacy. But doing that means somehow transforming the scripts from childhood, and forging a mutually created vision, a mature story of their own. Ultimately for Tanya and Geoff, the devil they knew won out over the devil they didn't. They left therapy after six months, elaborately thanking me for my questionable help. Their we story both satisfied and deprived them. I had the feeling that they would continue to complain but change nothing.

PEOPLE WHO STUDY marriage talk about the need for a we story in different ways. I call it the golden ring. Psychoanalytic therapists refer to it as the third, and the Gottman-oriented therapists call it the story-of-us. We're all referring to the same essential marital attitude: that each partner nurture, protect, and contribute to the relationship as an entity that exists apart from, and between, the two individuals. Creating a we story is a collaboration between partners about values, vision, and goals. It grows out of, and reflects, an attitude of care and interest. But if we're going to collaborate, we have to figure out how to have a productive conversation. A conversation—as opposed to a parallel monologue—involves two *different* people, each with a *valid point of view*, who are making an effort to *understand* each other. In the grip of emotion, conversations can be surprisingly hard to achieve.

Margaret and Ben had a big we-story decision in front of them. They were figuring out whether to move back to her native England to raise their children, who were now four and six. The choice involved economics, family, culture, and identity, and it necessitated collaboration. But when Margaret reached out to me for help, she told me, "Ben and I can't have a conversation." Each felt a looming pressure to set their course, but both felt stymied by how impossible it was to make a decision together. Every time they tried to make some headway, the effort broke down. They needed help figuring out how to talk.

To navigate a couple conversation successfully, it helps to think in terms of three phases. A useful opening move, deceptively simple though it may sound, is to ask your partner, "Is this a good time to talk?" If your partner's answer is "No, it's not," it's up to him or her to offer a timely alternative. This question is useful because we routinely broach complicated topics on the fly, while our partner is headed out the door to work, or puzzling out the income taxes, or trying to go to sleep. Then we become hurt or incensed that they "never" listen (and begin to weave a story about it). Embedded in this opening question is a golden-ring awareness that you are asking a complex, three-dimensional, *separate* human being to take *time and energy* to participate with you in a potentially *challenging and stressful*, although hopefully *rewarding*, interaction.

The second two phases represent the *feeling with* and *thinking about* process in action. Remember the example of falling off your bike as a kid? You needed both comfort *and* a solution. A universal source of breakdown in couple conversation is when partners offer or receive only one or the other: "I want you to listen, not try to fix the problem" or "Would you calm down so we can come up with a solution?" Couple conversations work best when there's room for both feeling *and* thinking. These can't necessarily happen at the same time, particularly in difficult conversations. It helps to begin with each person trying to discover and communicate what he feels, encouraged by questions but free of unsolicited commentary and interruption from his partner. This can take self-control. It's tempting to just go through the motions of listening, figuratively tapping the table while waiting to be the speaker, and getting antsy about making your case. But being a caring person in this moment *means* managing your own emotional state, so that you can listen with curiosity and compassion. After feelings have been shared on both sides—placed in the golden ring—partners can think together about how to address the problem. They may find, to their pleasant surprise, that fully articulating their feelings has revealed more overlap in their viewpoints than they initially expected. If not, at least they now have more understanding of what compromises they'll need to make to arrive at a solution they can both live with.

When I met with Ben and Margaret, I focused on *how* they were talking to each other because, in general, I believe that people are resourceful and creative problem-solvers once they can manage a collaborative conversation. I asked them to start having the conversation in front of me.

Margaret: [to Ben] Okay, so what have you decided about the move?

That struck me as a pretty confrontational gambit. Had they, unbeknownst to me, already agreed that the ball was in Ben's court?

> *Daphne:* Before you go on, could I just get clear? Do you have a
> shared understanding that it's up to Ben to make a decision?
> *Ben:* No, we don't.
> *Margaret:* Every time I try to talk about it, he ignores me, so I've
> told him he needs to decide.

Clearly, Margaret had not yet figured out how to initiate conversation successfully on this sensitive topic. Within three turns of the exchange, they were already in a seesaw situation. Frustrated by not feeling heard and not making headway on the timetable she'd hoped, Margaret tossed the issue over to Ben and behaved as if it were all his. He was now in a bind: damned if he accepted full responsibility for the decision (e.g., acting unilaterally, not caring about her feelings), and damned if he didn't (e.g., shirking responsibility, not respecting her need for progress). I needed to encourage a golden-ring, we-story consciousness.

> *Daphne:* This is a difficult, complicated decision, and obviously it'll
> only feel good to both of you if you can make it together. I think
> it helps to acknowledge that you are embarking on a challenging
> conversation, and to include that awareness when you approach
> each other. [to Margaret] Do you want to try that?
> *Margaret:* [to Ben] I'm thinking a lot about the move, and I'm
> getting worried. I'd like us to talk about it. Can we do that now?
> *Daphne:* Nice. Ben, since you're in a therapy session, I assume your
> answer is yes. But why don't you take it from there?
> *Ben:* That did feel better. [to Margaret] Yeah, sure, we can do it now.
> *Margaret:* So have you made those calls you were planning to make?
> *Ben:* Uh, it's been hard to make those calls because of the time
> difference. . . . But I do plan to do it in the next few days.

Ben seemed slightly intimidated, as if his response was overly determined by Margaret's sense of pressure.

Daphne: You know, Ben, part of getting across what you think and feel is going to hinge on you feeling you have a *right* to it and communicating clearly. I think you're so used to Margaret driving things that you end up reacting to her questions, and maybe even resenting her or dragging your feet in the process. I want you to try to figure out a way to respond that says, without being cowed or irritated, "This is what I'm feeling and thinking, and planning to do." Can you try that?

Ben: [breath] Let's see. . . . Margaret, can we back up a little bit? I think we should give each other a status report about where we're each at about this move. I'll tell you what I'm thinking, and I want to hear what you are thinking. I'm *not* trying to get out of anything. [He anticipated her likely fear.] I'd just like to take a minute to get a feel for where we're each coming from.

Margaret's face softened a bit, and she looked relieved and almost grateful. She also seemed a bit awkward, finding herself in the unexpected position of figuring out her own feelings, rather than demanding action from Ben.

As you can discern from this short snippet of interaction, Ben and Margaret had their predictable forms of breakdown. Confronted with an anxiety-ridden decision that evoked strong, confused emotions, they both struggled with their characteristic stances. Margaret became subtly critical and demanding, and Ben became both sheepish and oppositional. They needed to access a golden-ring structure both *within* themselves and *between* them. After Ben reacted in his characteristic way, I urged him to think about what he felt, and then take the risk of defining and expressing his point of view to Margaret. When Ben did that, it helped Margaret calm down. Margaret gained a visceral sense that Ben was doing his part, and she could feel more secure, such that she wasn't drawn to shut down or retaliate. When she calmed down, it helped him calm down.

One benefit of introducing a more structured conversational framework is that it can lead to a more neutral emotional tone, which does wonders for our nervous systems. The notion of cathartic self-expression that was deemed the path to emotional health in the 1960s and 1970s has been thoroughly discredited by our increased understanding of the role of emotional self-regulation in managing negative states. We now know there is a world of difference between emotion and emoting. With respect to couple interaction, the researcher John Gottman wrote, "Think about the relationship fights you have had. You'd probably agree that a neutral presentation of your partner's point of view by your partner would probably be an enormously welcome relief." Difficult as communicating neutrally sometimes feels, it is worth the effort. More neutral communication encourages less reactive and more cooperative interaction. It calms us down, which helps us to clarify our feelings and increases the chances that we will be heard and understood.

"TO TELL A story is inescapably to take a moral stance," wrote the psychologist Jerome Bruner. Every story we tell, of marriage or life, involves judgments about the salient facts, the details to amplify, the impression we wish to leave. The techniques that great storytellers use to draw us in are not unlike the ones that intimate partners use with each other to promote fruitful conversation. Both ease the listener into their story by speaking in terms of possibilities rather than certainties. When one partner wants to invite the other to consider his perspective, he signals his belief that he doesn't have sole access to the truth. He might use phrases like "I sometimes feel" or "I don't know if you really think this, but . . ." He presents his own interpretation as open to input and revision. In doing so, he invites curiosity. Troubled couples, by contrast, are strikingly consistent in their difficulty in doing exactly that. Rather than exploring implied meanings, they insist their partner's meanings are unambiguous (and often bad). They have trouble observing their own biases. They often use language to win their argument rather than to tell their story. They spend time arguing about *facts* ("Yes, you did say that!") rather than trying to understand intentions. They don't feel heard, but they find it hard to listen. Each partner feels too guarded to offer any thought in an open way, afraid of being misunderstood, blamed, or both.

Under stress we can all make a mess of even our most earnest efforts to acknowledge that we speak from our own perspective. "I" statements—those rusty gizmos clanking around in the couple-therapy tool kit—too often tack on a point of view by putting an *I* in front of every utterance. Sometimes it works, sometimes it doesn't. It would be humorous, were it not so painful, to witness how many ways people find to twist "I" statements into blame ("I hate when you . . ."). Riddling our speech with *always* and *never* is another type of attempt to coerce a single interpretation in our desperation to be heard.

But it is extraordinary to witness the impact when a partner expresses awareness that his feelings are *a product of his own mind*, rather than a direct result of his partner's behavior. It is instantly soothing and mentally organizing to the other partner, giving him space to consider rather than react. Impressively, this is true even when partners take perspective on their *inability* to take perspective. One wife tended to exaggerate when she became emotional—"My husband gets nasty, and then I feel abused," she would declare, oblivious of the hot buttons she pressed when she chose the words she did. It helped when she developed the ability to *notice* her rhetoric heating up, and to assess the validity of her own story. In that moment, her blind commitment to her story gave way to an attempt to understand.

When do we choose to tell a we story, and when do we choose not to? On any given day the story might change, and being an emotionally balanced person means not crediting any one variant too completely. Every we story isn't a story of staying married; some are stories of compassionate parting. Part of your we story might be how hard it is to *tell* one—how painfully at cross-purposes you often both feel, or how rarely those moments of intimate closeness or relaxed trust seem possible. But we have the opportunity, and the responsibility, to be curious about what kind of narrator we are, and how that shapes the story we tell. Even at those moments when the stuff of the marriage feels painful and conflict ridden, or boring and predictable, we can still be interested in understanding the story we are telling about it.

Affairs, Flirting, and Fantasy:
They're Never about Nothing

Martha and Aron came to see me after Aron had gotten involved with someone at work. A female colleague he liked had begun to confide in him about her unhappy marriage. Sexual electricity ensued. At the annual convention they'd both gotten drunk, and for six months they'd carried on at a hotel near their work. Martha found their texts on Aron's phone and felt she would be sick. She threatened to leave. Aron confessed and apologized, panicked he could lose her and their two children. At first he flung blame in every direction; he claimed he'd been seduced, then made a brief attempt to find fault in Martha—how buttoned-up she was, how hard it was to take any vacation from responsibility with her. When they first came to see me, they'd endured a week of tears, nauseating disorientation, and true misery. The worst of the storm had passed—they were talking, not just crying and yelling—but they felt spent, awkward, and confused, with no path forward.

In our first meeting, I was surprised by Martha's thoughtfulness. She was thin and serious, thirty-nine, with beautiful eyes. Their children were ten and eight, a boy and a girl. She'd stopped working two years ago, when their daughter had been diagnosed with Tourette's syndrome. "Helping her manage her anxiety is a full-time job," Martha said. The prominence of her daughter's situation in her mind, even in the current context, made clear how much it wore on her. I sensed that her apparent calm was her way of holding it together when tense. Aron was the opposite. Forty-one, with an athletic body going to seed, he exuded a restless vigor that, under other circumstances, I imagined would read as boisterous charm. Now he was awkward with Martha, and tentative, but I felt an undertow of impatience as well.

Aron, when he spoke, clearly wanted more than anything for the past to be the past, *to get back to normal.* "It's hard for me to sit here and not know what you're thinking," Aron said to me. "You probably think I'm a scumbag." He laughed incongruously, his eyes bright and wary. I wondered why he so quickly worried about *my* opinion. I felt pressured to lighten up.

"If I'm honest, the biggest problem for me right now isn't that I fooled around," he said. "It's that I don't feel *right* in myself. I haven't for a while. The happy guy I used to be is gone."

"Maybe this whole thing has affected how you feel about yourself," I said. "Or, maybe not knowing why you did it makes you feel a little disturbed?"

He looked at me. "I know why I did it. I was being selfish. I had an opportunity and I took it. I don't want to make excuses for what I did." It was important to Aron that the episode mean nothing, except that he was a "guy," selfish and sex driven; a scumbag.

After several exchanges like this, I understood that Aron wanted to take responsibility, and I admired the effort to be honest. But when someone is as intent as Aron to make a case for himself, even a damning one, I tend to wonder whether there is an alternative that is even more frightening for him to think about. Being "selfish" and "sex crazed" appeared to be a relatively comfortable picture for Aron. It meant he had lapsed, in a circumscribed "guy" kind of way, and it didn't have much to do with anything else. Nothing was shaken to the foundation by this indulgence; he could get back to normal.

"One thing your view of yourself doesn't completely explain is, why now? I mean, if this is just a selfish 'guy' thing, why not every month, or at least every year?"

My question clearly annoyed him, but he decided cooperation might be a better approach: "That's a good question."

Martha said, "You don't know what it means, and I don't know what it means, and unless we try to figure it out, we're going to stay on the surface."

On the surface was exactly where Aron wanted to stay. He wanted to believe that "it was nothing," both to save Martha from hurt (though he knew the damage was done), and to convince himself that nothing deeper was going on, that he could get back on track without major excavation and reconstruction. My vision was limited by my angle on the situation, since I was seeing them as a couple. But I detected more feeling in Aron, and more conflict, than he wanted to admit. He clearly felt the right thing to do was to reinvest wholeheartedly in his marriage. He wanted to return to his old story line. But the story had irrevocably changed; it now included new people and new emotions. His only hope was to find a new story, and to do that, he'd have to use the mess to come to some deeper understanding of himself and his relationships.

I gradually learned that confusing feelings roiled beneath the surface of his thrill-seeking, "guy's guy" persona. Family life—the stresses of work, the endless weekend to-do lists, the fraught discussions about the kids—had obliterated the time he used to have for blowing off steam, and the result was a churning anxiety in his gut and a shortened fuse. In the past, carousing with friends and flirting with women had generally kept his mood up. Now, even when he had the opportunity, it could only distract him so much, and he was beginning to run up against the limits of his own go-to diversions. External fixes became less effective, and the pressure increased to put his internal house to rights. Yet the confusion aroused by even beginning to approach his inner world had fueled more escapist tactics. Aron found himself, now, at their outer limit—not having blown up his marriage, but having come close.

He didn't like talking about himself. Even aside from his current predicament, the emotions he had to face from the past felt so impossible. How could he ever heal from the imprint of his mother's mood swings on his soul, from the chronic burden and fear of managing, comforting, and making sure he wasn't a problem for her—which meant keeping his needs hidden, even from himself? How could he ever come to terms with his father's apparent coldness? He was clearly vulnerable to feeling intensely responsible for the women in his life. When he let his wife down, which they both agreed he often did, he became ashamed, then angry, and then intent on pumping up his self-esteem through other sources. He'd stay in a cheerful, superficial, placating role with his wife, while indulging himself behind her back. If he could have made it work forever, he might have tried. But rough-patch crises force us toward discovering a deeper truth, even as we struggle to resist it.

Martha, I learned, had undergone an even more anguished childhood than Aron's. Her father was rarely there, and his extramarital affairs, supposedly "hidden," were a humiliating fact of life. Her parents divorced when she was twelve, and she struggled between her mother's demands for loyalty and her hunger for her father's attention. When she left home for college, she had found helpful mentors and done well for herself. Leaving work to cope with her daughter's difficulties had been a blow and a loss, and her mood didn't seem to have fully recovered.

Martha was deeply hurt and angry with Aron. Equally troubling, she said, was what she called "her Bill Clinton problem." "The sexual jealousy bothers me, but I'm even more bothered by Aron's lying and lack of self-control. I can't respect him." She still felt she loved him and was committed to keeping their family together, but the spark of admiration was gone. In its place, she envisioned a depressing future of living alongside each other, their ideals deflated. She also felt confused by something that surprises some postaffair couples: she and Aron were suddenly urgently attracted to each other. Martha's interest in the question of *why* appealed to me; unlike Aron, she neither tried to suppress her thoughts nor bury their consequences. "I'd be tempted to say the sex has to do with relief that I didn't lose him, but I don't actually believe it," she said. "I don't feel I've won him back in some kind of animal competition with a rival. It's weirder than that. I have some new knowledge of who he is apart from me, as almost as a stranger to me. It feels like something deeper is going on than our personalities."

*   *   *

WHEN I SIT with a couple after an affair is revealed, two questions hang in the air: Do you both want to find your way back, and what do you each want to find your way back *to*? Affairs are about so many things for the hurt partner: betrayal of trust, sexual jealousy, personal rejection, traumatic surprise, the sudden threat to one's grasp of reality, the excruciating question of what to do next. The unfaithful partners who aren't already on their way out are thrown into panic. They make desperate apologies, express remorse, plead to be given another chance. They try to attend to their partner's wounds and to put their partner first, but they often feel as if a truck hit them as well. They feel compelled to explain themselves, yet they're often deeply confused about what has happened, and why they did what they did. Their story has become too complicated to tell.

Months, sometimes years, pass as the couple tries to absorb the traumatic impact, make sense of what happened, and figure out how to go on. Recovery is rarely linear, and sometimes a horrible becalmed period sets in. The hurt partner continues to feel triggered (the spouse is late, he's inexplicably bought a new kind of underwear, there's a movie about strippers on TV—*isn't there always?*), and the unfaithful partner begins to feel increasingly trapped in a shameful role he cannot get out of. He will wonder aloud, at the risk of sounding callous, whether the hurt partner will ever get over the affair. He feels himself victimized by the hurt partner's continuing trauma and pain, unfair as he knows that to be.

One emotional source for this feeling harkens back to Henry Dicks's description of marriage as "a mutual affirmation of the other's identity as a *lovable person*." Feeling one has relinquished one's status as a lovable person causes a particular torment. The hurt partner justifiably feels that her sense of lovableness has been violently injured. But to recover after an affair, both partners must somehow be reinstated as lovable. The unfaithful partner faces obvious challenges. His behavior was not lovable, and now, to be restored as lovable, he's going to have to be honest, which commits him to revealing information that works directly against his lovableness. Tortured conversations ensue as a hurt partner seeks reassurances ("Was (s)he sexier than I am?" "Did you do [fill-in-the-blank sex act]?"), and the unfaithful partner tries to supply them. The unfaithful partner frantically wishes to reassure, and the hurt partner acutely wants to be reassured. But disturbing details are either revealed or suppressed, and in neither scenario do the partners feel relieved.

Couples desperately wish they could turn back the clock and return to "normal." Their life together and their story are now broken apart, and something different has to be constructed in their place. How they find their way through their feelings of loss—of trust, of their story of their marriage, of closeness—will determine whether they can find a way forward that works for both people. The sense of loss following a discovered affair is particularly searing—given the confusion, despair, and disconnection that now revolve around one's most central intimate relationship. It's not incidental that affairs themselves often occur on the heels of loss—of a parent, a hope, a job disappointment, or a child's illness. The mind alights on a seductive possibility at just the moment when it is in danger of falling into despair. And loss includes the feeling of limits. People come up against not only the limits of time and opportunity, but also their own psychological makeup. Like Aron, they may find that the adaptations they used to survive don't work anymore.

When confronted with limits and loss, and the pain they generate, there's a pull to come apart, to break down. The pressures can be huge. People may cast about for a solution and notice that in some new situation, with some new person, they start to stir, to come alive. The challenge is to find a way to think in the face of these pressures, and to act in line with one's values, even when one's desires feel conflicted. This is one way to define *integrity*: the capacity to withstand the impulse to come apart in the face of confusion and pain.

By definition, affairs coexist alongside one's "official" life. People lie because they simultaneously want two incompatible things. In some recess of their minds, they nurture the delusion that somehow they can keep multiple selves and incongruous story lines alive. When they are found out, or are forced to make a choice, it becomes obvious how incoherent the effort to live on two tracks was. Yet that awareness does not do away with the longing that one somehow could, or the grief that one can't. An affair has many meanings, but for the unfaithful partner it can include a last-ditch reaching after the possibility of more than one life.

This aspect of recovery from an affair was brilliantly addressed in the work of the late therapist Shirley Glass, who noticed that the welcome increase in gender equality in the American workplace had led to skyrocketing opportunities for sexual temptation. People not only come in contact with a larger number of possible sexual partners, but the workplace gives rise to a multitude of situations that can potentially be sexualized. Glass suggested that people who choose to have affairs do not differ from others in their *feelings*, but rather in their *choices*. In her now-famous formulation, people choose where to place their *walls* and *windows*. People can put their windows (openness, transparency, information flow) between themselves and their spouse, and walls (opaqueness, privacy, limits) between themselves and everybody else. Or, they can put a window between themselves and a potential affair partner—complaining over lunch about their spouse, confessing their complicated feelings, or interacting in plausibly deniable yet over-the-line ways—and put a wall between themselves and their spouse, keeping all these behaviors secret.

Glass's model went straight to the question of choice in an arena where people frequently feel they are not *deciding* anything. "It just happened" or "Before I knew it, I was in too deep" are commonplaces for a reason. When it comes to a potential affair, we often hide the element of choice from ourselves via a protracted series of microdecisions. These do not announce themselves; they are more like subtle shifts in perspective. They are likely to escape detection because their justifications can sound so reasonable and healthy: "Why can't I have a friend of the opposite sex, for God's sake?" or "What, now that I'm married, I can't even enjoy feeling attractive to someone else?"

The hair's breadth between self-deception and reasonableness, and our chronic difficulty in being truthful about the difference, is at the foundation of Glass's approach to healing. Models of healing from affairs differ on how much unflinching honesty is crucial to relationship repair. For the hurt partner, probing for gory details risks a secondary traumatizing effect. For the unfaithful partner, relinquishing every last shred of privacy can feel embarrassing and even violating. But in Glass's view, reestablishing walls and windows in their rightful place requires a couple to take the relationship down to the studs. To begin on a foundation of mutual honesty means prying up every rotting floorboard and purging every moldering closet.

Though Glass did not put it this way, the psychological logic of her approach is to shine a glaring light on the all-too-human wish to sequester and preserve the option of keeping two incompatible visions of the self alive. Glass's approach (and she is not its only advocate) amounts to a scarifying process of integrity building. It attacks just that place in the human psyche that yearns to be exempted from the limits of one story line, one life. We cannot be sure of our integrity unless we relinquish every last pocket of potential dissimulation, and our partners' seemingly endless capacity to be triggered keeps forcing us to turn back toward that task. One heartfelt apology does not do the trick. The hurt partners only begin to trust when they become convinced that the unfaithful partners are genuinely grappling with their own integrity. Glass insists that healing from an affair is tied to the recognition that our actions have to align with our values.

This is hard because who *doesn't* want more than one life? Who hasn't longed to be reflected back as beautiful in the eyes of someone new? Who has never imagined who they might *be* with someone else? These desires are fueled by a sense of limits, but also by curiosity and imagination and hope. Anyone in a committed relationship would have to be half-asleep not to occasionally wonder what it would be like to experience another version of herself, or to encounter an exciting new other. Each coupling is both an opportunity and a limit. We *would* be different with someone else, maybe better in some ways. Fantasizing about alternative realities is inevitable, a fact of life.

The *desires* that lead to affairs are universal and self-evident; and as

Glass points out, people who have affairs are no less "happily married" than people who don't. The *decision* to have an affair, by contrast, has to do with our personal way of *relating* to these desires—the excitements and fears we attach to them, the meaning we give them, our frustrations in resisting them, and our attitude toward those frustrations. Do we call to mind and keep in touch with the big picture in just those moments when we are vulnerable? Do we push inconvenient thoughts out of our mind, or do we attempt to consciously struggle with our conflicting values and motives? In other words, do we dissociate or integrate? We all long for a vacation from the responsibility of integrity from time to time. But the willingness to take a hard look at our desire for a vacation expresses our integrity. Integrity is, first and foremost, a particular kind of relationship to oneself.

Yet the reality that we only have one life, and the integrity it takes to face reality and live in it, does not do away with the haunting nature of our choices. To find oneself in a genuine love affair outside of marriage may be to find oneself in a world of two fundamentally irreconcilable visions of integrity. In one, integrity revolves around loyalty; in the other, around emotional intimacy. The triangular structure of affairs should always arouse our suspicion, since it's tailor-made for divvying up emotional roles in scripted and deluded ways—abuser and rescuer, savior and monster, madonna and whore. As an individual therapist I often counsel a person to spend time understanding his own mind, rather than succumbing to false comparisons or pressured ultimatums. At the same time, rough-patch affairs are often so painful because they bring to the fore our essential dividedness, and the extraordinary complications of trying to become more whole. When someone seeks my help in the midst of an extramarital love affair, I am often saddened by either potential outcome, because each entails a heartbreaking loss. I believe that a person will protect himself from a lot of pain, safeguard others, and feel more self-respect if he figures out the marriage on its own terms before deciding that the solution is to be found with someone else. (It helps sometimes to point out that most people don't end up marrying the person they left the marriage for.) Still, for some people, the very psychology of the affair is that it "can't be resisted."

Even if integrity might demand otherwise, they settle on the notion that they can't bear "to give up everything" if it means a jump into the void, but can if it's a jump into someone else's arms.

A TRUISM ABOUT affairs is that it is not the sex, but the deception, that hurts the most. Similarly, it is worth wondering whether in a marriage the *conversation* may be what's most important, not the sexual record itself. Affairs are not the most courageous, mature way to deal with marital alienation. Hurt partners are justly incensed by unfaithful partners' unilateral decision to change the terms. But if we grow by attempting to find a more genuine and generative integration between our conscience, impulses, and reality, we can understand why deceptive sex so often becomes a blundering way station in this process. We can understand too that for an affair to be more than a selfish and heartless mistake, we'll need to use it to have a different, more intimate kind of conversation with our partner, and ourself.

A more intimate conversation between marital partners, particularly one spurred by an affair, almost inevitably invites discussion of the meaning of sexual fidelity. If a marriage is to be a creation between two people, both people have the opportunity, and the responsibility, to think about what kind of creation they want it to be. Those who lament the sheer predictability of monogamous marriage should take a moment to notice the ways that they reinforce that predictability by choosing not to open up a conversation about the confusing borderlands of commitment, sexuality, and desire. Partners implicitly blame each other for the deprivations of monogamy, instead of facing their own mixed feelings about changing the terms. I don't tend to view tromping in new sexual pastures as the solution to rough-patch ennui. But rough-patch ennui is certainly made worse by the unarticulated expectations about sexuality that people bring to monogamous marriage. Free and fair discussion about the boundaries you mutually endorse offers the potential for a more interesting and intentional partnership.

The San Francisco Bay Area has a thriving community of "consensual non-monogamists." These people have non-monogamous marriage rela-

tionships of various kinds—open marriage, polyamory, swinging—and view their relationship's central commitment and point of integrity as honesty, not sexual exclusivity. What's bad isn't extramarital sex; what's bad is lying about it. Most of the consensual non-monogamists I've talked to say that they realized, either as young, unmarried adults or as sneaking married people, they weren't cut out for sexual monogamy. They decided that the most painful and alienating part of their relationships was their inability to be honest, and they sought to create relationships where honesty about sexuality was paramount.

"In our previous marriages, Ellen and I were the ones who lied and stepped out, and it didn't work for anyone," said Malcolm, now in his midfifties. "Early in our relationship to each other, we both knew that we were people whose interests sometimes wandered. At first, we had an 'out-of-town dalliance clause,' where we accepted that something could happen, and if it did, that we would come home and tell each other about it. We're both kind of rebellious thrill-seekers by nature, and by the time we got together, we knew that about ourselves and identified with each other."

Malcolm saw opening their relationship beyond the out-of-town dalliance clause as something Ellen initiated, but as Ellen describes it, she suggested it with Malcolm in mind. "When I went into menopause, I felt self-conscious about gaining weight, and I didn't have a lot of sexual energy. I'd always seen myself in very sexual terms, and menopause threw me into a bit of a panic. I was also worried about Malcolm having a sexual outlet. I asked, 'Would you be interested in seeing someone else?' I felt he would thrive more if he could express his sexual energy in that way. Which of course meant I could too." I asked Ellen what was important to her about having other men. "Every person reflects a different part of myself back to me," she said. "It's really an amazing path of self-knowledge and self-realization. Because I have a whole lot more sex in my life, my whole sexual being has come alive. If you turn that faucet on—it's a huge boon. My sex with my husband is awesome."

Both Ellen and Malcolm, by their own reports, ran wild as young people, had highly permissive and distracted parents, and experienced

what they described as inappropriate sexual attention early on. Both described themselves as "hypersexual" and were intermittently troubled by it throughout their lives. Coming to some resolution of those feelings, they seemingly needed to work through their shame at *wanting* to be sexual with a lot of people, and both of them found it meaningful to have a partner who accepted that.

Ellen and Malcolm see their relationship as "open," in that they permit other sexual involvements while their primary commitment and attachment is to each other. Whereas in many open relationships a pretty clear distinction is made between the primary love relationship and the additional recreational sex, Ellen and Malcolm's relationship includes their intimate relationships with other people of varying emotional and sexual depth. Their arrangement thus swerves toward polyamory because they allow and celebrate "many loves." When I asked Malcolm the question that invariably occurs to the monogamous among us—"What if you fall in love with someone else?"—he voiced a commonly held view: he and Ellen would treat the experience of "falling in love" or "crushing out" on a new sexual partner—also known as limerence or NRE (new-relationship energy)—as a passing mental state that they could decide to attach to or let go. If anything, Ellen told me, their relationship had deepened by virtue of helping each other through such episodes. "If Ellen really did fall in love with another man," Malcolm reflected, "I'd probably want to move in together and live as a threesome." Your average man would see such a threesome less as a solution than as a surefire route to agony, but Malcolm identified as bisexual. As for himself, Malcolm had no fears of falling in love with someone else. "Everything I am doing is spinning on Ellen. As a consumer of Ellen, it's enlightened self-interest. If she's happier, I get to be happier." He was saying that making her happy made him happy, but it left me feeling a little sad. It conjured an image of an eager little boy smiling nervously at his distracted mother in hopes of cheering her up.

"She's more innately polyamorous than I am," he continued. "What I love is *relationships*. I'm one of the undisputed masters of platonic dating. This life allows us to have deep relationships with people of

the opposite sex, something that's off-limits for most married people. I don't have sex with most of the people I have relationships with, but I love the depth. In fact, the most jealous I ever got wasn't even about sex. I heard Ellen laugh with a guy, and I'd never heard that laugh before. When I heard that laugh—I thought, 'He's funnier than I am.' Then I said to myself, 'Well, yeah, we get different things from different people.' He reached some part of her I don't, and it kind of terrified me. But when I talked to her about it, she said, 'Oh, baby, I love you so much, you are so funny. Ned is just a trip.'"

That story felt almost unbearable to me, and my first thought was how emphatically I would wish to *avoid* such an experience. But my reaction suggests a key, perhaps *the* key, difference between self-declared non-monogamists and the rest of us: the role and meaning of jealousy. Most of us treat jealousy as an emotion in a class by itself—something it is bad to cause, is worse to feel, and yet is a cherished proof of our beloved's unassailable value to us. Non-monogamists tend to treat jealousy as one of a range of negative emotions—such as envy, pride, or anger—that we build character through trying to overcome. Consensual non-monogamists like to talk about cultivating the idea of abundance rather than scarcity; and they speak of "compersion," which refers to an empathic enjoyment at one's partner's erotic fulfillment with others. Jealousy is, from this non-monogamist perspective, one of the main stumbling blocks to a more abundant erotic life. As Ellen put it, "To see Malcolm's joy at his freedom, it's a beautiful gift to give him." When Malcolm recounted to me the night he was "jumping out of his skin" with anxiety and jealousy when Ellen was on a date, or Ellen described crying one night on the kitchen floor, each followed up with describing the extraordinary closeness they felt when they shared their feelings and received the other's reassurance.

Such reassurance requires tons and tons and tons of *talk*. For Ellen and Malcolm, it was debatable which took more time—the dates with other partners, or the time they spent processing those dates. "This is a high-maintenance activity," Malcolm said. "You are constantly confronted with circumstances most people don't have to confront. It's a fast track to self-discovery and growth." Much as non-monogamy permits access to other partners' bodies, it permits unparalleled access to one's primary partner's *mind*. There's no room for secrets, and seemingly little room for private thoughts of any kind. For Malcolm, at least, I felt that the talking was an even *bigger* plus to their arrangement than the sex. Far more frightening than imagining Ellen having sex with someone else was imagining her having private feelings she didn't communicate to him. For him, hearing all about it afterward was an emotional reunion that recemented their bond.

Much as this might seem like an exercise in self-inflicted pain to many monogamists, the sheer level and intensity of communication required by non-monogamists may be something that monogamous couples can learn from. The basic relationship skills that make for successful monogamy and non-monogamy are pretty much the same. This was the take-home point that Dr. Yoni Alkan, a clean-scrubbed and enthusiastic thirtysomething doctor of human sexuality, promoted in his class "Opening Your Relationship." I attended his workshop at Kink.com, a pornographic-film studio housed in a former National Guard armory—described on Kink's website as a 1914 "reproduction Moorish castle" that "retains its original period details including wainscoting, stone staircases, sweeping corridors," and a "giant drill court spanning almost an acre." By day, Kink.com produces "fetish entertainment" such as *Hogtied* and *Ultimate Surrender*, but by night they offer workshops to "demystify and celebrate alternative sexualities" on topics such as rough sex and open relationships.

On arrival, the workshop attendees (a suburban-looking fiftyish couple and a smattering of hipster millennials) were led to a dungeon-like basement by a genial young woman with bleached-blond hair and a salacious Little Bo-Peep costume with black platform boots. Dr. Alkan sees his mission as bringing consensual non-monogamy into the mainstream, lifting its stigma, and instating it as a respected category of experience, analogous to the contemporary acceptance of gay and lesbian marriage. A genial and intelligent guide, he ended his lecture by discussing the personal qualities that are important if you are going to practice consensual non-monogamy. They were basically indistinguishable from the qualities any healthily partnered person would hope to have: self-confidence, self-esteem, a secure and healthy relationship, care for your partner, self-awareness, and communication skills. Dispensing some tips as to what kind of open relationship a person might be suited for—open, polyamorous, swinging, or relationship anarchy (no frameworks, no rules)—Dr. Alkan explained that "people who tend to fall in love with people they have sex with" might not be cut out for open relationships. I thought about this, since it seemed to decrease the population of possible practitioners by a sizable proportion. I decided to email him for clarification, and he responded, "Someone that ties sex with a strong emotional bond might not be suitable for an Open Relationship—because they might fall in love with every person they have sex with. However," he added, helpfully trying to find an open-relationship solution for all, "they might be suitable for a Polyamorous relationship or Relationship Anarchy."

Relationship anarchy? I must admit, I felt a creeping suspicion about all this sunny equanimity. A certain blasé nonchalance seemed even more pervasive among swingers, the couples who have sex together with other couples. I emailed Danielle, a woman in a nearby town who swings with her husband, to schedule a time to talk. In her reply, she evenhandedly enumerated her scheduling constraints, including volunteering at her daughter's school and preparing for her trip the next week on the Baltic Debauchery, a cruise for four thousand swingers. Our conversation was cordial and informative. She loved her husband and couldn't imagine their life without the novelty and pleasure of swinging. Like many female swingers, she was bisexual. When we talked, she ticked off with a certain lotus-eating apathy the foursomes and the "puppy piles" and the "sex room" her friends had built. I didn't know her well, so maybe she just had a deadpan speaking style. But I began to wonder if a transactional matter-of-factness was built into the culture itself. People described a party etiquette of asking each other politely if they want to "play" and moving on good-naturedly if they get a no. Proposals to complete strangers of specific and arcane sexual acts are efficiently negotiated in minutes.

To an outsider such as me, it sounded like a disorienting cubist pastiche of body parts and sex acts, less freeing and self-expressive than mildly psychosis inducing. But to its devotees, it clearly opens whole new doors of consciousness. If, as Jack Morin writes in *The Erotic Mind*, the basic structure of erotic experience is "attraction + obstacles = excitement," it's reasonable to wonder how erotic energy gets generated in situations where every last obstacle seems to have been removed. Maybe the erotic energy gets generated by the *group's* defiance of obstacles—a sort of reverse *Lord of the Flies*, where the group's agenda is to make love, not war, and rebellion leads to pleasure rather than mayhem. Perhaps the mass overcoming of social taboos is itself part of the turn-on. As people watch other live bodies copulating or join a group encounter, in the corners of consciousness may lie an excitement at doing what their "vanilla" friends or mainstream society don't have the guts to do. But the people I talked to didn't describe what they were up to as a transgression so much as a relief. They felt that overcoming the usual limits—of jealousy, of sexual monogamy, of self-categorization as hetero or bi—allowed them freedom to be who they were without a set of unworkable restrictions.

A striking aspect of the consensual non-monogamist lifestyle was how absorbing and time intensive it all seemed. I don't begrudge people their passions and pleasures, but the sheer calendaring involved made me feel exhausted. One man said it was a "big statement" when you shared your Google calendar with a potential partner; a woman said that polyamory was helping her "stay better organized." As a lifestyle between consenting adults, non-monogamy is one valid, if minority, compromise for dealing with the ongoing tensions inherent in sexual fidelity and long-term commitment. It seems fraught with peril and pain, but most of the people I met said they loved risk taking and were easily bored. People truly vary on the monogamy-polygamy spectrum, and self-knowledge and truth telling in this domain are valuable. All of us have twists and turns in our psychic and sexual lives, and there is no reason why two people shouldn't agree to adapt to those through opening their relationship.

My only abiding concern had to do with the children. Many of the people I met, including Ellen and Malcolm, had taken up non-monogamy as an explicit lifestyle after the children had left, or at least when they believed the kids were safely sequestered with the other custodial parent. But others were balancing jobs and marriages and small children—*and* multiple partners, hours crafting OkCupid responses, and sex parties that they flew across the country to attend. When I spoke to Emma, who was debating opening her relationship in response to her husband's inclinations, she said, "He thinks of it kind of like a fun hobby we could share. But sex isn't exactly like tennis or collecting stamps. It's private and intense. Kids can sense the difference when you are distracted versus entirely absorbed in something else. One of my husband's friends says that as long as his kids are taking their naps, it's okay to bring a lover home. I don't buy it. There's too much risk. If we decide to do this, we're going to have to be *more* aware and sensitive to the kids, not less."

FOR THOSE WHO aspire to live in a monogamous sexual relationship, yet have found themselves confused or tempted, curious or secretive, disconnected or shut down, questions linger: What is the optimal zone of privacy in a marriage? What, if anything, falls into the "don't ask, don't tell" category? What exactly does marriage commit people *to*? The interests of the individual and the couple never completely align. This goes for sex as much as for everything else. How do we deal with our individual sexual disposition and fantasy life, which necessarily expands beyond our monogamous physical relationship? How do we approach marriage as an opportunity for greater emotional and sexual risk rather than as a graveyard for sexual desire? How do we stay maximally alive yet not in chronic danger of acting out?

The romantic narrative of marriage tends to downplay a central feature of adult sexuality: people's sexual fantasy lives long predate and exist alongside their relationships with their intimate partners. Before they ever have sex with another real person, most people have an elaborate sexual-fantasy life, usually developed in the context of self-pleasuring. Its features are laid down young, and it is questionable whether anything is particularly voluntary or chosen about it. In sex with a partner, people strive to realize some aspects of their fantasy scripts, even if only partially. Sex therapists tell us that people routinely integrate their sexual thoughts into a shared experience by pairing intercourse with private fantasy, and by using fantasy images to trigger orgasm during partner sex.

We can think of fantasies as waking dreams. They are a fundamental part of us, the humming of our unconscious life. As we go about our day, we fantasize constantly, about everything from sex, to food, to sleep, to sports, to revenge. Like dreams, fantasies are psychologically necessary; without them, we would probably go crazy. Fantasies are momentary fragments that are designed to satisfy us. They are little packets of frustration relief, mini-movies that we direct.

Perhaps especially with sexual and romantic fantasies, it is not always easy to manage the relation of fantasy to reality. We're notoriously prone to mistaking a fantasy for an alternative reality (e.g., the movie romance that convinces us our relationship is deeply inadequate) or confusing a part for the whole (e.g., letting a sexual daydream sour us on our complicated marriage). Sometimes we forget the fundamental incomparability of reality and fantasy and entertain the illusion that we are stacking two realities next to each other and finding one wanting. But we also err in the other direction, overshooting on our inhibitions. We issue the stern self-instruction not to confuse reality with fantasy—"accepting" that it is not "realistic" to be attracted to our partner after fifteen years of marriage, for example, or declaring it is "silly" to derive pleasure from a short-lived flirtation.

Neither approach exploits the more vitalizing option, which is to find ways to pleasurably interweave fantasy and reality, to "enchant" reality with the excitement of fantasy. Doing that requires a fundamental shift in perspective. Too many of us secretly blame our partner for not living up to our fantasies, when, in fact, infusing our real relationship with the energy and pleasure of fantasy is an *internal* capacity. We hone and develop this capacity by maximizing awareness of the play of fantasy in our minds, and minimizing internal inhibition. The imagination is a playground, and one of its purposes it to entertain us. Fantasies are *thoughts*, after all, and the hallmark of a mature mind is the ability to recognize that thoughts are not actions. Where sex is concerned, most of us could put our daily fantasies and sensations to better use than we do in filling the fuel tank of our sexual self-image. The cute cashier, the song you heard, a wafting scent, how you feel in your clothes—they are all grist for an internal experience of yourself as a sexual agent. *Your relationship to yourself as a sexual person* is the single most valuable attribute you bring to the marital bed, and it is far more winning than the complaint that your partner isn't *making you feel sexy.*

Our sexual engines are fueled by many different sources, and the more we can enjoy those sources, the more alive we feel. Virtually all the sex experts agree that getting in touch with *yourself* is the first step toward a livelier partnered sex life. So far, so good. But how can we integrate all this "juice," presuming we manage to get in touch with it, into our actual long-term, (let's face it) familiar relationship? It's great to feel alive, but how does that translate into wanting sex with one's actual partner? This is where it's important to understand the link between arousal and desire, and to recognize the ways that men and women sometimes differ.

When we think of sexual desire, we tend to think of spontaneous, out-of-the-blue desire as "real" desire, and it's understandable why. Most of us experience this kind of sexual desire in a new relationship. But actually, people's typical styles of desire vary—some feel more "spontaneous" desire, others more "responsive" desire—and neither style is "better" than the other. Responsive desire may be more likely in certain contexts—for instance, a decade into marriage, with children underfoot. In those cases, people may only start to feel desire once they are *in* an erotic situation, so the challenge becomes *to create* erotic situations where arousal and desire can be kindled. "At the beginning of a relationship," said Ian Kerner, PhD, author of *She Comes First*, "there's a neurochemical cocktail that provides novelty and stimulation and general self-expansion. After that, things calm down, and couples tend to start relying on a very limited sexual repertoire. Then, the challenge is to increase avenues of arousal."

One way people try to increase arousal is by adding more sexual novelty, through more erotic talk, toys, movies, positions, whatever.

But another powerful source of arousal is *emotional context*. Given female sexual anatomy, many women in young adulthood are attuned to emotional context—feeling loved, beautiful, trusting—because they need to feel free to take plenty of time to become fully aroused. Men, whose youthful reflexes help them charge through the early sexual years, are often surprised when they find that these reflexes can't override emotional difficulties forever. Over time, they too need a loving, connected atmosphere to become fully aroused and emotionally satisfied by sex.

Research is moving us away from the stereotypical notion that men have a gender-linked higher sex drive. When desire discrepancies exist, they have more to do with whether the triggers for arousal are sufficient and effective for each partner. One approach to differences in desire, then, is for a couple to explore which sexual triggers *do* elicit each partner's arousal and desire, understanding that the cues for men and women may differ. Couples benefit from exploring the *actual* cues that excite *each* partner, and these are going to have a lot more to do with *context*—sexual, emotional, social—than with a hardwired trait for horniness. Particularly in long-term relationships, sexual desire is more of "a relational process" than an "independent libidinal state." Part of that "relational process" is each partner's being aware of the other's emotional world. Especially for women, the evidence suggests, anxiety, stress, and relationship conflict interfere with tuning in sexually. Knowing this makes a huge difference. A woman's partner can thus take seriously the need to listen to and understand what's stressing her out, fostering more relaxation and greater closeness. Women can also thus help *themselves* to actively tune out stress. One of the most effective ways to do this is by fantasy. "Fantasy is a potent, viable way to tune out stressors," Kerner says. "Women should permit themselves to enter a fantasy space during sex."

If people are going to keep their tanks full, their sexual imaginations will likely not be restricted to what they do or do not do with their partners. For this reason, people could grant themselves more freedom in their imaginations. But this leads to further complexities. When does the pursuit of private sources of pleasure slide into secretiveness or exclusion? Is browsing at a sex shop a secret you should tell your spouse, or a private outing that stokes your sense of sexual vitality? Is dancing too close to your friend's husband a harmless bit of fun that puts you in the mood later that night or grounds for a weighty confession? We all need an area of mental privacy where feelings can float in a fluid space of reality-fantasy, if for no other reason than to give a little poetry to life. On the other hand, private thoughts have a way of taking on a life of their own. What is the difference?

To answer this question, we need to step back and think clearly about the varying degrees of intensity that such thoughts engender. While it may be true that people have sexual thoughts throughout their day, most of the time the thoughts come and go without affecting people all that much. We're a bit like Teflon: they don't really stick. Sometimes, though, they do stick, at least a little. Individuals some-times arrive at a therapy session, coffee in hand, shaken by the electric moment of eye contact they just shared with the barista, wondering what it means for their marriage. The short answer is *exactly nothing*. But when people find such moments unduly scary or drenched with meaning or can't simply enjoy them and let them go, it's possible that they've entered the arena of their personal conflicts.

These take many forms. At the most benign level, people feel conflict between the pleasurable notion of getting carried away and the moral injunction not to. The conflict begins to scare people if they feel their longings are too strong or their brakes are too weak. People usually manage these moments through a subliminal balancing act—appreciating yet not amplifying, feeling yet not feeling too much. A bit of effort is in it, and a pinprick of loss in letting the moment pass. But equilibrium soon returns, and the day is brightened. When people feel hungry, or empty, that's not so easy. Too much is riding on these moments: the desire to feel appreciated is too strong, the impulse to resist too weak. People in the habit of overinhibiting their desires are also at risk of overreaction, since they don't benefit from the daily practice of noticing their desires and not acting on them. People's vulnerabilities differ in this area, and we will explore some of the psychological reasons for that in chapter 8.

The key difference between harmless and harmful private moments like these is *what we do with them*; namely, whether we elaborate a momentary feeling toward another person into a full-blown story. When someone begins to parse glances, decode phrases, and craft a narrative that reads meaning into interactions, she unwittingly chooses a perilous fork in the road. She develops into a detective of sorts— How come he is staying late at work when I do? Why has she started walking her dog in my neighborhood?—and starts to connect the dots in a way that promotes a story line of mutual feeling. She becomes increasingly preoccupied with confirming its reality. As she goes farther down this road, she starts to embroider into her tale deep sources of commonality. She notices the way he finds the same things funny and rues her spouse's unsophisticated sense of humor. Invidious comparison becomes a thickening agent in the story she is plotting, one in which it is just possible, she begins to imagine, that her marriage is fundamentally flawed.

A common feature of these scenarios is how innocuous they can seem—until they don't. People go along feeling as if they are doing what people *do* to keep themselves sexually vibrant and open to new experiences and realize too late that their alternative fantasy relationship is absorbing vast amounts of attention and energy. They find they are living on two tracks, the daily round of activities that keeps family life afloat, and the sequestered sparkling world of fantasized possibility. When they take a step back from the anxiety or excitement, they wonder what has happened to them, why their emotional life has become so unmanageable. Looking around, they see little in the way of cultural models to aid them. The "suck it up" model of long-term relationships equates "maturity" with hard work and sexual boredom. The romantic-love narrative reconfigures fantasies as clues to one's grand destiny of finding "true love," or at least greater sexual fulfillment. Next to nothing exists in the way of a road map for navigating the utterly normative, potentially destabilizing experience of extramarital attraction.

The question is, how do we deal creatively and sensitively with the daily reality of encountering other sexual bodies, other sexual minds, when we have chosen to commit ourselves to one other person? This is arguably among the more important life skills for remaining happily married, yet it attracts little in the way of subtle reflection or serious study. Bizarrely, no one talks about it until marital disaster strikes, then everyone acts simultaneously mystified and unsurprised. This question is not simply about the ubiquity of potential excitements, but about the emotional processes by which we skillfully manage them. We have a long way to go in generating a suitably complex answer to this question, but it seems safe to say that the answer lies in the direction of less moralism and more aesthetics. If we are moralistic, we regard the daily swirl of sexual life as something to be ignored, suppressed, risen above, or compartmentalized. Yet we know that this approach works in exactly the wrong direction for enhancing sexual feeling between two people in a marriage. An aesthetic answer, by contrast, poses us the challenge of staying open to the raw sexual material of life, yet transmuting it into more poetic forms.

Here, an analysis of sexual flirtation, and its uses and abuses, is sorely needed. Flirting between sexually committed people is a form of play that wrests maximal libidinal pleasure out of limited situations. It is considered an art because of its controlled use of technique to amplify feeling, and its skillful balance of possibility and limit, excitement and control. As a category of human experience and as a creative aspect of personality, flirtation transforms sexual energy into pleasurable yet noncommittal communication. Its success hinges on a pitch-perfect harmonization of feelings, aesthetics, and values. Without this harmonization, attempts at flirtation tend to be annoying, obnoxious, or sleazy.

Where is the line between flirting and fishing? How do people know when they are crossing it? What makes flirting different from fishing is our internal orientation to what we are doing, a key element of which is keeping in mind our partner's feelings and perspective. Sexual signaling is inherently exciting and absorbing and is rendered less enjoyable to people when the image of their spouse looms over it. At the same time, our subconscious dedication to our primary relationship keeps our momentary desires in line with our larger goals. Perhaps the most important way we keep our partner in mind is by choosing to keep our passing sexual thoughts about other people just that—passing. As in mindfulness practice, the thoughts pass through us, neither recruiting too much excitement nor too much guilt, and we let them go. Being able to *mentally* enjoy the electricity of everyday encounters, while in *reality* remaining boundaried, may make for the most constructive sexual approach in a long-term monogamous marriage.

WE HAVE EXPLORED the potential value of fantasies and private thoughts for a couple's shared sexual life. But what if these private strands cannot be easily integrated? What if they involve the tastes of one person that are not palatable to the other person, or that are not enjoyed together?

One of the more fraught expressions of this issue is the use of pornography. Pornography is ubiquitous. There are some 2.5 million adult sites, and internet porn accounts for 35 percent of all web traffic in the United States. Is private pornography use by one partner an "affair," which demands the high-octane integrity-building tactics that Glass supports? Or is it "fantasy," in which case it's rightfully seen as the private property of an individual's mind? Clearly, clicking on a pornographic website or opening an email enticement is a concrete action. Since real people are usually involved, who are subject to exploitation and coercion, it would be crazy and wrong to claim that pornography is "just" fantasy. Yet people do not always agree about where on the continuum of "cheating" the consumption of pornography falls.

Kira and Jacob, one couple I saw, argued over just this question. Kira happened upon a locked door one day and learned from a flustered Jacob that he had been watching internet porn. She said he had been lying and keeping secrets. He said he was doing something private. They became deadlocked on whether his behavior was something private that he was entitled to, or something secretive that betrayed her trust. Nothing less than complete exposure felt safe to Kira, which only provoked Jacob's guardedness and avoidance. His behavior then triggered her vigilance and insecurity. We can detect in their conflict an underlying attachment dilemma. The anxiously attached Kira worried at signs of separateness, and these worries were ratcheted up by the sexual content and the insistence on privacy. The avoidantly attached Jacob worried about intrusion, but his tendency to take care of himself, this time through solo sex, fed the anxious intrusive reaction from Kira that he dreaded.

Kira and Jacob's dilemma begs the question of what makes a sexual activity *secret* versus *private*. Most couples have an implicit agreement that having sex with another live person would fall into the secret category. But what about masturbation? One of the problems we have in thinking about pornography is that we tend to lump it in with the main purpose for its use. For some couples, the role of masturbatory sex is never fully worked out between them, and it comes as a shock when one partner discovers pornography is part of the other's self-pleasuring repertoire. People tend to see masturbation as a private activity, and pornography use as a secret one, but they never quite think through or reconcile the contradiction. In fact, for couples, making a distinction between private and secret is important. As Morin writes in *The Erotic Mind*:

> it is crucial to make a clear distinction between *secrecy*, hiding significant information, and *privacy*, the right to maintain a nonrelational sphere of existence. Secrecy hurts intimate relationships, privacy enhances them. Unfortunately, many people don't recognize the difference. They fear secrets, and therefore they resent privacy. Ironically, when they refuse to recognize legitimate privacy rights, instead of making themselves more secure, they create the very secrecy they fear.

We might understand Jacob and Kira's problem as throwing around definitions of secrecy and privacy to support what are essentially *emotional* positions. Kira is scared and threatened by Jacob's interest in looking at other naked women having sex, so she calls him secretive to protest. Jacob resists her characterization because, well, he likes looking at other naked women having sex, and he sincerely believes he's devoted to Kira, and he feels he's entitled to a private sphere of solo sexual activity. Masturbation can serve all sorts of positive functions in a relationship, such as smoothing over discrepancies in libido, learning about orgasms (generally for women), doing things in fantasy that you don't plan to do in reality, or exploring your "core erotic themes." Such positive functions can be misunderstood or drowned out by alarm over secrecy in pornography use.

But pornography remains an awkward topic for couples. Unlike an affair, pornography use does not end, to be followed by a clear-cut rebuilding of trust. It's an ongoing source of pleasure or release for one partner that can naturally arouse sexual rivalry in the other. Researchers debate whether women in heterosexual couples are enduring and adapting to their male partners' pornography use, or whether the women are enthusiastically joining in. Regrettably, studies in this area tend toward confusing terminology and subtle moralism. What we do know is that overall a climate of honesty around pornography mitigates distress and—unsurprisingly—correlates more highly to relationship satisfaction than dishonesty does. Thirty percent of pornography users are women, and about a quarter of women who have accessed erotic images online said it makes them more open to trying new things and talking about what they want sexually. Viewing pornography together tends to relate to greater couple satisfaction, on average, than when one partner (usually the man) is viewing it alone.

Pornography's chief advantage for a couple, sex experts agree, is its potential to create arousal between people who need more of it. Sources of arousal are what "responsive" desire responds *to*, and new paths to arousal are what pornography and erotica provide. Kerner offers his clients "pornography tours" of different sites, as well as various volumes of erotica and sexy movie scenes by male and female directors (who tend to produce better story lines and cast more realistic and relatable actors). On average, women respond more readily to lengthier narratives (think *Fifty Shades of Grey*, 100 million copies sold and counting), and men generally prefer less plot-driven visuals, but exploring both partners' erotic tastes can create a wider shared menu for them to choose from.

A spirit of sexual exploration is a worthy goal but can be hard to achieve, since sexuality is laced with such vulnerable emotions. Erotic tastes are deeply body based, out of one's conscious control, and susceptible to feelings of shame, which can make them challenging targets for self-revelation. Even if we grant that our partners have a right to their private desires, we may still have uncomfortable *feelings* about their private desires. Subjective perceptions vary. A wife may object to her husband's watching amateur sex videos of "civilians," who are, after all, "real people." At the same time, "reality" may be what her husband seeks in porn; as one of Kerner's clients put it, "When I look at porn, I just want something real. It's a wasteland of artifice." For a heterosexual woman, thinking about her partner fantasizing about women who are "real" *might* feel better than his craving sex with a pneumatic doll, or worse, going out and actually having sex with another live woman. But still.

Pushing the limits of the reality-fantasy divide is the online game *Second Life (SL)*, where you can buy, on the *SL* marketplace with *SL* currency, not only a variety of sexual organs to use for virtual sex, but also "animations" that enable avatars to engage in erotic acts. Some *SL* members pair their avatar's virtual sex with their own solo sex. Others have been known to have their avatars "marry" on *SL* and then try to make a go of it IRL (In Real Life). Hardly less bizarre was a research study that showed that "half of users felt they could communicate more openly with their *Second Life* partner than their real-life partner," and "more than a third said they have a 'stronger connection' with their online partner." In addition, "participants split on which context provided greater sexual satisfaction, with 43 percent more satisfied with sexuality in *Second Life*, and 42 percent preferring real life."

Back In Real Life, it can be particularly challenging to deal with different sexual tastes when one person finds the other's genuinely distasteful. Fetishes and kink—feet, leather, bondage, to name a few— are pretty fixed and unchanging sources of excitement, psychically set by adolescence. If partners share such tastes, they are in luck; but a relationship can also be rewarding in many important ways and not include this compatibility. Here, the best approach might be a tactful agreement to express certain fantasies in the private sphere (thanks to the internet, niche desires can now be safely satisfied at a distance). But we can also take a page from the radically open communication norms of consensual non-monogamists and recognize that couples can actually talk about this stuff and decide what activities to share. Specialized sexual proclivities may coexist fairly peaceably with a more "mainstream" sex life. Some people try to incorporate them, some prefer not to. But unless there's some understanding, they will be sequestered in secrecy, and secrecy can lead to distance and mistrust. If you talk, there's the possibility of acceptance and more closeness.

As we've explored throughout, many couple problems boil down to feeling threatened by difference. The struggle to *make you more like me and criticize you if you are not* can as easily play out around sex as anything else. Yet, if the marketplace is any measure of the sexual id, women and men, gay and straight, all *crave* difference. Heterosexual men scrutinize female anatomy; heterosexual women read romance novels populated with chiseled alpha males. Queer culture recognizes and celebrates individualized expressions of taste and breaks open the sexual and gender categories that limit us to certain kinds of (socially sanctioned) difference.

In fact, society's rethinking of categories and assumptions about sex and gender, unimaginable even a few decades ago, has created greater freedom to express individuality and difference. It's a valuable resource in questioning the expectations we bring to marriage. In sex, as in every other emotion-laced issue between partners, the challenge is to find a golden-ring approach to difference. This means trying to understand our own desires, apart from conventional notions of what we "should" desire, and collaborating to mesh them with our partner's. Perhaps in this process, a guy pauses to note, "Come to think of it, I do feel more attracted to my wife when I don't have images of twenty-two-year-old cheerleaders with fake breasts dancing in my head." He decides to turn to porn less and experimental sex more. Maybe a woman asks herself, "If I peer behind my knee-jerk indignation, is there a bit of politically incorrect excitement lurking in the shadows?" Each may conclude that the internet clicking (him) or a critical posture (her) detract from the possibilities for closeness and excitement between them. In the best case, they take the risk of coming together to explore activities that delight them both. Maybe they read erotica together, or they fool around with themes of power and objectification, freed from the fear that any of it commits them to a "real" position outside the bedroom.

These days, there's a lot of talk about "pornography addiction." There's the frantic perception that a pornography "epidemic" is siphoning off young men's desire for sex with actual women. We know that young men masturbate—a lot. They often use pornography to arouse themselves. Does this mean they are pornography "addicts"? Certainly yourbrainonporn.com and nofap.com would offer a resounding yes and might advise signing up for a "reboot" or taking a no-pornography pledge. But, in fact, little agreement exists on the validity of the "pornography addiction" concept. Addiction is not simply about *quantity* of engagement (e.g., eleven hours or more of porn use per week), but about *quality*—that is, persisting in pursuit of a substance or activity despite the accumulation of adverse consequences. Young men may well tune out the stresses of real life—jobs and relationships and future planning—by holing up and getting off. But that's not addiction, that's avoidance.

Young men's attitude of avoidance may portend an emotional coping strategy that will dog their later married lives, however. After all, middle-aged married men also click through erotic images to avoid the emotional stresses of their relationships. When pornography is used as an escape from the complexities of actual relating, it becomes an increasingly walled-off enterprise. People craft a disconnected world of self-soothing, which creates excitement and distraction while protecting them from revealing vulnerability, dependence, or need. Men who use online sex to deal with stress and create emotional distance are most likely to hide their habits and have partners who feel angry and betrayed. But their secrecy around porn is hard to disentangle from their general problems with intimacy. Like Jacob, some of these men are attachment avoidant—resorting to self-sufficiency and withdrawal instead of communicating about emotional need.

Whether we decide to define this behavior as addictive, it shares with the addict's approach the "assignment of great value to a false need and the depreciation of true ones," in the words of the physician Gabor Maté. It hijacks reward and motivation circuits that can only be genuinely satisfied through intimacy and effort. When one partner "gets their needs met" predominantly through nonrelational sexual activities, it leaves partners in unequal positions of need and power, since it decreases one partner's attention seeking within the marriage. Not a few men—and it is overwhelmingly men who use pornography in this way—have told me that porn is a pressure-release valve for the difficulties and conflicts of their relationship. While undoubtedly true, their interpretation minimizes and rationalizes their own part in a damaging cycle, since little provokes more difficulties and conflicts than a checked-out, disconnected partner who is downstairs on his computer rather than upstairs in bed.

At the extreme end of the spectrum, a partner whose entire coping apparatus is designed around taking care of himself through substances or other behaviors presents a formidable challenge to a marriage. The couple therapist Terrence Real has written important work on how to help couples where one person's narcissistic sense of entitlement to their addictions or affairs shows no sign of budging. I've seen enough such examples to cast a large shadow on my hopes. One couple came to see me after the wife found out that her husband was, while out of town on business, meeting up with prostitutes he'd found online. He unconvincingly maintained that if his wife would "liven up" their sex life, he wouldn't need the "outlet." They were back in my office three years later, and this time he was calling himself a "lust addict." As the addiction expert Robert Weiss incisively put it, "Is he an addict or an asshole?" The question for the wife was not whether her husband was a lust addict, but on a deeper level: Was there a "there" there? Did her husband have the integrity and goodwill to create a loving relationship with her? Our few meetings made it clear that he had grown up with cold, dismissive, and critical parents. It wasn't hard to identify a host of reasons for his problems. But he had to decide to wrestle with his problems, and he had no interest.

Prostitute-pursuing narcissists aside, male partners who engage in more innocuous online pleasures sometimes hide their activities to avoid their wives' displeasure. Men can find themselves frankly intimidated by their wives' disapproval, especially around sex. Certain unfortunate gender polarities intensify the problem. Women's anger in relationships is typically activated by powerlessness, injustice, and irresponsibility. Understandably, in light of unthinking sexism and the collective memory of male oppression, we women tend to be sensitized to not being listened to and understood. When we feel this way, we might point out to men that their approach to sex is not only objectifying and degrading to women, but simpleminded and unnuanced with respect to our desires and emotions. But when we condescend to men's "immature" attitude toward sex, is there any reason they wouldn't feel shamed and defensive?

This state of affairs leads us to consider one of the more stereotypical patterns of sexual breakdown in straight couples: the wife says she needs more emotional closeness to feel sexual, and she doesn't want to have sex when she perceives her husband as unaffectionate. The husband becomes less attentive and affectionate as he becomes more angry and hurt that his wife rejects him sexually. The more angry and hurt he becomes, the more irritable and disconnected he acts, and the less emotional closeness he expresses toward his wife, making her even less inclined to want sex. Down the spiral they go. One unfortunate by-product of this painful cycle is the gendered put-downs it can generate. Women can find themselves uttering clichés such as "All he wants is sex" or "He doesn't care how I feel." Men in this situation have been known to call their wives selfish, complaining, and cold. The man entirely misses that for his wife emotional connection and affection are the most direct route to feeling turned on and confident in her own allure. The woman entirely misses the yearning for emotional connection that her partner is expressing through his desire for sex.

Such male-female standoffs often involve an inflammatory rhetoric about feeling "used." Critical as they feel of their husbands' "using" them for sex, women might benefit from examining the way their own "use" of men gets hidden under a veneer of "relationship." Disappointed wives tell me that they wish their husbands would do more to put them in the mood. Women tend to regard the behaviors they want as more "relational" and "connected." But how different are they, really, from any other trigger for erotic desire? Is acting out the script of "sexy female" for his benefit really any different from his acting out the script of "romantic male" for her benefit? Women may view the kinds of things they say they want as more "relational," but just because they are less graphic doesn't mean they are any less scripted. Whether or not people's desires conform to gender stereotypes, men and women, gay and straight, *all* benefit from striving to honor and attend to, rather than ignore or criticize, their partner's *different* sources of arousal. In a loving relationship, we indulge each other's scripts, we're willing to play a part in them, because we understand their significance in creating good feelings between us.

On an emotional, and even spiritual, level, isn't this how marriage is supposed to work? Isn't the age-old purpose of marriage to contain our "baser" instincts and "selfish" desires within a relationship of love and concern? It seems that this is what marriage is designed to help us do. Marriage not only lets us have all kinds of sex—perfunctory, passionate, makeup, distracted, quick, slow, tired, electric—but is designed to allow expression of all the messy strata of personality. It is a relationship designed to find ways to satisfy the two *individuals* within it. Marriage is an imaginative creation, not a political manifesto, and its strength is its capacity to contain contradictions.

When married people fall into no-sex purgatory, it is almost as if they have reversed this age-old truth. Once upon a time the love relationship of marriage was designed to "house" sex, binding its unruly force for the positive purposes of pair-bonding and the protection of children. By contrast, the no-sex marriage treats sex as a rare and lofty pinnacle that will only be attained if the love relationship is perfectly executed. It would be tempting to see this tendency as women's strategy of revenge, lodged in the collective unconscious, for millennia of sexual duty. Except it is men, often enough, who deny sex to women, and same-sex couples struggle with sexless marriages too.

Intimacy tends to deteriorate in no-sex marriages, so to insist on even *greater* intimacy as a precondition for having sex is clearly a losing proposition. The only way out of this downward spiral is the counterintuitive move of increasing one's willingness to give. Genuine giving relies on expanding your empathy for the other person. It usually means leaving your comfort zone to try to give the other person something he or she wants, graciously and generously, if you can find it in yourself to do so. If you can't, address the aspects of the emotional climate that turn you off. Try what some sex therapists recommend: reframe the issue from "desire" to "willingness"; introduce more physical affection at nonsexual moments; consciously plan *not* to have sex sometimes and touch in other pleasurable ways instead. When we don't feel like giving, we often call up a host of explanations that cite the other person's behavior, or the flaws in the relationship. Those thoughts are a signal to consider whether our own empathy and generosity might be falling short.

Generosity toward the other person might not be so hard if we recognized it as generosity toward ourselves. A life in which you and your partner are not sexually engaging with each other is simultaneously a life in which you are not engaging with a part of yourself. We may regard our sexuality as tied to our deepest essence, but it's also possible to confuse our deepest essence with the trappings of our neuroses. In this sense, people may benefit from having a *less* personal view of sex. Treating sexuality as a natural force, as impersonal as the seasons or the sky, might help us refrain from holding it hostage to our damaged personalities. When you find yourself inwardly feasting on slights and grievances that quash your libido, turn your mind to the majesty of the life force. Try on the notion that awe and gratitude are the fitting emotions with which to gaze upon the erotic drive that courses through each of us. It may be one of the last preserves of untamed, untrammeled nature we have left. And if we've chosen to be sexually monogamous, there's only one other person on this earth with whom we can fully explore the terrain.

*   *   *

WORKING WITH ARON and Martha, I felt that Aron was lucky because Martha seemed to want to understand him, and herself. The outcome was unsure, but Aron's actions had not mired Martha in blame or rigidity. She saw that his actions were not all about her. This seemed to me like the most hopeful sign that they might find a way to get through this. I contrasted them to another couple I was seeing at the time, Dan and Jade, two teachers in their middle forties whose children were now twelve and fifteen. They were both Catholic, with large families nearby, and they had married young. Sports was a family centerpiece, with both children on track to pursue athletic scholarships to college. But despite their family support, their clear priorities, and their well-ordered home life, a current of struggle seemed to predate the crisis that had brought them to see me.

Dan had recently discovered that Jade was having an affair with a workout friend. He was profoundly wounded and angry, and Jade was repentant to the point of self-flagellation. On first glance, their situation departed little from many other scenes of postaffair wreckage I have witnessed: the traumatic shock, the chaotic aftermath, the uncontrolled swings of emotion. Helping them find some sense of safety was my first goal. Gradually, I tried to help them think about their relationship, how it felt to each of them, and what might need to change. But as the months wore on, I noticed myself becoming increasingly sympathetic to Jade's predicament. Week in and week out, Dan's reaction was as fresh as ever. Every time we created a bit of space to think together about what had happened, Dan seemed to reject the effort and return to rebuking Jade for breaking her vows and destroying their family. He exclaimed "how wonderful" their life had been until Jade had "ruined" it.

Increasingly, Dan's self-anointment as standard-bearer for the ideals of the relationship began to look like a barricade against his own deeper emotions. Dan's postaffair devastation began to feel like a retreat. He was entitled to his feelings, but he was locked within one narrow band of them. I worried that healing conversations wouldn't be possible. In the words of the psychoanalyst Adam Phillips, Dan seemed to be using his "states of conviction and revenge" as his "preferred self-cures."

Taking a stand of vengeful certainty felt safer to Dan, but if he was going to reconnect with Jade or repair the relationship, he'd have to bear that she was an independent person he couldn't control through his displeasure. Dan kept turning "sad" to "bad." This emotional atmosphere was what had alienated Jade in the first place and now diminished their chances for a reconciliation.

When both partners can accept that they create their marriage together, they have a chance to explore more honestly how the affair happened. It doesn't erase that one person lied and hurt people. But through a vulnerable and honest sharing of feelings, partners have a chance to move out of deadness and claustrophobia, and toward a more alive sense of connection. A person's feelings about his marriage fluctuate. One man interviewed by Shirley Glass put it this way: "On a good day, when things are going well, I am committed to my wife. On a day when things are just okay, I'm committed to my marriage. And on a day when things aren't so great, I satisfy myself by being committed to my commitment." At times the marriage is a structure we "comply with" but do not "feel." Even then—especially then—seeing the marriage as having a value and meaning bigger than our own fallible makeup and daily screwups helps us find a way through disruptions and breakdowns. As a golden ring, the marriage stands as a resource for stability as we work out the pains of alienation, discord, and repair.

Aron wasn't the most self-reflective guy in the world, and he'd entered therapy with guarded skepticism. He hated to "wallow in feelings"; when he felt sad, it made him feel powerless, weak, and lost. As he saw it, why spend time feeling bad when taking small actions around the edges—changing his exercise regime, cutting down on nights at the bar—felt so much more empowering and upbeat. Yet the affair had shown him that he wasn't always in the driver's seat of his own psyche. He panicked sometimes, or he felt oddly detached. The ghosts from his past would not let him rest, and he seemed to be running out of options. People in his position sometimes raise the stakes even higher, torching their lives more recklessly with each successive round. But Aron knew that he loved his children. He believed his wife to be a truly special person and that he was lucky to be with her. Knowing all that, he didn't understand why he'd jeopardized it. Despite his initial claim that he knew why he did it, he was utterly confused. He was facing directly, for the first time in his life, the fractures within himself. I often find myself telling people, "Confusion is good." They don't always like to hear it, but I believe it's true. Confusion is where we start to sort through all the contradictory experiences that we've tried so hard to smooth over. It's the first step to discovering what we really feel, and who we really are.

Dealing with the aftermath of an affair, as the hurt or the unfaithful partner, means feeling lost, fragmented, confusing even to ourselves. Growing from it means experiencing our conflicting desires, fears, thoughts, and values on the way to finding a livable, and livably coherent, sense of self. It's an ambivalent project, and along the way most of us stumble around, pursuing blind alleys, dead ends, and manic fancies. Aron and Martha touched me because they both took it all on. They courageously faced that their marriage had to make room for two people who were not always feeling or saying what the other person wanted to hear. They tried to appreciate each other's honesty, rather than punish it. They each took the risk of trying to respond to what the other wanted from them. Even in the feared context of sexual comparison, Martha tried to loosen up, knowing that even by her own lights she felt uncomfortably inhibited. Aron started to talk about his feelings in a different way, a gentler way. He almost seemed, in spite of himself, to *like* it. They relinquished their need for certainty and replaced it with a desire for presence. They managed the anger, the confusion, the insecurity, the judgment, and arrived at something else: a surprised, grateful awareness that they actually, really loved each other.

Alcohol and Other Attempted Escapes

"We can't drink like we used to." At forty-five, Paul was a compact, muscular man, dark haired and tan, with a pair of incongruously intellectual glasses. A whirlwind of energy, he was up at four thirty every morning running in the hills of Oakland, followed by frenetic days as a contractor. Twice a week, he played a pickup game of basketball with his high school buddies after work. He was tightly wound and funny and easily annoyed by his wife Nancy's long, digressive narratives about her needs. For her part, Nancy was charming, happy in her role as mother, in love with her husband, and earnest about improving their relationship. But they fought, combustively and nonproductively. They had two young children, Tessa and Liam, in front of whom they routinely pulled out all the stops. After the fact, they admitted feeling guilty, though they invariably blamed each other for starting the fight. Our sessions sometimes deteriorated into an accounting of who had lately issued more curses and insults. They rarely agreed.

Despite their fights, Paul and Nancy had a lot of fun. They were sociable and high-spirited, always hatching parties and celebrations. Paul sometimes complained, in a dramatic forehead-slapping show of exasperation, that Nancy crammed their lives too full, or that their social calendar was "out of control." Yet clearly, sociability was high on their list of shared interests. So was drinking. They enjoyed it, they ritualized it. There was rarely an evening when a wine bottle wasn't being opened or consumed. Their sense of fun was a genuine strength of their relationship, and alcohol played a central role.

Lately, though, Paul had mentioned that their drinking was starting to take a toll on him physically. He was gaining weight. He didn't bounce back from a night of drinking as well as he used to. He wanted to feel healthier. Nancy heartily endorsed the cause of health, so they promptly bought dual gym memberships, and she recommitted herself to daily Pilates. She loved to cook, so she threw herself into the time-intensive project of comparing the latest popular diets and preparing them down to the smallest detail. They agreed to cut back on their drinking, but their burst of shared enthusiasm soon gave way to disenchantment with the regimen. They offered vague, self-exonerating excuses about "life being so stressful," but the real issue was that neither was willing to give up their nightly bottle of wine or their drinking outings with friends.

"I don't think we're keeping our eye on the ball," Paul said one day in a moment of frustration. Their son, Liam, was beginning to disrespect his teachers, but neither parent was looking into whether he needed help. "We don't have any follow-through."

"What are you talking about?" Nancy snapped back. "We're one of the most together couples we know."

"Paul, are you worrying about the fog that sets in after a couple of drinks in the evening?" I asked. "It's pretty hard to care about boring but necessary tasks at that point."

"Yeah . . ." Paul's eyes darted toward his wife as if my comment were directed at her. "I just wish Nancy could take care of more of this kid stuff during the day."

"Wait a minute," she said. "You are the one who says we need to be a team, and the minute I try to get you involved, you become a control freak and we get into a fight."

They headed into a useless battle, caught themselves, then spent the rest of their therapy time pledging to drink less and exercise more.

To find oneself in the thick of marriage, children, work, and aging, sandwiched between generations, not having enough time to exercise, relax, or disconnect, is to find oneself in the precise spot where alcohol and other substances of escape offer themselves as a desirable antidote. Just the sheer challenge of domestic reentry after a long day, and the need to engage in what may be a tense reunion and embark on a second shift of family work, is enough to ring the Pavlovian "drink" bell for many people. How nice it is to be in a different state of mind that lends itself to "flow" rather than tension with people or pets. More mellow, more likable, more warm, less reactive, less irritable—these are all things we want and have a hard time attaining unaided. Substances not only help soothe anxiety and shift emotional states, but they can also make family life feel more interesting, or at least dull the feeling that it's not. Search *alcohol and marriage*, and you will come across a Norwegian study showing that married couples who drink roughly the same amount of alcohol are less likely to divorce than couples who drink different amounts. Search *marijuana and marriage* and you will discover a study that finds that couples who smoked pot together engaged in less partner violence. These utterly obvious findings seem newsworthy because they confirm an impression that many drinkers and smokers secretly share: Don't these substances help me make do in my marriage?

Paul and Nancy *liked* to drink together. I wasn't sure what I thought about that. As a mental health practitioner, I'm accustomed to looking through the lens of addiction, which has ascended in the past several decades as the key to explaining not only substance use (e.g., alcohol, prescription drugs, heroin), but a whole host of psychological difficulties now dubbed process addictions (e.g., sex, love, gambling, pornography, working, spending, eating). Since Alcoholics Anonymous was founded in the 1930s, the disease model has softened moral judgment, while capturing people's subjective experience of being victimized by an illness. Nancy and Paul were certainly pretty committed drinkers, sharing a bottle of wine over dinner, supplemented by one or two beers. It was taking its toll on the family—in their avoidance of unpleasant tasks, in fighting, and in what the children observed. The cost-benefit analysis was changing for them in midlife, as the physical and relational downsides of drinking became harder to ignore. But given the trouble so many couples have in the seemingly simple enterprise of having fun, I wondered if it might be a bit priggish of me to subject their practices to full-on suspicion. In thinking about their problem, I couldn't entirely discount their spirit of celebration. Perhaps Paul and Nancy might be better understood through an alternative interpretation of alcohol use, one that sees heavy drinking not simply as an illness but as a *central activity*.

A central activity organizes, influences, and inspires other life choices and time investments. Once an activity is central, it exerts an impact on our subsequent self-definition, actions, and values. A central activity expresses something about who we feel we are. Whether healthy or not, central activities have associated aspects of ritual and habit. For Paul and Nancy, where was the line between a pleasurable and meaningful activity involving ritual, and a dissociation or lack of self-control that could not be reasonably characterized as life affirming or healthy? Substance users make such an enormous point of their ability to "control" their use because they know that the inability to moderate is the sign that they have a problem. When the pattern of use crosses some line—the mental health field continually generates and refines instruments to assess the nature of that line—it becomes abuse, a destructive end in itself.

We can make better sense of drinking as a central activity if we recognize that altered states have always been a way that people transcend mundane experience and touch the sublime. A basic challenge in marriage is finding ways to incorporate both passion and structure, routine and surprise. So it's useful to consider substances not only in terms of pathology, but also as a way that couples augment their sense of vitality and connect to the sublime in each other. Whether it's through love, sex, music, religion, art, sports, or drugs, we all seek experiences that transport us beyond the quotidian texture of our lives. We yearn to pierce the veil, and each of us has certain things that have a power to move us in that direction. When we stumble across them, we usually feel a kind of cosmic connection has been made. These experiences feel meant for us—corresponding to some intimate contour of our being, embodying some kind of personal truth.

Paul and Nancy shared a gift for extravagant hospitality, a sense of occasion, and a contagious enthusiasm. Theirs was the New Year's party that everyone looked forward to all year, providing a festival of communal feeling in people's otherwise self-focused lives. Of course, things could get ugly (one year a guest who'd done MDMA was carried out on a stretcher), but the wild Dionysian energy was part of the fun. The party was more than just a party for the scores of friends who partook. The music, the drink, the once-a-year sampling of the drug du jour, engendered a breaking down of barriers and a sense of primordial bonding.

But if drugs temporarily satisfy the yearning for fellow feeling, their habitual use works against the very yearnings they aim to fulfill. Ritualized, repetitive intoxication is not a conduit toward openness to the world, but a closed and self-referential system where nothing new can happen. What begins with the prospect of exciting possibility deteriorates into numbing repetitiveness. While the drinker (or smoker, or snorter) may feel he is gesturing toward oceanic empathy, the more he imbibes, the more he can't help but eventually become enclosed in narrow solipsism. This is a big problem for relationships. From the imbiber's point of view, substance use may be categorized as a central activity. But for the partner (and ultimately for the children), the committed drinker's or pot smoker's most important relationship is clearly to their drug. The user's rhetoric about "choosing" to ingest because it's "enjoyable" rationalizes their disregard for the impact of their habit on the people around them. Drinking and drugs are counterfeit means of deepening inward and expanding outward. While they seem to lead to both goals, they actually lead to neither.

THE ROUGH PATCH is an opportunity to face our emotions and take an unflinching look at how we're showing up in our relationships. In this light, let's consider the most common reasons people give for drinking: (1) to be sociable, (2) because it's fun, (3) to forget worries, and (4) to fit in. Substances help us lose self-consciousness, which is why we feel they connect us to the sublime. But the primary purpose in helping us lose self-consciousness is to rid us of painful and conflicted feelings. It's no coincidence that the strongest predictors of problem drinking are self-enhancement (it's fun) and coping (forget worries). People's strongest reasons for problem drinking are for *regulating negative emotions.*

Substances offer a chemically enhanced method for not dealing directly with emotions, creating their own big, swirling self-perpetuating reward system *on top* of the already-problematic emotional strategies a person has come to rely on. While the reward system dispenses the person a short-term pleasure surge (or at least relief from pain), it also doles out the longer-term penalties of corrosive mistrust, emotional deprivation, and fearful uncertainty. That's why substance abuse gen-erates a Great Wall of China–size barrier to the basic challenges of relationship growth. It generally involves secrets and half-truths and rationalizations and excuses. It embroils us in a miasma of denial—of the harm we are inflicting on ourselves and others, and of the crash that will follow the high.

It's easy to see why the impact of drugs and alcohol on marriages can accumulate so ruinously in middle age. Houses have been pur-chased, jobs are being endured, children are being reared, and finances are being stretched. We've made our beds, for better or worse, and now we are lying in them. Our daily stresses end up stressing our marriage. There are too many demands and not enough time. At the end of a long day, we may seek oblivion. Ten p.m. is hardly the time to tackle our relationship issues. A beer goes better with work emails or mindless TV than with sensitive emotional conversations. Maybe we self-medicate because it's always been our main coping strategy. (It worked a lot better and was a lot more fun in our courtship days. It led to sex instead of snoring.) Or maybe we self-medicate because we despair at getting on the same page with our spouse in any meaningful way. We may even justify our choice to do so ("I'm going to keep doing this till something happens or falls apart"), forgetting that our children's entire lives could fit inside what we call biding our time.

Where did we come up with these anesthetic coping strategies in the first place? Role modeling, for one thing. As children, huge numbers of us were exposed to adults who used intoxicants as coping methods.

More than half of US adults have some form of problem drinking in their family history. Many of us know from experience that parents don't fully grasp the impact of their drinking on their children. They hold themselves to fairly crude standards ("I wasn't really drunk," "they didn't see me drinking"), blocking out the extraordinary sensitivity children bring to their interactions with those on whose care they depend. The memories I hear from adults in psychotherapy reflecting on their drinking parents provide a painful perspective: the feeling that Mom was "gone" after 5:00 p.m., the affected accent Dad adopted late in the evening, the harshly oblivious bonhomie of their parents' gatherings, the sloppy sentimentality of Mom's good-night kiss. The impact of parents' substance use is sometimes traumatic or even tragic (sexual and physical abuse come to mind), but even in its milder forms it is still alienating and subtly neglectful.

We also now know from scientific evidence that certain childhood experiences predispose people to seek comfort through substance use. Drugs are powerful precisely because they recruit the natural reward centers of the brain. These centers include our opioid system, where our endorphins, naturally produced opioids, generate early emotional bonding, soothing, and relief from pain. Oxytocin, a key bonding hormone, acts in concert with endorphins to increase our sensitivity to our natural opioids, as well as to decrease our reactivity to stress. Our dopamine system is responsible for motivation and initiation of pleasurable activities critical to our survival, such as eating and sex, but can be activated by any anticipated reward, be it shopping, drug use, or *Game of Thrones.*

Consistent and attuned emotional nurturing directly affects children's dopamine and oxytocin levels, as well as their developing capacity for self-regulation, including the regulation of stress. The early childhood environment forms the human brain, and relationships with caregivers *are* the child's early environment. Parental presence and attuned emotional contact mold the child's development at the biochemical and emotional levels. A biochemical surge of oxytocin translates into subjective *feelings* of security, closeness, and of calm. Evidence suggests that when a parent is "physically present but emotionally distracted—a situation that has been called proximate separation"—children experience levels of stress that are equivalent to levels experienced with physical separation. Lack of nurturance, whether physical or emotional, results in the neurochemical and psychological deficits that render children more vulnerable to seeking chemical replacements later in life. And parental absence, physical or emotional, is one huge by-product of *parents'* use of alcohol or drugs.

If early relationships do not help a child to develop self-regulation and self-soothing in response to stress, she grows up with more easily triggered stress responses, and fewer coping skills for dealing with them. The addictive impact often sets in when kids reach adolescence. Emotional reactivity and weak self-regulation make for adolescent impulsiveness and risk taking. Eighty percent of teenagers have some exposure to alcohol. But kids who take their first drink before the age of fourteen have four times the risk of a substance use problem in adulthood. And the younger a person starts drinking, the more impaired is emotional growth. This is because when people rely on a drug to manage negative emotion, they lose a vital opportunity to develop other, healthier coping strategies. It's a truism among recovering alcoholics that they are stuck at the emotional age they were when they started drinking. One man told me when he became sober at age thirty that he had "entirely missed" his twenties; in his emotional growth and development, he felt a ten-year lag.

When I observe couples, I am curious about what makes some people fall into the family tradition of their parents' drinking habits, slotting into a life of conviviality well oiled by drink, whereas others develop a diagnostic critique of their family dysfunction. It doesn't seem to relate to the actual severity of the family drinking itself. Some people join the family culture readily and without question. Others break with it, though often enough they marry someone with whom they continue to argue about the dangers and irresponsibility of drinking. In both cases, couples may have started out bonding over drinks in the early days of their courtship. Gradually, substance-related attempts at stress relief and harmless pleasure run the risk of cumulative damage—to health, certainly, but to family life and marriage as well.

Behaviors have by now solidified into patterns, and the patterns have their recurrent problems. All this occurs within a life structure that is itself hard to change or dismantle without its own kind of fallout.

Which brings me back to Paul and Nancy. They didn't like fighting, and they didn't like dropping the ball on important life tasks. But they closed ranks if I confronted them with how both behaviors related to drinking. Ultimately, it seemed, changing their drinking represented too much of a loss. They preferred to regard it as a shared central activity rather than a dysfunctional holding pattern. Since their lives hadn't dramatically deteriorated, it was hard to get either interested in looking at how they were hurting themselves or anyone else.

I've been a therapist long enough to feel what I believe to be justifiable worry about the ways parental drinking patterns eventually weave through children's lives. Thinking about Paul and Nancy, I couldn't help spinning a story about the paths that Liam and Tessa might take. After all, their family and social world prepared them to treat alcohol as an entirely expectable part of family life and relationships. Mom and Dad polished off a bottle of wine every night, followed as often by melodrama as by glazed silence in front of the tube. As in countless other families across America, barely used bottles of opiate medications lay around in bathroom cabinets, there for the taking. Everyone in the family agreed that convivial drinking with friends was one of the high points in life. That's when people were at their best, their funniest. Hangovers, an unavoidable by-product, were a source of humor and family commiseration.

Perhaps, I thought, as Liam grows, he'll be a bit of a rebel, and by high school he'll be one of the more charismatic partiers. Tessa might be the straight arrow, working hard in school but binge drinking on the weekends by tenth grade. Both Liam and Tessa might go off to party schools and find there's never an occasion to have only *one* drink. Once they move past the mystery-punch and beer-keg days of freshman year, they'll graduate to "adult" drinking—wine and Jack Daniel's. After college, the drinking won't abate, it will just take place more often in business casual. It will move from an unthinking rite of passage to an occasion for conspiratorial mirth ("Should we go for that fifth glass of wine?"). Now that they are "responsible adults," they'll know that something about their drinking is a bit juvenile and reckless. But this is pretty much what the "responsible adults" in their lives have always done. Navigating life means turning to chemicals when feelings become overwhelming. And feelings become overwhelming quickly, since healthier coping strategies haven't been given a chance to develop. Tessa, the overachiever, will eventually stack her life with parenting and work demands, intensified by her anxious perfectionism, and she'll know how to keep things going as long as she doesn't peer into the sinkhole of her emotions. But if she begins to feel that the muddy waters are rising and threatening to drown her, she might add daily Klonopin to her nightly wine. Liam, the bon vivant, might spend his twenties partying and hooking up, but once he settles down, drinking will continue as a central activity. When he and his partner begin to think about having a baby, they will agree, briefly, that it's time to clean up their act. Nancy and Paul's marriage may eventually blow up, since drinking is a major culprit in failed marriages. Either way, Liam and Tessa will confront years, maybe decades, of their parents' drinking-related health problems, their mother's cognitive slippage and their father's failing liver. And their own children, as they grow up, may continue in the family tradition.

IF YOU HAVE ever heard anything akin to the line "I'm so unhappy in this marriage, I need to dull the pain," you already know that tuning out through substances amounts to its own freestanding Rationalization-Generating Machine. Yet even as a mental health professional exposed to these issues daily, I occasionally deny or forget that truth. One reason it's hard to keep in mind is that it's unbearable. The sorry fact for anyone who is the child or partner of a serious substance user is that their most important relationship is to the substance, not to us. Who wants to believe that? Who wants to accept that a chemical trumps a person? Trumps *us*? In a sober state the user would never endorse this view. But if we observe his or her behavior, it is hard to conclude anything else.

The inner workings of the Rationalization-Generating Machine are not immediately visible to the naked eye. However, the powerful core processor of the entire apparatus is that the user will always prioritize the drug as *the one thing that will not be done without*. As the user's partner, you may think you are indispensable, but he will offer any number of crazy-making quasi arguments to justify why *you* are his biggest problem. Criticize his behavior and you will be met with a counterargument, which masquerades as a legitimate reason, as to why you are unfair, judgmental, overreacting, etc., etc. This will include a minimization of the use, and a justification of it. "She's such a nag, I need to zone out." Yes, but would she be such a nag if you *weren't* zoning out?

What is the problem with rationalizing in this way? First, even when you sound as if you are speaking honestly about your emotional experience, you probably aren't. It's likely that you are lying to yourself and manipulating your partner. But the even bigger problem is that it keeps you from dealing with your actual emotions. If you ever curb your consumption, or stop, you will be forced to face the dispiriting truth that you have been spinning your wheels while others around you (aside from your drug friends) have been developing as people.

This dynamic points up one of the most formidable challenges to recovery: admitting you have a problem you can't control. Growing up in the drug-addled 1970s, I remember a couple in which, every few years, the wife would be drunk at the end of a holiday party. Her husband seemed steadfast and loving, and something in his manner conveyed that he was dealing with an invalid rather than an embarrassment. He knew she was ill; she knew too she was ill. As I got older, I learned that she had tried over and over to recover. In situations like hers, the model of alcoholism as a disease fits because she knew she had little control over her behavior. She accepted that she suffered from a physical and spiritual sickness and had relinquished the denial aimed at protecting her habit. By contrast, when a person hasn't shifted to accepting his lack of control, what ails him looks more like a psychological problem. His rationalizations, denial, and blame are center stage. Only when he's admitted that his motivation to take drugs exerts a powerful effect on his *thinking* will he be able to progress toward taking responsibility for his *actions.* The addiction specialist Gabor Maté described the challenge in starkly physiological terms: "The brain, the impaired organ of decision making, needs to initiate its own healing process. An altered and dysfunctional brain must decide that it wants to overcome its own dysfunction."

Facing the inability to control one's addiction gives rise to a second formidable challenge: the need to take responsibility for one's development as a person. We've identified self-awareness and self-responsibility as central necessities in midlife and marriage, but they take on special importance in recovery. Substances notoriously distort healthy relations within a family. Spouses make dysfunctional attempts to adapt, whether by excusing, overcompensating, staying silent, blowing up, or taking on unwarranted guilt. Building a healthier personality and building a healthier couple relationship both require the same thing: more differentiation, more individuation, and more autonomy. While it's an understandable impulse, insisting on "more intimacy" early in recovery tends to mire couples in their old maladaptive patterns. Paradoxically, prioritizing separateness and individual healing may be a couple's most direct route to eventually finding their way back to each other. But it's hard. It can take years of ambiguity, uncertainty, and having no clue of how the story ends.

Lucy and Thomas, a couple who came to see me for therapy, got together while partying pretty hard, but when they decided to marry and start a family, the pattern shifted. Lucy stopped drinking and smoking during the week, though sometimes she consumed to excess at social gatherings. Thomas loved listening to music, which usually meant having a joint. After a hard day at work he felt he deserved a few hits, the first of which he'd sometimes snag with a friend before he came home. Thomas wasn't the heaviest user out there, but any time of day he deemed leisure time would include a toke or two.

Many couples struggle over their dueling definitions of leisure time. People justly wish to have their long day crowned with a tasty imbibable and mindless entertainment. But parents have eighteen long years of less instantly gratifying evening fare. Under stress, they draw their battle lines over who is being "bossy" or "controlling," dodging the real question of how to shoulder fairly the burden of family work. When drugs enter the mix, tensions escalate.

Lucy complained that Thomas was checked out in the evenings when the kids, in fourth and sixth grade, needed help with their homework. Not an easy criticism to hear, but I hoped Thomas would at least consider Lucy's point of view. Instead, he mounted a full-throttle counterattack to defend his right to be checked out: "You know, Lucy, the *only* way to do it is your way. Everyone's supposed to be as anxious and controlling as you are. The kids are *thrilled* that I'm not breathing down their necks. They wish you would lighten up too. It's like the whole house is supposed to tremble before your rules." Of course, when Thomas was checked out, Lucy increased her demands. Thomas then claimed her demands made his life feel "joyless" and "controlled."

Thomas's most straightforward strategy for decreasing his wife's anxiety would have been to stop smoking. But that would have forced him to confront that he had a problem. The addiction and recovery expert Stephanie Brown has identified a tension between two realities: although drug use is the organizing principle dominating the daily life of the user, the user needs to deny this organizing principle in order to keep using unimpeded. To manage this tension, the user rationalizes his use with "a personal accounting system" ("I don't use before noon," "I don't need it, I just enjoy it," etc.) that keeps his behavior within his own "definition of 'normal.'" The accounting system is designed to obscure what sets dependent users apart from others, namely the extent to which using the drug structures and dominates the user's life.

And dominate it did, whether Thomas was actually smoking or just thinking about it. A drug user's behavior does not begin with ingestion of the substance, but with the anticipation and rituals that precede it. That's when the dopamine release kicks in. Induction into the addictive state begins with the rolling of the joint, with the ceremony of the five o'clock cocktail, with the call from the dealer. There may or may not be a separate emotional precursor, such as a difficulty at work. Drug users tend to feel anxious or frustrated leading up to their use, which serves as a "reason" for the drug, but also signals a lack of coping strategies for normal human emotions. When a substance is the default response to discomfort or anxiety, it reinforces its own use and contributes to an addictive cycle.

Tolerating emotional discomfort in a relationship is a capacity we all need to develop continually throughout life. For drug users, the task is doubled: they need to stop medicating discomfort through drug use, and they need to learn to withstand the normal pain of negotiation in emotional relationships such as marriage. Like a lot of substance users, Thomas saw pot as a method for tolerating problems in his marriage. But substance use disorders are "primary" in the sense that they are separate conditions that then interact with other emotional and relational problems. It wasn't as if Thomas's perceptions of Lucy's behavior had no basis. But for me to follow his lead and turn my attention toward helping Lucy soften her behavior would have amounted to protecting his habit. There wasn't going to *be* a way for Thomas to confront the problems in his marriage, let alone his life, shrouded in the haze of pot smoke. Until he admitted that he was not in control of his habit, he'd continue to off-load responsibility and blame his emotions on others, in ways that sometimes sounded reasonable, but almost never were.

"From what you are saying," I said to Thomas one day, "you see the evening as a time to relax, so you choose not to participate in things like cooking dinner and watching over the kids' screen time?"

"It's not like I never do that stuff," Thomas said, "but I don't think it takes the level of micromanaging that Lucy seems to think it requires."

"So would you say, you cook dinner . . . half the time? Do the dishes maybe half the time?"

I could see Lucy working hard to muzzle herself.

"No, not that often," Thomas said.

"So when it comes to evening's necessary tasks, do you think you do your fair share?"

"No, probably not."

"So if I get what you are telling me, you find yourself choosing to relax and smoke in the evening, but on some level you know it's unfair."

"Yeah, I guess that's right. But once I enter the house, there's so much tension, and I don't feel like I created it. I feel I shouldn't have to have my life dictated by her stress level."

"There's something about that blast of emotion you expect when you come in the house that's really hard for you to take. It makes you want to get away somehow. But let's leave Lucy's stress level aside for a minute and focus on the kids. Looking through your kids' eyes, are you present and involved in the evenings?"

Thomas shifted in his seat, visibly trying to manage the dissonance of two clashing perspectives on himself. "I think they are relieved to have one parent who isn't so tightly wound."

"That may be. But Lucy says that she's tightly wound partly because you are high and not fully there. I'm asking you whether you think you *are* fully there, and whether your kids see you as fully there."

"I don't know. I do know that Lucy puts everyone on edge."

"Do you notice how you keep shifting the topic from yourself to Lucy? You seem to think that your problem is an overly anxious wife who makes the evenings too tense. You seem to believe that Lucy's anxiety level is what causes your need to avoid the evening's stresses, including doing your share or helping with the kids."

"Pretty much."

"Smoking is a solution to the problem of *her* anxiety, a problem that can't be solved in any direct way—like helping with the kids more, for instance, or talking to her about the effect her mood has on you, or smoking less pot."

Thomas couldn't easily answer. Affirming my statement would mean he was agreeing that smoking was his only response to stress. That, in turn, would reveal that smoking was a necessity, rather than an optional source of relaxation. He was caught in a bind.

"Until you accept that you have an addiction and reach out for support to address it," I said, "you're not going to be able to get to a better place, personally or in the marriage. Blaming Lucy for your behavior isn't going to help you."

We spent some time looking at how he and Lucy slotted each other into long-standing family patterns. Thomas saw his mother as irrational and overly emotional, and when his mother started acting "crazy" when he was a child, Thomas would feel frightened, then contemptuous. Along with his father and brothers, he developed a veneer of indifference toward her, as both a defense and a put-down. But underneath, he was highly sensitive to the emotional turmoil his mother instigated. In his marriage, "mellowing out" was intended to cope with his tension around Lucy, but ended up adding to it. Lucy grew up with an ineffectual mother, and her father—a drinker—left when she was seven. She became hyper-responsible, almost mechanically taking care of everything, but feeling angry, hurt, and abandoned. When they met, Thomas was struck by how competent Lucy was, nothing like his irrational mother, and Lucy was struck by how steady Thomas was, nothing like her absent father. Yet, gradually Lucy "became" the "overly emotional" wife-mother, and Thomas "became" the "checked out" husband-father.

As we unraveled some of these threads of marital difficulty, Thomas and Lucy gradually gained more understanding about each other's reactions. Thomas began to see how alone Lucy felt, and therefore how scared, when she felt she couldn't reach him or get his help. Lucy saw that Thomas's first priority was staying on an even keel and *not* being affected by her emotions. Once they experienced some compassion for each other, their mutual blame could be interrupted long enough to return to the question of Thomas's habit.

"Smoking lets me not get all wound up and worried about tiny details," he said. "It helps me look at the big picture."

"Big picture?" I asked.

"It lets me see what's beautiful in the world and enjoy it. When I was growing up, it felt like everyone was paying attention to the wrong things. Not putting your clothes in the laundry was a three-alarm fire. I got so fucking sick of hearing my mom go off."

"That's tough. You had to spend a lot of energy keeping yourself calm. No one was helping you with it."

"I guess I have the same reaction to Lucy when she starts getting uptight. I just want to get away." Thomas said this almost gently, feeling the weight of it. He looked sad for a change.

Over many conversations focused on his pot use, Thomas came to accept that he had a problem of his own. He started thinking about the extraordinarily challenging task of tackling his marijuana dependence. Having acquired some insight, he entertained what life would be like if he didn't manage his emotions with a joint. He decided to cut back, restricting his use to once per weekend. Two months later, he stopped using and began attending Marijuana Anonymous meetings.

As Thomas began to work on his recovery and develop his support system, I played the role of witness, coach, support, and sounding board. My job was to help both Thomas and Lucy not demand too much of their relationship while they got their bearings, and to support their differentiation from each other and their development as individuals. It's natural for couples to imagine that once the addicted partner abstains from using, the main problem has been solved. But as Thomas and Lucy soon found out, the hardest work was ahead. They had entered what addiction specialists call transition, the phase of recovery that follows the commitment to abstinence. This tough phase can at once dash inflated hopes that the problems will now be over and reveal emotional fault lines that the drug use obscured. One of my most important functions during this period was helping them accept the need for *taking time*. Addictions tend to breed a sense of crisis. In recovery, people face the difficulties and frustrations of making lasting change. Just when they think they'll feel relief, people are surprised by a sense of loss: the loneliness of personal responsibility, even the loss of the false intimacy that fighting affords. Sometimes it was all I could do to accompany them in the long, hard struggle, reassuring them that their turmoil was normal and necessary.

Even after they stop taking a drug, people still have their personalities to contend with. Some of the personality traits that lead people to substances in the first place are the same traits that make relationships unrewarding and difficult. As the AA literature puts it, "Defective relations with other human beings have nearly always been the immediate cause of our woes, including our alcoholism." Thomas had problems with expressing emotions, inchoate dissatisfactions, blame, irritability, and impatience. He oscillated between self-inflation and self-loathing and was prone to turning his discomfort with closeness into criticism, condescension, and distance. Aside from her residual resentment about Thomas's habit, Lucy struggled with anxiety, and she reflexively took responsibility for others' emotions. Her own reactivity, fear of abandonment, and difficulty setting limits only made their bad emotional cycles worse. She recognized she had work to do and decided to pursue a recovery support group of her own.

Recovery meetings, therapy, and their commitments to exercise meant that Thomas and Lucy were preoccupied with themselves, which created a challenge as parents. We talked a lot about how to create basic conditions of security for their kids, including talking to them about what was going on, and responding to their needs. Collaborating as parents had always been a challenge for Thomas and Lucy, and a chronic source of stress. We talked about tense situations—normal events in a marriage and in a family—to help Thomas stay involved rather than withdraw. Lucy tried to become aware of her feelings earlier in the chain of reactions, and to talk to Thomas about what she needed before she became frantic. Daily life provided plenty of opportunities to practice.

"Why is it that if I ask you to fill out school paperwork," Lucy said one session, "suddenly it's *me* who's too concerned with every niggling detail? I mean, it's the *school* that's demanding the paperwork. I'm not making it up just to hassle you!"

"Yeah, but the way you ask, you've got this angry tone, as if I already screwed up."

I worked with them to find a way to live together, to take good care of their children, but not to put pressure on each other. At times, they felt they would have benefited from living apart, but financially that wasn't in the cards. We came up with agreements about how to live somewhat separately within the same house for a period of time. Because it meant negotiating their separate roles with the kids, this had a beneficial effect on balancing their parenting responsibilities. Thomas felt more involved as a parent, and Lucy could allow him the room he needed without interfering. The same went for household responsibilities. Staying out of each other's hair and taking charge of their own duties helped dismantle the enmeshed, blaming dynamic that had dominated their relationship. We were able to use each "Who does what?" dilemma as an opportunity for honest discussion about when it was good to pick up the slack for the other person, and when it was good to resist bailing the other person out.

It took three arduous years for Lucy and Thomas to create a stable, calm home life. Thomas remained sober, the children were in good shape, and Lucy and Thomas hardly fought. They had both developed more autonomy, and their relationship was more collaborative. They were a good coparenting team. They continued to be committed to their support groups. Lucy and Thomas were proud of all they had accomplished.

But they struggled to discern what they had together as a couple. As they'd grown in emotional health, the old script, the dysfunctional story of their relationship, became less and less compelling to them. The push-pull that had gotten them together, and that underwent its highest magnification in their conflict around pot, had lost its painful allure. That their entire relationship had involved drugs meant they had never known each other as partners without one or both using drugs. When couples are fully engaged in recovery, some partners are confirmed in their motivation to forge a new and different relationship with each other. They have enough in common, they are emotionally compatible, they truly like each other, and they want to work through their disappointments. But sometimes, as partners develop as individuals, it becomes clearer that they want different things. For Thomas and Lucy, it was becoming obvious that each wanted to be someone *other* than the character they'd been cast—and cast themselves—to play in the story of their relationship.

For the most part, they'd fortunately moved beyond setting up their emotional differences as a battle, claiming that they "would be" intimate "if only" one or the other "stopped" or "started" doing this or that. They could now approach each other with more respect, openness, and honesty. Each grappled with questions of basic compatibility, and what it would take to bridge their differences. They were trying hard because of the children. They didn't want to stay together *for* the children, but the children drastically shifted the costs and benefits of splitting up. For their children's sake, they both were invested in keeping things going, unless and until it was absolutely clear that they couldn't.

Their fundamental struggle was about intimacy. In working toward a more solid sense of himself, Thomas became unsure how emotionally intimate he wanted to be. "I actually think I'm saner if I'm not deeply emotionally engaged," he said. "I'm as close as I feel comfortable being. I don't know where that leaves us, but I think that's the truth." Lucy, on the other hand, longed for a closer love relationship. She wanted more physical and emotional engagement. She wasn't sure that seeking it out was worth breaking up their family. Things were so much better now than they had ever been. But the longing wasn't going away, and she wrestled with the costs of burying it. Many, perhaps most, people believe that ideally marriage is close and intimate. But not everyone feels equally capable or desirous of that. My own values lead me to try to help a reluctant partner see the benefit of moving toward greater intimacy. But he may choose against that move and have to accept the consequences, including that his partner will not feel loved or will leave.

In marriage, as Lucy and Thomas discovered, the *desire to try* is profound and fragile. No feeling is quite like the alienating realization that you've lost the *desire* to try, and you have no idea how to get it back; when a voice from within says, "I'm done," even if you can hardly bear to accept it. After months of talking and working and looking at it from all angles, both Lucy and Thomas had to face that their hearts weren't in it. The realization came in a two-steps-forward, one-step-back kind of way. But when it was finally clear to us all, they both felt it as an embodied sense of relief—his blood pressure decreased, her gastrointestinal pain remitted, their insomnia abated. I physically felt more space was in the room, more air to breathe.

It was almost excruciating at times for them to feel that they had come so far and yet couldn't seem to go the final distance. But all their struggle had taught them the preeminent value of trying to tell the truth. When they "gave up," compassion and mutual forgiveness crept up on them. "Unconditional acceptance of another person doesn't mean staying with them under all circumstances, no matter what the cost to oneself," writes Gabor Maté. "Acceptance in the context of adult-to-adult relationships may mean simply acknowledging that the other is the way he or she is, not judging them and not corroding one's own soul with resentment that they are not different." Released from trying to turn each other into a person who would give them what they wanted, Lucy and Thomas could more fully accept who they actually were.

"This is so hard," Lucy said one day, after they had decided they were going to separate. We were in the midst of talking about what they would say to the children. "I'm not angry or hurt anymore, but sometimes I'm so sad. I look at you"—Lucy turned to Thomas—"and I can see the person I fell in love with again. It's easier, somehow, now that I feel I don't have to be in love with you. But it's still sad."

"Yeah, accepting reality is a big relief, but it hurts," said Thomas, returning her gaze.

They smiled at each other. The way forward would be filled with difficulty, but because of all the work they'd done, they could be friends in facing it.

WHEN PETER AND Bess first entered my office, he struck me as the more eccentric of the two. They both looked to be on the cusp of sixty. He was rumpled, with a pair of inexplicably thick-soled black shoes. She looked cast to play his opposite: her hair colored auburn, stylish glasses, her outfit sleek and almost prim. A highly successful academic, she instantly appeared the more put-together and attractive, and though he looked as if he would fall apart, he induced in me a feeling of comfort. I noticed that it took me effort to turn my gaze toward her; something about her self-containment almost rebuffed it.

"Well, where should we start?" Peter said, smiling at Bess. He sneezed, and after searching his pocket and coming up empty, he crossed the room and raided my Kleenex box, though a conspicuously similar box was on the table next to him. I felt amused rather than annoyed and wondered if his overly relaxed manner gave me a subtle sense of relief in the presence of her stiffness.

"Peter's the one who initiated this visit. He thinks I'm in my head too much, and we don't have enough fun."

"What do you think?" I asked.

"I think he's being unfair." Bess spoke thoughtfully and looked at me with an even gaze. "I have very demanding professional responsibilities, and that's nothing new. This year I am the chair of the department. It's a lot of meetings and political maneuvering. I resent it too sometimes, but it is what it is. If I'm going to do my job, I have to put in the time. With Peter, I've really tried to initiate more things. I cook three nights a week, we go to a movie on the weekends, and I often suggest outings on weekend days when I don't have to go into the office."

She didn't seem angry or hurt; she seemed cooperative and sincere, but distant. Or rather, anger and hurt had fused with her character so fully that they created the atmosphere, but couldn't be directly approached. I found myself feeling oddly desperate in the face of her calm.

Peter's outward intensity reverberated with my inner state. Agitated and leaning toward her, he looked into her eyes. "I can't figure out what you are thinking half the time. It's not like I can't entertain myself. I have plenty to do. Yes, we have dinner together, and yes, you tell me about your office politics. But I'm alone." I admired the directness of his emotional appeal, his willingness to convey real hurt. I also saw that I was watching an exchange that had happened many times before and had become, for them, rote and ineffectual. As he spoke with her, she looked at him hard, though her body almost imperceptibly retreated. That small trace of fear gave me my first sense of heartache for her.

With a full professorship, successful children, and a workable marriage, Bess was getting along fine, more than fine. She had been responsible and steadfast her whole life; control was paramount. Her career made good use of her workaholic tendencies. She was devoted to her family, if a bit at arm's length. When the children were young, Peter had been their emotional North Star. It had happened seamlessly, since her career had always taken precedence and the family had adjusted to its requirements. His role felt natural, similar to the one he'd had in his family growing up. It had been up to him to deal genially with the messes, of whatever kind. I wondered if his slapdash, run-ragged appearance, particularly when contrasted to her punctiliously groomed demeanor, showed something about how well schooled he had been to meet the needs of others with eager solicitude, and to prioritize their care at his own expense.

Yet he obviously loved taking care of people. He was warm and funny and childlike in his own way. His kids adored him, and he was already hankering for grandchildren. He'd also gotten a lot out of taking care of Bess. When he'd met her, he said, she'd been "a fragile flower who ran the literary magazine with an iron fist." He'd always been proud of her public achievements and privately satisfied by her reliance on him.

When the children had been at the center of things, they'd provided Peter with endless preoccupation and a lot of affection. Now, his jolly, easygoing attitude was giving way to a repetitive and urgent plea. "I can't stand the distance anymore. I always thought that by sixty I'd be too old to even *have* feelings, for Christ's sake," he said one day. "But life is just life. I still want the same things I always wanted. I want to be close to Bess." For Peter, their physical relationship, always sporadic, had become almost unbearably disconnected. Their problems had started way back, with the birth of their second child, when Bess's exhaustion and tenure process had resulted in a years-long dry spell. In recent years, some health setbacks and waning libido had made physical affection even more important to Peter. Bess's principled agreement that she "should" express physical warmth toward him didn't go far enough. This was when, for the first time in a thirty-year marriage, Peter called Bess out on her drinking and said he wanted her to stop.

"Most nights, Bess's first old-fashioned gives way to two or even three. At dinner, we talk about our day, but by then she's gone. I've lost any chance of reaching her. After dinner, she generally disappears into her study, and I clean up."

I glanced at Bess to see how she was taking this revelation. "Is it hard to hear him say that?"

"No, not really," she said. "Pete's a person who relaxes through interacting and talking. I'm a person who needs my alone time. Having a drink or two helps me relax. It's actually a very enjoyable part of my day."

"Peter, can you tell her more about how that feels to you?"

"I feel like she calls the shots—no pun intended—because I need something from her that she doesn't need from me. It's unfair. She gets to tune out, but I don't get to talk. Shouldn't there be some way that we both get something?"

"I *do* talk to you, all the time." Bess's voice went quieter. "We talk about the children's lives, we talk about work. I ask you what you want to do on the weekends. I sometimes feel that it's hard to tell exactly what you want or what would satisfy you."

No matter what approach I tried, I felt a palpable pressure *not to touch* Bess's drinking, as if she was protecting an extraordinarily sensitive relationship. "Alcohol is special to the alcoholic," wrote the recovery expert Stephanie Brown, "like a secret partner. It is an intruder to the rest of the family members who must make major adaptations in their personal relationships within the family and outside it." Given the zone of unreachability that Bess had constructed around her drinking, I could see why Peter had avoided confronting it. But for so many years? At what cost to himself, and to the children? Couples strike unconscious bargains to steer clear of those things that frighten them both. As the couple therapist Warren Colman wrote, marriages can be constructed "to ward off conscious and unconscious anxieties of both partners. . . . Often these anxieties are shared, so that partners have the same vested interest in avoiding particular situations." Every marriage is developmental *and* defensive, encouraging growth in certain ways and limiting it in others.

Addictions introduce an additional overlay of dysfunction into this picture. Peter had long had his own problem with codependency, which had led him to automatically adapt to the emotional requirements of Bess's habit. During his younger years, Peter had felt, as many spouses of alcoholics do, that something was specifically and uniquely wrong with *him* that resulted in Bess's drinking. With time and experience, though, that view of himself had lost its power. He knew his good-natured solicitude was a lifelong reflex, and he'd replayed his childhood emotional dynamics in his marriage. But the important thing right now was that he wanted to do something *different*. He wanted to shift the bargain, change the unspoken contract. Whenever, and however, that happens, I see it as a positive. The contract *can't* stay the same forever because people change. Sometimes, though, when one partner pushes for change, the other partner sees it as betrayal. Dramatic protests were not Bess's style, but with a bland expression she persisted that her drinking was not any kind of problem. According to her, Peter was exaggerating. But Peter kept advocating for more closeness and less drinking, and I was squarely behind him to not back down.

I began to wonder whether Bess, with her attitude of retreat, was subtly dissociated some of the time. At times I felt I was unwittingly joining her in a kind of lulled, unquestioning remoteness, and I had to shake myself loose. We all occasionally check out, but Bess's disconnection was a more pervasive aspect of personality. In trying to find some new angle, I reread my early notes and was astonished to discover that in our initial meeting I'd learned that her father had been killed in a car accident when she was ten. How could this have disappeared from my mind? I was stunned that I'd forgotten such a pivotal event. Traumatic events lead to dissociation, so it made sense that Bess's memory of her father's death had not been brought fully into conscious connection to other parts of her life. I wondered how this had affected my own ability to remember it.

Just as I was thinking about how I would reintroduce this terrible loss, Bess startled me by beginning to reminisce about her father. She indicated a world of love and grief that we hadn't ever touched. She remembered times as a young girl when her father had listened to her ideas, and how proud she had been that he took her seriously. She relished her memories of talking with him in his study, as her mother cared for the younger children upstairs. I wondered whether a whiskey and a wish to avoid his wife had accompanied her father's grand intellectual discourses with his bright-eyed daughter. ("Was the car accident drinking related?" I asked. "I have no idea," Bess replied.)

Bess's remembering her father opened a trove of loving feeling, but I noticed it was hard to stay in contact with Bess when she began reminiscing. I felt that as we gently probed the past, she went down into a well of grief, and nothing much was brought back up. Her eyes filled with tears, and we touched the watery boundaries of her loss, but her grief stayed deep and contained. More and more, I felt her drinking was a ritualized way to cherish a deep communion with her father. But in drawing the link between drinking and communing with him, she strengthened the illusion that drinking provided her an important connection that would otherwise be lost.

I wanted to help her question this illusion, and to consider how her drinking might instead be getting in the way of connecting to her husband, her children, even herself. One day when we were "in the well," I said to her, "Part of you is so vulnerable, still so devastated by losing your father—that's the part you soothe when you drink. But do you see that when you turn to drinking to solve it, you don't have the chance to turn toward Peter? You are so frightened to really *feel* the feelings of wanting and giving love. It is too scary, the risk feels too great. You feel that drinking can never let you down like a person can. It is always there, when you want it." I thought Bess heard me that day, and that she felt understood. But even as I tried to suggest that she might long for love and connection in real time, I felt as if she was blocking her resonance with me. There was a dead spot, not unlike her blank expression. I knew she depended on Peter hugely, and that she appreciated him. She even felt sentimental about anniversaries and the like. But it was hard to access her passions; those emotional frequencies were jammed.

Peter and Bess had spoken shockingly little about the impact of her father's death over the years, nor of her mother's subsequent behavior, which included erratic rages that intermittently bordered on cruelty. Bess had tried to suppress it, and Peter didn't want to hurt her by probing. But as I considered her painful childhood experiences, and the ways she dissociated from their emotional impact, I began to think about Bess's alcohol use both as an addiction and as a way she medicated her unresolved trauma.

"Once you recognize that post-traumatic reactions started off as efforts to save your life," wrote the psychiatrist and trauma specialist Bessel van der Kolk, "you may gather the courage to face your inner music (or cacophony), but you will need help to do so. You have to find someone you can trust enough to accompany you, someone who can safely hold your feelings and help you listen to the painful messages from your emotional brain." Van der Kolk is talking about therapy, but people also long to find support from their partners to heal from past wounds. It can be complicated, though, as Bess and Peter's situation made so clear. Partners are invested in each other's well-being and have a lot to gain from each other's emotional healing. But decades can go by in a tacit agreement that the trauma will not be broached, even as its effects play out day after day in disconnection, emotional volatility, sexual problems, or self-medication. Unprocessed trauma leads to over-reactivity or numbing out, both of which work against intimacy. Traumatized people need the same things from their partners that we all need—understanding, acceptance, and attuned response—only more so. But it can be hard when, as the couple therapist Sue Johnson writes, "trauma survivors may need very little confirmation in present interactions with partners to evoke negative attachment models from the past." The traumatized partner may be intensely sensitive to her partner's occasionally nonoptimal responses and experience them as "threats"; the partner is frustrated, in turn, by what he sees as her exaggerated overreactions.

Bess's strategies of disconnection had protected her for a long time. But with Peter's continued plea for more closeness, and with my presence adding to her sense of safety, we tried to talk about the feelings that her drinking was helping to medicate. She began to feel her way into her darkest and most painful places. It was frightening for her to explore her memories, to feel exposed and yet to resist the impulse to retreat to abstraction and self-reliance. We developed a ritual. Every time we met, Peter took her hands in both of his. He gently questioned her about things, but let her set the pace. He engaged

her with a quiet, tender voice. These signposts of comfort helped
Bess get in touch with, but not feel overwhelmed by, her emotions.
Gradually she began to shield herself less, and to feel more viscerally
Peter's love and support.

They had enough strength in their partnership that their conversations could unfold sensitively. They got closer as a result. Over time,
Bess felt more comfortable in her own skin. She took up yoga, and
before too many months had passed, she said, with uncharacteristic
enthusiasm, that she felt "one hundred times better." One day she
smiled at an offhand joke of Peter's, and almost involuntarily I said,
"Wow, I've never seen that smile before." She had a beautiful smile,
and it had taken almost a year for me to see it.

Bess's drinking didn't stop, though maybe she did a bit less of it. It
was on the table, and she knew where Peter stood. But she remained
unconvinced it was a problem. I told Peter that he could pursue an
exploration of its impact on him. In what I saw as an impressive show
of autonomy given his lifetime of enabling, Peter took up my sug-
gestion and decided to go to Al-Anon meetings. A partner married
to an addict, or to someone mentally ill, or to—well—anyone, must
determine the kind of relationship he or she is ultimately willing to
live with. Devoting one's life to trying to change one's partner into
someone one *can* live with is a recipe for bitterness and resentment.
The guiding philosophy behind 12-step programs is that no one can
change another person. "Would our help, good looks, higher income,
or cleaner house, overcome the progression of Alzheimer's disease?"
queries the book *How Al-Anon Works.* "Our compassion and support
might make a loved one's struggle with illness easier to bear, but it
is simply not in our power to cure someone else's disease. We are
powerless over another's alcoholism. We didn't cause the disease, we
can't control it, and we can't cure it." We can only do our own psychological and spiritual work, decide what we can and cannot accept,
and communicate our limits and needs with honesty and compassion.

"I can love her as she is," Peter said, "and we can see this differently.
Heal myself and treat Bess with love. That's my view of marriage in
a nutshell." I think that Peter thought, "Who am I to take this away

from her?" He appreciated Bess, he had compassion for her. He was not interested in taking the drastic actions, or issuing the ultimatums required to test her willingness to change. But he did begin to talk honestly with his children about the impact of Bess's drinking on their lives, and he let Bess know he was doing so. Over time, perhaps Peter's shifts would begin to change Bess's behavior and thinking. When Peter added it all up, he felt they'd had a successful marriage. Their daughter was getting married; soon, they hoped, there might be a grandchild. Yet too, Peter's longing to be closer, physically and emotionally, remained unfulfilled. "If I'm truthful, there's a third, or maybe a quarter, of this relationship that isn't good," he wrote in a note of thanks when he and Bess ended couple therapy. "It's a good, solid marriage, and a loving marriage. We have a very rich life, and I'm grateful. But there are ways we've been separate that make me sad, and I think they'll always be there. You read obituaries, where people talk about their 'wonderful wife—she was my best friend, my partner, my lover.' We've come out pretty well, but I won't be able to say all of those things."

ONE OF *SATURDAY Night Live*'s most popular skits of the 2013 season was "Xanax for Summer Gay Weddings." Structured like a standard prime-time drug commercial, it features schlubby straight people gazing out rain-flecked windowpanes or pausing in mid-dinner preparations, while the singsong voice-over asks, "Do you suffer from feelings of anxiety? Are you worried that you'll never be good enough, that you'll never measure up?" The reason, the voice intones, is that "this summer you must have been invited to a beautiful gay wedding." The skit humorously juxtaposes two unrelated social trends: the growing cultural acceptance of gay marriage and the definition of social anxiety as a problem to be medicated. "Usually at weddings, I'm the best dancer there," Bill Hader frets. "But at gay summer weddings, everyone knows a choreographed dance from a Beyoncé song that hasn't even been released yet." The voice-over interjects, "Because your gay friends have it all figured out. And you don't."

No class of drugs may be more seemingly suited to addressing our culturally induced ills than the benzodiazepines—Xanax, Klonopin, Ativan, etc.—known as minor tranquilizers, whose purpose is to relieve anxiety and stress. "We're the most anxious country in the world," according to a psychiatrist quoted in *Vogue*, who claims our culture is tailor-made to be "anxiety-producing, stress-producing, mood disorder–producing, and stressful to the self-image of girls and women." (Benzodiazepine use is twice as common among women as men.) Adderall and other stimulants also occupy a central cultural position, though for the opposite reasons. If benzos help us calm down and mellow out amid our jacked-up, frenetic, multitasking lives, stimulants help us focus, stay up later, and get more work done. Cadging stimulants from each other in college, kids get through exams and papers, then watch Netflix and chill with a combo of Xanax and weed. Busy parents juggling marriages, children, houses, and jobs seek a prescription of Klonopin for feeling overwhelmed, then find that it makes trips to the supermarket, cooking dinner (especially with a bit of wine), or having sex a little more relaxed. Older people struggling with anxiety or loss are prescribed Librium by their primary-care doctors and stay on it long term, even though benzodiazepines are addictive, are recommended for short-term use, and pose risks of bone fractures and cognitive decline.

Between 1996 and 2013, the total quantity of benzodiazepine prescriptions filled tripled. Often the drug is prescribed in response to a circumscribed problem—fear of flying or job loss—and imperceptibly it becomes the calming antidote to life's continually stressful situations. It can help you be less reactive with your kids, or calmly handle a crucial business meeting, or greet your spouse with a more pleasant expression. People who decide pharmacology enhances their lives will attempt to keep their use within limits. Some people believe they can respect the downsides of the drugs while using them judiciously in the long term. However, long-term benzodiazepine use is highly controversial, since discontinuation after just three or four weeks precipitates withdrawal symptoms. Unlike opiates such as oxycodone and fentanyl, the dangers of which are publicized almost daily in the news, tranquilizers largely fly under the radar. But visit BenzoBuddies .org and you will encounter an avalanche of evidence for why benzo-diazepines are risky. People become dependent on even therapeutic doses, and withdrawal can be hellish. Many users report hearing insufficient warning from their doctors about the downsides, including the insidious buildup of tolerance over time. An entire, dedicated board in the forum is "Planning Your Taper," since abruptly stopping the drug can result in anxiety, nausea, convulsions, hallucinations, and a host of other hideous symptoms. Benzos are "getting by" drugs that have entered the mainstream as something between a necessary evil and a boon for meeting the demands of modern life. As the historian Andrea Tone put it, "Our need to calm down fast is bound up in our harried race to do it all as effortlessly and quickly as possible, with minimal stops (who has time for therapy or vacation?) on our way to the finish line." Yet for every few moderate users, there is someone whose habit slops over the sides, whose kids suffer, and who crashes their job or their marriage.

This is what happened to Sheila, who told me her story of addiction to both alcohol (for twenty-five years) and Xanax (for six years). I met her when she was in her midsixties, when she had a couple decades of sobriety and AA under her belt. But the Xanax years had been nasty. "When the kids left home, a huge chunk of me went away. I'd been raised to be a perfect wife, a perfect mom. The appearances on the outside were always great—I was good at my job, good at entertaining, the girls looked adorable. But I didn't really know who I was. I was a quiet drinker, pouring gin while talking on the phone at night. I didn't make scenes. When my second daughter left, I had stomachaches. My doctor said, 'I'll give you Zantac for the stomach and Xanax for your anxiety.' We all had so much faith in doctors back then—I feel like suing him now. I was still very high functioning, but totally out of touch."

One Christmas, her grogginess, slurred speech, and stumbling alarmed her husband and her daughters, who were home from college. "They asked me what was going on, and I said, 'Nothing,' and acted offended. They'd grown up with me drinking, so they were used to having to act like they bought into my story. But I dozed off at a stop-light on the way back from a holiday party and was picked up by the police. My husband let me have it. He screamed at me, as if all those years of silently suffering and suppressing his feelings were over. He was beside himself, and there was nowhere for me to hide. No one in my family had ever expressed that kind of emotion—ever.

"The next morning, the whole family confronted me together. My husband said he'd leave if I didn't get help. He'd spoken with our daughters about it beforehand, and they supported him. It was a watershed moment for me. To this day, I'm not sure why. Certainly my husband's show of emotion was part of it. It was a moment of grace. I'm not a religious person, though I think there's God in all of us, our higher selves. That day, something made me give up the ghost. I knew I was an addict. I knew I needed to do something. I honestly don't think my family thought I'd do it.

"I went into rehab, and I remember the doctor telling me they'd have to taper the Xanax so that I didn't have seizures. I remember looking behind me, thinking he was talking to someone else. I still didn't get how bad it was. My family came to meetings, they sup-ported me all the way through." Sheila paused and became tearful. "My husband's a tremendous guy. He was big enough to give me the space to figure myself out. It's not a foregone conclusion it'll work out that way, believe me. You don't always know what will happen when you get honest. I had a lot of years of struggle, getting sober, and figuring out why I am on this earth. He was beside me at every step. He's a really good person, he had my back. I feel we've had about eighteen different marriages, all told. But I think our best ones started then."

Aside from her husband's loyalty, Sheila felt that his confrontation that Christmas had led to the other two great blessings of her sober life: friendship and community. "I belong to a group of twelve women, all from AA, and we meet once a month. There are four generations of women in the group, and between us we've been through pretty much everything: death of a spouse, children with serious problems, terrible worries about grandchildren, marital problems, divorce, illness, you name it. It's about being there for one another, trying to do our best, telling the truth, and walking through life together with honesty and dignity. The willingness to be open, to always keep your side of the street clean by not keeping secrets—it's unbelievably precious.

"Then there's the extraordinary friendship with the woman I've sponsored all these years. She's twenty years younger than I am, but she's my mother and my daughter and my friend all at once. Have you heard that saying '*Intimacy* equals "into me see"?' What we have is above and beyond . . . an honesty and love that nothing in my life taught me to expect."

IN 2016, THE Napa Valley Wine Train introduced its new Private Reserve Vintner Dinner, a five-course gourmet meal in its exclusive thirty-six-seat "restyled Pullman railcar," where guests would have access to winemakers "on board to discuss the pairings and tasting notes in depth." The rollout featured a photo of a dashing French vintner with a faintly lascivious twinkle in his eye, a tuxedoed James Bond/Daniel Craig wannabe, intended to attract the ladies, no doubt. In my part of the world, wine has a special status—as an organic product, wholesome and of the earth, conferring a healthy California style of drunkenness. As one of my Bay Area friends said, "Have you ever noticed that people around here don't really consider drinking wine *drinking*?"

Wine tasting is big business, monetizing the ritual elements of leisure—travel, luxury, romance—through a "relaxed," "natural" drinking experience. At $299 a pop, the Private Reserve dinner is a decidedly exclusive affair, purveying a particular strain of wine-drinking prissiness and dressing up alcohol consumption as a rarefied "cultural" experience. In general, sociologists say that travel and leisure promote a form of emotionality called *communitas*, "a state of intense emotional fusion among members of the same group." The same might be said of drinking. The world over, from beachside communities to "Margaritaville" vacation destinations, drinkers greet "beer o'clock" as the moment to indulge their urge to break down barriers, to shed the armor of self, and to merge into the vast, thumping human organism.

Yet most of us realize at some point—and addicts learn the hard way—that it's an illusion. Even though the connection between us on ecstasy *felt* deep, it wasn't; even though it *felt* as if we were kindred spirits during that marathon drinking session, it turns out I pissed you off. In recovery, people start learning about the real nature of community. We lose our grandiosity and our crippling sense of specialness through engagement with others. The community then helps us to navigate our intimate personal relationships with more integrity and humility. As with raising children, couple life "takes a village." A man who has been in AA for over three decades said that the community of men has been crucial in supporting each other in their relationships with intimate partners. "It takes talking to other men to get the emotional grounding that we all are dealing with the same kind of stuff," he said. "Our struggles aren't just about our own personal problems, it's the nature of the beast. That can be incredibly calming and helpful."

So much of marriage, and life, is about sitting with uncomfortable feelings, and not reaching for the quick fix that won't work in the long run. This sometimes means confusion, lack of control, or feeling broken before you feel whole. It means understanding "not knowing" as a positive capacity, rather than as failure or ignorance. People who pray, people who meditate, have a model for this. They assume that it takes time for mysteries to clarify. The artist Georgia O'Keeffe famously said, "Nobody sees a flower—really—it is so small it takes time—we haven't time—and to see takes time, like to have a friend takes time." A spiritual practice helps us to know that seeing takes time; and that sometimes it can take a long time to see because we resist painful realities.

All this can be hard, and it isn't made any easier by the demands of the culture: to shift our moods by the clock, to treat impatience as a virtue, and to confuse self-certainty with emotional health. Addictions run in families via genes, behavior patterns, and the interaction of the two. Regardless of the source, one of the overarching features of addiction-generating households is a vacuum of healthy coping with emotions, and a tone-deaf demand that people ignore their feelings as the price of being accepted and cared for. It can take a lifetime to see this for what it is, and to heal from the harm. But, when a person begins to peel away the layers—whether through being confronted by a loved one, or finding the strength to confess secrets, or going to therapy, or hitting bottom—the self-awareness the person finds is lifesaving. As one recovering alcoholic said to me, "Once you have this self-awareness, you can't ever go backward. You can't pretend you don't have it. Things change forever."

A core difficulty of the rough patch is finding that our usual coping strategies don't work anymore, including our use of drinking and drugs. We know from the recovery and addiction fields that the basic precepts for overcoming an unhealthy relationship to drugs are pretty much the same precepts that underlie healthy relationships to other people. We try to see, accept, and understand our emotions. We try to look at the big picture about where we've been, where we are, and where we're headed and try to align our actions with our values. We speak the truth to our partners and to our friends, and we make amends for harm done. We support and are supported by others in community. Once we relinquish our substances, we'll have to face ourselves before we can discover what's possible in our relationships. The hope is that, as we explore our own destructive patterns and cope with our demons in a way that opens the path for growth, we can turn to our partner and discover a friend.

Money: The Knife in the Drawer

Money, sex. Sex, love. Love, power. Power, gender. Gender, money. Money, sex. People can get pretty crazy when it comes to money, playing out the most primitive parts of themselves. It's certainly a significant source of rough-patch distress, and one of our most glaring theaters for marital dysfunction. According to Karly Mitchell, a financial planner in Fairfield County, Connecticut, "There's a high percentage of people who don't deal with money, other than on a day-to-day basis. They don't do planning, they don't understand it, they don't know how to deal with it, it's not talked about. Couples don't set goals. So often someone will come in and say, 'I was trusting my spouse to deal with this.' But they don't sit down and give each other a goal or a pathway: Where do we want to be in ten years, in twenty years? They don't check in—ever."

In marriage, money easily becomes a hidden currency for pressing emotional and spiritual questions: Am I worthy? Will I be cared for? Can I care for myself? Do I have enough? This gives rise to two types of confusion. First, people mistake their emotional needs for financial needs, freighting their spousal money conflicts with projections of childhood wounds and past grievances. Our attitudes toward money reflect deeply embedded messages that we pieced together from observing our families in childhood. One Bay Area "money coach" I spoke with spends a large part of her time with clients delving into these messages. Using Jungian-style archetypes (the Warrior, the

Victim, the Fool), she tries to help people recognize and then rectify their troubling scripts. The second confusion is that, when money differences arise, couples mistake them for thoroughgoing marital incompatibility. Money stress has a striking power to feed an atmosphere of marital gloom. It so seeps into our consciousness that we have a hard time identifying accurately the distinct marital concerns it contaminates. Money worry makes all our other worries feel worse, which is why it's no surprise that couples that have high levels of debt also tend to experience greater conflict about other marital issues such as sex and in-laws.

Having money doesn't seem to help nearly as much with these problems as one would expect. In the leafy precincts where Karly Mitchell plies her trade, affluent professionals and high-net-worth individuals struggle with financial discord and duplicity just like everybody else. At the extreme, stealthily refinanced mortgages cover gambling debts, inheritances are jealously hoarded, or family businesses are run into the ground. More mundanely, a gaping canyon of noncommunication separates the family's designated "earner" and designated "spender," and into the void drift "Holy shit!" levels of credit-card debt, pricey leases of status-mobiles, and a deluxe dollop of mutual resentment. Some women, whose feminist consciousness is otherwise fully functional, give themselves over to deer-in-the-headlights panic or princess-style unconcern when confronted with the concrete reality of dollars and cents. Some men who otherwise consider themselves enlightened boomerang between tyrannical control and emasculation anxiety.

When one or the other pulls the plug on the marriage—it's usually the woman—the grim extent of the financial chaos is revealed. A quarter of those seeking divorce cite "different financial priorities/ spending patterns" as one of their reasons. (It's one of the top five reasons for men, but not for women.) But once a couple has determined that their different priorities rank as a deal breaker, they move into the two-household zone of compounded financial stress. Money conflict can fan the brushfire of mediation into the inferno of litigation. Then, the escalation of the couple's rage is matched only by the depletion of their bank accounts. "Some folks don't have the gene for it," one divorce lawyer said to me. "It's like they can't perceive financial reality. They are mentally unequipped to process the fact that they will *run out of money* if they don't come to an agreement, or get a job, or save, or invest."

Money differences in marriage can be handled effectively in all sorts of ways—pooling or separating resources, rethinking divisions of earning and nonearning labor, creating priorities and savings plans. But they all depend on *thinking together*. What enables a couple to collaborate about money, or anything else, is being able to look together at the big picture. Then they can discuss, compromise on, and integrate their ideas. They can set shared goals, financially and otherwise. A nerdwallet.com columnist wrote that the best way to build wealth is by following the "one house, one spouse" rule. It's a glib little phrase, but it also economically captures how a shared, coherent worldview— emotional and financial—is what helps couples prosper over the long term. There may be no area of marriage where the golden-ring model is more challenged than in the area of money. Not having enough creates intense fear in people, and it is hard not to deteriorate into a seesaw mind-set, where it's every man for himself.

Money is an acid test of the we story. Couples who can't place their momentary feelings within their larger goals tend to have trouble. They act on impulse and hope for the best. The lure of short-term gratification, and the use of purchases as emotional nourishment, can stoke this culturally endorsed form of madness. Middle-class couples can look pretty similar from the outside—houses, kids, jobs—but peek into their bank accounts and you discover that money is an exacting measure of whether two people are genuinely collaborating or whether they are just putting on a good show.

SAM HATED HIS job. Really, really hated it. He'd survived the bloodbath of 2008, hanging on by his fingernails, and his reward— hallelujah—was the stupor of staring at his computer screen, his head throbbing. The website of his financial services company showcased the soulful profile of a guy gazing at his triple monitor as if he were Columbus pondering whether the earth was round. But people in his office only felt they were doing their jobs if they were screaming. Casual brutality, a sense of crisis, a hair-trigger temper—these were the signals that a man was hard at work.

Willa, Sam's wife, had no idea what it took for him to get through his day. She had no *clue* how normal it was to feel pummeled and abused. If she tried to put herself in his shoes and imagine how he felt, he knew it would help. But when she cocked her head with stubborn optimism, trying to pass off her "We'll just make the best of it" attitude as camaraderie, he could tell she was subtly refusing to empathize. He was wearing himself down into a strange, stunted version of himself, ghostly and depressed and angry. Yet her response—"If it's too much, we'll figure out something else"—felt belittling. Basically, she thought his bad mood was his own damn fault.

Willa popped out of bed every day at 5:30 a.m. for thirty minutes on her treadmill. Her days were full to bursting, every moment accounted for. The twins were a delight, but Jacob had ADHD and Lucia was moody like her dad (tantrums still, at eight years old). Willa's to-do list was a mile long, but she tried to make the walk to school special, asking the twins to name the flowers that were in bloom. Lucia sometimes refused to answer, but Willa tried to stay positive. She strove to brighten people's days without even thinking about it. She'd spent her entire youth as a cheerleader for her mother, helping her put one foot in front of the other. Willa's antics had always made her father laugh and tousle her curly hair, at least until he was too far gone.

Lately, though, Willa felt tired of cheering everyone else up. For a while she felt she'd made it work, repaired her past. She married a responsible man and gave her children the attention her own mother hadn't been able to give her. But when Sam was anxious about his job, he became sleepless and irritable. His unhappiness started to feel selfish, even a little mean. Her sympathy did nothing to comfort him; he seemed to hold her good mood against her, as if it were damning proof that she didn't feel his pain. One day she looked at him, slumped in his chair—his favorite chair, a ghastly glob-shaped burnt-orange thing he'd proudly retained from his student days. Her eye landed on his shoes, the sole pulling away from the leather toe. It's time, she thought, it's time to deal with the sorry state of this house.

Enter the remodel. Sam and Willa had bought a house in the most affluent suburb they could afford soon after their twins arrived. The 1960s ranch was a basic dwelling built when people had neither the need nor the money to treat their houses as castles. It appealed to Sam's long-range planning and belief in a good address. Willa dreamed of applying her artistic skills sometime down the road. They both agreed the house was in a wonderful community for raising kids.

Over the years Willa had become more and more uneasy about the house, its lack of light and its disrepair. The kids hadn't yet noticed, but how long would it be until they did? Her friends had lovely houses, and she was embarrassed by hers. Sam gave her mixed messages. He said she was "the CEO" of their family life and that care of the house was her domain. So why did he treat a request to fix the kitchen faucet as one more in a string of endless demands for cash? ("Hear that sucking sound?" he'd say in a sarcastic mood. "That's you bleeding me dry.") Sam was so negative, she decided she'd wring pleasure from wherever she could; she wasn't going to deny herself everything out of fear of his reaction. And who knew? Maybe a pleasing environment would buoy his mood. In any case, she knew she had to do something to bring in more *light*.

Sam respected his wife's efficiency. He appreciated the energy she invested in jump-starting their remodeling plans. He even recognized that a piece of valuable property such as theirs deserved some improvements. It was hard for him to admit, but he secretly felt a little relieved that Willa could mobilize on something that required such an exorbitant outlay, knowing that left to his own devices he'd languish in paralysis. Yet as a result of the remodel, he was even more crushed by money worries than before and more tightly tethered to his hated job. Predictably, the scope of the improvements had ballooned, the delays had lengthened, and they'd had to move out of their house for an inauspicious thirteen months. Now, with construction finally completed and their savings duly drained, Willa was suddenly talking as if landscaping their garden was an immediate necessity. Where was *that* money going to come from? Evidently straight out of his hide, in longer hours, ass kissing, and the bad diet and insomnia that went along with them. She was even on the brink of insisting he get rid of his *chair*. In proof that no good deed goes unpunished, his willingness to defer to her had convinced Willa that it was "her" house now, and he was henceforth expected to live with her high-handed decrees about bulb wattage, cleaning methodology, and even where he was allowed to relax.

When Willa and Sam showed up at my office, they weren't exactly on the same page about whether to spend money on therapy. For Sam, therapy was one more item in a long list of expensive goods and services that Willa seemed to require to feel good about her life. Each of those goods and services was paid for by a job he despised, at a cost to his emotional and physical health. For Willa, Sam's reluctance to try to work on their relationship was just one more way he shut her down and dismissed the importance of feeling close and connected in their marriage. Having spent an admittedly shocking amount of money to make their family home more comfortable, she feared that Sam would insist on keeping their emotional life dark and dingy. She was trying so hard to find a way to be happy together.

As I began to try to understand Sam and Willa's problem, I knew that I shared the same bourgeois social apparatus. We partook of the same set of conventions, nested like so many Russian dolls, about houses and school systems and safe communities, about marriage and intimacy—a set of conventions that for them was resulting in shelling out money to get help with the problems that shelling out money had exposed in the first place. As if to remind me of our mutual conscription in that world, I found myself standing in line one day at Macy's several people behind Willa. Her arms were laden with merchandise—clothes for the twins, judging from the garish hues. I was there to return some ill-considered purchase, bought in the haze induced by coupons algorithmically generated to appear at exactly the moment when I had been about to swear off being doped up by deals.

Aside from occupying the same consumption-driven world, we were poised to enter into an economic arrangement as well. Psychotherapy, barely one hundred years old, has gobbled up, without so much as a hiccup, a role once filled by ministers and kinfolk. Psychotherapy is an emotional relationship whose commercial underpinnings are not entirely comfortable. It bears some resemblance to marriage. Marriage is an "I-Thou" relationship, in the theologian Martin Buber's terms, where we care for the other as a person who has the same personhood as ourselves. But it's also an exchange economy, with money, sex, and labor among the elements exchanged. Ideally, we imaginatively enter our partner's experience and act with concern on her behalf. We express our care *through* goods and services such as money, sex, and labor. But every relationship of dependency includes some form of use, and marriage can never entirely rid itself of this element. It's not always an easy tension to navigate.

Perhaps money is the conjugal arena where use is most blatantly on display. Money lies so close to what we might call our core of survival, our self-preservative impulse that seeks satisfaction of its own needs above all else. Money can lead to nastiness because it pulls so readily on our primitive drive to *live*, even if at other people's expense. One colleague called money in marriage "the knife in the drawer," alluding to money's menacing potential to turn the always tenuous relationship of equals into occasions for primal displays of dominance and submission, powerlessness and control.

Economic issues—Who is consuming? Who is producing?—were at the forefront of how Willa and Sam presented their marriage to me. If awkwardness inevitably clings to therapy because it entails *paying* for a relationship, Sam and Willa resisted the idea that they were paying for a *relationship* at all. When I explored with Sam his reluctance to pursue therapy, he confessed that he would be less wary about the cost if I could guarantee that some useful "tools" would come out of it. Willa worried that with all their expenses, it would be important to "work quickly"—as if my understanding of them should be accelerated if possible.

If I saw myself as offering a brand of purely technical expertise, I might have earnestly tried to speed up the production line, as it were. I was not averse to offering suggestions, and I let them know that they could access many of the common tips and tools far more cheaply in books. Privately I mused that Sam and Willa expressed two contrasting archetypes of the American approach to money. Sam was the do-it-yourselfer, the sufferer-in-silence, whose stoicism was hard to distinguish from martyrdom, and whose frugality looked at times more like a puritanical stinginess. Willa was the can-do spirit and self-improvement seeker, whose aspirations led, at the margins, into entitlement and heedless consumption. They were united, though, in their shared pragmatism—which had them asking me for strategies before I had even grasped their situation and pressuring me to package my insights in a way that they could cost-effectively take away and use.

The urgency with which both Sam and Willa wanted me to deliver the goods felt like part of the mentality that was getting them into trouble in the first place. Sam felt misunderstood and unloved because he felt that Willa just wanted him to "produce" so that she could purchase her gratifications elsewhere. Willa felt that Sam treated warmth, humor, and affection as "luxuries" he couldn't afford. They unthinkingly shifted the possibilities of therapy into the idiom of getting their money's worth, even as they were trying to find a way to rescue their relationship from its economic ensnarement. To my mind, the capacities they needed to develop would be found in the opposite direction from where they were looking. The challenge would be to help them discover the *emotional meanings* that were carried by landscape designs or year-end bonuses or new chairs. And to understand why money and things seemed to offer the only currency with which to express them.

"You are such a doomsayer," Willa said one day as she and Sam were arguing about spending money to landscape their yard. "You act as if we'd all be better off if I just did what you say. But you are the one who said it was fine to live with a broken downstairs toilet for a *year*. Am I supposed to sign on to your depressing point of view to prove that I'm responsible? I don't think so. I refuse."

"My 'depressing point of view' happens to be the reason we've saved as much money as we have. Besides, we're talking about the landscaping, not the toilet," Sam said. "Remember, we *agreed* that we weren't going to fix *anything* leading up to the remodel. This is what you always do—you exaggerate and try to make me look cheap so you can get your way."

Willa's face colored at his harshness, and I could sense, in her subtle shift in posture, an internal struggle between asserting herself and losing control. "What do you mean *my way?*" she said heatedly. "Our way, it's *our* way. You *agreed* to this remodel. We worked on it together. Every time you get uptight, you turn it into *my* project and start acting like it's my nutty scheme. It's not fair."

"That's because every time you take the reins, I discover that your idea is five times more expensive than what we agreed to! Case in point: Since when has landscaping become a family necessity? How'd that get slipped in there?" Sam slumped back incredulously, then replenished himself with angry sarcasm. "Sure, go ahead, knock yourself out, with your hot tub and your pergola and your sport court or whatever the hell they call it. I give up."

"I know this is complicated," I said. "But just so I'm clear, do you have a shared vision of the budget for the landscaping?"

"Are you kidding?" Sam burst out. "There *is* no budget for the landscaping!"

"That's not true," Willa retorted. "I distinctly remember our conversation last December when we talked about using your bonus toward fixing up the yard. Are you now going to act like that never *happened?*"

"*Aaghh,*" Sam sputtered, "*the yard wasn't the only one thing we talked about!* We talked about college funds, and retirement savings for you, and an emergency fund! We talked about when I might be able to leave this friggin' job! Is the landscaping part *all you remember?* Jesus!"

By now, Willa had decided Sam was a bully and a tyrant, unwilling to compromise or even listen. She looked at me helplessly, seeking support. *See what I mean?* her face seemed to say.

"You know," I began, "I can see how hard this is to think about together. It's as if you've allocated roles here, and so neither of you feels responsible for seeing the whole picture. Starting with you, Willa, when you look at the whole picture, do you have a sense of what you believe is most important? Do you have your *own* idea about how these different priorities should fit together?"

She looked at me, a bit frustrated that I hadn't come to her rescue. She drew a sharp breath, but then she stopped and considered. "I guess I think that . . ." She didn't seem sure what she thought. "I think Sam is a bit of a doomsayer."

"I'm not asking what you think of Sam. I'm asking you about what financial priorities you think are important, from your own point of view."

"My priority is to give my children a good childhood. I want them to feel happy where they live. I never had that. A nice outdoor play space is part of that, I think that's my top priority. It'll mean a lot for them to have somewhere to play with friends. They haven't had the easiest road socially in some ways—Jacob can't always control himself, and Lucia's moody and fights with her friends." Willa looked at me earnestly. "If that means Sam has to work a while longer at his job, I think that's a reasonable price to pay. If he's going to be at work most of the day anyway, why wouldn't he want me and the kids to enjoy where we live?"

Willa's declaration was heartfelt, though she had skirted my question about financial priorities. I pushed a bit: "From what I can tell, Sam doesn't feel this arrangement is entirely fair."

"But we *agreed* on it, early on. We *agreed* that he could make more money than I could, and that I would manage the kids, and it hasn't been all fun and games, even if he likes to act like it has, and then he just blames me for doing what we agreed I'd do in the first place. I *appreciate* how hard he works, I *appreciate* that he supports the family." Two tears brimmed over and trickled down her cheeks. She paused, steeling herself to speak. "But sometimes I wish he would stop being so negative and just do what needs to be done." Her voice caught on a half sob. "I have friends who take their kids to the beach for the summer and the dad stays in the city to work. Can you imagine Sam doing that? He'd miss the kids too much, I know. But shouldn't he be thinking more about them? I just don't think it's *good* for them to be here all summer and have nowhere to play."

Before I knew it, I found myself thinking, Okay, we have now officially entered the land of Rich People's Problems. Images leaped to my mind of the sparkling open spaces and beaches in our part of the world, not to mention the parks that could serve just as well as a landscaped backyard for children's social needs. I tried to figure out how to ask Willa to spell out her thinking a bit more, but Sam jumped in. Or rather, jumped down her throat.

"This isn't about the kids. It's about you. You just want a yard you can brag about. Sure, you'd love to guilt-trip me into bankrolling a vacation for you and the kids somewhere far away while I sweat back home. You'd love to hang out and have girl time with Libby and Joyce and get away from the husbands. This is what I mean! Why won't you just be honest? What matters most to you is your *lifestyle*. Period."

I had to admit, I sympathized with Sam. Willa seemed to have no idea how entitled she sounded. But I also remembered her wounded disclosure a couple weeks earlier that Sam wouldn't have sex with her. I could see how it made her more frantic, and although he pleaded exhaustion from his relentless work demands, I sensed he had an inclination both to protect himself and punish her. Listening to the music and not the words, I heard the despair each felt at not being able to find some understanding in the other. Neither felt the other was interested in, or willing to, share their reality. Instead, both were trying to survive by winning the argument and establishing the superiority of their version of the truth.

Deep down, I believe, Sam and Willa both knew that their claims to being right were suspect. In the heat of a fight, most of us portray a situation with a dose of dishonesty. We try to drown out the other's perspective while treating our own actions as entirely produced by the other's actions. We channel our scared, sad, confused feelings into a harsh, decisive claim about reality. When we are highly emotional, these distortions seem real and crucial to our survival.

What's lost in these moments is not only an honest picture of our own reality, but a picture of reality that makes room for *both* people's emotional truth. The couple therapist James Fisher said that to be intimate with another person we must be able to face the truth, by which he meant two things. We need to face the reality of our own experience, and we need to face the reality of someone else's experience while not losing or denying the reality of our own. In his language, "marrying" is a continual emotional activity that takes place between partners throughout life, defined as the ongoing effort to recognize the needs and feelings of the other while keeping in touch with one's own.

What an extraordinarily difficult thing this can be. It was certainly Sam and Willa's painful challenge. Under perceived conditions of emotional threat, they violently intensified their struggle over whose truth would prevail. Each said, in effect, "Your attempt to get your reality heard cancels out my reality. So, of course, I need to yell louder to try to get heard." In such states of mind, people start to justify their egocentric behavior as a legitimate response to their partner's egocentric behavior. They get confused about what constitutes sticking up for themselves and what constitutes blocking out the other person. People are so quick to locate the problem in their partner's behavior, or feelings, or viewpoint, that they fail to recognize the prior problem in their *own pattern of thinking*.

Sitting in my office with a couple, I will watch one partner hearing the front edge of the other's complaint and trying to shut it down before hearing any more. Why is this? Why is one partner's feeling or thought so unbearable for the other to hear, or listen to, or take in? People supply all sorts of rationales for why they find their partner's utterances unbearable: "She's said that a million times before," "He's trying to lord that over me," "That's not true!" But none of these responses answer the question: What is so painful and desperate and provocative about *hearing the other's point of view*? I think that what's unbearable is feeling that our partner's utterances either negate our feelings or blame us for their feelings. These are the quintessence of a seesaw model of marriage.

Money lends itself perfectly to these kinds of struggles. Two people's "truths" can feel genuinely incompatible because spending is, indeed, a zero-sum proposition. If I get what I want, you might not get what you want. My buying a new bike *is* at cross-purposes with your springing for some new clothes. Plenty of couples smooth over incompatible spending "truths" by going into debt and kicking the financial—and emotional—can down the road. Or they share a worldview in which both tacitly agree to ignore financial reality. But sometimes we're talking about genuinely incompatible *values*. It's a problem when my new ski equipment conflicts not with your spa weekend, but with "your" roof repairs. Mutual respect breaks down when partners feel they can't get each other to appreciate their values.

In conjugal arenas other than money, couples can float unhappily along defending their respective truths, injuring the emotional atmosphere but not their pocketbooks. If a wife says to her husband, "Hey, when you call the pediatrician's office, can you ask if she thinks Susie should be taking vitamins?" and he responds, "I don't believe in vitamins; you call them yourself if you want," the husband is clearly not extending himself to consider his wife's reality. He's giving himself permission to treat her concerns about their child as solely "her problem." Gradually, left unchecked, behavior such as his will deplete their closeness, trust, and mutual respect, but it may take a long time.

Money conflicts also have the potential to become repetitive and corrosive, but because they're about a finite resource, they can't drag on indefinitely. Money flows into bank accounts or doesn't, accrues toward retirement or doesn't, is available to fix a roof or isn't. You can try to solve the problem with "Oh, I'll just do it [work, budget, worry] myself." Or with neglect. But there's usually a limit. Then joint decisions of some sort will have to be made.

That's where Sam and Willa found themselves. Neither liked or respected the other's approach to money. They were infuriated and pained by each other's blind spots. But landscaping would have to be okayed or vetoed, and a summer vacation would have to be planned or not. To act, they had to find a different way to think and talk to each other. Money is a rough-patch issue that naturally invites a seesaw mind-set, but it also desperately screams out for a shift to the golden ring. The hopeful fact is that even when differences in values seem unbridgeable, the right kind of conversation can lead back to mutual respect and feelings of warmth. The *process* of conversation can restore respect and warmth, even if the *content* remains contested.

Let's imagine a more constructive version of Willa and Sam's summer-vacation fight. In this version, Sam doesn't charge Willa with selfishness. Instead he tunes in to his softer emotions: "I feel hurt when you talk as if you want to go away alone with the kids. I feel like you want to get away from me. Maybe you do that because you feel like I'm a downer. Is that true?" Sam allows himself to know and express his fears and doubts—to face his truth—as a first step to facing Willa's. This creates a different atmosphere, one in which Willa can begin to reflect on her own, and Sam's, emotional experience. Perhaps she does feel that he's a downer, or that she needs to advocate for herself, or that she's tried to be empathetic but he's met her efforts with criticism. If her answer conveys self-awareness and an interest in her husband's feelings, they can move from the assumption that one person has the power to determine "the truth" toward one in which two people are curious to discover their own and the other's truth. Fisher identified the essential capacity as "tolerat[ing] the truth of another's experience, acknowledging and taking in the meaning of the other's experience without losing the meaning of one's own, especially when these experiences not only differ but conflict." When couples can do this, it's a major developmental achievement.

SAM AND WILLA played out the tension between the seesaw and the golden-ring models of marriage in the seemingly pampered realm of house remodels, but across social class levels, money issues mobilize similar tensions. We know that money and "I got mine" states of mind (narcissism, entitlement, arrogance, etc.) tend to go hand in hand at the high end of the socioeconomic spectrum, but they can be also linked at the lower end. When I encountered Linda, she conveyed how tired she was of "living like this"—by which she meant, in silent discord with her husband about money. She had three children and was working in her semirural school district as a tutor, driving long, punishing distances between sites. Though her husband had a union job, they scraped the edge of poverty. She grew her own vegetables, kept her own chickens, cooked from scratch, eschewed a clothes dryer, didn't have cable or cell phones, and worked her hardest to keep to a budget. Her husband, she said, frequented pricey convenience stores for snacks, trolled eBay for impractical purchases, and told her "it would all work out," while accepting loans from her parents. If she pushed him to feel her level of desperation, he said she should work harder or get another job. He let off steam by drinking beer. She let off steam by snacking. If she confronted him about his beer (it made him more "sloppy" in his spending), he criticized her weight. Listening to Linda, I found it easy to imagine her husband retreated to selfish pursuits and let her carry the bulk of their shared burden. His behavior was deeply corrosive to their mutual trust and respect, but I found it hard to know how Linda contributed to their dynamic. Clearly her inability to confront him effectively was a huge problem. As stressed as Linda was by their finances, she was even more stressed by their inability to work together.

Money is an issue *within* marriage, but it's also a major variable in who marries, and for how long. Joblessness, employment insecurity, and lack of education contribute to both lower marriage rates and higher divorce rates. Wealth inequality in the United States has skyrocketed in the past forty years. Financial strain—not to mention graveyard shifts, multiple jobs, and lack of benefits—is known to weaken the stability and quality of marriages. It results in less family and spousal time, less flexibility, and more emotional stress, all powerful drains on relationships. Conversely, the people who are most likely to marry and stay married are those who have the most to gain, and the gains are largest for those who can tie their fate to another person with education, health, and opportunities. Today, the most educated Americans marry more and divorce less than the moderately and least educated groups. Their advantages both result from, and reinforce, what used to be called middle-class values: hard work, delayed gratification, and educational pursuit.

Statistics show that the white-picket-fence dream of marriage is increasingly out of reach for the majority of the population. Yet Americans from across different wealth, ethnic, and age categories continue to highly value marriage as an institution. They regard it as "extremely important" and hope to enter into it (about 90 percent of Americans marry at least once). They aspire to invest in their marriages, even if their circumstances make it difficult to do so. Among the poor, where marriage rates are lowest, maintaining flexibility in partner arrangements is one way to avoid the very real chance of being further disadvantaged by a nonearning, dependent spouse, or to improve one's economic position through association with a solvent spouse. That people across classes aspire to sustain marriage, yet are impeded by social and economic realities, clearly deserves more concerted attention and resources than we as a country are willing to give it.

It might seem that even to contemplate the kind of fine-grained emotional communication I advocate in these pages is a luxury that most people can't afford. However, in the dynamics of marriage, people's subjective experience of how economics relates to emotional satisfaction is neither simple nor self-evident. On the one hand, the impact of objective economic hardship is sometimes primarily emotional. For example, divorce risk rises in cases of spousal job loss but not spousal disability. Layoffs and disability both result in financial instability, but when a spouse loses his job due to a layoff, it prompts doubts and anxieties that focus on personality or character, and catalyzes doubts about the "fitness" of one's spouse. These emotional responses then render the marriage more fragile.

On the other hand, even when couples command economic resources, emotional scarcity can obtain. Researchers have hypothesized that marital dissatisfaction in our era arises from the gap between the amount of time and effort that's required to approximate our ideal of an emotionally rewarding marriage, and the amount of time and effort that people actually put in. This trend is not only a problem for the economically disadvantaged; it exists across the socioeconomic spectrum. The phenomenon has cultural causes, as well as emotional and psychological ones. Human beings are complicated, even when they are economically secure. They don't always act in their own best interest, they don't always see the big picture, and they have maladaptive relational patterns that get in their way. Whether rich or poor, developing an intimate, trusting marital bond takes place in the fullness of time, as we work through our fears, vulnerabilities, bad habits, and old scripts. *Taking our time* is essential for emotional deepening of every kind, but for both practical and emotional reasons, paid work can stand in the way of taking that time. Across social classes, people agree that time is their most depleted resource.

The emotional "economy" of marriage is such that people invest time, energy, and resources with the expectation of a return on their investment. We downplay this underlying dynamic due to its unromantic connotations, but morally, the issue is one of fairness and justice. It's a painful rough-patch moment when people start to feel that their investment isn't paying off, or that the trade-offs aren't fair. Social-exchange theorists have applied to marriage the concept of the "comparison level for alternatives." In this framework, relational commitment is calculated by comparing the rewards of the current relationship to the rewards one might receive in another (imagined or real) relationship. The more favorable the comparisons, the more commitment. The more unfavorable the comparisons, the less commitment. Anyone talking about his or her marriage this way in public would be viewed as a superficial, heartless ass. But people *do* have to feel that the investments and returns in their relationship are fundamentally fair. Partners feel closer, and luckier, when each partner pulls his or her weight. There are many ways to uphold fairness, and many forms of valid caretaking. What works for one couple might not work for another, and ultimately what's fair is a personal, subjective evaluation. But if partners feel they are giving more than they are getting, they may, over time, find their feelings of love eroding. They may begin to feel they are staying in the marriage out of duty rather than fulfillment, and even then, they may wonder what responsibility they bear a partner who they feel hasn't been responsible toward them.

Investment also lies at the center of how people weigh marital costs and benefits in considering divorce. When we consent to the marriage contract, we pledge to share our future. In principle, spouses agree to even out each person's individual investments over time. Spouses will have different bargaining positions at different points in marriage, but if they stay together over the long haul, neither one will unfairly profit when they happen to be "up" or unfairly lose when they happen to be "down." But this bargain can collapse in several ways. First, within the marriage, one partner can take advantage of his stronger bargaining position to *exploit* the other. For example, a woman who's at home with children may feel she has little bargaining power because her dependent position makes staying in the marriage she's in, whatever its faults, preferable to leaving. An exploiting husband can then use her relative powerlessness to renege on household duties, stay out late with his friends, and expand his me time. Second, by divorcing, one spouse can *appropriate* the investments the other made in the marriage. One such instance is leaving after your spouse has spent the last three years putting you through school. Another is when a woman with young children files for divorce and appropriates her husband's (future) time with his children through a custody arrangement that favors her and appropriates his (future) labor through alimony and child support.

In the traditional narrative of marriage and divorce, men leave women. They benefit from women's early investment in rearing children, pocket that investment, and move on to greater financial and matrimonial advantage. But this story doesn't hold up. For one thing, gender roles and work patterns have changed. For another, women file for divorce roughly two-thirds of the time. Researchers have surmised that women lose interest in reaping the future benefits of marriage if they feel trust eroded early on, due to perceived unfairness or their husbands' insensitivity to their needs when the children were small. It may also be that as women age, they're less interested in the benefits of being married than men are. They may depend less on men than men depend on women for social life, community networks, and domestic structure.

What are the most common money-related reasons for divorce today? Oft-cited candidates are women's freedom to leave marriage due to greater economic independence, and the stresses of limited family resources. But one of the most robust financial predictors of divorce appears to be husbands' lack of full-time employment. As we saw above, either spouse's job loss can spur divorce. But if husbands' underemployment has the *strongest* association to divorce, it's hard not to infer that conventional gender norms are alive and well, at least where men's breadwinning roles are concerned. This reflects less than brilliantly on our progress toward gender equality, but it does help account for men's acute suffering and women's anxious frustration when husbands don't work for sufficient pay, or at all. Wives can feel critical, even if they know it is unfair or uncompassionate. Husbands can feel inadequate or ashamed. Power shifts, and neither the men nor the women tend to be happy about this. Depressingly, men's unemployment correlates with sexual problems in a marriage, as well as physical violence.

Women's feelings about men's unemployment take an even more negative turn when men renege on remunerative employment, especially when they persist in astonishing levels of finickiness as to what employment suits their talents. It is painful to sit with a woman on whom her partner's titanic disregard is slowly but inexorably dawning. It's not unusual for her to realize that her marriage closely traces her history of shouldering unfair burdens growing up. Yet facing the specter of living alone with her children, supporting the family, and relinquishing a husband (as he garners child support and takes up with an adoring young thing) fills her with dread.

On the flip side, some women are not above an infuriating sense of entitlement about their husband's earnings. Sometimes it grows out of a true naïveté about money, though maintaining oneself as a naïf well into adulthood is its own kind of cop-out. One of the more painful situations is when a husband suffers a job loss and his wife seems alternately oblivious and blaming about the need to cut back on spending. For every husband who unilaterally decides to quit his job and become an indie-film director, there's a wife who says to her husband, "You figure out how to pay for the kids' college. It's your problem, not mine." But women get more cultural cover for this kind of irresponsibility, whereas men confront more directly the shame of falling down on their "masculine" obligations.

Such displays of selfishness exist on a continuum with more extreme marital money scenarios, where compulsive spending by one family member imperils the group, or ostensibly self-sufficient middle-aged adults feed off the "green umbilical cord" of parental support. Unsavory class dynamics reverberate through people's psycho-fiscal arrangements as well. "We all know," as one friend put it, "that some people marry résumés, houses, and teak chairs." People keep tabs on whether they are marrying "up" or marrying "down" and harbor strong identifications with their family of origin as sources of pride or shame. People have been known to subtly torment each other with family fortunes that feather one partner's nest but not the other's or end up failing to materialize at all. A husband from a lower-middle-class family worked hard while his wife drew on her sizable family wealth and complained that he was "boring" because he was "never around." A wife worked two jobs and paid the price physically, while her husband, addicted to pot, waited to receive a windfall he'd spent his whole life expecting. (Turned out, he didn't get it.) Lives are built on assumptions that are never spelled out in black and white, money being for many people an unspeakable topic.

In the less dramatic middle, where most people live, money can be a chronic source of rough-patch discord, and a lot of it has to do with the kids. Kids are *expensive*. Life is expensive. The cell phone bill, the car payments, the property taxes, they're one thing. But then, what about the travel soccer team at $2,000 per season, or the price tag for a year of music lessons, or the summer science program? This stuff isn't taken care of by skipping Starbucks or never eating out. The sociologist Annette Lareau coined the term *concerted cultivation* to describe the middle- and upper-middle-class approach to childrearing. Through enrolling their children in a roster of athletic and cultural activities outside the home, parents commit "to childrearing strategies that favor the individual development of each child, sometimes at the expense of family time and group needs." This approach makes for a hectic family life, contributing to the well-known "time fam-ine" that sociologists have long decried. But it also makes for a bind about money and values. If parents decide to opt out of concerted cultivation, they worry about disadvantaging their children and dis-connecting from the larger childrearing culture. If they opt in, they risk feeling stressed and strapped. We know from research that money and time stress can directly feed into subjective feelings of marital dissatisfaction. So, despite the proud moments at the piano recital and the Little League championships, all this concerted cultivation can come at an emotional cost.

Money stresses parents because it funds the cherished goal of giving children the best possible start in life. Their conflicts about money inflame their own childhood wounds and incite anxiety about community belonging. Parental disagreements about money can instigate remarkably corrosive rifts. A breadwinner husband controllingly reviews all purchases, while his wife finds his behavior tyrannical and feels it creates a negative emotional environment. An extravagant parent inculcates materialistic values in the children, and the frugal parent, despairing of getting any traction, becomes alienated from the spouse and worried about her children's character formation. A middle-class couple, distressed by the gap between what they want to give their children and their financial constraints, find themselves fighting with each other. They worry it's leading them toward the even more expensive outcome of divorce. A father wants his children to have what he had growing up and resents his wife's foot-dragging about getting a job, while she thinks he minimizes the value of her unpaid labor at home. Children can stress a marriage by revealing to parents their deep differences over money, differences they may not have even known they had.

In a perfect world, our social arrangements would support a work-family balance that caused less money and time stress for couples with children. Laura Carstensen, one of the leading lights of longevity research, extols the benefits of spreading out work and other obligations more evenly between "Act II" and "Act III" of our lives. She suggests "creating an employment 'arc' in which employees can gradually ease into the workforce as young adults, working fewer hours during the years that they're caring for young children, completing their educations, and trying to find the right careers." "A slower, longer work phase," she writes, "would mitigate time pressures on middle-aged adults and allow people of all ages more options for how to spend their time." Putting Carstensen's vision into practice, even partially, would have a powerful impact on the "normal" levels of life (and money) stress faced by midlife couples and parents. But social norms change slowly. In part, it's because people are steeped in the customs of their social group, and their identities rest on their economic profile and patterns of consumption in ways they are loath to admit. Society is unlikely to reengineer itself overnight, and if we wait for the heavy cogs of workplace culture to shift, we'll be waiting a long time.

A more near-at-hand countercultural approach can be found in the blog posts of Mr. Money Mustache, who advocates a radical frugality based on a personal amalgam of stoicism, Buddhism, and "badassity." Like many of his enthusiastic followers, I spent a week one summer binge-reading every post of his since 2011 and became hooked on his singular brand of humor, needling, and inspiration. He defines his mission as "to try to get the people of the world's rich countries excited about separating the idea of *lifetime happiness,* from the idea of *buying expensive shit with which to pamper yourself.* . . . It's a human psychology problem as much as it is a financial or technical or political one."

His approach turns what social scientists call time discounting on its head. For most people, "the power of now" means that they'll choose to enjoy something in the present rather than defer gratification. Mr. Money Mustache (aka Peter Adeney), by contrast, believes that one of the most useful concepts to apply to personal finance is a form of big-picture thinking he dubs "the idea of a past, present, and future self." He writes:

> Every financial transaction you make today is not so much a deal with a mortgage company, car dealer or department store. It's a deal with your future self. After all, when the 20-year-old version of you borrowed $32,000 to buy that fully loaded Honda Accord, who ended up having to pay it back? The past self got the new car with no responsibility, and her successor in the present holds the result: a debt hangover and a car that's now worth only a tiny fraction of the new price. Past You gave Present You the shaft.

Adeney's point about integrating your past, present, and future self into your current financial perspective lines up with the golden-ring mind-set we've discussed, where the needs of the individuals and the couple are integrated into a big-picture approach. But taking account of your past, present, and future self, and becoming a financial "badass" as Adeney suggests, pretty much guarantees you'll feel unintegrated into the mainstream consumer culture. He doesn't believe in commuting, new cars, expensive extracurricular activities, debt, eating out, and any number of other fixtures of bourgeois American life. What he despises most is affluent Americans complaining about their money woes, and he's happy to help cure us by pouring a big bucket of cold water over our heads:

> In almost every tale of financial woe, the real villain is the victim's Past Self. . . . What the newspaper describes as a medical bankruptcy could in fact be a Caribbean vacation bankruptcy "victim" who happened to have the bad luck of getting sick when almost out of money. A foreclosure caused by the recession could very well be more attributable to commuting 25 miles to that job for the preceding 10 years in a GMC Tahoe. In fact, if you've ever blown a dollar on frivolous spending, and years later find yourself a dollar short due to the arrival of hard times, it's not the hard times that broke you. It was that dollar blown long ago.

SAM AND WILLA'S "summer vacation" fight happened on a Tuesday evening. The subsequent Friday they asked for an after-hours session. Willa wept throughout our meeting. Her sobs turned gasping as she imagined they were heading toward a divorce. Sam was quiet, pained by a mix of sadness and guilt that made him choked and unable to speak.

"He sees me as such a user," Willa said. "How can I be married to someone who sees me that way? How can I be married to someone who never sees the good, who always sees the bad?"

"I don't always see the bad. I see the good," Sam said miserably. "I'm trying."

Willa sobbed harder. "You see all the efforts I try to make for the family as *selfish*. Nothing I do makes you happy, but I'm trying to make you happy *all the time*." Her shoulders shook. Her crying gradually slowed. A minute passed in spent silence. "I'm tired of marriage. I don't want to try."

Sam made a brief half attempt to look skeptical, but concern overtook him. "I know how hard you've been trying. I really do." He looked deflated, and as if he might cry too. "It's just—I'm drowning over here."

We sat in silence. For a while, I felt any attempt to solve the problem would be paltry and absurd. Their fury had subsided and left them guilty and sad. Horrible as they felt, I saw a bit of hope in their change in tone. It opened the door to reflecting on their fight, and what it might be able to teach them about their old wounds.

Over the next few weeks, feeling afraid they might be reaching a point of no return, they began to have more patience with looking deeper. Until now, Sam's portrayal of his family of origin had been almost formulaic, seemingly fed to him long ago by his moralistic father and never fully revisited until now. Sam's father was a "hard worker" who "never missed a day in his life" at the Midwestern tool-and-die company where he'd spent his career. Sam's mother had been a "spendthrift" who took off with the church choral director (of all things) when Sam was eleven. In his description, his mother came off as shallow, his father stoic, but behind the labels, I sensed his father was dark, even depressed. When Sam's mother left, a ray of light vanished. Sam saw it as his duty to join forces with his father in the war of responsible men against capricious women. Yet he longed for his mother even as he and his father rained down contempt on her recklessness.

In the desolation brought on by Sam and Willa's most recent battle, Sam felt a bit broken and became more open to looking at himself. I talked with him about how pressured he had felt to take sides between his parents. In their dramatically polarized world, there was only one right way. He sensed his father needed a comrade in his bitterness toward his wife, and in any event, Sam's mother had left.

Sam's father's feelings blinded him to his son's need for his mother. For Sam, loving his father meant downplaying his need for his mother. Needing his mother hurt his father. It was one or the other.

The crisis with Willa drove Sam to revisit, for the first time, the internal reflex to reject and judge the softer, more indulgent qualities that his mother represented. His images of his mother as affectionate, unreliable, and childish melded in his image of Willa, rendering her, he realized, both deeply attractive and mildly inferior. The important movement, from my perspective, was that Sam began to notice and turn over in his mind the ways that the voices from his past so harshly stepped in and defined his current perceptions. In certain moments, he felt he couldn't even separate his adult self from his father's messages. He realized that softening his view of Willa brought him face-to-face with a painful sense of disloyalty to his father. Sam's condescending judgment toward Willa was a real-time reiteration of his agonizing childhood position. "I guess my dad had his own fears of loneliness," Sam said one day. "It's as if he couldn't see me as separate from him."

For Sam to admit that he loaded all this onto Willa was hard, but he felt relieved at the freedom to finally begin to take his own adult perspective. Hurt as Willa was, she also felt relieved that he was letting her out of the box he had put her in. Willa started to think about why Sam's projections had felt so normal to her, even deserved. It took her back to her own earlier life. Her parents had parted when she was six, and as the youngest of three girls, she enjoyed the reputation as the "cute one." Her parents each relied on her for comic relief and precocious competence in detecting their needs. She was, truly, their "ray of light," all blond bounciness and easy smiles. She knew she got more than she deserved, partly because she caused fewer problems for her parents than her sulkier older sisters. As Willa grew up, she became adept at giving each of her parents what they wanted and thereby was relatively privileged in the family. That she was more adorable than her sisters was at once a claim to specialness and a source of guilt. She got more things, and thanks to her flair for clothes, she always looked stylish. Her corner of the shared bedroom was her evolving masterwork. Her sunny disposition and practical smarts impressed the rest of the beleaguered crew. But her needs for nurture, comfort, and parental protection were met at unpredictable intervals, and she felt vaguely sullied by the power of her charm.

Throughout her twenties, she expressed her emotional needs indirectly through caretaking an alcoholic boyfriend. She was proud when she extricated herself from her seven-year relationship with the man, who in every particular resembled her father in his youth, down to the sandy hair and preference for rum. When she met Sam, he had seemed like a mature choice, a man who could support a family and not make excuses. She admired his work ethic and fell naturally into making sure he felt happy and relaxed during his time off. With him she had a clear understanding about roles, without a lot of mixed messages and murky dependency. What a relief, she thought, to start her adult life in earnest.

Neither of them expected the arrival of children to deplete them so thoroughly. Twins were hard, for sure. Fatherhood kicked Sam's provider anxiety into overdrive. Willa now needed more help herself, but Sam was completely spent and unavailable. The weekends offered neither of them a chance to recoup. Exhausted, they snapped at each other and made fewer gestures of empathy, and each retreated to a posture of self-preservation. For Sam, this meant putting his head down and joylessly slogging through his workweek. Offering warmth to Willa felt like one too many demands. He got mad that she harped on what he didn't do, rather than appreciated what he did. Willa came to feel that Sam used his financial responsibility as an all-purpose excuse for not connecting with the family or expressing affection toward her. If he wasn't going to be involved, she'd concentrate on making life as pleasant as she could for herself and the twins. In her world, this meant spending—an anesthetic pastime that balanced the scales in her mind, compensated for her deprivation, and bought off her unhappiness.

Both felt mounting anger and frustration at not being understood, which led to alternating bouts of protest and retreat. The protest would come out in their flaring fights, which escalated as each tried to get heard. The retreat would take the form of a self-justifying decision to turn away. Neither Sam nor Willa had ever witnessed a couple constructively managing the tension between self-seeking and concern for the other. None of their parents had been able to think about what Sam or Willa needed apart from what the parents needed of them. As a result, neither Sam nor Willa believed that in their hour of need the other would make the leap of imagination to empathize, comfort, or help them. Under Sam and Willa's emotional conditions of scarcity—and parenthood only intensified that scarcity—each decided that the best they could hope for was to care for themselves.

Money became a substitute currency for care. Willa felt entitled to spend because she had to find some comfort in her depriving marriage. Her spending made Sam feel "sucked dry" and used, which made him more depleted and less giving. His detachment intensified her need, which found its way into the pursuit of ever more creature comforts. If he questioned her, she blamed him for her deprivation. That made him conclude she was selfishly pursuing what she wanted at his expense, with no regard for his feelings.

A bit of perversity lurks in the financial corners of some marriages. As in "creative accounting," people allow themselves leeway in holding incompatible ideas. A divorce attorney tells me about marriages that never seemed to be about much more than money, though not until the divorce does that become completely apparent. It might seem that the couple married for love, but love was indistinguishable at first from the feast of indulgence that attended courtship. Beauty in exchange for wealth, youth in exchange for paternalistic support (one woman called her husband "Papa"), marrying a catch and supporting her expensive tastes—a centerpiece of such arrangements is how often assumptions go utterly unspoken, and how little consciousness, let alone conversation, there is about any of it. Then there's the primitive spectacle of marital arrangements that are about little more than monetizing gender. The men are valued in their "masculine" capacity to earn big bucks, and the women "get paid" to perform femininity— with all the clothes and cosmetic surgeries that it requires.

As the quintessential symbol—and asset—of domesticity, houses are a key arena where fiscal irrationality plays out in marriage. There's the ill-judged purchase of a house that is too expensive for the couple, but which fulfills what one partner "owes" to the other or what the couple "owe" to themselves or to their future children, or what kind of house they "really need." Only when the finances finally unravel do recriminations start flying about people being "misled" or "duped." But at no point did anyone actually *seek the truth*. For a couple intent on financial self-deception, the market's cycles will usually provide an opportunity for borrowing way too much money and entering the cultural swim of overspending, overreaching, and keeping up with the Joneses. One couple took advantage of the real estate market's upward climb by moving from house to house, buying and selling for the purported reason of extracting equity needed to support his business. When the wife brought the husband to therapy to talk about how upsetting these moves were, and how she couldn't take it anymore, it took me weeks of painstaking investigation to arrive at the reality that these upheavals came about primarily because of their lifestyle, on which she fully insisted. The support of that lifestyle *depended* on outlays derived from this constant selling of houses. The disconnect in their minds between their spending and their upheavals was stunning.

Sam and Willa were at least *trying* to find some clarity, and to behave in a more loving and collaborative way. Although they spent a lot of their time unable to understand where the other was coming from, under the right conditions they would have moments of meeting. When they had an experience of empathy for each other, they strengthened the hope that it was possible. As Sam began to perceive the rigid wall of martyred anger he'd erected in identification with his father, he could gradually allow himself to genuinely enjoy the warmth and beauty that Willa endeavored to bring into their family life. In line with the idea of maturity I discussed in chapter 3, Sam began responding to his *own* softer emotions, and in so doing he found more freedom to respond to hers. As he appreciated and dignified her love of beauty in this way, Willa was increasingly freed from her own shame around "taking advantage" of him. She could claim her aesthetics and warmth as strengths in her adult personality and more actively assert their value in creating a feeling of home for both of them.

Several months into therapy, they had an interaction that heartened me. The week before, Willa had made a big effort with her appearance for a school fund-raising dinner. She had bought a new dress and highlighted her hair. She came to the session complaining that Sam had not even noticed her, much less expressed pleasure or pride about her appearance. This struck me as a tailor-made incident to produce a breach in empathy. As a child, prettying herself was one of the few ways Willa had to break through the usual inattention. Parental oohing and aahing tended to be a pretty low-demand (on them), high-reward (for her) form of attention. As poignant as it was that she longed to please Sam, her expecting that spending money on her appearance would mean the same thing to him as it meant to her was a bit childish. She seemed unaware that Sam's first response to her expenditures was more likely to be anxiety that they weren't on the same page about money, and fretfulness over their next Visa bill. His mind was likely to travel to his mother's merrily greeting mail-order purchases piled at the doorstep without a thought to the burden it placed on the family finances.

Luckily, they each managed to step back from the brink and notice what got going between them. The night of the dinner, Sam's thoughts included all the same criticisms he might have leveled in the past, but having progressed, he managed to suppress them. In our session, he said his first impulse *had* been to comment on the expense and their lack of agreement on money matters. But he waited to express these thoughts until he could blend them with some more generous ones. He ultimately said he understood that she was trying to please him, and that he should have complimented her at the time, but that he also wanted them to have a bigger conversation later. She said she understood why he felt the way he did, and why his mixed feelings had made it hard for him to compliment her. In our session, they agreed they should come up with clearer agreements about discretionary spending. They also agreed she should start looking for a job.

IT WOULD HAVE been easier if Willa and Sam had been more compatible in their philosophies about money in the first place. As couples go, they were not unusual in having spent virtually no time up front contemplating how they differed, or even defining what their personal views were. Hard-nosed money discussions are not a natural fit with new love. In the glow of idealization, people may even welcome a novel approach to spending ("He frees me up," "She makes me more responsible") as a corrective to their own. Courtship is an expansive (and expensive) time, and even the most steadfast skinflint will likely relax his standards out of sheer excitement or to signal appropriate ardor. When the inevitable moment of reckoning comes—a wedding to be planned or a budget to be drawn up or an apartment to be chosen—the trade-offs and limits can chafe against romantic enthusiasm and the illusion of seamless compatibility.

I remember sitting in a Chicago restaurant with friends, overhearing a conversation at the next table. A young woman announced to her dinner partner that she had decided to quit her job to plan their wedding. An excruciating silence followed. As I casually buttered my bread, I was riveted out of the corner of my eye by the pivotal relational moment unfolding. It felt terribly saturated with all the couple's future misunderstandings and unspoken disappointments. This was the moment that something difficult had to be said, and I was mutely rooting for the man to say it: *How come you didn't talk about it with me? Shouldn't this be a joint decision? I don't know if that's the wisest move. We have to figure this out together.* Instead he remained quiet, and the mood remained tense. I thought I saw him reposition himself in light of this new information, as if he were rearranging his internal emotional furniture. Something in the hardness that entered his expression was heartbreaking. He seemed to be making the fateful decision not to fight and to withdraw—here, at the very beginning of their life together. And she, from the sound of her brief statement, was making two fateful mistakes by which money issues come to doom a marriage. First, she was avoiding thinking about limits; second, she posed the issue as a fait accompli, thus choosing not to think *together* about the choices in front of them.

In part, money is stressful because it is frustrating to confront limits and to live within them. It requires willpower, taking the long view, and doing without; it means making choices between different goals. In a couple, money decisions need to take into account the other person's thoughts, wishes, and tendencies, which are often in conflict with one's own. We are always at risk of turning what should rightfully be considered internal conflicts about reality's limits into fights with our partners. Willa had difficulty budgeting and denying herself things, yet when Sam told her his opinion that they were over-spending, she focused on calling him a "downer." Exaggerating my partner's position allows me to fight with *him*, rather than ask *myself* the hard questions about what *I* believe we can afford. I delegate certain attributes to my partner—for example, recasting his reasonable concern as his "negative" approach to money—while claiming other attributes for myself—I spend as a way to "stand up for myself" in the face of my partner's "control," or to express my "sense of adventure" in the face of my partner's "inertia."

When we project onto our partner, we're not developing an inte-grated perspective within ourselves. People are going to have different opinions about money, but each person ideally comes to the table willing to struggle internally with the difficult trade-offs. Only when I struggle within myself to reconcile my desires with the limits on my resources do I begin to take an honest perspective. How human, if delusional, to try to locate the pain of reality in the failings of a spouse. We adopt this strategy because thinking about reality is hard. In reality, we rarely get to have our cake and eat it too. In reality, awful things sometimes happen. Apart from the hideous crises and losses, the usual problems of life—about children, money, jobs, houses—are difficult and frustrating to talk about and often hard to solve. It takes effort to remain self-aware and self-controlled enough to continue to think together about the problems. It takes effort to resist the temptation to cast our partner as our obstacle, and instead to face that life *itself* presents obstacles, and that remaining in conversation with our partner is sometimes our best hope of meeting them.

Willa and Sam demonstrated, no more dramatically than many other couples, the ways money can become an antigrowth black hole in the rough patch. Anxious to give their children the best possible start, concerned with career success and security, wanting to fit in with their community, couples confront real economic challenges and a raft of anxieties. The difference between deadlock and collaboration has everything to do with how people manage these anxieties, and whether they face them constructively.

My work with Sam and Willa lasted several months. Bit by bit, we managed to turn the volume down on the blame and criticism and create a safer atmosphere for exploration. That safer atmosphere helped them each admit their own conflicted feelings and resist the tendency to attribute the conflict to the other person. Willa realized and acknowledged that her motive for painting Sam as an incurable stick-in-the-mud was to rationalize her abdicating responsibility for figuring out what they could and couldn't afford. She empathized with his misery at his job, and Sam became less defensive as a result. He realized that his tendency to play the angry victim repeated his own family's dynamics and put Willa into a role she couldn't escape. I was impressed by their efforts to understand the parts they played in the cycle. Their self-awareness ultimately allowed them to collaborate in figuring out a way to mesh their different financial styles. When they left, I was glad they weren't headed toward one more post-remodel divorce, the newly refurbished house summarily sold and the children, a bit dazed, continuing their childhoods in a suburban apartment complex with sparse furniture, frozen food, and newly single parents. Sam and Willa were beginning to see and appreciate each other for who they were, and to be seen and appreciated for what they most valued in themselves.

Lovesickness and Longing:
Putting Them to Use

When Christina sat down in my office for the first time in sixteen years, she looked very much the same as before: petite, expressive, tending toward nervous thinness. I had seen her in psychotherapy when she was a graduate student who, by her own account, was working too little, drinking too much, and sleeping with too many men. Since that time, she told me on the phone, her life had gone well. She loved her job at a local research lab. She'd been happily married for more than a decade and had two "apparently well-adjusted" kids. After her friendly preamble, she said, "I'm having some trouble," with tears thickening her voice. "But I'd rather explain it in person."

When she came in, I felt happy to see her. She sat and gathered her breath, looking as if she was trying to find a way to begin her story that was truthful and complete. She was a scientist, and despite her youthful excesses, she valued precision. "I guess the way I want to start is to describe what happened. Because I don't really know what happened." She told me that two months before, when her husband and daughter were visiting his parents across the country, her five-year-old son, Ethan, had woken up one day with a high fever and had seemed incoherent. She got worried, and when she called the doctor's office, they told her to bring him in right away.

"I was driving down the hill from our house, totally distracted, and I drove over a garbage-can top that had blown into the street.

I stopped, even though I was freaked out and tempted to just keep driving. My neighbor Michael came out of his garage. He picked up the top and gave me a big, warm smile. I felt shocked at how beautiful his smile suddenly seemed to me. I remember the words *bright spot* went through my mind. It felt like some weird kind of otherworldly moment, looking into his eyes, in that light."

After two days of blood draws, urine samples, and consultations among herself, her husband, Ben, and her son's doctors, Ethan's health picture was clearer and his recovery assured. But she kept returning to the "otherworldly" moment, like a secret source of security. During the hushed, long days when her son slept, she wandered around the house, unable to focus, replaying the memory of Michael and his smile.

"At first it felt like a harmless vacation in my mind. I'd think about Michael, and it felt comforting and exciting at the same time. Taking care of Ethan in the house all day, I almost felt like I was recuperating too. But then, when Ethan got better and went back to school, I kept feeling this way. A few weeks ago, I ran into Michael at the supermarket, and I started *shaking*. The day was pretty much shot. I felt like I was going crazy." Christina wept. Struck by her tears, I asked if she was aware of feeling depressed, something she'd struggled with earlier in life.

"I cry a lot, but I don't feel depressed," she said. "I feel anxious when I see Michael, but I don't walk around anxious all day. My problem is I *feel too much*. Sometimes I feel like my body is being turned inside out by all this intensity, like I want to crawl out of my skin. And then I start feeling that I'll die unless I can *do* something. I'm obviously here because I needed to tell someone."

We agreed to meet again later that week.

In the days after our meeting, I let her feelings, her *rawness*, work on me and tried to notice what arose in my mind without my trying to impose order. Why now? I wondered. Why so intensely? I kept returning to that vivid moment when Michael smiled at her. My mind alighted on the way that geese instinctively bond after birth with the first moving object they see. It reminded me of Christina, in her fragile state, latching onto the beauty and goodness of the first human face she saw. It was as if she had fleetingly returned to a time when her protective barriers had not yet formed.

When we met again, Christina's mood had lifted a bit. She seemed more like a person in the grip of a crush. "Maybe the problem isn't so much your feeling of attraction," I offered, reacting to her more lighthearted mood. "Maybe it's the sense of danger you attach to it. Perhaps you can let yourself be playful and enjoy a bit of harmless banter when you see him."

She let me know this was exactly the wrong thing to say. "I feel like I'm falling off a cliff, emotionally and physically. It doesn't feel like play." Suddenly looking worn-out, she informed me about the current shape of her days. She would set her sights on a productive workday each morning and find herself preoccupied instead, and on the brink of tears. If she ran into Michael when picking up the kids at school, she spent hours trying to right herself. Routine school functions triggered high anxiety as she anticipated making small talk with Michael and his wife, Shauna, and dealing with the private emotional fallout afterward.

I asked how she had managed the past few weeks before coming to see me. She reported thoroughly on all the efforts she'd made to snap out of what she knew to be a distorted state of mind. First, she dipped into the popular writings that try to explain complicated emotions via hormones and brain activity. She learned that "nature has bred philandering into our genes," and that perhaps her sexual intensity was due to "high testosterone levels." Evidently, her brain's dopaminergic reward system was being activated, since the intense cravings of love and cocaine both worked through that system. From sociobiology, she learned that she was evolutionarily programmed to fall in love again every four years, and her interest in another man might spring from the ancient evolutionary imperative to garner resources by confusing men about their paternity.

Maybe these general facts were true, she thought, but what could they possibly explain? Obviously, all emotional states have biological underpinnings, yet these underpinnings could tell her nothing about the psychological meaning her emotions had to *her*. The writers' glaring lack of interest in human subtleties and complications left her dispirited. Yet one day she exclaimed, "I almost wish I *were* convinced by these books. At least then I'd have an explanation." She found their reductionism shallow, but also strangely relieving, as if it held promise of some world where the personal meanings in her life could be dismissed as insignificant specks, dwarfed by implacable and timeless evolutionary forces. Christina so wished to be rid of the sense of meaningfulness that oversaturated her interactions with Michael—the very meaning of which made no sense.

She'd also turned to therapeutic books on love addiction, hoping she might recognize herself in their pages. Christina felt powerless over her longings, and the addiction paradigm could perhaps explain why. She had struggled earlier in her life with the seductive lure of drinking, and she could well imagine that her thoughts of Michael offered a similarly self-destructive form of escape. But again, she was disappointed. "Love addicts" obsessively focused on partners who couldn't love them back. Christina had no such pattern. She wasn't repetitively attracted to withholding, "love avoidant" men, and she didn't habitually look to love as a drug that temporarily allowed her to avoid her problems or blur healthy boundaries or shun adult responsibility or feelings of emptiness. She could not reasonably slot herself into any love-addict type or pattern.

In the midst of her recitation, she blurted to me, "I have this image of Michael confiding his marital troubles to me, and I can't get it out of my mind." I saw firsthand the unnerving intrusiveness of her thoughts, the way they broke through her normal consciousness, and the effort it took to counter them. She continued miserably, "I see us on a park bench, and we're both telling each other what we're going through. We're understanding each other, and feeling so close." Despite her earnest attempts to insist on its senselessness, her episode starkly revealed the tortured logic of the love triangle. I had the thought that lovesick yearning almost invariably involves both love *and* exclusion. These exquisite doomed loves noisily leave other people out.

Demoralized in her search for intellectual understanding, Christina tried to exert more self-discipline. She plunged into the widening pool of willpower books, which helped her fend off "ego depletion" ("people's diminished capacity to regulate their thoughts, feelings, and actions") by getting enough sleep and eating at regular intervals. Exercise also helped. But she found that even the willpower experts didn't claim that you could actually change your *emotions* through willpower. As one book explained, "Emotion regulation does not rely on willpower. People cannot simply will themselves to be in love, or to feel intense joy, or to stop feeling guilty. Emotional control typically relies on various subtle tricks, such as changing how one thinks about the problem at hand or distracting oneself." Christina was certainly not above deploying some "tricks" and distracting herself. But changing her way of thinking amounted to more than a trick and was proving extraordinarily hard to put into practice. She turned to mindfulness meditation as a deeper method of emotional control, and though she could barely follow one breath without getting lost in a wayward thought, she felt somewhat calmed by the effort to center herself.

With characteristic practicality, she had tried constructive self-talk to avoid exposure and flare-ups. She wrote Post-its to herself and read them each day: "Minimize contact. Be aware of responses and check them. Practice discipline." "I don't judge myself, I earnestly try to help myself and don't criticize myself for my confusion." "This is always, ultimately, about me managing my own feelings. That is my highest and only priority."

Christina tried to approach her problem systematically, but the methods she turned to had ended up feeling like piles of dry leaves, empty of any meaning or relevance. We agreed we would meet twice a week for a time. As she spoke, I listened, questions coming and going in my mind. Was she revisiting early emotional wounds, trying to repair miscarried love from her childhood? Was she a forty-four-year-old woman being preyed on by a welter of confusing endocrine events? Was she, as she entered middle age, trying to recapture a younger version of herself, for whom new love was still in her future? Christina told me that when she was driving alone in her car, she had taken to listening to music from her early teens. She found herself lost in nostalgic reverie, collecting up bits of her past that she hadn't remembered in years—deep talks with her father, her first high school heartbreak.

"I don't know why I'm so *absorbed*," she said one day. "Sometimes I walk around with a brick of grief inside. It's as if all my available internal room has been filled with this brick. My children talk to me, and I feel like I'm listening from the end of a long tube, echoing, far away, hard to hear. This is their childhood, and I don't feel present. And I feel terrible about Ben. Obviously, he knows something is wrong. What can I say? That I've fallen in love with another man? That's an awful thing to say. And it's not even really true. Sometimes I feel my heart will break if I have to 'give up' Michael. But then I think, I'm not giving up a real person, or a real relationship." I felt acutely Christina's effort to contain her feelings, and the strain of trying to manage them in her relationship with Ben. It felt to me like one of the true limit situations of marriage, where, in the face of unexpected and unexplained emotion, the interests of the individual and the marriage, though still fundamentally aligned, feel as if they are blowing apart. I also imagined, with a sense of aching worry, the tormented uncertainty that Ben must be going through.

What would it mean for Christina to "give up" Michael? I wondered. *What* was it that she would be giving up? A feeling? A fantasy? An idea? I began reading to try to discover something more about the state Christina was in. At first I was astonished to find how little had been written on lovesickness. As a phenomenon in Western culture, it is everywhere. Novels and films fairly burst with brilliant portrayals of love triangles, adultery, and ambivalent longing, but it hardly shows its face in scholarly or clinical works. In literature, from Greek mythology to *A Midsummer Night's Dream*, the *irrational* element of love is portrayed as an experience as much to be feared as craved. Being touched by Aphrodite, or being swiped with Puck's magical potion, meant you were going to fall in love with the next person you saw—to your detriment. The irrational can neither be summoned nor banished; it simply appears, and we must bear it, handle it, and guide it. It opens us to creative possibilities, but also to destruction. In the 1960s, the existential psychologist Rollo May wrote, in *Love and Will*, of the power of the "daemonic" and Denis de Rougemont's 1940 classic, *Love in the Western World*, endures as a thoughtful treatise on the dangers and allures of romantic passion. But in the current psychotherapeutic era, it seems, states of longing and lovesickness have been largely redefined in terms of addiction.

As I was bemoaning this gap, I realized that a precious source was hiding in plain view. The field of psychoanalysis was founded on the discovery of *transference*. Freud observed the situation, which "occurs so often and is so important," of a woman patient who "shows by unmistakable indications, or openly declares, that she has fallen in love, as any mortal woman might, with the doctor who is analysing her." At first glance, such behavior seemed unfitting and potentially destructive—an unfortunate impediment to the work at hand. But Freud came to understand transference as the vehicle of the cure itself. If the love that arises in the therapeutic relationship "has the character of a 'genuine' love," he wrote, and if it seems "lacking in normality" in its intensity, blindness, and unconcern for consequences, it's because "these departures from the norm constitute precisely what is essential about being in love." The very fact that people brought the painful irrationality of their love lives—their love *sickness*—into therapy created the opportunity for them to rework their troubling emotional scripts from the past.

Falling in love is a common feature of transference, and transference is a key aspect of falling in love. The powerful sense of recognition that underlies both transference and falling in love is the kindling spark that lies at the start of virtually every meaningful emotional relationship. It hooks us in and sets the stage for something new and real to happen. Recall what we learned in chapter 4: we are healed by love relationships because they reopen the channels between our early emotional experience and our conscious story of self. Love is what catalyzes a subjective sense of emotional receptivity and loosens the grip of the psychic compromises we've made to forge our personalities. A truth of emotional life is that we only learn how to do things differently in relationships by actually *doing* them differently in relationships. Love relationships enable the imaginative reorganization of self and story by generating a fluid interplay between past and present, between conscious and unconscious experience, and between embodied emotional memory and the articulated story of self. Through this process, we re-create ourselves, gaining a sense of psychological wholeness and the feeling that our life is meaningful.

How does all of this help us understand lovesickness? As we discussed in chapter 5, people continue to fall in love in adult life with people and things, and these experiences must find a place. Marriage is no protection against the "kindling spark," nor should it be. We certainly don't want our "love affair with the world" to be dominated by the currents that make actual love affairs exciting, but we don't want these currents to be entirely absent, either. Our openness to people and things *out there* provide moments of poetic joy at being alive, and they connect us to ourselves in new and surprising ways. Sudden attraction, yearning, a mutual spark—these are all true on the level of human feeling, on the level of the soul. Any subjective experience of love is real in the sense that it offers, for whatever enigmatic set of reasons, a profound feeling of fit between one's desire and the world. For people in committed relationships, the question isn't "How could this happen?"—of course it *can* happen. The question is "How do I understand *what's* happening?"

Our answer depends on whether our story is basically working. When happily married people come across a pull with someone other than their spouse, they tend to simply notice and appreciate, rather than intensify or pursue. They may permit a drip-drip-drip infusion of loveliness into their day, but they refrain from turning on the spigot. They don't start weaving the moment into a full-blown alternative story because they don't feel the need to do so. What they perceive as their authentic emotions fit with a generally coherent, satisfying story of themselves and their marriage.

But as we've seen, not everyone's story works in the rough patch. People's sense that their emotions and their story don't fit together might be its defining feature, its central problem of meaning. Some portion of these people will use a "falling in love" experience to begin constructing an alternative story line. They'll allow the deeply evocative meaning of another person to crack open the personal and professional personae they've built until now. They may begin to feel as if things are actually starting to make sense, to fall into place. Perhaps they feel unshackled, for the first time, from the shame- or guilt-based emotional contracts that have, until now, constrained their choices. For them, weaving a new story feels like growth and personal evolution. Ideally, for the children if for no other reason, this moment will activate searching inner questions: What's not working? Patterns in the marriage? Unfinished business within the self? And how do these fit together? In a mature approach, one engages in the difficult balancing act of accepting chaos while not being broken by it, finding a way through bewilderment to ethical action.

And then there are cases like Christina's. Christina was in distress and sought me out precisely because she had fallen in love—at a time and place in her life when it made no sense to do so. It was not just that she felt it was ill-advised; she felt it was crazy—unbidden, irrational, and terribly disruptive. She hadn't chosen the feelings, they'd chosen her. She knew that her feelings for Michael were "transferential." As she said, she wouldn't be "giving up a real person, or a real relationship." She was clear in her mind that her fantasies about Michael did not alter her basic belief in the value and satisfactions of her life with Ben. But knowing all that didn't seem to help; it made her feel worse.

Musing about the particular character of Christina's potent and self-destructive longing, I came across an article by the French Canadian psychoanalyst Allannah Furlong that used the films *In the Mood for Love* (2000) and *2046* (2004) by Hong Kong director Wong Kar-wai as the medium for examining the "compulsive plight of some lovesick individuals." By way of introduction, she wrote:

> The incapacitation connected with dammed-up passion has been brought forcibly home to me by several patients—at one time five simultaneously. . . . For all of these patients, falling in love was a

trauma, exposing them to tides of unmasterable and repudiated excitement. . . . In each of these cases, the outbreak of passion occurred against a backdrop of chronic depression, leading to paroxysms of short-lived elation followed by existential collapse. The torment of these lovesick patients was severe, despite high-level functioning in other areas. Caught between irresistible longing and implacable interdiction, their despair reached occasionally to the verge of suicide. What kind of object elicits so much passion and doom?

Two aspects of Furlong's account stood out: the idea that falling in love is a trauma, and the connection of lovesickness to depression. As to the first idea, is the "trauma" in lovesickness due to the duress of "dammed-up" passion—the need *not to act* on powerful sexual desire? Or rather, is something inherently traumatic in sexual love *itself*? Sexual feeling is shot through with an experience of excess, including, in the words of the psychoanalyst Ruth Stein, "an excess of physical sensations beyond regular containment, an excess of desire over sensible judgment, an excess of meaning beyond symbolization, and the other's ungraspable excess over me." The entire experience of excess draws on "the sense of overbrimming with inordinate arousal that makes one feel it cannot be encompassed."

We make much of the sorry diminishment of this state over the course of marriage, but it's worth at least a nod to the difficulty of sexual intensity, and why people might feel a trace of relief at its dwindling. Still, "everyday" sexual experience is also characterized by "overbrimming"; it's an inherent quality of sex. The unique power of sexuality derives, in part, from the urge to "fill a gap," and to "grasp the elusive, ineffable quality of the sexual other." This quest begins in early life, when our mother first ministers lovingly in a sensual way, both soothing and exciting us. She inescapably sends us messages from her unconscious, both seductive and nurturing, and our sexuality is built up through our "translating" these not-wholly-translatable messages. The longing to reach the mysterious other enduringly imprints our sexual lives. Sexual feeling can express a range of bodily experience and emotion, not only pleasurable. An overbrimming of any kind of excitation, even those that are traumatic or painful, can seek discharge in sexual excitement; these can flood, overwhelm, and sometimes make us feel ashamed. But even "normal" sexuality involves some degree of shame because of its inherently excessive, unmodulated, and exposed character. One reason love helps us with sexual shame is that with a loved person we validate each other's excitement and transgress together against its prohibitions.

Christina felt such sexual excess, and it destabilized her sense of herself and her relationships. She viewed herself as a happily married and sexually satisfied woman and wasn't in the habit of having unmanageable sexual feelings for neighbors and friends. The alien quality of her feelings, their distance from her experience of her adult self, speaks to the indistinct yet inundating force that the deep currents of our early eroticism can impose on our otherwise orderly existence. Our unruly erotic core animates us from a realm beyond the reach of symbolic thinking and language. It must be lived, borne, and worked with, but it can't be rationalized, fully explained, or explained away.

It is also true that, in general, physiological arousal can feed many different subjective emotions, and its interpretation depends on context. When I camped in Yellowstone National Park, the edge of fear introduced by the presence of bears and the eerie midnight chorus of coyotes seemed to feed my vividly *positive* memories of the experience. We are not always able to identify how our states of physiological arousal relate to specific emotions. Highly emotional events also lead to more vivid memories. Emotional arousal triggers both rehearsal of stressful events in their immediate aftermath, as well as the repeated return to these memories over the subsequent hours and days.

Christina had felt a moment of intense fear that initiated her obsession with Michael. She was alone with her son, her husband was far away, and she was terrified. She felt unprotected and urgently distressed, defenseless and exposed. Though she managed as an adult pragmatically—she got Ethan into the car and drove to the doctor—

emotionally her normal coping methods were weakened, and she felt like a frightened child desperate for safety. If her husband had been present, the intense stimuli of the situation might have been discharged through seeking comfort with him. Instead, in her naked fear, she had encountered Michael, and his smile pierced her with its message of a wordless, primal safety, linked perhaps by powerful body memory to the vital smile of the soothing, exciting mother that shows all is right with the world.

If this were true, Christina's obsession with Michael might still have dissipated once Ethan was well, Ben and her daughter were back in town, and life was restored to normal. But Christina's problem did not end with the short-lived experience of being flooded by intense fear, its merging with a sense of sexual overstimulation, and a romantic sense of rescue through Michael's face and smile. It became, rather, an ongoing unmasterable loop. This characteristic of her experience evokes the linkage Furlong observed between lovesickness and depression. Depression and lovesickness both render their sufferers unable to do what's best for the self and engender a flagging spirit of self-preservation. We may one day discover that lovesickness and depression share an underlying physiological-emotional state, or perhaps that lovelorn longing provides specific imaginative content to preexisting feelings of depression. But even when a lovesickness doesn't begin in depression, certainly something is depressing about the endless repetition of longing that lovesick people are compelled to endure.

Christina said she was not depressed; but she did feel a kind of aching nostalgia and sense of loss. "Sometimes this feels like the most real thing I've ever felt," she said, "but it also feels like a dream." As we explored the dreamlike, saturated vividness of her feeling state, she noticed her sadness connected to the thought "I'll never be able to tell him." "It would be such a relief," she said, "to somehow acknowledge with Michael what we've 'been through' together. Hearing myself say that, though, I know how ridiculous it must sound."

Her dreamlike feelings resembled the nostalgic reverie that figured prominently in the stories of Furlong's lovesick patients. Each patient in childhood had had a parent who longed for a lost love of some kind—an abandoning parent, a distant brother, a lost homeland. As a child, the patient had therefore experienced a parent who was chronically mournful, and whose gaze was turned elsewhere. Seeing one's parent in an endless and unresolvable pining, Furlong suggests, imparts to the child a sense of helplessness as well as a painful insufficiency. It may instill an ongoing hungry longing in which stuckness and irresolution are centrally meaningful features. The child, like the parent, keeps looking for something she never finds.

When Christina had first come to see me in her late twenties, it had been over problems with men, complicated by a family crisis during which it came to light that her father had had an affair many years before. She'd always wondered what had gone on during her childhood, and she secretly sympathized with what she imagined was her father's desire for more love. In my work with her when she was a young adult, I'd learned of her parents' separation for a year in her early teens. Seeing her again now, I realized that her father's affair had taken place when he was exactly the same age she currently was.

Her beloved father had likely transmitted the message that he was absorbed elsewhere. But her relationship with her mother also made Christina vulnerable to longing. Temperamentally, her father had been the "warm one," and her mother, an artist, had been a bit cooler. Christina admired and shared her mother's seriousness and precision, but Christina also felt her mother had bristled a bit at the needs of her children. Though she'd borne four, she prized her solitude, and she'd molded in her children, with few words and disappointed glances, a precocious maturity. A lonely part of Christina felt that she hadn't been able to consistently elicit her mother's nurturing attention. Christina had sometimes compensated by spending inordinate time strategizing about getting her mother's approval. She'd generally kept her emotions under careful control, and she feared being seen as "childish," even by her husband. She had long felt conflicted about the yearning, hungry part of herself and was painfully shocked to find it was now running the show.

Most lives are riddled with loss, and one readily imagines that many sufferers of lovesickness had parents with unresolved losses. In my clinical work I've come to view certain combinations of events and emotions as disposing people to lovesickness, and as operating quite apart from how viable they deem their marriages. A critical dimension is a recently experienced loss or threat of loss. Examples of people whose losses tripped them into romantic or sexual thralldom include the sixty-two-year-old man who, confronted with his wife's cancer, spent his time absorbed in a friendship that became a tortured emotional affair. A forty-year-old husband and father of three who commuted for months to visit his mother as she died a slow and painful death became obsessed with a dancer in a strip club. A forty-three-year-old woman, after years of infertility, adopted a child and then became preoccupied with longing for her college boyfriend. None of these people wanted or intended to break up their primary relationship.

Like Christina, their equilibrium had been tampered with, and the emotional balance they had struck was now precarious. Perhaps all of us walk around in a more needy and vulnerable state than we think, ready to be undone by jarring losses. People can also have a subtle sense of being "emptied out," which feels more like low mood or mild depression. They find themselves inexplicably and powerfully moved by someone when they least expect it. Only in retrospect do they piece together how depleted they felt, sometimes for years, without knowing it.

On the other end of the spectrum, a manic mood can also induce lovesickness. A risky new business venture or a sudden success can catapult people into unexpected infatuations. Psychologically, both depressive and manic moods alter our relationship to loss and limits. In depression, we're suspended in chronic sadness, unable to grieve loss and move on. In mania, we feel so self-expansive as to deny the limits that normally structure our lives. Both immoderate gratification and immoderate loss can deplete us in different ways, making our higher mental functions, and our contact with the big picture, harder to access.

* * *

GOOGLE *ASTRONAUT DIAPER* and the top search result is a *Wiki- pedia* entry on Lisa Nowak. In 2007, Nowak, a NASA astronaut and forty-three-year-old married mother of three, drove 950 miles from Houston, Texas, to Orlando, Florida, with "a black wig, a BB pistol and ammunition, pepper spray, a hooded tan trench coat, a 2-pound drilling hammer, black gloves, rubber tubing, plastic garbage bags, approximately $585 (USD) in cash, her computer, an 8-inch (20 cm) Gerber folding knife and several other items." Her intention was to "do severe bodily harm or death" to navy captain Colleen Shipman, a rival for the affections of fellow NASA astronaut Bill Oefelein. Nowak was apprehended by police at the Orlando International Airport after accosting Shipman with pepper spray in the parking lot. On her arrest, Nowak told the police that she had worn diapers during her car trip to hasten her journey. (Her lawyer later claimed that the diaper was an "absolute fabrication.") When the story broke, it was accompanied by various before and after photos: an official NASA image of Nowak in her orange flight suit, posed lovely and smiling before an American flag and an image of a rocket launch, side by side with a disheveled, distraught booking photo of Nowak at the Orange County jail. The pictures were fascinating and horrible at the same time. It was hard to bear thinking about the cause of Nowak's apparent descent into such a desperately unhinged state. Yet, a common reaction to news of the incident was laughter—emanating, I think, from the unnerving juxta- position of disbelief and recognition. That may be a reason Nowak's story caught on in the culture, finding its way into television series, popular songs, and late-night comedy routines. We couldn't *imagine* being her, yet with a disturbing flicker of doubt, we wondered whether under certain circumstances any of us *could* be her.

Nowak's lovesickness was stratospheric, incomparable to the strug- gles of most other mortals. But by middle age, many of us have had a "What the f*** is going on with that person?" experience with some- one in our broad acquaintance. It can be hugely disquieting; it can rearrange friendships, create awkward silences, and disrupt our sense, even from afar, of what we know and don't know about life. I think the experience says less about some new collection of behaviors that grip us in the "midlife crisis" than about the basic disjunction between outward appearances and interior life. Inside, everyone is teeming with needs, fears, and dreams and trying his or her best to strike a balance. We're perennially looking to find our personal equilibrium between stimulation and calm. Mostly, people try to manage these challenges internally, out of view, or in confidential conversations with relatives, friends, or therapists.

"When I think of what a good girl I've always been, I can't even believe what I did," said Rita, in what was our first of only three therapy sessions. Lively, pretty, and stylish at fifty, she had femininity down pat. The ease with which she seemed to assume she'd win me over put me on guard. She began her story with a furrowed brow and a look of pleading charm. "This trainer at the gym, Stan, he literally took me over. When I was in front of him, I couldn't function. It's like *my skin* couldn't even protect me. It's like he got *inside* of me, by just looking at me. When he texted me in a flirtatious way, I didn't even really *think* before I answered. I've never, ever done anything like this before, and I have to figure out why I did it."

Rita had two daughters in their teens and had been married to Brent for twenty years. "Until Brent had his heart attack, I don't know if I even really thought that we *had* any problems. Brent was always the ultimate type A achiever. He ruled the roost and had opinions about everything. Honestly, I was doing the kid thing and kind of stayed out of his way. Plus, I felt so lucky to be with him. Everyone loves Brent. He's a winner in everything he does. Since his heart attack, though, he's gotten even more particular. His sense of humor is gone. He tries to control everything, and he's demanding and superior about it."

"Superior?" I asked. Her note of criticism seemed to provide an opening.

"He always has to be right. . . . But then I think of how I've been so wrong." She short-circuited her own thought, shifting from a complaint about her husband to a criticism of herself.

I stayed quiet, waiting to hear what would happen next.

"Once Brent discovered the text-message trail, he came down

hard. He told the children without asking me. He just did it. I felt horrible. Exposed. Yet, I know I deserved it."

I know I deserved it. I found the comment disturbing. In the system they had created, her "badness" entitled him to shame her. Before her husband's heart attack, Rita seemed to have signed on to the shared fiction of his invincibility. They had basked in their mutual specialness. But she also accepted as normal her husband's incursions into her autonomy. His heart attack jarringly shook their defensive collusion. He no longer provided a fitting target for her unthinking idealization. He was more rigid and vulnerable. Was there room in their relationship to shift the balance of power, to actually change their status quo? It seemed that maybe she wasn't yet a person who could truly stand her ground—controlled by her overbearing husband, and then by her tantalizing seducer.

From the shards of her story I was left with after our meetings, I thought about the quality of Rita's attraction to the trainer at her gym. Though she described her experience as acutely physical, a disruptive, mysterious plunge into seemingly untamable arousal, the body is never a straightforward messenger. Our experience of its messages is always molded by our minds. Some people tirelessly generate a sexualized zone, and Rita's trainer might well have been one of those. An offhand comment she made about him—"I felt a fierce chemistry, even though I wasn't even that attracted"—suggested the possibility that she was dealing with a brand of sexual mind control. A powerful psychological process can get going between two people where one person projects his feelings into the other person and controls her "from within" by pressuring her to behave in accordance with his projection. Although conveyed mentally, it is a *real* pressure, exerted through genuine, if subtle, interactions between the two parties. It can operate in every domain, not just the sexual. But the confusion it sows in situations like Rita's can be profound. While Rita was trying to figure out why sexual excitement was taking her over from within, she also had the uncanny feeling of being controlled from without. She felt unable to tell what was "hers" and experienced shame and self-criticism at being so absurdly affected.

Sexualizers and seducers tend to project a blend of sex and aggression that simultaneously manipulates and excites. It can feel as if they have entered one's inner sanctum and helped themselves to one's juicy pulp, all the while seeming to engage one in a swoony sexual merger. *Merger* may sound blissful, but when it takes over an adult's mind, it packs a wallop of insanity. Erotic thralldom operates in a psychic space from which loss and separation are banished. It temporarily allows us to experience a kind of dyadic haze, and to obliterate our relentless aloneness. But it also makes us feel a bit mad, untethered to the grounding features of our lives. When we are pulled in this way, it can feel as if we were falling through a trapdoor we didn't even know was there.

Rita was dealing with two simultaneous stressors, the appearance of the seductive trainer and Brent's heart attack. Given the evident importance of her feminine charm to her self-esteem and self-concept, I saw the two events as meaningfully linked. The trainer was skilled at messing with her mind, but her mind was also vulnerable to being messed with. Brent's heart attack created more load on her psychic system. She was more fragile, and therefore more susceptible. Brent's ill health also imperiled the satisfaction they both drew from their value to each other as sources of masculine and feminine power. The impact of his heart attack on their physical intimacy deprived them both of needed affirmation.

Perhaps it was also a source of awkwardness that just as Brent was feeling less sexually driven, Rita was feeling more so. Some people in midlife—in my anecdotal experience, it is mostly women—begin to experience themselves sexually in a new way. Perhaps it's related to having been released from the need to protect themselves from the onslaught of objectification that characterizes young womanhood, as well as having gotten through the reproductive gauntlet. A woman's sexuality may have developed into a more known and freestanding aspect of self, more available to her and less encumbered by notions of romance or subtleties of interpersonal dynamics.

In some cases—again, in my observation, this is an almost-exclusively female phenomenon—this newly intense sexual fervor switches genders, redirected toward a woman rather than a man. Anita, a forty-five-year-old married woman with two children, found herself intensely sexually attracted to Jen, a woman at work. Anita had not identified as bisexual, nor had she had a sexual encounter with a woman; but the intensity of her desire had no equivalent in any previous relationship. She'd felt herself to be relatively happy, if a bit bored, with her husband, and she still felt she was. But she reported to me that the relationship with her husband and her feelings for Jen were two entirely incomparable realities. When she and Jen began hanging out as friends, Anita's confusion fueled a gnawing sense of anxiety and excitement; around Jen, Anita said to me, she "felt like a drug addict." Anita felt so impelled to act on her urges that she and Jen began a blistering sexual relationship. Anita moved out of her family home (and left therapy) in their first week of cohabitation.

In this instance, I felt the less destructive path would have been to have had an affair, even if it remained secret for a time, as Anita figured out what she planned to do. I thought she needed time to sort out her sexual desire, her marriage, her specific relationship with Jen, and her evolving sense of self. If she'd taken time to manage her complicated and conflicting emotions in a less combustible way, the explosion in her children's lives wouldn't have been as traumatic. As it was, I feared another major meltdown might be in her not-too-distant future.

In Rita's case, her attraction to the trainer, like her marriage, was extreme. Having boomeranged from an idealization of her husband to a flirtation at the gym, Rita's growth would probably lie in understanding who she might become apart from the desires and demands of men and her investment in pleasing them. I felt it would be a hard challenge for her. After all, her most meaningful roles had been as mother, wife, and general life-manager for a busy and seemingly self-important husband. As she headed toward her children's departure, a huge part of her maternal job description would evaporate. Her role as wife was apparently tipping away from "object of desire" and toward "caretaker." The part that worried me most, though, was that nagging detail about her husband's shaming her in front of her kids. Given her reflex to blame herself for his reaction, I wasn't sure she would come to question his dominance, and I doubted he would tolerate it if she did.

WITH THE HUGE proliferation of communication channels in the internet age, the opportunities for rough-patch romantic longing expand apace. What does it do to our brains to be reminded on Facebook of our college sweetheart's birthday, or to be able to find past loves on Instagram? Most of us have jobs, children, and an endless string of petty frustrations. At the end of the day, our willpower is routinely tested by incredibly easy access to all manner of fantasy escape. Aside from porn and shopping, the internet provides a treasure trove of opportunities for reconnecting with people from the past.

I remember an email I received a few years ago. "Hello old friend!" read the subject line. I wasn't used to seeing a personal salutation in my business email account, so I assumed it was spam, perhaps a request for money from someone who had pirated a name from my address book. Then I noticed that the sender's name looked familiar from my college days, and I clicked open the message. In it was a photograph, taken on a porch somewhere, of a man my age. He was surrounded by four children, ranging from a girl about six to a baby nestled in the crook of his arm. I squinted at his image—graying hair, a bit of a belly. It was hard to entirely make out the face through the filter of time. Below the picture it said, "So, there I was, for some reason, thinking back over the years . . . places and people . . . and you popped into my head . . . and I smiled and thought, now she was really something." Huh? That last bit seemed like a slightly suggestive choice of words. I barely knew the guy. His evidently dreamy state of mind couldn't have had much to do with me.

That this person took a moment to savor the past and share a warm reminiscence was nice, I supposed. Even in the midst of a contented life, an exhausted fiftysomething father of four children under six might be expected to indulge in a bit of (alcohol-aided?) nostalgia. Still, it got me thinking: What if this man had been my first love, or someone who haunted me from time to time with thoughts of what might have been? How would I have reacted to his musings then? What if I had been looking for an escape or distraction? Might I have studied his words, mentally amplified them, even spent hours crafting my response?

My thoughts turned to the various patients who'd reported over the years their struggles with Facebook stalking, risqué email repartee, and escalating text exchanges that seemed friendly until they got confusing, creepy, or carried them away. People drained entire afternoons of productive activity in just such pursuits—and often weren't even sure what they wanted or why. Unexpected blasts from the past can't help but deliver a particular piquancy, marinating us in a bath of memory, desire, and nostalgia. They feed our midlife urge to reach back through the decades of our lives, whether to pick up threads or to stir old pots—we're not quite sure. Online communication adds an unprecedented charge, since messages launched into the void lend themselves to fevered anticipation, not to mention runaway fantasy and an inflated sense of significance. Intermittent reinforcement is the most powerful shaper of behavior; when rewards come at variable intervals, it's habit-forming. We never know *when* we might be rewarded, so we repeat the behavior more and more often in hope of a hit (think slot machines). Unfortunately, the obsessive quality of infatuation can become paired with the conditioned rewards of email checking, creating a supersaturated energy suck. People feel horrible about themselves but seem powerless to put on the brakes.

Despite the depressing nuisance of such habits, they express a deeper dilemma. By midlife we can't help but feel aware of the roads not taken. Our awareness can prompt anything from leisurely curiosity to profound regret. We look for ways to incorporate the dreams of our youth into our present reality. It's not simply boredom, though it might be that too. We want to reconnect to people from our pasts, to set things straight or understand events from a different angle. We want our life stories to add up, to make sense.

For some, these desires draw on the memory of what life felt like when they were young, and this can't help but invite invidious comparisons to how life feels now. The family-building phase pulls people toward a conventionalized set of roles that can feel repetitive even when we're basically contented with them. We run from home to work to school to home and repeat the cycle when we rise the next day. No wonder people lack the time or energy to develop a subtler and more pleasurable mix of relationships. And life throws all sorts of exhausting and difficult things at all of us. Fatigue, stress, and anxiety make it notoriously hard to access a creative state of mind that generates new possibilities, and too often we end up stuck in the same old mental grooves. When things feel stressful or confusing, sometimes all we want to do is shut down, stop trying, and click into automatic mode. It's also entirely natural to imagine escape. A Caribbean cruise would be nice, but we'll settle for junk food, binge-watching TV, or a harmless flirtation at work.

Even under the best of circumstances, there lurks a larger midlife question: How do I both pursue excitement and maintain a stable relationship? It's hard to figure out how to fit together the structures we've built and the passions that stir us. If we open ourselves to excitement and challenge, we feel. When we feel, we risk. When we risk, we don't always know what the outcome will be. One problem of reaching out—toward a wider circle, more excitement, greater connection—can be navigating the boundaries between romance and friendship.

This was the quandary for Roger, a married man who after many years ran into an old friend, Marian, also married. Their meeting led to an email exchange ("It was a wonderful surprise to see you"), which led to an increasingly revelatory email correspondence ("I feel like I was my best self around you"), which led to heartfelt conversations ("We have to figure out what this is"), which led to a kiss, which led to pained marital reckonings and, ultimately, to their decision to cease contact. When trying to explain the slippery slope of their involvement, Roger said, "I couldn't stand the idea of not having her in my life after all these years. But I didn't know *how* to have her in my life. In hindsight, I ask myself if there could have been another way. A way that didn't lead where it did."

Roger's romantic reaching out, which looks from one angle like an attempt to expand his horizons, looks from another angle like a kind of retreat, because it used romantic infatuation as a means of greater connectedness at exactly the point in life where the challenge is to broaden the base. Too often, the impulse for greater connection gets funneled into romantic feeling because people haven't found a way to transition out of the one-point focus that our excitement about romantic beginnings sluices us into, and toward the biodiversity of relationships we need to survive and flourish in a long life. Youth, vitality, possibility, and intensity, all seemed linked with romantic love, and it is not always easy to see how these qualities might be accessed through other means.

The fancy psychological word for accessing these qualities through other means is *sublimation*, a term that references a core paradox of healthy adult life, namely that we need to *give up* in order to *get*. When we accept the limits and structure of a role—be it parent to child, husband to wife, teacher to student—we paradoxically gain freedom to express the full range of emotions within that role. This bargain can be surprisingly hard to strike because the gain is tied to the loss. Accepting the need to behave within the limits of roles involves relinquishment, for sure: the frustration of wishes, the loss of a fantasy of infinite possibilities, even grief at what we cannot have.

But all told, it's a productive and creative exchange. Reinvesting time and energy into our limited life often yields the greatest bounty of fruits, even if we are aware that somewhere over there is an exotic varietal we'll never get a chance to try. Holding on to limits, even when they are tested, is what allows us to conserve and preserve those things we care most about nurturing, whether it's a stable home for our children, the time and energy to pay attention to them, or the pleasure of developing our interests. Having confidence in our boundaries also allows for the flourishing of much more diverse relationships.

By contrast, witness the chaos that ensues when we lack such boundaries. Tia came to me for help because she fell in love with a coworker every time she was hired for a new job. When she became excited about collaborating and sharing ideas, she invariably found herself pulled into a blur of erotic feeling. She couldn't rely on the structure of her work role for any semblance of a safe emotional harbor. Her relationships became confusing and complicated, and she felt she was in constant emotional turmoil. She lost out on the very real pleasures of collaborative creativity, teamwork, and friendship. Her lack of boundaries meant that every relationship was "fair game," but far from offering freedom and gratification, she found herself stuck, over and over, in an ironically self-depriving situation.

As extreme as Tia's situation sounds, it may have more in common with Roger's situation than it initially appears. The midlife pull toward romantic exploration makes sense as an expression of the desire to try on new selves, to collect up old selves, or to rewrite our story. The longings from our youth are powerful stuff, an important aspect of who we are. But the impulse to interpret those longings within a romantic formula may derail us from moving into a life that is lived in less sexualized and more sublimated terms. Maybe our need for love, admiration, and appreciation is best farmed out to many sources. Where human connections are concerned, perhaps diversification is the key to a rich emotional life.

When we reach out, it's propelled by the desire to appreciate the people who have mattered to us. Connecting with old friends serves an earnest craving for an enlarged sense of community and a connection between our past, present, and future. As we all know, reaching out through social media presents a challenge. One minute, our phones and computers function as a mood-enhancing drug; the next, a mood-deflating intrusion. Disconnecting means depressive pangs at turning off our pings. And it's not easy when the main communication channel for our social causes is the same one our exhibitionistic friends use to report on their weekend getaways with new lovers. The trick is to figure out how to disentangle the lure of addictive rumination from the healthy desire to engage and widen our circle of concern. Perhaps, when we catch ourselves trying to rekindle an old flame, we can ask ourselves whether there might be a way to redirect our passion toward rekindling a *bigger* flame—doing something creative, or broadening our interests. If that's too grandiose, we might turn toward a more modest, yet gratifying, goal: remembering that many of the good things in our lives come from our ongoing conservation and protection of what we already have.

NINE MONTHS AFTER our first meeting, Christina came in and said, "I think I've finally stopped believing in this feeling. I think I'm letting it go." I remember that I felt the urge to cry. The image that came to my mind was that we'd been in a storm together, and we'd managed to swim ashore from the wrecked boat. In the storm itself, my role was akin to that of a steadfast parent: to accept and contain her unbearable feelings, and pull for her survival by keeping my own mind when she felt she was losing hers. Until this moment, I hadn't allowed myself to feel how worried I really was. She had so much to lose. But she'd put faith in our relationship; she'd kept reaching for me, using my encouragement of her curiosity about the reasons for her turmoil, and leaning on my interest in looking for ways to approach it. What helped her to manage the storm was our relationship, and what I can only honestly call my love for her and hers for me, transference or no.

Together we came to believe that her fear at Ethan's health scare, with the background of Ben's absence, had lowered her normal defenses. Her mind had played the trick of dramatically intensifying the saving grace of Michael's smile, and like a traumatic memory trace, it seared into her psyche. Unmediated by her higher mental functions (judgment, a sense of reality), her high-arousal state of fear had jumped the tracks and fueled her subjective flood of excitement. Her ongoing, deepening well of lovesick preoccupation, though, drew on family-of-origin themes and transferences, for which the "love" of Michael provided an enigmatic symbol. Her emotional position was that of a dependent child pining for the gaze and attention of the loving other. Whether any of these retrospective stories carried historical weight could never be decided, and in any event their accurate reconstruction didn't provide the healing. Rather, *trying to make meaning together* helped her. She couldn't process her experience by herself; she needed a caring person outside herself to help. My bearing witness to her confusion and shame, my accepting of her intense emotions, and my meeting her nagging excitements with interest and calm, all helped transform the roiling forces into something more tolerable.

Christina loved her husband and was loved by him. She enjoyed good relationships with her children, friends, and siblings. All this said to me that she had gotten the essential love she needed as a child, despite the family's difficulties. Given this, that she had developed such a deep obsession for another man remained puzzling to us. Few of us believe our need for love is *entirely* satisfied by reality, but for someone such as Christina, it would seem to have been satisfied enough to avert an obsession such as the one to which she fell prey. She and I explored whether, despite her compatibility with Ben, anything was missing in her experience of *herself* in her marriage. She came to feel that there was something important within herself that she had not yet found a way to express in her marriage, a kind of secure and unashamed spontaneity. She began to realize that she'd constructed her marital bond in the mode of coping and competency, and she hadn't tested with Ben how necessary her stance actually was. Delicate as it was to consider given her wayward attraction to Michael, we began to appreciate an underdeveloped passionate side of her that she'd never felt the luxury or freedom to fully explore.

At first she'd been embarrassed to tell me, but she eventually divulged that a welcome by-product of her thoughts about Michael had been a more intense sexual connection with Ben. When we looked closely, she noticed that it wasn't fueled by specific fantasies or thoughts of either man, but resulted from her feeling different in her body, in her *self*. Her confusing emotional state of the past few months had so often felt to her as if her personality had been destabilized. But it may have also allowed her to experience a more fluid, less controlled circulation of feeling. Even with all the turbulence, she somehow felt less worried, less stuck in her cognitive mind. In her life more generally, this shift spurred her to experiment with a freer, more relaxed approach.

Christina was coming out of it, though for a while she felt as if she were convalescing. I thought about the curative function of mental rest, and how different it is from the therapeutic goal of digging to the bottom of things. Perhaps her experience would have been called a nervous breakdown in another era. Not depression, but a cousin; not a trauma, but a deep, quasi-physiological event. As her mood became more even, she missed the highs and lows a bit, but mostly she felt relief. "I was dropping off some political flyers at Michael and Shauna's house," she told me one day, "and I happen to see a pile of books from the library on their table in the entryway. They looked like the kind of books Michael would read, socially conscious and a bit boring. It hit me, he's been having a regular, humdrum life, and enough peace of mind to actually read and pay attention to these books. I didn't feel any longing for him; I felt more of a hollow feeling, like the world isn't as intense and vivid a place as it was when I believed we had a special connection."

As her feelings diminished, she felt ashamed and wrong to have left Ben wondering alone about what the hell had been going on when he'd seen her distracted or in tears. She missed him as a friend, but she didn't want to selfishly unburden herself, either. We talked for weeks about what it would mean to tell him what she had been through; how she thought he would understand it; and whether the closeness she was seeking from confessing to him was realistic. She went back and forth, fearing that the conversation itself, though undertaken with the hope of understanding, would create its own inescapable misery. She particularly worried that just as she was beginning to feel greater emotional freedom within herself, their inevitably shame-inducing conversations would put an end to it. She knew it was a big risk, but she also felt that she didn't want to keep going on with him in the way she had been.

"When I told him," Christina recounted to me, "I was careful to lead with the fact that the entire episode had occurred only in my mind. I told him how much you and I had talked about it, and that if he and I agreed it would be easier to talk with a third party, you'd help us find someone to do that with. At first, he surprised me, because he felt relieved. He'd worried that maybe I was having an affair. I felt so bad. After that, he was hurt, and angry. He really doesn't like to be angry, with me or anybody else. But he was."

It was a hard time for them. They felt awkward and oversensitive, and it was nearly impossible to find time to talk. When they did manage to talk (she felt guilty about how much time the kids spent on their screens during those weeks), it was tough going. Ben wanted to know, in detail, what had been going on in her. She told him that she hadn't felt in her right mind for much of the time. She listened to what he'd been feeling and thinking, and was moved by his interest in what she had gone through. At times, he was even sympathetic. After several weeks she said to me, "I feel I'm almost stunned by his actual love." From Christina's telling, it seemed that she and Ben were managing to listen to each other and bear each other's feelings. Christina was genuinely sorry that she hadn't protected herself or Ben or their marriage better, yet she didn't collapse into shame. Ben was genuinely hurt and angry at her feelings and her secretiveness, yet did not get stuck in chronic blame or coldness. He could accept her remorse, she could accept his disappointment. It was a lot to process, and it took its own time.

I'd never witnessed something unfold in quite this way. It impressed me to see a couple where one partner put such a painful experience into the golden ring of the marriage, and where they could both then struggle so persistently together toward mutual understanding. I was impressed too with their acceptance of the need for patience, sustained effort, and the passage of time. Neither was trying to solve the problem by hurrying up their feelings. They intuitively understood that working through this would take time, and that the marriage had a rhythm of its own, a seasonality, that deserved respect.

"I would never, ever wish what I've been through on *anyone*. Never." Christina and I were reflecting on where she'd arrived. "I feel like I've had to piece myself back together, bit by bit. Ben didn't deserve this, and I still wonder what I could have done to stop it." She paused for a long time. "Awful as it's been—and it has been awful—I'd almost say we've put it to good use."

"What do you mean?" I asked.

"I never expected that what I went through could be remotely accepted in a marriage. I feel I've discovered something about what marriage is, and who Ben is. I think being married is about helping each other along. Not blaming each other for being crazy sometimes. Ben's done that for me."

The summer came, and with it the expectable scheduling complications of camps and vacations. Our meetings slowed, then stopped, and I wondered whether Christina resisted formally ending our meetings out of some faint superstition that she'd be tempting fate. But when I saw her once more in the autumn, she seemed, despite a fresh crop of trials, to have reached the other side.

"My mother has had surgery, and we've moved her here for the time being," Christina said. "For now, the prognosis isn't clear. I feel closer to her. I feel like I'm seeing her as her own person for the first time. I feel sad for her when I think about her rigidity and fear. Michael calls sometimes with a message about carpooling or something. I leave it on the voice mail for a couple days, just to test myself and see what it's like to listen to it. It makes me happy to feel nothing."

She looked at me with a heartrending smile. "Thank you. It's like you've seen me naked. Now—finally—I've got my clothes on, but you've already seen me."

"That's only a problem if you think there is something wrong with you naked," I said.

We were both silent for some time.

"I've seen you human," I said.

Body, Health, and Age:
The Stakes Only Get Higher

"I have a beautiful cousin," Raymond, a fifty-four-year-old lawyer told me. "I see her at family functions every couple of years. Last year, it seemed when I looked at her that something had changed. It was something around her mouth. I felt like I couldn't relate to her as easily. I felt distracted. Like I couldn't quite *see* her face anymore. It was disturbing."

Those who study robots, computer-generated imagery, and cosmetic surgery talk about the *uncanny valley*, "a vague eeriness" or revulsion we experience when presented with "nonnatural" human faces. Our exquisite face-reading abilities have evolved over millennia, so it stands to reason that an "operated-on" look creates some interference. People perceive faces through a complex process of integrating features into categories, and certain kinds of facial changes make for category "uncertainty." We detect emotional meaning in tiny muscle movements and share emotion through micromimicking each other's facial expressions. Given all this, we can see how the emotional benefits of aging—subtle shades of feeling, nuanced expressiveness, authenticity—might collide with our efforts at physical damage control and augmentation.

My friend Kanade Shinkai is a dermatologist in San Francisco. She does not perform cosmetic procedures, despite the opportunity to make four times more money than she does in this wealth-ridden city. Laser, Botox, chemical peels, reconstructive facial surgeries—she can do them all. But she has chosen not to, partly because she is interested in serious dermatological diseases, and partly because, she says, "I don't want to do them without knowing why.

"It's extraordinary to witness the different meanings skin has for people. A man can feel that hair loss is literally ruining his life. Yet I treated a patient who needed portions of the lower half of his body removed due to an aggressive cancer, and he and his wife still happily watch TV together on their couch. In our waiting room, there are people with large tumors who are sitting next to people coming for their Botox injections. All of the patients are in that waiting room for important reasons *to them*. I want to understand the reality of the person." Kanade is a practicing Buddhist, which might help explain her thoughtfulness about skin and time and self-acceptance. "Any desire is a source of suffering. I am happy to talk to people about healthy, evidence-based practices—avoiding the sun, not smoking. But I don't want to occupy a position of authority about what people should desire or what should make them suffer."

" 'I feel young but I look old' is the chronic lament," writes the sociologist Virginia Blum in her study of cosmetic surgery. Surgical patients tend to frame their stories as a mismatch between the real (youthful) person within and the shocking external appearance. "You have a right that the 'real you' be seen, recognized. It's locked in there, clamoring to get out and announce itself." But why is it, Blum asks, that our vision of the "inside self" is youthful? One reason, surely, is that at some deep stratum of our mental life, we regard ourselves as never changing. In a hidden corner of our minds, we safeguard an image of ourselves at peak adorability. It comes as a rude assault when the reality of time forces an adjustment in expectations. We experience aging as something that somehow wasn't supposed to happen to *us*. Another reason is that, looking in the mirror, it can be hard to square our present self and past self. It's as if there is a rupture in our story, some pages are missing, and rejuvenating our appearance is a way to build a bridge between then and now.

Kanade is not critical of cosmetic procedures or naive about the ways appearance defines us. "Appearance is our public face, our business card," she says. But in ten-minute conversations she simply can't know the patients she's talking to, or their fantasies about how this or that dermatological procedure might relate to their inner struggles. She's intuitively doubtful that an external change can fix an internal state. Yet as she poignantly describes, people are hoping that having their bodies restored to a more youthful state *will* help them cope with, and even undo, their suffering and their mistakes. "Our skin reminds us of what we've done," Kanade said, "tattoos and scars, yes, but also sun damage and smoking and stress." Among other things, she reminds us, skin can confront us with regret. "The most common question I am asked by healthy, middle-aged patients is 'What should I be doing?' There are so many choices and so many levels of intervention now. People struggle, and I wonder, 'What are they really asking?' Underneath the self-criticism, the main feeling I hear in these questions is regret. Regret that they were too hard on their bodies, or that they didn't take good enough care of themselves. They mourn their youth and want someone to bring it back."

Reflecting on Kanade's words, I was struck that aging makes the body into another factor in a marriage. For healthy people lucky enough not to learn this lesson earlier, aging represents the slow transformation of the body into a "problem." It may become an aesthetic problem (to oneself or one's spouse), or an athletic problem, or a more general functional problem. It creates an oddly doubled self, where the "me" that I bring to the marriage is now "me" and "my body." We are charged with finding a graceful way to live with the changes in our bodies, in much the same way we have worked all these years to find a graceful way to live with the differences of our spouse. All the while, we are each trying to live gracefully with our spouses' bodies. Our bodies become new sources of limit, and need, and strident opinion, and they demand to be heard and have their due. They need to find a place in the golden ring, along with all the other feelings and concerns that the two individuals in the marriage put there.

*   *   *

ELSA AND MITCH were a fiftysomething couple that came to see me during the fall that their daughter was applying to college. The ordeal seemed to be bringing out their worst tendencies. Elsa was blamefully pushing for more support and closeness from Mitch, and Mitch was absorbed by work and guilt ridden yet resentful about her demands. Mitch expected Elsa to oversee the college applications, yet Elsa and their daughter were similarly high-strung and constantly provoked each other. I thought Mitch's stance was a bit shirking; the logistics and emotional storms of college applications struck me as an all-hands-on-deck proposition, and it deserved at least a good-faith effort from him. But it also seemed strange that just as Elsa was shepherding their daughter toward leaving home, she was devoting such elaborate attention to all the ways that Mitch neglected her. Was her neediness distracting her from the somewhat thankless parental work presented by her current stage of life?

With her cascading hair and slender physique, Elsa signaled that her attractiveness was a core concern. Mitch had an unassuming air, but it registered as a counterweight to his lifelong experience of being the best-looking guy in the room. They looked like people who'd spent the bulk of their lives being envied for their sex appeal, and I found myself wondering whether this factored into their difficulties somehow. As if on cue, Elsa declared herself upset that Mitch had lapsed in their years-long ritual of going to bed at the same time.

"You just *aren't* prioritizing our *time* together," Elsa said in a somewhat plaintive tone. "Is it so hard to understand that I'd want some attention?"

"One of us needs to stay up to make sure the girls get home safely," Mitch said coolly, hinting at Elsa's selfishness.

"If we don't watch it, we'll have nothing left between us once the girls go," she said, ramping up.

Elsa's focus on romance seemed a bit intense to me, given their current parental demands. But like a lot of people, she worried about the marital void that would follow their children's departure. She was the more voluble about this concern, but their intimate life was bothering each of them in different ways. Elsa felt rejected by Mitch's lack of romance, and Mitch felt weighed down by Elsa's inflated and insistent romantic expectations. The argument about responsible parenthood concealed anxieties about their growing physical and emotional distance.

As we analyzed their frustrations, a fairly common age-related problem emerged. For most of their relationship, their sex life had taken on a rhythm set by his desire. He'd "wanted it" so reliably that she always felt desired and never had to take much initiative. As Mitch's sexual responsiveness slowed, Elsa was thrown off-balance, and she became anxious, then demanding. In a move that seems at least as common among midlife men as women, Mitch was quietly avoiding sex, and even at risk of giving up on it. He'd pretty much stopped expressing affection, fearing that it would lead to sexual expectations. Now, their predicament felt less like a period of psychological adjustment than an existential threat.

Mitch and Elsa were not alone in having fallen prey to a particular brand of thinking about couple sexuality. People tend to subscribe to an "ideal" model of heterosexual sex: men have reliable and lasting erections on demand, women's sexual desire is responsive to male initiation, and men's sexual interest is sustained by women's attractiveness. This model becomes increasingly untenable with age, with the result that people feel they've fallen short. When men display less driven desire or physical performance, women become worried about not being attractive enough. Men worry about their "masculinity" and how they *function* sexually, and women worry about their "femininity" and how they *look* sexually. This causes distress for couples, sociologists observe, arising from the anxiety at no longer being able to perform sexually on the model coded as *youthful*. Spooked by the specter of waning attractiveness and youthful energy, widely signified by the accomplishment of vaginal intercourse arising from male desire and female desirability—people cast about for physical fixes. Viagra offers itself as a producer of sexual function (though not of desire), and an entire beauty industry, including plastic surgery, is available to "treat problems" of female attractiveness. "Aging well" becomes understood as maintaining youthful sexual and gender norms.

Notably, distress about age-related sexual changes is more pronounced in the forties and fifties than in later life, because that's when the norms of youthful sexuality begin to bump up against the physical realities of aging. Despite visions of doom, however, research indicates that across the life span sex continues to be an important part of relationship satisfaction. Between the ages of forty-five and fifty-four, 80 percent of men and 75 percent of women consider sex important to the happiness of their bond; at the age of seventy, 66 percent of men and 50 percent of women do. The frequency of sex decreases with age, but if people's health and sexual self-esteem are good, age *itself* does not lead to a decrease in sexual desire. And contrary to the familiar "sexual boredom" hypothesis, the length of a marriage does not predict a loss in either sexual desire or frequency, for men or women. In fact, evidence suggests that satisfaction with their sexual relationship tends to lead couples to be happy in their marriage, and that their marriages are more stable as a result. The causal arrow from sexual satisfaction to happiness in marriage appears to hold true for both men and women.

So, sex continues to matter to a lot of couples, and desire doesn't go away. A subset of couples may agree that they don't want to be a sexual couple—though a subset of that subset might be in for an upsetting surprise when one or the other backs out of the agreement. Elsa and Mitch both knew that sex was important to them, but they hadn't yet figured out how to think outside the he-man conventions of male initiation to which they'd long adhered. Doing something different can feel frightening. People have their tried-and-true methods. The amazing thing about relationships, though, is that doing something different, even something small, can be big. Almost any spouse who still has feelings for her partner is touched when her partner takes a risk. The bravery of trying counts.

With Elsa and Mitch, we worked on two fronts simultaneously. One was accepting the time-intensive and not necessarily rewarding aspects of parenting teenagers, something they each seemed to be avoiding—Mitch through his work and Elsa through her slightly hyperbolic need for attention. The other was helping them to move out of avoidance and toward exploration in sex. One of the more hopeful findings about the age-related shifts in sexuality is that men and women begin to approach sex on a more equal footing. Men can find that a less goal-driven model of sex creates a potential for more emotional connection, and more relaxed, whole-body sharing of pleasure. Women, who are used to variability in their sexual responses (i.e., sometimes turned on, sometimes not), can put this awareness to empathetic use in accepting men's more variable sexual responses. With age, women become more comfortable with expressing what they want sexually. This is an opportunity for men, not only because they've always wished their wives would initiate sex more, but also because they can use their wives' arousal as a source of excitement.

When partners operate as an intimate team in this way, they can throw off constraining ideas about sex and collaborate on what pleases *them*. The spirit of collaboration extends to using a variety of arousal methods, and not treating one method as better than another. In partner sex, people generally get aroused in three ways: partner interaction, self-entrancement, and role enactment. Partner interaction is what we consider the usual way, namely becoming aroused by one's partner's looks, feel, and behavior. Self-entrancement is focusing on one's own body sensations and accepting touch. Role enactment is becoming aroused in your private imagination (fantasy), or through role-playing or props. When sex becomes boring, it's often because couples limit themselves to partner interaction as a source of arousal. The antidote is to vary arousal styles.

Treating the current era of their sexual life as something they could figure out together tempered Elsa's tendency toward complaint and Mitch's tendency toward disengagement. Then, as if visited by the goddesses of twenty-first-century middle-aged womanhood, Elsa's recently divorced sister persuaded her to add yoga to her exercise regimen. Elsa thus joined the 14 million yoga practitioners over the age of fifty, and her practice became the seed of the sense of community that she had been yearning for. Elsa tended to be frenetic and reactive in daily life and felt at sea and agitated when alone. In class, the quiet, the mood, the music, and the gentle voice of her instructor, all helped to settle her nerves. Yoga also helped fill the growing empty space she felt in her family life. It gave her an avenue to the sacred and a deeper sense of self-compassion. Finding "bottom-up" awareness and appreciation for how she felt in the moment; balancing effort and ease; uncovering layers of physical tension—these were a huge boon to her daily well-being and an antidote to stress.

Along with its many other benefits, yoga became a bridge back into sensuality. It helped Elsa approach physical affection with renewed confidence and calm. The trappings also had their charms. Her yoga clothes made her feel cute and sexy. Websites such as girlsinyogapants .com and the widespread semifetishization of women in workout clothes helped her feel in the game. And it didn't hurt to have a shirtless twenty-eight-year-old yoga instructor at her Tuesday-morning class, who took his job of adjusting women's pelvises very seriously indeed. But most of all, the actual practice helped her feel more centered, and the breathing made a huge difference in her state of mind and body. "It's all about the breath," she informed us, and I was glad to see her new yogic wisdom replacing the blaming tone that had characterized her previous bids for Mitch's attention. "Yoga is helping me be a better partner," Elsa said one day, "because I'm more willing to be patient and listen." Once aggrieved at Mitch's dearth of romantic gestures, she now asked whether he would be open to candles, essential oils, and exotic scents. He even tentatively agreed to a mindfulness-based yoga retreat for couples. ("Lucky you," said Mitch's brother, on hearing of these developments.)

THE RUEFUL "CAN you fix me?" that Kanade Shinkai hears in her dermatology office is not all that different from the "Please fix yourself" that we as marital partners sometimes deliver to each other. Aging is a demand and a pressure, not unlike having children. It taxes the system in a new way. It's simply human for our deepest anxieties to return as our vulnerability increases, not to mention our characteristic defenses against those feelings. As the visible aging of our bodies puts our sense of self-preservation under threat, we inventory our sources of self-esteem and become more sensitized to their depletion. A marriage vow is an agreement to make the marriage the chief story line of our intimate relational lives. We can't promise never to feel or act in ways detrimental to the marriage, only to choose to interpret those feelings and actions in a way that treats the marriage as our relationship life's central narrative. Yet the feelings that the changes of aging will generate cannot be fully predicted. While some of the changes are foreseeable and inevitable, the feelings will be difficult anyway. (As one man sheepishly confessed to me, "I feel like I want my wife to stop aging *as soon as possible*.") Other changes can't be foreseen, and we'll have to struggle with the fear and disappointment they arouse. Either way, we'll need to engage all the skills we've been exploring—self-awareness, self-responsibility, curiosity, compassion, control—and then some.

An uncomfortable question lies hidden in love relationships: How and why does loving someone continue to support and promote our self-love, and how and why does it start to diverge from, and threaten, our self-love? Narcissism threads through healthy married love as mutual pride and admiration, so it's not always easy to distinguish its more pernicious forms. It's also hard to distinguish excessive self-regard from the ideal of "taking care" of oneself. I remember one couple where the husband, in his midsixties, reported that he had a new lease on life due to his strenuous exercise routine. Though he and his wife had both been competitive athletes in their college years, the wife had not joined her husband in his new athletic enthusiasms, largely because she'd had a knee replacement a little under a year ago.

They had recently taken a trip to Europe and explored some major cities, mostly on foot. When they returned, they were barely speaking to each other. I learned that this silence had begun as they were making their way to the metro on their last day in Paris. The husband had rushed down the stairs to catch a train arriving in the station—he had them on a tight sightseeing schedule—and when his wife failed to keep up with him, he yelled from the subway-car door, "Hurry up!" She felt humiliated and enraged by the way he spoke to her. She sat down then and there on the subway stairs, despite her pastel-yellow capri pants.

They had not talked to each other for the three days since that moment—on the metro, at dinner, in the cab to the airport, and on the flight home. She found his treatment deeply inconsiderate and offensive. I sympathized. Honestly, though, his behavior was not exactly a surprise to me, even if it was a more extreme iteration. He had always exhibited an unsavory dose of narcissism, and the hard truth was that in the past its glow had more reliably included her. As aging introduced its inevitable rumble of decline, he was resorting to fitness as a culturally approved and personally preferred program of immortality. For it to function smoothly, his wife would have to get on board. Yet she couldn't.

In the husband's mind, his wife's problem was that she "wouldn't" take her fitness seriously, and he was simply urging her to reach her potential. He appeared unable to see that twisting his wife's genuine vulnerabilities into matters of willpower was self-serving. It also conveyed a veiled reproach for their differing genetics. Both physically and in appearance, his wife had clearly aged faster than he had.

To expand his sympathy for his wife, the husband would have had to reflect on his own defensive strategies, and he showed little taste for this painful prospect. It seemed obvious to me that being stronger, faster, and better could not remain his answer to every problem forever. Yet people are surprising. According to his proud report, his ninety-year-old mother was still living on her own in a three-story town house on Boston's Beacon Hill, driving herself to the symphony on Fridays and scorning her less robust, easily defeated friends. Who knew how long he could go on maintaining his fiction of superiority, and at what point even his wife of thirty-five years could become its casualty?

"JESUS, NO ONE told me about this," Louis erupted one day. He and his wife, Amanda, were fifty-three, and the parents of two teenage sons. "Her mood, her irritability. Her sex drive's evaporated. I don't know who I am dealing with from one day to the next." The subject was menopause, and he was referring to his wife in an exasperated third-person way, even though she was sitting right there.

"It's incredibly annoying to hear you talk about me like that," said Amanda. "I suppose suddenly *you* don't have anything to do with my mood or irritability."

"This is different. It's a new low. Or a new high. I don't know what to call it."

Amanda and Louis were what's known as a "passionate" couple. They'd started seeing me, on and off, six years earlier, to deal with the effect of Louis's ADHD on the marriage. Louis was creative, a lot of fun, and a frenetic multitasker. He ran a successful chain of restaurants and was widely beloved. But he was also easily bored, and a self-confessed "disaster" when it came to the multifarious tasks of family life. He, along with their teenage sons, Reed and Cal, relied on Amanda to delegate, orchestrate, and have sufficient executive skills for all of them. Now that the boys were adolescents, Amanda found her role more stressful than ever. Her emotional self-control, never strong, had always flared when the pressures of her floral business ramped up. But now she was in chronic emotional overdrive.

"These days, I have three man-boys in the house instead of one," she said. "I feel like my head is about to explode. I'm tired of it. And I just feel so *over* having to micromanage everyone—"

"I *hate* you micromanaging me," Louis injected.

"Yeah, but not enough to keep track of anything yourself!" she cried. "You and the boys treat me like your personal maid service! I'm not going to keep trying to keep the peace and stuff all my feelings and get sick all the time as a result."

Whether she'd read the popular books on menopause or not, Amanda was articulating a major line of thinking about the effect of "the change" on women's psyches. Leading up to menopause, the argument goes, women's brain chemistry changes as the hormonal balance shifts. Throughout the fertile years, estrogen and oxytocin are the "tend and befriend" hormones that stimulate women's nurturing, conciliatory behavior. But in perimenopause, these hormones are on the wane. As children grow and their need for physical tending decreases, so too does the reward of oxytocin release, leading women to feel less inclined to prioritize the care of others. They begin to experience their desires and goals differently; they feel more autonomous and empowered.

Men, meanwhile, are blindsided and befuddled. If women have given little thought to menopause before it hits, men have given it less than none. People generally avoid thinking about aging, and a kind of cultural smoothing obscures the disturbing details. But with menopause, there's also no normal course, and no one knows what to expect. There's the usual stuff that even men have vaguely heard of (hot flashes, night sweats). There's the uncomfortable need to countenance "female problems" that were heretofore blessedly irrelevant (vaginal dryness, the pros and cons of hormone-replacement therapy). But then the various wild cards include sleep problems, weight gain, dry skin, sex-drive changes, and all the issues of mood: depression, irritability, anxiety, unexpected swings, crying jags. Both men and women can find themselves in uncharted territory with respect to women's fluctuating physiology and psychology.

The notion that waning tend-and-befriend hormones unleash the full power of women's discontent spins a biochemical tale of female empowerment, but also oversimplifies the picture. What looks like a "sudden" personality change in menopause generally has a long lead-up. Sylvia, fifty-four, a character in Louann Brizendine's book *The Female Brain*, asks herself, "What is it about my life that isn't working?" She regards menopause as the prime mover of her reassessment. We've learned a few pages earlier, however, that for *decades* she'd yearned to have a job, but her husband, Robert, "had made it impossible by denying her household help." Under what draconian marital regime might a husband issue such an edict, and under the sway of what benighted consciousness might a wife accept it? Perhaps menopause incites Sylvia's rebellion, yet she didn't simply *tolerate* her long-standing arrangement, but helped *construct* it. Earlier in her marriage, her husband was "telling her" she couldn't have what she wanted; now her body seems to be "telling her" that she can and should. The dominating force may have changed, but her basic orientation toward it hasn't. In either case, she'll only make personal progress if she struggles to recognize and claim her own legitimate voice.

For Amanda, hormonal changes were only the latest wrinkle in a complicated relational picture. She certainly felt her hormones gave her a bit more license to be a "moody bitch" and fight for what she wanted. But she'd struggled for a long time with shouldering the emotional burden of keeping the entire family on track.

"Amanda's story is that my ADHD has totally ruled our family life," said Louis. "But I think her moods have been running the show for years." He turned to her. "You won't cop to it because, according to you, I'm the reason you're always so irritated."

We were back into a seesaw state of mind, Louis and Amanda volleying blame as they often did when tempers were high. Amanda *was* irritated a lot, I could see that. But she'd also heroically coped with Louis's disorganization. I felt a bodily sympathy with Amanda's wish to be *done* with managing all these other people and empathized with the self-blame that attended her thought of having somehow created this many-tentacled family-dependency monster. But it wasn't much of a stretch, either, to see why Louis was caught off guard by her abrupt indignation and intolerance. A new force was behind it, and who could say whether the push was from hormones, or personality, or the accumulation of years, or an unholy alliance of all three? Yet, entitled as Amanda felt to a new world order, and energized as she was to make some changes, she also suffered and wanted back her old, more tolerant, less fed-up self.

She wanted her sex drive back too. Was her sex drive off because of hormones, or because she'd finally reached her limit with family demands? And did she feel she'd reached her limit with family demands *because* of what her hormones were doing? Sex had always been one of the ways she and Louis worked off irritation and quelled the nonstop sources of personality friction in their marriage. He could be fun, he was good to look at, and he had an uncharacteristic ability to focus on details when it came to her body. Now sex wasn't as effective an outlet, and she missed it.

For some women, libido drops off the face of the earth at menopause, and it can be a painful and mystifying loss. Others feel freed
up, almost happy. Whether a woman is coupled or single can make a
difference. A partner's dissatisfaction can be the main problem that a
woman has with her loss of sex drive. Couples can aim for a pragmatic
compromise (e.g., Saturday mornings with a lot of lubricant on hand).
It may not satisfy the yen for romance, but at least it keeps them from
wanting to kill each other. Some women want it to be accepted that
they don't want sex after a certain age. By letting go of striving to be
an object of the sexual gaze, they can feel their inner freedom expand.
But women's discomforts with the realities of their flesh can also stem
from their own self-persecuting version of that very gaze. It is hard
watching oneself grow older, and hard to distinguish what might be
a healthy, even brave, relinquishment of the need to sexually attract,
from a defensive closing of the door on a potentially pleasurable realm
that has become overloaded with self-judgment.

Other women in their forties, fifties, and sixties want more sex
than they are getting—menopause having, if anything, intensified their
interest in sex. They might endorse Princess Metternich's response
about the fate of sexual interest in older women: "You'll have to ask
someone else, I'm only sixty." Some women in harmonious, committed relationships report having the best sex of their lives. Occupying
the panoptic position of a therapist who sees people at all phases of
life, I sometimes have the Ghost of Marriage Future impulse to tell
women in their exhausted thirties, who currently feel hounded by
their partners' sexual demands, that in a decade or two they might
be hankering for a bit *more* attention, not less.

For some women, the exhausted thirties give way to the sexual
forties in ways that actively discombobulate the marriage. Still feeling
young and attractive, capable of getting fit and looking hot, feeling
more comfortable in their own sexual skin, and often having finished
with the intensive childbearing and little-kid phase of parenthood,
they look up and wonder, "What else is out there?" Evolutionary
explanations abound—"There's just enough time to have one more
baby"—and perimenopausal hormonal changes may play a role in

women's subjective sense of being more revved up. In the early forties, the communication between the brain and the ovaries becomes less tightly choreographed, and hormonal swings become broader. With more variability in estrogen production, the brain's alarm goes off when estrogen levels get low, and the body's production of estrogen and testosterone go up, resulting in weeks of the menstrual cycle when hormone levels surge. The subjective experience of rushes of sexual feeling can be empowering or destabilizing. A woman gives off a different vibe. Her body starts yakking, and she has to figure out what to do about the din.

Amanda's sex drive wasn't completely gone, but it was muted. We started there, trying to talk about the annoyance they each felt at their sex life being less easy, and the irritation with each other that the disruption had engendered. Those conversations gradually helped Amanda get in touch with her affection for her husband, even when he drove her nuts. Once she could calm her emotions a bit, her menopause-fueled impatience goaded her to think more pragmatically and constructively about strategies to share family responsibilities more equitably. Louis made a point of expressing more gratitude, even when it brought up feelings of shame at his inadequacies. They both valued depending on each other, a need that neither, at least in their softer moments, felt compelled to deny. Needing each other physically, even if sex wasn't the same, was part of that.

They could also laugh. One day they burst into laughter together about the ridiculousness of something, seemingly to do with his Russian ex-brother-in-law, whose ill-fated sexual exploits could be relied on to offer a burst of ribald humor between them. I had a feeling of being partly shielded, partly left out, as they spoke in code, two decades of shared meanings and allusions encrypted in their smiles. They'd have to adjust to the new normal in their intimate life, but somehow the menopause storm clouds were now moving on. The sun was out until the next marital weather system came through. Nothing fixed, nothing solved, I thought. The same old insoluble problems. But they could play, and sometimes they lit each other up in a real way.

*   *   *

"WE'RE HERE BECAUSE Henry won't get his act together," Marla said abruptly, once seated. Henry laughed as if she'd made a humorous comment that had nothing to do with him. A friendly couple in their midforties, they entered my office for the first time that day and both offered jokey greetings that fell curiously flat. "Helloo, helloo, helloo," Henry had cheerily said, by way of introduction. "It's a zoo out there," Marla chuckled, referring to the crowded waiting room. I was put on edge by their jauntiness, and the feeling compounded when I watched Henry lower himself into one of my chairs. Prompted by the complaints of unhappy couples that felt forced to sit too close together, I had recently replaced a couch with two chairs. Now, I saw that the sides of the chair slightly squeezed Henry's girth, and I was embarrassed by my insensitive choice of furniture.

" 'Won't get his act together'? What does that mean?" I glanced at Henry.

"Well, for one thing, Henry's gained a lot of weight in the past few years." Marla had beautifully smooth skin and was curvy and plump, on the voluptuous side of heavy. "Now he has trouble performing. And he's not doing anything about it."

Her openness was almost refreshing, but I also felt a bit taken aback by her speedy directness about sensitive matters. I looked over at Henry, curious how he'd respond.

"She's right. I've had problems with weight, and my performance, for a while. I can understand why she's not happy about it."

"How do you feel about it?" I asked.

"I feel bad that I haven't made it a priority. Marla's been telling me I should get it checked out. But now that our insurance has changed, I don't really have a doctor. I'd do anything to make Marla happy, she knows that. But I'm kind of at a loss."

I felt a ripple of frustration with Henry's way of talking. In two minutes, layers of obfuscation and self-erasure had enveloped whatever nugget of truth lay within his words. Despite his imposing presence, I couldn't hear *him* in what he was saying. He was eager to accommodate and quick to absorb blame, yet it seemed like a reflex to protect him from something—perhaps from being cut to the core by the reality of his problems, or from facing his paralysis in dealing with them. Was this what Marla's unvarnished mode of speech was meant to disrupt?

In the first few sessions, I took the role of forthright adviser, helping Henry and Marla clarify the steps to address his weight and sexual issue, and exerting a constant, mild pressure on Henry to follow through. This met with all manner of genial resistance, yet after two months of my patiently refusing to accept his roadblocks—the difficulties of sorting out his insurance, finding a doctor, etc.—I was rewarded by the news that Henry had found a doctor he liked, and a month later he had had a full examination. His blood tests revealed high cholesterol and insulin resistance, both of which related to his obesity and sexual performance. Problems with performance certainly contributed to his lack of desire. But body fat too was a culprit, since it meant higher levels of a body chemical that binds testosterone and thus diminishes desire. Henry's doctor prescribed exercise, weight loss, and a healthy diet as the first line of attack. Now that Henry had solid medical recommendations, the ball was in his court. On the psychological front, I recommended some books and the possibility of sex therapy, to help them chart a course for dealing with their sexual issues. Marla felt relieved to have a support and ally in me.

"I love Henry a lot, and I care about his health. I don't like to see him basically killing himself. It's not fair to him, it's not fair to me, and it's not fair to the kids. I'm glad he's doing something about it," said Marla. Then she turned to him. "It's not easy to say, but now I'm so used to sex not working that I can't muster much enthusiasm. I'm afraid that one day it's just not going to be enough, and I don't know what I'll do. It's like a ticking time bomb."

Henry's amiable veneer didn't crack, and I was struck by his lack of response. If he had registered more hurt, or worry, or any kind of emotional reaction in response to what she said, perhaps she might have softened her language by now, or they might have found a way to take up the substance of her concerns. I tried to help them talk about this raw issue in a way that was considerate of each other. I suggested that if he responded to her questions and concerns with more self-disclosure, she might feel less frustration and express herself more tactfully. I stopped him when he tried to deflect through lighthearted humor and began to probe the feelings of shame and inadequacy that kept him so bottled up. I was trying to help them find a more expressive language with which to discuss the hurt, anger, rejection, and shame that had coalesced around his sexual problem and the issue of weight, and to approach it with a vulnerability that it seemed they had long ago armored themselves against.

As dutifully as they listened to me, their exchanges continued to be ineffectual. Marla's directness and Henry's impermeability clearly fed on each other. Had it always been this way? As things went along, they reminded me of some other couples I'd seen where they seemed to be able to talk about physical facts, but unable to translate their experience into emotional language that successfully communicated how they *felt*. Sexual acts and exercise regimes and dietary restrictions and even bowel habits were discussed openly, laid out without a trace of reticence, while the language for emotions remained underdeveloped. Each week as I tried to grab hold of an issue, it would strangely evanesce. Henry intended to exercise, but he was so busy at work. He had been trying to implement some portion control, but nighttime snacking set him back. He and Marla meant to do their partner exercises to address the sexual issue, but they were too tired at night.

"I guess I feel at this point I should either accept you for who you are or decide I can't tolerate things the way they are and leave," said Marla a few months in, plainspoken still. "But to hang around and keep badgering you, that seems a little sick."

"It's hard to know where the line is," I said. "When does confronting your partner end up feeling like punishing them for something they can't help? Henry, do you feel badgered?"

"I don't feel badgered exactly. I guess sometimes I feel judged." He hesitated for a moment, as if considering whether to say what was on his mind. "But just for the record, I think Marla actually contributes to my eating habits. She's the one baking the cakes and putting the butter on the popcorn. It's not a one-way street." It was a relief to see him assert his viewpoint.

"If you can't beat 'em, join 'em," Marla declared flatly, parrying his cliché with one of her own.

I remembered a conversation we'd had early on, when they'd talked about their shared pleasure hanging around in their pajamas on the weekend (had I remembered right that they'd said "*matching* pajamas"?), eating and watching movies, in a kind of cocoon of similarity and friendly gratification. I'd thought, at the time, how much like siblings they seemed, somehow inhibited in being different, separate, and sexual. Their relationship to food was shared, even if the genetic lottery meant that its results showed up more on Henry's frame. Despite Marla's admirable qualities as a straight shooter, this story said something to me about how difficult it was for them to create a differentiated, adult bond. The matching-pajamas vignette had overwhelmed me a bit at the time with its aura of fusion. But I was beginning to wonder whether, for complicated and still mysterious reasons, there wasn't a way to turn their relationship into anything else. I tried to look on the bright side. In our months of working together, they'd taken classes together in French, Italian, and Indian cuisine. Food was truly a source of creativity, pleasure, and playfulness between them too.

Two years after they'd left therapy I saw Henry and Marla on an airport shuttle back to our home city. They had just visited their older son, they told me, who now lived in Pittsburgh. Henry looked much the same, a little grayer; Marla had gained about fifty pounds. We exchanged pleasantries, and for days afterward I found myself thinking about them. What emotional deal had they finally struck? Had they tacitly agreed to match themselves up, or down, on their degree of body vitality? Perhaps to stay together, they'd aligned their desires and longings, settled on shared methods. Perhaps they had decided to give up together, or to simply enjoy what they had.

Weight is tricky. There may be no marital complaint that lights up internet comment boards with more vitriol, misinformation, and gender warfare. Some complaining partners are conflicted, guilt-ridden, even mournful. They love their spouse, are concerned for his or her health, want to be more helpful, and wish they felt differently. Others seem insensible to glaring evidence of their obese partner's depression, alcoholism, or crippled self-esteem. One common refrain is men's trouble accepting their wives' weight gain, conveyed via agonized or angry declarations that they *just aren't attracted anymore*. They disrespect their spouse's "lack of willpower," but their bigger beef is that they feel disrespected *themselves* by their spouses' indifference to the necessary conditions for sexual desire. These pronouncements are routinely met by four kinds of responses: the pile-on male response, emphasizing the visual basis of male sexual attraction and blaming wives for laziness and lack of willpower; the disgusted female response, targeting these complainers as "shaming," "shallow," and even "pig-gish"; the sympathetic response, that both spouses owe each other an effort to stay attractive; and the "spiritual" response that love is more than flesh deep.

The "lack of respect" model conveys real pain, but it also displays a psychological tone deafness. A retired pediatrician from East Texas penned a defense of disgruntled husbands called *Gain Weight, Lose Your Mate* (the sole review on Amazon: "This is a great essay on the state of the American wife. . . . Unfortunately, it will never reach its intended audience. . . . [My wife] wouldn't crack the cover, and got angry with me for reading it"). As a long-form version of the sputtering diatribes on the internet, his opus shares an oblivious-ness of the human effect of criticism, blame, and personal attack. "Daryl," a thirty-eight-year-old mechanical engineer, "began to complain at every opportunity and shared with Jeana that he was very dissatisfied with the way she had begun to look. . . . He began to feel that no matter how much he complained or shared his feel-ings with Jeana, she was not going to lose weight." Since when, exactly, did complaining about how another person manages her body result in cooperative responsiveness? The issue is further confused by the pervasive cultural misconception that obesity is due to lack of willpower, and solvable by diet and exercise alone. Even the more tempered of those commenting on the internet tend to misconstrue their partners' failure to lose weight as a stubborn refusal to respond to their wishes, completely overlooking the empirical evidence that self-help is often insufficient.

Buried in this inflammatory debate is a real dilemma on which people genuinely disagree: What, if any, is the appropriate way to bring up concern about one's spouse's body? If you are living with another person 24-7, you are going to have feelings about his or her body, negative and positive. I don't believe that bodies are a special, off-limits case, but rather are just one of the whole range of sensitive topics that couples need to become skilled at discussing. I also believe that putting off such discussions doesn't help. People avoid talking because they are afraid of hurting feelings, and because they are afraid nothing will change. But waiting is likely to make both problems worse: your reactions will have built up covertly and will therefore hurt *more* when they are confessed. The problem will also have become a more entrenched part of the relationship. It is harder to come back from there, and you will be less able to deliver your message with compassion.

So how do people successfully approach these sensitive topics? No single approach works for everyone, but I favor a combination of strong support and honesty. The challenge is to balance truth with tact. Incrementalism is your friend. There's no gain in blunt declarations of waning attraction; but there's value in voicing prospective worry if that's an important part of your emotional reality. So, regarding weight, one might say, "Hey, I feel a little anxious bringing this up, because it's so important that you understand how much I love you for who you are inside, and that hasn't changed at all. I want us to have a long, healthy, active life together, and to keep being able to do all the stuff we love to do, and as we get older, it's not as easy. So I'm wondering if we can find a time to talk about how to stay in decent shape and maybe support each other in doing it." Presumably your partner knows you pretty well, and (s)he may smell a rat. "Are you telling me I'm fat?" (s)he says. "I do notice your weight," you respond honestly, "but that stuff happens with age. It doesn't change the fact that I love you. I'm no perfect physical specimen, either. It's just that I think we're a great team and I want us to stay as healthy and attractive as we can for each other. Do you think maybe we can work something out together?"

To create the best context for understanding, especially with sensitive issues such as weight, we lead with the positive whenever possible. Leading with the positive helps the listener to consider the more difficult part of the message, to *think* about it rather than simply reacting to an "attack." In this, as in so many difficult couple conversations, the goal is to dwell in the golden ring, finding a spirit of collaborative problem-solving at just the moment people are most vulnerable to feeling criticized or misunderstood. When partners share their thoughts and feelings in this mind-set, they can both look at the issue, mull it over, and figure out how to respond. This contrasts with the runaway train of reaction and counterreaction.

These conversations sometimes break down because no matter how tactful the one broaching the topic tries to be, the partner's response is something like "How *dare* you think you have any say over *my* body [drinking, smoking, eating, etc.]?" I think this exchange bears a closer look because embedded within it are important questions about the individual and the marriage. It's true that decisions about one's body are one's own. Adults' attempts to manage other adults' bodies range from patronizing to controlling to perverse to downright sadistic. In a marriage, respecting the other person's autonomy in decisions concerning his own body is *basic*. But how a given partner manages his body will have *effects* on his partner, and those effects will have to be honestly dealt with if alienation is to be avoided.

Sometimes, in exchanges like the one just described, the partner who attempts to tactfully broach the awkward topic is voicing concerns that are actually *shared* by the target partner. The target partner's indignation, while a valid defense of bodily autonomy, operates as a deflector, converting into an argument about insensitivity or intrusion what could more profitably be understood as a sad, scary discussion about vulnerable feelings. Being mad instead of sad is one common way we deal with a lack of control and a sense of failure, feelings that often accompany destructive physical habits. (Women in particular, barraged as they are by toxic cultural messages about their bodies, can easily feel crushed when versions of these same messages are delivered by their male partners.) Here is where being able to think *both* about your own *and* your partner's reality becomes both critically important and highly challenging. For the target partner—let's say she's a woman—the emotional task is to analyze what piece of her offended reaction derives from her discomfort at being confronted with a feeling that she *herself* shares. When she discovers that her partner has expressed a highly uncomfortable message with which she nonetheless *agrees*, her highest-leverage focus is her relationship to *herself*.

Much has been written about the self-critical voices that women direct toward their own bodies. A raft of feminist and psychological literature plums this complex phenomenon, including its links to the mother-daughter relationship. Women's relationships with their bodies and appearance are private, complex, and often tortured in ways that transcend the reactions of husbands and lovers. That's not to say that men play no part. As troubling as the male gaze may be to women, losing it creates troubles of its own. Enlightened men want to treat their wives as complex individuals subject to unforgiving social pressures to be youthfully attractive. Evolved men who love their wives also tend to be aware of their own tendency to objectify younger female forms, and they refrain from becoming too absorbed in doing so. In my experience, men are much less judgmental toward women's bodies than women themselves are. Men have their individual tastes and predilections, but the vast majority of them seem less distressed by a love handle or a bit of cellulite than women are. I wish I had a nickel (okay, a hundred-dollar bill) for every time a man expressed to me his fervent wish *not* that his wife lose her baby weight or alter her less-than-perky breasts, but that she be less *self-conscious* about the baby weight or the shape of her breasts; in other words, that she feel freer and more confident in the sexual body she *has*. While she's busy hiding due to her ostensibly lost attractiveness, he's busy bemoaning that her *hiding* is what's making her less attractive.

It takes a lot of energy to hide, and the truth is, feeling attractive starts with yourself. It's great to get a compliment, but if your sense of well-being hinges on it, you don't stand a chance; it's a bottomless pit. Attractiveness starts with going *inside*, and asking, "What brings me *joy*? What would it mean to feel satisfied, to satisfy *myself*?" It's easy to get distracted by starting an internal argument with your partner or your mother, or by launching into a litany of negative self-talk. You create a lot of mental space by stopping the self-nagging habit. Encourage yourself, be gentle toward yourself. The key is, don't get stuck; take just one step forward, then another. If your mate is more attracted as a result, great. But do it for *yourself*. When you feel more whole, you'll feel more graciousness toward everyone else. No one escapes the loss of youth and the passage of time—male, female, gay, straight, he, she, they—so the question is, what are you going to do? If you're lucky, you may have *thirty or forty more healthy years* on the planet to enjoy beauty, joy, and vitality. One answer might be *Step it up. Don't waste the present moment.*

MANY YEARS AGO, I was stuck in a car for two hours with a couple, perhaps in their late sixties, who had offered me a ride home after a multigenerational social event. As we ensconced ourselves in their Volvo sedan, they couldn't have been more genial; so when they let loose a few innocuous jabs at each other, I dismissed it as normal bickering. But an hour in, they were hopelessly embroiled in a baffling but obviously time-honored battle about the wife's favoritism toward their son. Their parries were cut with a hateful sarcasm, and I wondered if they'd forgotten I was there or didn't care or truly had no idea what they sounded like. By the time they spit me out of the car, their vitriol had reached Shakespearean intensity.

I remember thinking at the time, with the smugness of youth, why do these old people even bother to fight anymore? It seemed a little pathetic that they were still arguing over ancient grievances, and odd that they still regarded themselves—and each other—as worthy of so much energy. Maybe keeping their wounds fresh was how they managed to feel vigorous. In the decades since, I've jettisoned my misconception that people age out of being at the center of their own dramas. I'm convinced now that with age, the stakes only get higher. If we've acquired psychological maturity and skillful modes of interaction, aging can lead to more serenity and satisfaction. But if we haven't, aging only compounds the existing problems in our relationships.

Think of the pressures. Eyesight, hearing, stamina. Hips, knees, feet, shoulders. Mental acuity, word finding, names. Stairs, laundry, computers, cooking—eventually, they all become challenging. And these are just the mundane, entirely expectable arenas of aging. Then there's cancer, diabetes, heart attacks, early-onset Alzheimer's, intractable pain. Vulnerabilities proliferate, and the confrontations with diminishment expand. We might hope that declining energy or mental vagueness will aid our acceptance of our partners and ourselves. But too often it works in just the opposite direction, with the anxieties of decline heightening our tendencies to take things out on each other. Ask anyone with aged, infirm, unhappily married parents. Or recall Stephen and Diana from chapter 3. If nothing ever changed between them, we might easily envision them in old age, their impatient commands to "Grow up!" now replaced with "You're losing it!"

Worries about survival dispose us to a seesaw state of mind. It makes everything worse, but when we're scared, we can't see it. We become like drowning men dragging down those who might save us. With age, we need a golden-ring consciousness more than ever, but the hurdles are newly daunting. Our anxieties are existential. If we're lucky, the slow pace of aging can help us work out our relation to it. "Let me tell you about my doorknob problem," said a friend. "My wife started complaining about the doorknobs in our house, and how hard they are to turn. At first, I saw it as just the latest edition of an ongoing marital quarrel: I think she's all about comfort regardless of the expense, and she thinks I'm cheap and a bit judgmental. It felt so familiar that it took me a while to realize that, in fact, she was saying something new. It *hurt* her to turn the doorknobs, and it had to do with her aging wrists. This wasn't our usual tug-of-war about expenses. This was reality, moving in one direction and one direction only. I could pretend it was the same old conflict, but that wouldn't be compassionate or fair. I was sad to realize that. Then I changed the doorknobs."

My friend chose reality over delusion, acceptance over blame, and that was a loving move. We depend on our bodies, just as we depend on other people. And like other people, our bodies aren't entirely under our control—they let us down, they get sick, they die. What helps us face these realities is love—emotionally secure relationships, and a nurturing attitude toward ourselves. Both were palpable for Susan and Laura, a couple in their late forties, who struggled with Susan's multiple sclerosis (MS). They had been together for seven years and were raising two children together, each from a previous marriage. Susan had been diagnosed with MS in her midthirties and had enjoyed about a decade relatively symptom-free. More recently, the relapse-remitting type had transitioned to a secondary progressive type, and both women felt frightened by Susan's worsening symptoms. Her fatigue and intermittent depression, as well as her occasionally blinding headaches, were features of her illness that she and Laura had developed systems to address. But her pain, spastic muscles, and bowel and bladder problems were worsening and leading to more overall distress. Their burdens were substantial, with jobs, kids, pets, a house, and a demanding, difficult illness. Life together was now made up of continual modification, tweaking, and fine-tuning. The chances for miscommunication were vast. But they seemed to manage so relatively well that I became fascinated by observing, at close range, what exactly they were doing right.

First, they were good at asking for help. They had contacted me proactively, saying they wanted to use me "as a sounding board" to make sure they weren't "missing anything" as they headed into a period of new challenges. They depended on their larger community, fully expecting people would want to support them, and expressing gratitude when they did. Second, they were both funny and had a talent for defusing tension through finding a comic element in almost any situation. They could crack each other up, even in grim moments. Third, they both had a refreshing attitude of acceptance toward themselves and others. For couples dealing with MS, or any other illness, the caretaking partner is always at risk of abdicating her own needs, and the relationship inevitably suffers. Laura was honest but compassionate in expressing her difficulties with Susan's illness. Finally, though their tempers flared sometimes, both were good at apologizing and accepting apologies.

Those who have given a lot of thought to living with a chronic illness such as MS suggest that coping is enhanced by regarding the *illness* as akin to a "third person in the marriage—one with demands, desires, and a disposition all its own." Making space for the illness's presence is not so different from making space for a child or a job or a relationship—or for that matter, an aging body. Susan and Laura were unlucky in being hit with Susan's illness, but they were lucky in their basic psychological health. They were "good at being dependent," as the couple therapist Dan Wile put it. " 'How dependent is that person?' is the wrong question," he writes. "Everyone is very dependent. The question is 'how skillful is the person at being dependent?' . . . People who are good at being dependent don't even look dependent. They just look like engaging, appreciative, responsive, and loving people who are successful in getting you to want to comfort and take care of them. They make it fun to do so. They are people you'd want as friends. They are people you'd want to marry."

HOW DO WE age well? We accept the things we've lost, or never had, in order to fully embrace and *live* with those that we do. The psychologist Peter Levine, an expert on trauma, likens us to trees whose "gnarls, burls, and misshapen limbs speak of injuries and obstacles encountered through time and overcome. The way a tree grows around its past contributes to its exquisite individuality, character, and beauty." Letting go, whether of a person, an illusion of self-sufficiency, or a dewy, youthful version of self, takes courage and effort and sometimes even a period of despair. But sometimes it is the only way to go forward fully alive.

Aging well also means staying in touch with *youthfulness*—not the look, but the feeling. The best symbol may be found in music. We can all remember adolescence, when "our" music had urgent, even mystical importance to us. When we listen to it decades later, we're instantly dropped down into our youthful selves—in body, feeling, and memory. It's possible to get stuck there, of course; ask Christina, lost in her nostalgic loop, or any middle-aged person who can't seem to get interested in listening to anything other than the same old grooves. But think, too, about all the ways people turn toward music in midlife when they're seeking more intensity and adventure: joining a band, taking singing lessons, taking up a new kind of dancing, digitizing entire music collections, sharing music (when they let us) with our own teenage kids.

Music is all about time, yet it takes us out of time. It evokes the memory of our youthful selves, but connects us to youthful energy in the now. The novelist Nick Hornby wrote about it in terms of rock music:

> Youth is a quality not unlike health: it's found in greater abundance among the young, but we all need access to it. . . . I'm not talking about the accouterments of youth: the unlined faces, the washboard stomachs, the hair . . . I'm talking about the energy, the wistful yearning, the inexplicable exhilaration, the sporadic sense of invincibility, the hope that stings like chlorine. . . . Rock'n'roll was and remains necessary because: who doesn't need exhilaration and a sense of invincibility, even if it's only now and again?

Music offers more than a distilled essence of youthfulness; it also delivers an almost overwhelming sense of joy and *rightness* when musicians we love echo, vary, sample, and respond to their influences, paying homage to the past with original and fresh versions of their own. It's not a bad model for marriage, or for life. We seek out variation on enjoyable themes. We render the familiar more exciting, and more cherished, by experimenting and improvising. We keep listening for everything we ever loved in each new thing we hear. Perhaps we're not talking so much about youthfulness as the joy of being *alive*. It's still available, always available, until the moment it's not. "Soul clap its hands and sing, and louder sing/For every tatter in its mortal dress," wrote Yeats. Yes, our bodies ultimately fail us, but in the meantime, we're *here*, and there's no end to great music.

The Empty Nest: Children, Parents, and the Turning of the Generations

"There's something scary about being left alone with your spouse," said Eric, who'd agreed to speak to me about the empty nest when he was feeling deeply dejected about his son's departure for college. A friend of a friend, he was the fifty-seven-year-old father of two children, a twenty-six-year-old daughter and an eighteen-year-old son. When I suggested coffee, he jumped at the chance.

"Middle age is *nothing*," he said, fiddling with the foam on his drink. "The real challenge is when the kids leave. Middle age is a gentle, rolling hill. The empty nest is Mount Everest. I said to my wife, Hannah, the other day, 'Why are people like us still married?' And we're actually pretty compatible. She joked to me, 'I guess if we don't keep each other from doing anything we want to do, there's no need to get divorced.'"

A friend's mother says that your fifties are about escaping the "two D's," death and divorce. Unlucky friends and relatives have been hit with terminal illnesses. Divorces are commonplace. Our kids begin to see us age, and we see them becoming full-fledged adults. Our parents get sick and die, and we know *this is going to happen to us*. Yet, just as we begin to contemplate the end of the line, we are also looking at a period of great potential. If our health holds, we can put our time, skills, experience, self-knowledge, and even wisdom to productive and satisfying use.

In the midst of it is the complicated emotional matter of getting the kids launched into adulthood, and that can be easier said than done. Just as parents of babies nurture the illusion that it will get easier when their children are older, empty nesters delude themselves that launching their kids is a one-shot deal. In fact, it's protracted, mysterious, and often messy, for children *and* parents.

Perhaps the most apt symbol for this complicated leave-taking is what happens to kids' rooms. "Hannah and I have gotten pretty feisty over Tobias's room," Eric said. "She wants to clear it out and make it into a guest room. To her, it feels like a mess waiting to be cleaned up. To me, it's a bit like a shrine, or at least a comforting reminder. I like going in there and looking at the old piggy bank on his shelf and the books he was reading in first grade." Loving parents are in both camps: those who keep their kids' rooms indefinitely, and those who convert them immediately. Practically, there are the realities of limited living space, but emotionally, there's a delicate drama of beginnings and endings, inclusion and exclusion, authority and equality. When parents unilaterally repurpose a room with no discussion, I sense a dismissive attachment style is at work, a minimization of dependency and emotional need. Parents sometimes appropriate a child's room to emphatically break from their own identity as parents, as a way to launch *themselves* into a new life stage. "I'm done!" the mother cries, as she commandeers the room to finally start her new business. They can also have less-than-savory memories about the uses to which the adolescent put the room ("Is that the smell of pot? What are they doing in there?") and desire a cleanup.

Overall, I believe that a bit of negotiation between children and parents, out of respect for the multilayered meanings involved, has a psychological benefit. Children have strong feelings about what happens to their rooms. For them, as for parents, leaving home doesn't happen all at once. They want to come back and enter the repository of their childhood memories from time to time. Coming home on holiday breaks, they regress in the setting of their childhood and adolescence. Both sides may feel a trace of annoyance, but also comfort. For young adults, it's a form of refueling, drinking at the well of security so they can go explore again.

"They leave, but they still need us," said Eric. "In fact, I'm amazed by how much they keep needing. The focal length of parenting changes, but not the basic need for attention. My daughter borrows the car regularly. We still pay her cell phone bill. When she needed to get her own health insurance, she asked for a lot of hand-holding to figure it out. Hannah and I don't always agree on the right level of support." They didn't agree on how much independence to require, but they were also different in what they sought emotionally from their relationships with their children. "Hannah said that when we took Tobias to college, I was acting as if we were shipping him to the far end of the Siberian tundra," Eric said. "Toby and I are texting daily about little things, jokes, stuff we see online. If we ever get to a point where he wants to move home after college, Hannah and I are going to have a conflict on our hands. I'll be thinking, 'How nice,' and she'll be thinking we ought to put a limit on it. She wants a cleaner launch—more privacy and freedom for us, more independence for him. I get it. She feels that when he's twenty-two or twenty-three, it'll be time to push the baby bird out of the nest. But I feel the whole thing takes time, and you can't really rush it."

Haunting the bittersweet saying of good-bye to children is the worry that they will fail to launch. Some can't find direction, some can't find a *job*. Families are complex systems, and a child's success in leaving also depends on the ability of those left behind to let her go. It can be a painful and revealing moment about the marriage. A mother might realize that she's come to rely on her son for emotional sustenance that she's stopped seeking from her husband. A husband may fear the renewed focus on his marriage once the clamor of childrearing has drawn to a close. Yet, just as parents are beginning to adjust to the new normal and hope to feel satisfied by a job well done, their child can introduce a whole new set of needs—for financial support, for psychotherapy, for housing. Even in less pressing circumstances, young adults need practical and emotional support, and the "not-yet-empty nest" can last for a decade.

When a sense of "home" isn't solid, it's harder for young adult children to push away. Yet the divorce bump that attends the empty nest indicates that some portion of couples wait until kids leave to break up the family home. *Gray divorce* refers to the trend of people over fifty leaving their marriages, and the numbers are greater than ever before. Waiting makes sense in terms of parents' desire to live with their children full-time until the end of childhood, but it also puts kids in a complicated position. Just as they are trying to separate, they are pulled back into the family fray by disruption and pain. Affairs complicate things still further. Despite their best intentions, parents can become needy and rely on their children at a time when children's primary job is to individuate and begin their own lives. Ironically, the child-focused, couple-neglecting model of contemporary marriage is one likely cause of down-the-road marital disaffection, which then contributes to gray divorce and disrupts the lives of late-adolescent and young-adult children.

Even those who hope to stay married echo Eric's trepidation at being "left alone" with their spouses. They don't always know what to expect. They may be quietly afraid that there will be nothing left to salvage. One woman worried that, given what workaholics she and her husband both were, the departure of the children would lead to their almost complete disconnection. A man said he could still call up the traumatic surprise of his "happy" parents divorcing when he left for college and wondered what precautions he could take in his marriage as his own daughter approached college age. One lithe woman said she'd spent the last twenty years managing children, home, and social life while her high-powered husband made the money. "With my last kid leaving, a big part of my job description is going away. It makes me insecure. It's embarrassing to admit, but will my husband see me as 'obsolete'?" Another man spoke of how extraordinarily trying for his marriage his son's autism had been, and how hard it was to feel hopeful or excited about the future of the marriage. A woman said simply, "We just don't know how to talk anymore."

THE EMPTY NEST gives us a further push toward individuation. When Sadie and Sean's third and last child left for college, Sadie was itching to begin her creative life in earnest. She wanted to lose herself in her studio and focus on her art. She no longer wanted to be the family caretaker. She wanted the freedom to work through the night, to not be home for dinner, and to not even *think* about cooking dinner. One day, after she'd left early in the morning and didn't get home till late at night (she'd powered down her cell phone for the duration), Sean went to bed, turned out all the lights, and didn't speak to her when she rang the bell at ten forty-five (she was notoriously forgetful about her keys). That was when they sought me out.

"She just—disappeared," Sean said with an exaggerated eyebrow-raise of disbelief. A fifty-nine-year-old director of a nonprofit, he was a devoted and caring family man who was easily irritated. He seemed to be trying to cast general aspersion on her judgment.

"I really should have called or left a note. I'm sorry about that," Sadie said. "But you knew I was at my studio. And you know I get lost in my work." Sadie's manner was charming and conciliatory, but her eyes were sharp and unwavering.

Sean began noisily moving into place a phalanx of justifications for his right to be the center of Sadie's attention. *He* had largely supported the family all these years and hadn't had time to develop "hobbies" (conveniently forgetting that diapers and PTA meetings and cooking dinner had not exactly been Sadie's "hobbies"). He skimmed over the many sacrifices and adjustments she had made to further his career. He offered his own workhorse mentality as a reason she should continue to be available. Reasonable as he tried to sound, I felt he was defending his disinclination to change. He was dependent on his routines and his ruts, and though they were in the service of adult responsibility, they also served as one giant comfort zone. I felt he should have been following her example, rather than insisting that she follow his.

Was Sadie neglecting her husband? Was she trying to escape the echoing emptiness of her home or her marriage? No, she was *developing an interest*. She finally had more time, and she threw herself into it. Sean and Sadie's dilemma gets to a core question of the empty nest: How does being an individual fit with being part of a couple? What interests and capacities do you want to develop as an individual? How do you continue to create closeness in your relationship? And how can these be integrated to each person's satisfaction?

Hearing about Sean and Sadie's situation reminded me of what defines a good childhood. You get to become completely absorbed in playing with your LEGOs or your dolls because you feel secure that, in the background, there are people who love you and take care of you. Shouldn't a long marriage offer a similar opportunity for *play*? The psychoanalyst Donald Winnicott was the twentieth century's most astute commentator on play. He thought that people live in three worlds simultaneously: the inner subjective world, the world of external reality, and a third, "transitional space" where we suspend the question of whether things are "real" or "not real." Play belongs in this transitional space. He coined the term "transitional object" to refer to those things in life, like a child's teddy bear, that exist in a zone where what's "pretend" and what's "real" can remain undecided. Winnicott believed that we retain this area of experience throughout life "in the intense experiencing that belongs to the arts and to religion and to imaginative living, and to creative scientific work." According to Winnicott, this "intense experiencing" begins with trust. Being relaxed is a precondition for the creative activity of play, and in childhood we first experience being relaxed when in the presence of a trusted other. Paradoxically, we learned to take pleasure in being *alone* from having confidence that the person we depended on was reliably *present* in the background; even when we forgot her, she was still there.

In a couple, allowing each other aloneness is part of allowing each other to explore, have interests, and play. One puts oneself in the other's place through sympathetic imagination. Each person recognizes that "my partner has to do this to be who (s)he is." Each can tolerate the idea "you will forget about me, will forget I'm alive" for some stretch of time, and each accepts, supports, and respects that. At the same time, they share an understanding: "I need you to come back and remember I'm alive, and that I need things from you." In a good relationship, we are constantly calibrating and adjusting the elastic band of distance and closeness. Sometimes it's pulled tighter and sometimes it's more slack. But the security built over time allows for solitude and immersive experience.

I spoke to a devout Baptist, Anna, who'd grown up in a conservative community and married young. But despite her traditional roots, she and her husband had always agreed to make room for their own interests. "I think the hardest thing to negotiate in marriage is time for yourself," she said. "I think both people have to stand up and claim it. When you do that, there might be a struggle, but there won't be resentment and blame." Anna took up djembe drumming after her last child left home. "I want to learn things, not just watch other people," she said. "There's a thrill in being a novice. It's really joyful, the feeling that the brain can still learn things. I hear rhythm everywhere now, even in the supermarket, and it's exciting to realize I can be aware of hearing new sounds. Drumming is communal by nature. My teacher said that in drumming groups, the heartbeats of the drummers become synchronized. Whether it's a metaphor or not, that's the feeling. It's bliss." Her interest in drumming was *hers*, and her husband was outside it. But he could accept and tolerate being outside, neither disengaging nor intruding. He could also appreciate what it meant to her. "Last Christmas, my husband got me a beautiful pink djembe," she said, "much nicer than the one I'd found on Amazon. It meant a lot."

A research study of empty-nest couples found that for some, the challenge was feeling guilty at spending time on individual pursuits when they "should" have been spending more together time with their partner. Yet, interestingly, people's sense of guilt arose from their *subjective worry* about their partner's objections, rather than the partner's *actual interference* with their individual goals. This tells us that a big part of the adjustment is *internal*. Our evolving understanding of our individual desires needs to be shared in conversation, not buried under fears and projections. Anna and her husband had a shared understanding of the high value they both placed on individual pursuits. Sean and Sadie were in more conflict, which is why they ended up in my office. They had to struggle to figure out their preferred calibration at this stage of life. Messy as their negotiations were, though, they ultimately benefited as a couple from Sadie's conviction. At times in a marriage, one partner carries the banner for the interests of the individuals. It may elicit protest, but suppressing individuality also corrodes the bond and isn't viable over the long term.

Not all play is solitary; playing is also something couples do together. Like many couples, Sean and Sadie felt they had lost a certain lightness and playfulness over the years. As we talked, I inwardly mused about how incredibly important, and yet how perishable, a sense of lightness and playfulness can be. A couple seeing a sense of play in each other is a potent source of connection. "Going through some old home-movie clips," a man recounted to me, "I found some footage of my wife flying a kite with our son. They were totally involved, and laughing together. I showed it to my wife—to give her the pleasure of remembering it, but also to say, 'I see that playfulness in you.'" Even when things are bleak—especially when things are bleak—humor is a saving grace. A friend of mine said that when she and her husband were on the brink of divorce, black humor would get them through; they'd agree they couldn't split because neither wanted custody of the kids. Problems and preoccupations, losses and disappointments, can so easily encroach on our moods, and we increase our own suffering when we refuse to lighten the mood.

A couple who enjoy each other's company can feel, once the kids leave, that "it's like dating," and sex becomes a more central source of play. A boon of the empty nest is more privacy, more freedom, and more fun. There is no one to hear, no one to interrupt, no one to worry about walking in late at night. The fear of pregnancy is long gone. For couples with entrenched patterns of disconnection, though, the departure of kids can be like staring into a chasm of uncertainty. For them, trying to plunge straightaway into the high-vulnerability arena of sex may not be the most effective way back into an intimate relationship. The avenues for play are endless, travel being a big one at this stage of life. But music, sports, art, humor—any shared area of play primes the pump of shared pleasure.

Social psychologists have shown that when couples share in novel, arousing activities together, their satisfaction in the relationship increases. We don't tend to think of long-term relationship experiences—being in year fifteen of a marriage, for instance, or raising teenage children together—as forms of *novelty*. However, the researchers' findings aren't about extreme sports or pricey adventures, they're about the conditions that encourage a sense of self-expansion. A new intimate relationship is exciting because couples have frequent and intense conversations that involve risk-taking and self-disclosure. The problem in long-term relationships is not that these kinds of conversations aren't possible; it's that people stop *having* them. Conversations at *any* phase of a relationship can contribute to a sense of excitement and positive feeling if they include emotional vulnerability and self-revelation.

Life presents us with novel experiences just by virtue of time going by. Our position and perspective keep changing. The question is, can you experience new facets of yourself and express them with your partner? You'd be surprised how many people can't, no matter how many river-rafting expeditions or treks in Nepal they can muster. Whether thrill seekers or homebodies, plenty of people avoid opening up to something new happening. Filling their minds with distractions or holding on to past injuries, they can't or won't play.

Couple pleasures do not even have to be as "dramatic" as a self-disclosing conversation to be satisfying. Winnicott wrote, "Being able to enjoy being alone along with another person who is also alone is in itself an experience of health." Younger people find nothing quite so terrifying as "the old couple at the restaurant who have nothing to talk about." It floats as a dreaded specter on the road to loneliness, decrepitude, and death. Yet, if we explore such a scene from Winnicott's perspective, it may not be what it looks like from the outside. The enjoyment of shared solitude is an emblem of confidence in the other's presence, and in one's own capacity to be alone. The relationship pendulum need not only swing between desire and excitement, and boredom and disengagement. In an in-between place, being together in a state of trust is possible. We trust in the expectable return of desire, stimulation, and initiative within the relationship. When we truly play, or truly relax, we feel secure enough to let things unfold in their own way and in their own time.

Remember our discussion of marriage as a story? The critic Jonathan Gottschall observed that stories are about "great predicaments." Love stories qualify—whether on the screen, on the page, or in our lives. But how does making coffee, loading the dishwasher, or having the flu figure in? As a couple therapist, I observe all these "insignificant" activities turning operatic when they make their way into the "great predicament" of people's marital discord. But I don't shudder at the silent couple at the restaurant because I celebrate that for some couples a blessed point arrives when their "great predicaments" can become located in their "play." They can leave things unsaid, alone together in the "transitional space" of imaginative and aesthetic experience. If we are gaining any wisdom as we age, melodrama and grandiose self-stories tend to lose their appeal. The basis of meaning shifts from individual self-importance (great! passionate!) to the cherishing of relationships (good, ordinary). The surface of a couple's interaction may look fairly serene, even *boring*. But inside, they feel both each other's nurturing presence *and* the freedom and security to become absorbed in something other than each other.

If the core empty-nest question is how the individual and the couple fit together, in some marriages clearly they don't, at least for a time. Consequently, perhaps we should make more room for phases in long marriages where people seek more independence from each other. Some relationships, by common agreement, do well with a lot of separation; for others, time apart is a way to keep the commitment going in the face of confusion and uncertainty. Alternative marital arrangements require a high degree of self-knowledge, courage, and creativity, with each couple charting its own course on how to nurture and protect their attachment in the face of separateness. But given the forms of escapism people routinely resort to in marriage—drinking, TV, the internet, work, their phones—taking time apart may be a braver and more effective way to engage questions about commitment and connection than is disengaged cohabitation.

The Chicago-based family therapist Karen Skerrett and I talked about this issue. "People seem to think there's only one way to be in a long-term marriage," she said. "When I talk to couples, they sometimes feel they are burnt out, and one or the other needs a reset. I tell them that given their age and their point in marriage, this makes total sense. They get it intuitively. But trying to package the idea in the public domain, that's a lot harder. I often ask myself why we don't have categories for stop-outs or separations to help people reset. Why is this not done? The reason is hard to pin down. I think that trying to tease out what is genuinely developmental and progressive from everything else is a huge challenge."

"What seems to one person like a chance to refresh," I said, "might seem to the other like the first step toward divorce. I see couples in therapy sometimes where one wants some time apart, and the other says that if they do that, they want a divorce. It isn't always clear whether time apart will ultimately be pro-relationship or anti-relationship. Sometimes people don't know, but they feel they need to take the risk to find out."

"It's a risk for sure," Karen said. "But the key to making this work is that the couple comes at these conversations not just from the vantage of 'what I need' or 'what you need,' but what the *relationship* might need at a particular point. Sometimes people need to take time apart to find a way back into the relationship. Space and time can allow people to see themselves and their situation in a new light. There could be value to tipping the balance in our picture of long-term marriage toward a more spacious range of approaches, without a lot of stigma. But all that's likely to work best for people who can think about themselves *and* the relationship."

I told Karen of a sixty-three-year-old therapy patient who had divorced her husband when they were in their late forties. The reasons had centered on their sexual problems. "She grieves that she didn't take a longer view," I told Karen. "She said to me, 'The most important thing to me now is friendship, and I miss my ex-husband as my friend. At the time, I focused on feeling sexually dead in the relationship. But I think back and I wish we'd found another way to manage it. Maybe if we'd taken a bit of time apart, I could have struggled with how much I needed him in the context of the other things I thought I needed. What seemed like such a big problem then now feels like it was just a blip. If I had to do it over, I'd have made another choice.'"

*   *   *

THE DEPARTURE OF children is one common turning point in adulthood. The death of a parent is another. Because the death of a parent is so inevitable, we can be surprised by its shocking reverberations, including its profound effect on marriage. We enter a new stage of adulthood where a bulwark of elders no longer stands between ourselves and the end. Parental death brings us face-to-face with the clock. We perceive in an even more immediate way that our own time is limited. Matriarchs and patriarchs vanish; parents who were supportive are no longer there to offer support; high-maintenance parents who drained way too much energy now leave us relieved and strangely empty. The impact is unpredictable and not restricted to the death itself. There are the difficulties of the parents' aging and infirmities, the heavy burden of travel if they live far away, and agonizing decisions about moves and medical interventions, shadowed at times by complications with siblings and money. The sheer amount of energy required, and the depressing nature of the effort, take their own toll on people's inner resources. When death comes, people may be wholly unprepared for how it affects their attitude toward their spouse.

"The body. I still can't get it out of my mind," said Carolyn, a fifty-four-year-old wife and mother of two teenagers. She was sitting in therapy with me, replaying her father's death. "In those last moments, when I could tell he was going, I yelled, 'Daddy, Daddy, give me your arms!' It was this childlike pleading. I was saying, 'Don't leave me!' from somewhere deep in my gut. I had the crazy thought that he wouldn't leave me if I could just get him to give me his arms. It was like a dream, the endless seconds passing and his eyes not opening. I haven't called him Daddy in about forty years." Carolyn cried.

Her father had died six months before. She came to see me when he was dying, because she was terrified thinking of how she would live without him. His illness had pitched her into an awareness of how utterly she relied on him, even as he was, in her words, a "control freak." He was larger-than-life in her mind; both her parents were. She said drily that they'd always seemed "like people who would never get old and die." Carolyn reflected, "My parents created our world," referring to her siblings and their families. "Until now, I didn't realize how much I still saw myself as their daughter. Their friends, their social life, their vacations, their holiday celebrations—we adopted them all."

Partly Carolyn had been struggling because, under the threat of her father's impending death, she had felt a mounting disappointment in her husband. As a young woman, she'd been attracted by her husband's easygoing nature. He exerted no powerful counterforce to her family and didn't interfere with its agendas. She could relax with him, then head back into her family's stimulating fray. But now, anticipating her father's death and watching her mother's slower demise, her perception of her husband was changing, as if the marriage worked only within the larger family ecosystem.

"I've always been the manager of our family," Carolyn explained one day, "and now that I'm dealing with my parents, I need my husband to take more leadership. I need him to *figure out* what needs to be done and do it." We talked about the ways she'd subtly disempowered him over the years—summer vacation plans had always been made in concert with her family, and the kids' activities had followed her own family's interests. She also realized she was changing the terms on him, now that the prospect of losing her father meant losing a dominant male force in her life. "I sometimes think I'm mad at him because he isn't my dad," she admitted.

Choices about our marriages inevitably reference our parents in some way—the marriage our own parents had (or didn't have), the views and opinions they proffered, the kind of support or understanding they led us to expect (or not expect). Research suggests that people recover best from the death of a parent when they view their parents as loving but not the most important source of love in their lives. It is harder when a parent persists either as the main source of emotional support or has been a disappointment. For Carolyn, her parents had remained emotionally central, long after she'd had a family of her own. We reflected together on her father's status in her emotional world, and how it had limited her relationship with her husband in certain ways. Had she chosen someone to marry who would never compete with her father in her mind? She was trying to face the reality of her marriage at the same time she was trying to face the reality of her father's death, and the two were psychically intertwined.

As she was working with me to understand all this in the months after her father's death, her ninety-year-old mother took a fall. Within just two weeks, Carolyn was also having to face her mother's inexorable decline. "My mother was a robust, athletic woman, and lying in the hospital bed now, she's a tiny wisp." Carolyn sat crumpled in her chair, weeping and twisting her Kleenex. "It takes no strength at all for the nurses to turn her over. It's like lifting a bunch of twigs. My mother had these gorgeous breasts, and now they're like dangling empty tubes." Her mascara running, Carolyn looked at once like a child and an old woman. "I'm so scared and sad. . . . And I feel completely baffled . . . going along thinking I was figuring stuff out as I grew older . . . then my parents get sick and shrivel and die . . . everything's more confusing than ever. Even though I've known for my whole life what's coming, I'm thinking, 'How could this be? How could I be *here*?' . . . It's like vertigo."

Two weeks after her mother's fall, talks with the palliative-medicine team made it clear that hospice was the next step. Carolyn was relieved there was a plan, but felt overwhelmed in every other way. She cried when she was alone in the car and was barely able to hold it together in front of her kids. She felt that losing her mother so soon after her father might break her. In turmoil about her marriage, she was blindsided at odd moments by an unbearable sadness that it might not survive. She could see that the feelings of abandonment went both ways. Her grief rendered her less available to her husband too, and he obviously missed her. Intermittently, that realization gave her a small spark of hope.

Near the very end, as her mother lay in her hospital bed in Carolyn and her husband's first-floor living room, Carolyn had an unexpected experience watching her husband with her mother. Sitting in a chair next to the bed, her husband stroked her mother's hair, making her smile with his low-key humor. Carolyn welled up with tears. "It reminded me of his gentleness and his kindness," she said. We talked about her husband's comforting *presence*, something she tended to dismiss when she identified with her active, impatient father. She had to admit that her husband had always been a more comforting parent than her, and his supposed "inertia" was also the source of his nonjudgmental and receptive approach with their children.

People we love do not die all at once in our minds. There is the death, and then we do the internal reworking to move into a new life in which the beloved person is no more. The actual loss of her parents was excruciating to Carolyn, and the pain of relinquishment was physical. For a time, Carolyn felt as if the past were full of riches but irretrievably gone; and that the present, while still here, was empty. Her relationship with her parents had kept her young in her mind. She felt a bleak recognition that everything ends. Sometimes she felt crippled by futility.

But her parents' deaths forced Carolyn to face that her life was *her* life, apart from her role as her parents' child, and the mutual idealization that had buoyed her for so long. In her grief, she had the unusual, and strangely relieving, experience of feeling "useless"—wanting to be alone, not wanting to socialize, and pulling back from her usual hyperactive approach to her tasks and roles. And as she pulled back, her husband managed family life and gave her space to "not function." A parent's dying and death is a watershed moment in a marriage because the emotional support we do—or don't—give and receive becomes the basis for appreciation and gratitude, or disappointment and hurt. Carolyn's customary pattern of ruminating about how her husband was letting her down was disrupted by this new experience. She felt his emotional support in a deeper way. She realized that she couldn't evaluate the potential of their marriage without understanding the ways she'd slotted her husband into her inner emotional world while her parents were alive, and how that might change now that they were dead.

We think of mourning as something we do when we lose someone we love. But more generally, it refers to the mind's process for letting go of something we are attached to. We come to terms with the inescapable finality of the loss, and we preserve in memory and make part of ourselves the loved aspects of what we have lost. The attachment may have been conflicted, and making peace with what exists *in reality*, both the good and the bad, is part of the work involved. After mourning her parents' death, Carolyn eventually found a surprising sense of freedom. It was as if a spell of identification were broken, leaving her at first unmoored, then more able to own herself. She said, "This is a veil of time you go through. Things are different forever. In it, I really couldn't have known which direction the marriage would go." Laying her parents to rest within her inner world freed energy for her present life—which included mourning what wasn't possible, and appreciating what was possible, with her husband.

The psychological capacity to relinquish and mourn the dead is what allows us to love the living. Ideally, we use our experience of loss to invest more fully in the here and now. Development in adulthood, and in marriage, requires using the past to animate the present. We lose many things in life. We lose people we love, our younger selves, our children's babyhoods, and the crazy-in-love phase with our partner. We mourn the losses and keep the memories and past selves alive in us—through rituals, reminiscence, and loving action toward others. The backdrop of mourning is perhaps why generativity is by its nature bittersweet. Being generative—sharing our skills, mentoring others, investing in the future—is one of the great gifts of mature adulthood. From midlife onward, perceiving oneself as generative gives people not only a sense of meaning, but appears to relate to greater health and longer life. Expanding outward is also a crucial antidote to rough-patch disaffection, as it uses our agency to make positive pragmatic or spiritual contributions. Yet we're diffusely aware that nurturing the growth of those who come after us gains both its urgency and pleasure from the knowledge of time, its preciousness and its passage. Talk to people about mentoring, and you can hear them voice this poignancy. "It helps me age to help younger people of my gender," said one fifty-five-year-old artist I know. "I feel parental toward them, and it helps me accept the order of things, rather than get lost in competition." Another man, a professor, spoke of the satisfaction that came from mentoring young women scholars, particularly in the sexist climate of his field. "When it works, it's wonderful," he said. "There are these quiet moments of redemption that soften the suffering of aging. It connects you too to the experience and memory of people who mentored you, and there's a huge internal satisfaction to that."

No moments in adulthood may be more universally saturated with the close-to-the-bone sense of transience, with the doubleness of grief and beauty, than the leave-takings of children and parents. Each pitches us, overnight, into a new stage of life. Despair at one extreme, and denial at the other, perennially beckon. But passing time can lead to internal development, an increase in our ability to recognize and bear paradoxical and mixed emotions, and a more philosophical appraisal of both what is lost *and* what is gained. As Tennyson's Ulysses said, "Though much is taken, much abides." Going forward fully alive, engaged in living a life that counts, means staying balanced on the narrow yet welcoming edge where awareness of limits fuels the urge toward possibility.

AT A WORKSHOP I gave on the empty nest, people were talking about children's departures and parents' declines. But they were also asking questions similar to those that people ask in their twenties: "What am I doing?" "What is my purpose?" Listening to the group, one man said, "We sound almost embarrassingly lost." Among the surprising aspects of this phase of life is the humbling realization of how little you know. One of people's biggest barriers to change is the illusion that they should have figured things out by now. The reality, though, is that we're facing weird, new stuff, and the most fitting orientation might be disorientation. After all, the cost of believing we've got it figured out is often a sense of stasis. One benefit of recognizing our confusion can be an openness to exploration and change.

With age, it's worth keeping a lookout for the ways we're letting our past approaches define us. What you've done so far in your life is just that: what you've done so far. As long as you live and breathe, you can be open to doing something different. Just as we were "beginning parents" when we first had children, we are "beginning empty nesters" when the children leave. Jim, a fifty-seven-year-old workshop participant, described a problem with his wife that had intensified since the departure of their children: "Sometimes I'm immersed in work, and I'm not paying a ton of attention to my wife. I love the level of focus I achieve. But she feels it. She gets mad and ramps up and says, 'I'm not sure you even want to be with me.'" In the past, he said, this familiar problem had been jointly understood as his problem with closeness. This emphasis was helpful to a point. His wife's ongoing bids for reassurance and comfort had helped Jim remember all those years the importance of connection. As we've explored throughout these pages, attachment needs never go away. When couples keep comforting, touching, and turning toward each other, their emotional communication keeps working.

But whereas Jim used to feel guilty and a bit inadequate about his absorption in work, now he felt more impatient, and he was trying to figure out why. At this stage of life a good couple relationship enables, rather than obstructs, devotion to interests, goals, and experiences beyond the dyad. We don't only need closeness and attachment; we also need other sources of satisfaction and meaning. In the generative thrust in midlife we derive satisfaction, and even joy, from interests and concerns beyond the personal. It's not only about whether Jim gives his wife enough attention; it's also a question of whether his wife is uncomfortable with the intensity of his other interests, or the paucity of her own.

"Until fairly recently," said Robert Levenson, one of the major researchers on long-term marriage, "the view was that with age, the lights go out, relationships become more lifeless, mundane, and companionate, and the passion is gone." All that *can* happen, but Levenson's studies have shown that for many people, it doesn't, and the reasons relate directly to continued emotional development. Older couples have often acquired the skill of reducing their negative interactions with each other and are able to recover more quickly. They have refined their ability to shift to positive emotion and soothe themselves and their partners. Over time, if people evolve in complexity, the marital bond is not a case of diminishing returns. The empty nest is a chance to actively take on a change, rather than slink into oblivion with the rationalization that couple problems are "here to stay."

As longevity has dramatically increased, psychological research has helped shift our paradigm of later life. Individuals and relationships continue to develop throughout life. The "life design" gurus Bill Burnett and Dave Evans say, "You never finish designing your life—life is a joyous and never-ending design project of building your way forward." Extending their metaphor, if we know our materials and possess the right emotional "tools," we can look at our marriage and think about how to best broaden and elevate the vistas. It may involve some load-shifting here, some cantilevering there. But if we know where the loads are, and which pillars can't be moved, we can think creatively about the most beautiful design that lies within the possible.

The realities of the "longevity dividend," and the productive confusion of the empty nest, bring home the value of allowing yourself to be a beginner at any age, including in your marriage. In the life of the couple, that'll take a lot of talk. Just because you've never had certain conversations with your partner before doesn't mean you can't have them now. In fact, you'll have to have them now. What you each want now that the children are gone, or the parents have died, are huge questions. Confusion is not blameworthy; "not yet knowing" is an entirely valid state of mind. You always have the chance to try new things, rethink problems, and ask each other for help. Ideally, amid sorting through tuition bills, cleaning out the basement, and deciding whether to downsize, the empty-nest agenda will continue to include the question "Can we play?"

Staying or Leaving

William and Patty had been married fourteen years when they came to see me, and they had two daughters, one on the cusp of adolescence. William was friendly, a people pleaser, while Patty was more reserved and wary. I soon saw that his alacrity was a reflex, and once he dropped the habitual smile, his face looked almost slack. His perception was that for years nothing he had done made Patty happy, despite his working full-time, cooking dinner, and doing everything he could to accommodate her. Patty said that while William worked hard for the family, he was "distracted and checked out." She lamented that their weekend sex had fallen away (she slept in another room with earplugs all week to protect her sleep), and that he didn't remember, even after repeated reminders, that it mattered to her that he did the dishes in the sink before he left the house or brushed the dog every night to manage its shedding.

William had brought them to therapy because he felt that they had never gotten over an incident that had happened about seven years before, and that it continued to affect their interactions. When their younger daughter was a toddler, William had taken her for a walk in a stroller, and a driver on his cell phone had run into them both. Their daughter was thankfully ahead of the impact; the stroller tipped over but their daughter was unharmed. William was directly struck by the car and suffered a broken hip, ending up in the hospital for the better part of two weeks. The injury was difficult, but mostly he felt profoundly shaken by the danger to their child. He felt scared, he felt fragile, and for once in his life, he was *aware* of needing comfort. He was deeply hurt when he felt Patty couldn't muster sympathy or concern for him. The accident left her feeling that William was careless and untrustworthy. She began to treat the incident as a time he had hurt her by being inadequately attentive to their daughter. She was terrified, but had expressed it as blame. William felt she virtually ignored not only his broken hip, but his fear.

The episode became a negative touchstone in William and Patty's relationship—an "attachment injury," which comes about when one person in a couple fails to respond to the other at a critical moment of vulnerability or need. Typical moments include labor and childbirth, illness, trauma, loss, and times of transition. If a person feels betrayed, neglected, or uncared for by his partner in such moments, relational trauma occurs. The incident then becomes an organizing event and recurring theme that stands in the way of understanding and repair. Such injuries may be single incidents that concentrate and catalyze ongoing disappointments. Or they may be ongoing patterns, such as drinking or serial affairs, that create repetitive cycles of hope and disillusionment. In either case, the longer they go unrepaired, the higher the risk of disengagement and ultimate detachment.

In the difficult aftermath of the stroller incident, William and Patty had sought out couple therapy in an attempt to heal from their mutual hurt. Who will be able to heal from an attachment injury and who won't is never entirely clear at the outset. People with similarly difficult backgrounds, or similarly troubled marriages, can differ on how able and willing they are to use a crisis as an opportunity for healing and growth. One component of successful repair is what some therapists refer to as "softening," in which the more critical or withdrawn partner asks for reassurance from a position of vulnerability. When it works, a softening leads to an experience of greater connection. But it is also a common point of impasse and one of the most difficult challenges to navigate.

William's faith in their marriage had been worn down by their never having successfully put the traumatic stroller incident to rest.

To hear Patty describe it, they had "moved on," though it seemed her story had never changed. She wove the accident into her story about how William was always letting her down. She still said that William had endangered their daughter due to his "distraction" crossing the street, but she wasn't "going to hold it against him forever." This was the attitude that William was having such trouble getting over.

To my mind, the attachment injury couldn't be laid to rest because it was just a more dramatic version of the problem that arose daily between Patty and William. Patty felt that William's "nonresponsiveness" (not doing the dishes in the sink, not prioritizing her requests) *hurt* her. To repair these hurts, she believed, he should admit wrongdoing, feel some shame, and apologize. He agreed he should acknowledge the *effect* of his actions on her feelings—"I know it means a lot to you for me to wash the dishes in the sink, and I'm sorry I don't tend to have time to do it, but I'll try." But he didn't agree that he *caused* her feelings, or that her expectations were fair. In other words, he didn't agree with the meaning she assigned to his actions, nor with her equating his actions with indifference and neglect. He was not willing to accept her view that his failure to do what she wished constituted a "betrayal." They had different beliefs about the truth of the situation.

For years, it seemed, William had dealt with the dissonance by placating Patty. It had felt like enough to him, if barely, to be taken back into her good graces. But I could see he'd lost respect for her sense of proportion. It cost him his own self-respect to live in a world where the conditions of being accepted were that he deny his own beliefs about truth and fairness. His integrity hinged on holding on to his point of view—not in the sense of denying *her* truth, but in the sense of not having to choose between her truth and his. They were stuck in a seesaw mind-set, and William kept trying, seemingly singlehandedly, to move them into the golden ring.

Patty and William's problems could not be solved simply through more "responsiveness" to each other. In adult relationships, each person needs to be able to reflect on his own responses. Rough-patch marital distress obliges both people to try to untangle the complicated knot of feeling and interpretation. Both must find their way to think about what they bring to the table, so that they don't simply attribute their emotional reactions to the other person's actions. Turning every issue into a referendum on the other's *responsiveness* risks blowing past the equally necessary duty to take responsibility for one's own *responses*. It gives people a pass on their tendency to blame their partner for their own feelings and behavior.

Despite my gentlest and firmest attempts to confront her, Patty continued to expect William to heal her wounded sense of self-worth through more attention, more effort, and more remorse for his failings. I pressed her to seek individual therapy, saying that I thought the problems went deeper than the marriage. She said she was too busy. If she had changed nothing else, but had mustered the self-awareness to say to William, "I know I feel bad about myself and I tend to blame you for not fixing it," it might have engendered shared compassion and some hope. But the tragedy of Patty, and partners like her, is that she *couldn't*. She would cry bitterly at how she could "do nothing right" according to William, as if his heartfelt distress were a dart of criticism aimed at her. Deep down, I think she was crying because nothing he did succeeded in healing how she felt about herself. But against her innermost longings, she stuck with her story that the problem was him.

Self-awareness and self-responsibility are the critical prerequisites for realistic hope in a struggling marriage: "I see what I am doing and I am working on changing it." When one partner refuses to grapple with his deficits in this department, he is probably going to need to be confronted. Sometimes marriages limp along because a partner who needs to use leverage won't. (S)he is too scared, too guilty, too bullied, too confused. (S)he rationalizes and procrastinates ("No marriage is perfect," "Didn't I read that everyone marries the 'wrong person'?"). Or, (s)he is frightened that once the unproductive fighting ends, nothing will be left. But not all problems are created equal. Sitting across from people, I am pained when they don't take responsibility for themselves. But I am almost more pained when partners fail to confront the view that they alone are to blame for their partner's behavior and feelings. Though it made me feel less hope for the marriage, I felt it was right for William to refuse this role.

As I continued to work with William and Patty, I found myself less and less able to hold off the conclusion toward which events were inexorably leading. Months went by in our conversations, and a gloomy stasis settled in like smog. The islands of rapprochement became fewer and farther between, surrounded by coldness and blame. William continued to feel that every conflict left him with only two choices: he could either capitulate to Patty's view or fight it. Nothing short of his agreement made her feel "heard." I told them I wasn't honestly sure they had a way forward together that they could both feel good about. In a panic, William hastily arranged a trip to Hawaii at their anniversary, a move geared to answering Patty's ongoing refrain that he never did anything to "nurture the relationship." They hoped that a vacation alone together, an occasion for romance in the past, might kindle some warmth. When they returned, they agreed it was awful.

In the next weeks, William started to get the ashen look I've come to associate with terminal forms of marital distress. The physical symptoms of marital alienation can be impressive. People gain weight or become gaunt, their skin becomes pasty, their faces ragged. More than once, I've noticed someone start to seem less attractive and more stressed looking than I've ever seen him before; misery has subtly contorted his features. I find myself worrying for people's health. Years ago, an older colleague told me that her marriage was "making her sick," and I privately thought she was rationalizing leaving her marriage for an affair she'd begun. That may have been true, but I've also seen enough over the years to convince me of the dramatic physical manifestations of marital unhappiness. A man said that once he got divorced, he no longer had the wish to stay out of the house as long as he could doing errands, a pattern he'd developed so as not to share physical space with his wife. He now felt a bodily relief on returning to his empty house. One woman said she'd assumed she didn't like physical affection because she couldn't stand the feeling of sleeping next to her husband. Only later, in a new relationship, did she realize she loved sleeping entwined.

The body sometimes encodes truths that our minds can't accept. As the thought of divorce floats at the margin of awareness, people do everything they can to overrule their bodies for the sake of their conscious intentions. People may try to work out more, drink less. But they feel they've hit a formidable wall. The force can be immense, like a punch in the stomach; people find it hard to breathe. The old coping strategies stop working, not only in the marriage, but in life. Pleasing others, checking out, keeping one's head down, avoiding conflict—whatever they've been doing all this time, it no longer works, in the marriage or anywhere else.

But even under such duress, William and Patty both struggled with competing values. They shared a painful and pessimistic sense of the emotional reality of their relationship, but they also felt attached to the comforts of home and the value of an intact family. They both wanted to live with their children full-time. They still admired some of each other's qualities and at times felt terrified at being alone. They shared history and a sense of familiarity. Staying married was a central life goal. So, like others who reach this point, they asked themselves, how would divorce affect the children?

On the effect of divorce on the well-being of children, certain findings have remained fairly consistent across the decades. On average, children with divorced parents, when contrasted to children with continuously married parents, tend to score lower on a number of measures of behavior, health, emotional well-being, and academic performance. Factors that appear to lower children's well-being after divorce include decline in household income, parents' psychological problems, ineffective parenting, lack of contact with nonresident parents, and continuing conflict between parents. In young adulthood, children with divorced parents do not exhibit higher levels of anxiety or depression than those from intact families. They do, however, more often describe "their childhoods as being difficult, wish they had spent more time with their fathers, feel that their fathers do not love them, and worry about both parents attending important events such as weddings and graduations." Children's concern about fathers' love is heartrending when considered alongside survey results indicating that fathers' biggest worry about divorce is not seeing their children. (Interestingly, 50 percent of mothers said their children "were supportive" of the divorce, while only 22 percent of the fathers did.)

However, the picture of how divorce affects children has become more nuanced over the years. It's less informative to look at *average* differences between children from divorced and continuously married homes than to consider what makes divorce more and less negative for children, and how divorce relates to other complex family factors. For example, chronic negativity and conflict contribute the most to poor child outcomes, whether these occur in nondivorced or divorced families. Those parents who eventually divorce have higher rates of depression, antisocial behavior, addiction, and financial problems before the divorce and are more likely to exhibit poor problem-solving skills. Parents who eventually divorce demonstrate more contempt, denial, and withdrawal, as well as conflict escalation and negative attribution toward partners. An implication is that, much as divorce inflicts its own stresses on children, many of the same difficulties that lead to divorce are already exerting their ill effects on children before a marriage dissolves.

We know that a high degree of marital conflict has more bearing on children's behavior problems than divorce per se. A lot of research in the last twenty years has focused on the mechanisms by which family discord and conflict affect children's development. Unhappily married parents want to know which is worse for children, a conflict-ridden home or a divorce? The answer is not simple. Divorce can bring its own sources of disharmony, and it involves the same two individuals who were fighting as married partners. It's important to remember, regarding children's welfare, we are not generally comparing a happy, harmonious home life to a divorce, but rather a difficult home life to a divorce.

Conflict and anger are inevitable aspects of family life and marriage. They can be necessary aspects of working out differences, and observing parents work through conflict to resolution is a valuable lesson for children to absorb. The critical issues are how anger is handled, its intensity, and its underlying meaning and negative emotionality. From the child's point of view, the key question is, does what's going on right now affect my safety? Children are "almost like emotional Geiger counters," and they are exquisitely sensitive to, and discriminating about, the tenor of angry expressions between their parents. They can sense the difference between destructive and constructive conflict. Intense expressions of anger are more distressing than less intense ones, and physical aggression is uniformly damaging to children's mental health. Not surprisingly, children's emotional security is negatively affected by parent conflict tactics such as threats, insults, hostility, withdrawal, and physical distress, and it is positively affected by conflict tactics such as calm discussion, affection, and support.

In the face of parental conflict, children have varying strategies to regulate their emotions and seek emotional security, based on inborn qualities as well as age. Some become appeasing, some aggressive, and others attempt to manage their parents' conflict. The most important thing to understand about children's responses to parental conflict is that their uppermost goal at all times is *security*. When their emotional security is threatened by parental conflict, or their attachment security is threatened by separation, all their other emotional and behavioral systems tend to be affected. Breakdown of parents' attentive caregiving underlies the negative effects of both marital conflict *and* divorce. When children worry about the continuing presence, attention, and kindness of their parents, their sense of security is compromised. Conversely, if parents can create security and safety for their children even when the parents themselves are struggling, the effects on children of both marital conflict and divorce are diminished.

Whether in divorce or marriage then, *how* parents *manage* their conflicts has a huge impact on children's sense of security. Most obviously, it's detrimental when children are put in the middle of their parents' fights, a role that risks turning them into adults who neglect their own feelings in the service of others. Overall, children's negative reactions to parental fighting are reduced when parents reach some resolution. Complete resolution is rare; research is inconclusive on whether satisfied-couple interaction depends more on resolution of conflict or on the ability to recover quickly from conflict or to let issues go. What's important for children is that they perceive a positive attempt at a constructive outcome. Resolution may happen behind closed doors, or after the fact, and explaining that the conflict was resolved can be calming to children as young as five. Emotional positivity, compromise, and apologies are optimal resolutions from the child's vantage point. Children tend to perceive resolved fights on par with friendly conversations; according to the main researchers in the field, "resolution appears to act as a 'wonder drug' on the children's perceptions of adult fights."

Parents' attempts to turn toward each other and manage their conflicts together, then, are a relief to children. This calls into question the benefits of the strategy of disengagement that some parents adopt to avoid overt discord. Parents may feel they are taking a more "mature" approach by not fighting; but it's inaccurate to assume that children are blithely unaware of the emotional mood. Research indicates that parents' marital withdrawal and ongoing nonverbal hostility resulted in children's negative emotionality in much the same way as verbal hostility and personal insults did. Children interpret nonverbal anger and marital withdrawal as destructive, even though parents sometimes assume they are protecting their children by avoiding conflict. Many of us remember parsing the subtleties of parental fights and standoffs as children. And why wouldn't we? Our safety depended on it. When parents avoid emotional exchanges through withdrawal, they not only lose an opportunity to tackle their own problems, but model for their children an unhealthy strategy for coping with feelings.

How parents manage conflict also has a long-range impact on their children's future relationships. Children whose parents divorced are more likely to divorce themselves when their parents' interactions were *low* conflict, rather than high conflict, prior to divorce. This may seem counterintuitive, until you consider that low-conflict unhappy parents are less likely to be confronting problems directly. They're more likely to employ sarcasm, engage in passive-aggression, or utter things under their breath, transmitting dysfunctional modes of conflict resolution to their children. Young adults whose parents *stayed* in high-conflict marriages expressed *lower* commitment and satisfaction in their romantic relationships than did young adults whose parents *left* high-conflict marriages. This suggests that as difficult as divorce can be, it represents a decision that the emotional climate of a relationship is unworkable and may give children a road map of sorts about the kind of relationships that are worth fighting for. By contrast, something is confusing and demoralizing about a parental unit that is chronically mired in conflict.

Patty and William went back and forth on how divorce would affect their girls. He believed it was not good for them to see Patty treat him with disrespect when she became so angry, but he also worried whether the children would bear the brunt of her outbursts if he left. She said he was exaggerating her behavior and minimizing the affronts that triggered it. But finally talking concretely about the effects on the children seemed to shift something in William. Not long after these discussions he stopped expending the energy to disagree with Patty's story; he was letting it stand. From his matter-of-fact attitude, I sensed he'd ended his effort to change Patty's mind about him. He seemed to have become exhausted by, and ultimately uninterested in, the role of assuaging her feelings so completely.

"I don't want to do this anymore," he said one day. "I'm sorry." With that, he gave up on resolving problems within the marriage and embarked upon ending it as skillfully as possible.

At first, Patty protested: it was wrong to break up the family, he was acting selfishly, and this was one more instance of his not stepping up in the relationship. He kept saying he was sorry in response and stood firm. She escalated. But William had spent almost fifteen years on the receiving end of her onslaughts, and now he appeared less pained than relieved at having given up on trying to reconcile their glaring disjunction of worldviews. I could see that all his effort was now concentrated on shepherding them toward a divorce with minimal damage.

After about a month, Patty's tears and recriminations lessened. It helped that William could bear to sit and listen, something he hadn't been able to do nearly as well when he was still trying to depend on her. I felt sad watching Patty, trying at this late date to foist onto William the need to change. Gradually, though, as Patty realized she could get out of the marriage with her pride intact and her story unquestioned, she seemed almost at peace. They had been good savers, and it helped them that money wasn't a point of contention. As we discussed their next phase, I even wondered if Patty felt a certain relief at not having to try to be close to William anymore.

THE QUESTION OF responsibility is often at the core of people's conflicts about whether to stay or to leave. What can my partner help in his behavior, and what can't he? For some percentage of couples, one spouse will have an identifiable mental illness, addiction, or personality disorder. If that spouse can't help it, is it fair to leave? Even if the other spouse feels she should stay, can she realistically bear to? What are the ethics of staying in the face of loneliness and disconnection? What are the ethics of leaving when the disruptions will be so enormous, or one's partner wants to keep trying? You have an ethical responsibility to your children and to the commitment. And you have a responsibility to the emotional truth of the situation as you see it. These conflicts can be tragically difficult to reconcile.

When partners reach their physical, emotional limit, as William did, is there a way back from there? Should there be? Or should we turn instead toward acceptance? As at a death, perhaps we should discontinue heroic measures at some point and turn our aspirations toward a graceful and dignified demise. We can't control our feelings entirely. None of us has superpowers. People do come to a point when the truth of their situation conflicts with their ability to regenerate a feeling of love. When they are honest with themselves, they may realize that they can no longer respect their partner's behavior or view of reality. Or despite their efforts, it will never be enough. It leaves them feeling that the limits they perceive in their relationship are real. It is profoundly humbling, and unbearably sad.

Some people will tell you these emotions are "soft" reasons for divorce. But at times a deepened honesty about your emotions leads you to understand why the marriage can never work for you. You may come to view the expectations as profoundly unfair or find it ultimately too painful to live in an intimate arrangement with a person you are not intimate with. Far from being "soft" reasons, the dead-end impossibility of restoring loving feeling is among the more "solid" reasons to divorce.

Even in the face of such feelings, people don't want to disrupt family life. There may be fighting, or disengagement; and they may have a vague sense that the marriage will someday be untenable. But for the time being, if things aren't terrible, people will tell themselves that their discontents are normal and expectable. They'll tend to maintaining the infrastructure and its many moving parts—homework and year-end reviews and laundry and visiting grandparents and birthday parties and sporting events and teacher conferences and bedtime stories and family time on the weekends. How irrelevant, almost, it can feel to focus too much on one's personal happiness; as long as it's possible to stay on this side of a clinical depression, it's better to sit tight.

But just as they have resolved to do so, some couples are assailed by the unwelcome reminder that seemingly every negotiation—of which there are many per day—bears the painful stamp of misunderstanding. The tranquil moments are few and far between. The demands and disappointments are repetitive, without any sweetness to compensate. Still, they can't imagine how parting would work financially; the sacrifices would be huge. Would it really be worth it if it meant living in a crummy rental with no savings? The thought feels disorienting and almost absurd. Neither can they bear to even think about living with the kids half-time. In our generation the entire marital project centers on children. Under what shroud of selfishness would one willfully decide not to give the children the best possible start in life? Divorce would feel like a personal failure, but even more, it would feel like failing the children. People deal with a lot more adversity in life than feeling misunderstood or disregarded by a spouse. Food, a roof over your head, healthy children . . . given all that, dwelling on the insufficiencies of marriage is almost embarrassing, a decidedly first-world problem.

Often enough, people use this line of thought to guilt-trip themselves, or their partner. One couple couldn't stop fighting about every little thing, the wife saying her husband was "negative," the husband saying his wife was "never happy." But he always tacked on an additional jab: they had everything, they lived in the most beautiful place in the world, and it was ridiculous that she couldn't take more pleasure in what was right in front of her. It's a useless notion. She couldn't, and for the record, he couldn't, either. That's because people's emotional dynamics with their partners color their worldview. Changing one's experience of one's intimate relationship is an emotional and relational achievement; it's often hard-won, and it's not always possible.

When not applied as a cudgel, though, thinking about what's valuable to you and recognizing your good fortune is a constructive guide and motivator. Children—and even money, especially if you have children—are excellent reasons to turn back toward the marriage and try harder. For a lot of people, two domiciles exhaust resources for college, vacations, clothing, even doctor's visits. The emotional and economic costs of divorce, to children and to one's success as a parent, are real. Sometimes it's the responsibility for children and the constraints of money that keep people around long enough to realize that there might be something to salvage. Whatever you can lean on to motivate you, do it.

Love, dimmed even to William and Patty's level, may still return. One or the other person might not want to try; (s)he may have reached the point of no return and decide to pursue another path. Sometimes it is too little, too late. But given the smallest inkling of self-awareness and self-responsibility, a meeting of the minds can occur one day out of thirty, then twenty, then ten. "Things have felt better to me for the last couple weeks. Have they for you?" "Yeah, they have." "Do you feel like you want to stay married today?" "Yes, I do." "So do I." If something that basic and simple can occur, there's hope. If each person can think about his or her part, seek genuine understanding, and make the effort to change, there is a chance of coming back from the brink. There is a chance you can again feel close to the person you married.

*   *   *

THE PAST COUPLE years Belinda had been struggling with what it meant to spend the rest of her life with her husband. "He really just wants to be left alone," she said. "He doesn't want to disappoint me, and he even defers to me. But I feel like he does it so I won't ask more of him."

When Belinda first sought me out fifteen years before, she'd been feeling resentful and alone in her marriage. Before having children, she and her husband, Justin, had had a great relationship, which had rested on their high degree of independence. Children had meant more mutual dependency, and that had proved a hard transition to navigate. She had been disappointed that Justin hadn't seemed terribly interested in sharing the burdens and joys of childrearing. In therapy all those years ago, she'd decided that they had enough history and compatibility, not to mention the shared need to care for two young children, to try to make the marriage work. She threw herself into her community, her friendships, and her children's school activities. She continued her work as a tax lawyer, and despite its moments of frustration and boredom, she found the work rewarding.

Now, at fifty-five, she was returning to see me because her good friend Alice, who looked enviably young at fifty-one, had pulled the plug on her marriage. "I don't know why I am so shaken by this," Belinda said. The women had been close since their children were in preschool and were part of a group of six women that went out to dinner for their birthdays every year. "Part of me feels my reaction is justified. I mean, Carrie is on her second round of chemo, Louise's son is addicted to heroin, and Alice is busy reveling in her newfound freedom. But I know I'm being petty. I'm jealous that Alice has such a dramatic reason to leave"—her husband was a "sex addict"—"and seems so blameless. She gives off this aura of having done everything right. She makes a big deal of having waited till her kids were gone, confiding to us all, 'I realized I couldn't have lived apart from them,' as if that's some kind of blinding insight. She's the least psychologically astute person I know, but now she's saying she's going back to school to become a therapist."

I was struck, as Belinda talked, at how rarely she revealed this kind of raw, unflattering emotion, and how much it upset her to be out of control. "You know me, I'm a *doer*, I don't dwell," she said. "But these days I feel eaten up about Alice, to the point that I'm numbing out with cheesy country music and bad TV shows." I laughed, in spite of myself, at the incongruity of the image, since Belinda characteristically presented herself somewhat formally—silk scarves, modest gold hoop earrings, and pumps that didn't show her legs to best effect. I found myself dressing her in my mind, and wondering whether it was time for her to liberate herself from the overly dark hair dye. I wanted her to feel every bit as attractive as Alice, and my spirit of competition was engaged on her behalf. She had a delicate, pointed face, with intelligent light blue eyes. With age, she'd come into her own. But for her, self-expression held no allure. Why would she want to wear her heart on her (literal) sleeve? She was an observer at heart, embarrassed by any trace of exhibitionism.

I'd known Belinda long enough to recognize that her tendency toward quiet observation and even self-suppression had played a role in creating the marriage dynamics that she lamented. I also felt that Justin had always sounded like a basically decent guy. They had now been doing their dance for almost thirty years. Belinda had fluctuated between attempting detachment from Justin and trying to engage him, but with a blaming edge that conveyed he'd already let her down. Justin, it seemed, had stoically continued, as many men do, to be devoted to Belinda and committed to the marriage, but at a slight emotional remove. The remove was at once self-protection, philosophical acceptance, and comfortable default. I imagined he saw virtue in compartmentalizing the difficulties of their marriage and appreciating the good; he likely felt the marriage was workable enough since he could pursue his other interests relatively unencumbered. Belinda perceived his position as rejection.

In talking to me about her reaction to Alice, Belinda admitted that proximity to a person excited by new vistas aroused her envy. Another friend was also newly single. Her husband had died suddenly of a heart attack, and though devastated, she had quietly confessed to

Belinda an awkward relief at having another chance after her largely sexless marriage. Belinda ached for her, but had no trace of envy. Embarrassing as it was to admit, Belinda realized that she didn't feel Alice was suffering quite enough.

But Belinda knew that Alice didn't have an easy road ahead, and Belinda herself didn't particularly want to be single. She wasn't hankering after sex with other people. Alice's situation unsettled Belinda because it seemed to support the idea that the strong, courageous thing would be to strike out on her own. So much of the time Belinda was inert in her marriage. She almost felt that she could take it or leave it. But she knew that if she ever left her marriage, she would lose a lot—including financial security, her standard of living, history, the pleasures of an intact family, and physical contact.

Women, as we know, initiate most divorces, including gray divorces, and people generally don't regret their decision to divorce. But in terms of financial hardship, loneliness, and depression, experiences are mixed. A third of divorcing women in their fifties say one of the best things after divorce is "not having to deal with another person." A third also say that the worst thing after divorce is "nobody to do things with." Sixty-nine percent of married women say they kiss daily; only 6 percent of unmarried women do. In the desire to leave behind the painful parts of a marriage, people sometimes minimize the pain of what they'll miss. Belinda was carefully trying to weigh all this and was annoyed by what she perceived to be a simplistic narrative of liberation. "There's this idea that if you leave, you'll find something better. Better how, exactly? People say, 'I'd rather be alone than lonely in my marriage.' But I'm thinking I'm likely to be alone *and* lonely, at least when it comes to sleeping with another warm body."

When I see a patient who is agonizing about whether to stay or to leave, I sometimes ask if she can commit to try for the next two months to behave like a model marital citizen. The experiment is useful, first, to see if she can do it; and second, to find out if behaving differently helps her feel more loving or induces panic that she won't now have a reason to get out. Belinda gave it a try and developed a catalog of her irritations and trigger points. She was surprised to notice how many of them had to do with Justin's vulnerability or signs of aging, rather than his long-standing introversion and nondemonstrativeness. We discussed whether she benefited from noticing the apparent mobility of her complaints. Trying to behave well toward her husband calmed her down somewhat, but her negative behavior had never been her biggest problem. She was more prone to a fatalistic giving up.

"If you could magically erase the history of disappointments in the marriage, do you think you'd wake up in the morning liking him?" I asked. For marriage to work well, we must at least have it *in us* to like being around our partner, even if it's gotten tarnished over the years. At times she did like him. They'd share a laugh, or they'd both feel delight at one of their kid's successes. At such moments, though, something would rise up inside her that told her not to give herself over to the moment. She said it had to do with "not wanting to be hurt again," and she would rehearse a host of past incidents when she had opened herself up to Justin and had been disappointed.

But I sensed she felt something deeper and less definable. Belinda tended to view her efforts to detach from Justin as self-protective, but they were also based on a sense of grievance. She had to acknowledge that her feelings of grievance didn't begin and end with him. She had old wounds from way back in her own life, which we revisited. There was also the inevitable gap between aspiration and reality. She harbored the idea that somewhere inside her was a treasured version of herself that her husband didn't bring out. Belinda felt grief at not having "another chance." But her constant rumination about "Should I stay or go?"—and her inability to ever settle it—was also one way to avoid the difficult finality of choice.

Part of our work was to disentangle the grievances she felt toward her husband from those she felt about the limits of her life. I shared with her in a lighter moment that women are more likely to blame their partners' behavior for divorce. Men are more likely to want to stay married and are less likely to blame their wives for the marriages' problems. "But isn't it obvious that men are actually more at fault?" she joked. It had felt natural to blame her husband for her life going by. It took time and talking for her to begin to measure the present by the reality of the future, rather than measure the present by the hopes of the past. But as she began to question the story that justified and legitimated her sense of grievance, she took more satisfaction in her current life. Revising her story felt like a death of sorts, but it also felt like a kind of waking up.

Insight led to small changes in her perspective. Her feeling of annoyance at her husband's aches and pains, she realized, was a way to deflect anxiety from her own. She noticed that when she found herself critical toward him, she would float into a fantasy about the better life she could have, then realize that she was comparing reality to a fantasy. Relinquishing grievances meant coming face-to-face with this being her one and only life. The sense of being in a living relationship returned—hard and frustrating at times, but meaningful. "I made a mistake at work," Belinda told me, "and I was afraid it would have bad consequences. My first impulse was to call Justin. In the past I would have vetoed that thought. But instead of starting my mental gymnastics to protect myself, I tried to enjoy the feeling of wanting to reach out to him, and to even feel grateful for it. I ended up calling him, and I consciously kept the edge out of my voice. I said simply that I needed his help. He tried to help me. I felt closer to him."

She realized how much she'd focused on their relationship as the central problem in her life. It was liberating to wrest her mind from the tally sheet of slights, to choose to see herself and Justin as square with each other. Her disappointments didn't evaporate; they'd probably always be there. But when she stopped treating him as if he had already disappointed her, he was happy to get along and didn't seem to have any interest in loading up ammunition of his own. Whereas in the past she might have viewed that as evidence that he didn't care enough, she was glad, and even a bit admiring, of his lack of interest in holding a grudge.

"I've been editing old videos of the kids when they were little," Belinda said. "I have adorable footage of them at two and four, then four and six, then six and eight. While I watch, I also remember the stories I was playing in my head at the time—resenting my sister-in-law, or feeling mad at my husband. I think to myself, so much of that beautiful time *went by* with me *stuck in my head*, distracted from the miracle that was playing out in front of me. How I regret it. And then I tell myself, the only solution is to be awake to the miracle *now*."

LIFE IS LIVED forward, but self-knowledge takes time and experience. We all come to marriage with the completely valid hope of being loved for ourselves. We have the right to expect love, and the responsibility to give love. That is the sacred human compact at the heart of marriage. It's what we strive to commit to, honor, nurture, and remember, in good times and bad. My advice to every newlywed, to every new parent, and to every busy work-family juggler is *don't let that die*. Once it dies, once you've closed your heart, it's *really, really* hard to open it back up. It may prove impossible. Like everything else in life, investing early works better than trying to catch up later. Every single day, it's important to look at the long game, and to keep your eye on what you want: to give and receive love.

But when marriages die, I don't believe that it is only out of neglect or error. Sometimes marriages die because they cannot be sustained except at too great a sacrifice for one or both partners. Sometimes, the bargain at their core was flawed: *I will absorb your abuse as long as you never leave me. If you love me, you will let me do what I want. We can be together as long as we leave each other alone*. Though the marriage may be *possible* to sustain, the costs may be great. Some will decide the costs are worth it, some will not. But these emotional, ethical, and existential decisions are profoundly personal and can't be decided on universal principles.

People who grow up in families where the parents loved each other and treated each other and their children well come into marital life with a huge advantage; they are, quite literally, born into privilege. They are less prone to feeling responsible for everything that goes wrong. They are more likely to believe their feelings are accurate, valid indicators, rather than something they need to adjust and second-guess. They don't spend so much time trying to forgive themselves for being human. By contrast, people who grow up in families with dysregulated emotions or scarring breakups don't witness at close range a workable or desirable model for meshing emotional fulfillment and family life. They risk repeating the chaos of their pasts, or hunkering down in "safe," child-focused marriages, only later to risk being destabilized by feelings they squelched to provide predictability. Children from happier families learn young, in their viscera and in their minds, the lessons about relationships that the rest of us need to learn through conscious effort and a more intentional journey toward self-integration.

Even when a marriage is basically good, people are not always happy. Marriage is a crucible for becoming a more mature, compassionate person. It offers an unflinchingly up-close-and-personal example of how we treat another human being. We see our minds in action, both our worst tendencies and our best. In this light, how can we even judge the viability of our marriages without making sure we've gotten enough sleep, exercised, eaten right, and developed some means of reflection, prayer, or meditation? Our emotions and bodies whip us around, and we're so often mystified as to what's causing a given mood. It's so easy to blame the person at hand, which in marriage, unfortunately, is often one's spouse.

Whatever the rumblings of marital discontent, many of us put that aside to focus as much as possible on our children's happiness and sense of security. Giving our children a good childhood is, for many, the most cherished goal of family life. This is where our private emotional conflict runs up against what we may regard as a universal principle: that divorce is bad for children. In evaluating this principle, it's key to remember that if it's done right, divorce takes all the same interpersonal skills that marriage does. All the same old dysfunctional patterns *plus* divorce will probably create more stress for your children. So, the decision to divorce should carry with it a private pledge to function *better*, not worse. A tall order, made taller still if you are the person being left. It will take every shred of maturity you can muster. But how you act makes a world-altering difference for your children. And if you act well, you will feel much better about yourself—more effective, more empowered, and prouder of the person you are becoming.

Here are a few thoughts about children that may help. For those whose parents divorced, being parents who inflict divorce on their children carries a special pain and guilt. If you do not want the divorce, you may do anything you can to avoid it. If your parents stayed married, you may feel that getting divorced will deprive your own children of the benefits you enjoyed. In either case, you may carry a monolithic, catastrophic picture of divorce in your head, a picture that expresses your worst fears and, if you are being left, justifies your ongoing anger toward your parting spouse. To navigate divorce skillfully on behalf of your children, you need to recognize the monolithic picture in your head for what it is: a broad-brush view of reality that blinds you to the crucial subtleties. What your children need most from you is sensitivity and attunement, a clear-eyed attention to the business at hand that is not clouded by crude categories of good and bad, victim and perpetrator. Your main job is to manage your own emotions so that you can continue to provide sensitive care. Divorces can go vastly different ways for children. They can be awful nightmares, or necessary, if complicated, improvements. *It all depends on how you handle it.*

It can be challenging at the very beginning. The evidence suggests that the first year after a separation is usually disruptive and painful, even if after that people are more satisfied. All are going to slip up as they find their bearings. I worry more about the ongoing issues. For instance, parents may try to banish their feelings of guilt by not listening when their kids express their sadness or their anxieties about the other parent. Parents can be too preoccupied to help their children solve the inconveniences and practical concerns they inevitably shoulder when they live in two homes. I also worry that parents gloss over the extraordinary complexity of love interests, stepparents, and stepfamilies. Sometimes the newly divorced are so happy and relieved to have love in their lives that they expect their kids to somehow get with the program. But pairing up with someone new is fraught with emotional complication. You owe it to yourself and your children to take your time. Recognize your temptation to rush and to ignore red flags. Give a new relationship time to develop, and give yourself the room to discover if you can talk, understand each other, and struggle through hard issues. The goal is not only to find someone to love; it's also to choose an excellent stepparent for your children—someone who is warm, loving, secure, not threatened or possessive, not caught up in loyalty battles or favoring of his or her own kids. As the research shows, divorce isn't simply about the *event* of divorce. It's about all that leads up to it, and all that follows. At every stage, you owe your children your most thoughtful and compassionate approach.

We've all heard about worst-case scenarios. In a horrific subset of divorce cases, parental narcissism, envy, and hatred make for hellish, protracted custody wars. But can benefits accrue to children on the other side of divorce? Constance Ahrons, the author of *The Good Divorce*, says yes. Parents may be restored to greater well-being and greater focus on their children. Children may live in more harmonious domestic environments and potentially experience better role models for intimate partnerships. One parent's home can be a haven of sanity if the other parent is disturbed or dysfunctional. An oft-repeated chestnut is that children "don't care if their parents are happy." Children thrive in security, stability, and routine, and it's good if parents can avoid letting their own unhappiness disrupt their children's lives. But just as children are immensely attuned to the subtleties of their parents' fights, they are also highly sensitive to their parents' happiness. For every patient who has come to see me with a painful parental divorce in her background, someone else speaks of her parents' difficult marriage. In adulthood, people sometimes struggle with guilt at having a better life than their parents. They sometimes engineer marriages for themselves that replicate in every miserable detail the marriages their parents couldn't manage to end. There is real benefit to having a parent who had the courage to live a happier life. Given how many narcissistic, self-justifying versions of this story we see in novels, films, and life, I hesitate to champion it, for fear of being misconstrued. But I also think the fear of being seen in a selfish light can prevent people from honestly exploring their thoughts and attending to their emotions. That isn't a good outcome, either.

People leave marriages without any insight, having learned little or nothing, sowing destruction in their wake. People also stay in marriages without any insight, and with little hope that a more satisfying relationship is possible. There are healthier and less healthy ways of staying *and* leaving. Both depend on the same basic capacities of self-awareness, self-responsibility, and emotional regulation that we've discussed throughout. We sometimes delude ourselves on this point. Tired of doing what we're doing, and not sure how we got here, we vaguely hope our plight has an escape hatch. There might be, sort of; but it is incremental. There's no alternative long-term relationship, after all, that doesn't take place in *reality*, on *earth*. That means that a lot of the same challenges we face in this relationship will be present in the next one. A lot of the same ones; but not all of them. Into that gap we pour our longings and hopes and our tormented deliberations about whether to stay or to go.

A final thought: a research study on relatively satisfied couples observed that most marital conflicts ended up "unresolved," in the view of at least one of the partners. Even when a conflict was "resolved," it was uncommon for it to result in an actionable, agreed-upon change. We tend to regard conflict resolution as a necessary condition for marital harmony, yet for these relatively satisfied couples, resolved conflicts and agreement weren't what mattered. What mattered was *understanding*. Whether partners left the interaction feeling understood was what determined whether their problematic patterns of behavior had any negative impact. To my mind, the moral is that happy couples fight, and unhappy couples fight. Happy couples don't resolve conflict, and unhappy couples don't resolve conflict. Happy couples don't reach agreement, and unhappy couples don't reach agreement. What makes the difference is trying to understand the other person. Whether you are happy, unhappy, marrying, divorcing, or stuck in between, start there.

Love Is a Conversation

You are young. You are in love with the person you are going to marry. The physical attraction is intense, of course. But what's extraordinary, almost magical, is the way it feels to *talk*. Time feels dense, expansive, precious. You are effortlessly curious and endlessly intrigued. You want to go deeper, to know and to understand the person you now love. When you talk, it's about so much more than conveying information. There's cadence, rhythm, intensity, silence. Bursts of laughter, expectant pauses, the enthused tumbling of words. It's a delicious, delightful whole-body experience.

Now here you are, ten or fifteen or twenty years later. Family life is full of demands. Children, along with their pleasures, limit your time to talk to each other, while adding to the topics to be discussed. Logistics crowd out emotions; bad habits carve conversational ruts. Your tender inner voice that whispers, "Turn toward him," or "I need her," is drowned out by the din of frustration or the tasks of the to-do list. It feels almost foolish to continue hoping that conversation might lead to sharing and meaningful connection. You find yourself searching for a story to make sense of what you've lost. You look back wistfully on the blissful days of early love, and wonder if you're just too different.

Time wears on, you feel it passing. Your repetitive, fruitless spousal exchanges start to feel like a drain on the life energy you have left. If this is what talking is going to be, you'd rather garden, or cook a good meal, or watch some football. Do you still even truly desire to talk? Did you both let that desire die? Perhaps. But if you're honest, you don't think so. Deep down, you still yearn to find your way back to the nourishing, beautiful conversation you once shared.

All my talk of self-realization and conversational skill is in the service of helping you attain that goal. Throughout these pages, I've encouraged us to look within, particularly when things feel urgent, or difficult, or dead. At such moments, if we can allow our defenses to soften, we can find a golden ring awareness. We each bravely offer our feelings into the shared space of the relationship, and we think together about what's before us. In this space, we take our emotions *more* seriously, not less. We don't try to grow out of, or get past, or get over our feelings; we try to increase our skill at expressing them. I've discussed the extraordinary power of self-awareness ("I see what I am doing") and self-responsibility ("I'm trying to change it") to shift almost any marital interaction from a standoff to a collaboration. When we cultivate our capacities for compassion, curiosity, and self-control, we can speak, and listen, in a richer and livelier way.

In a good relationship, the early bliss lives on as a wonderful memory and inspirational resource and returns from time to time, unbidden, surprising you with its potency. But what matters most is what's possible on the *other side* of love's first blush: conversations that are rewarding, intimate, and real. It's not that we come together in electric recognition and pure understanding, then fall away from that through conflict, difference, and the reassertion of selfish needs. Rather, we come together in a rush of passion, then we *achieve* love through the ongoing conversation we're able to create, one body to another body, one mind to another mind, one heart to another heart. The conversation by which we engage each other *is* love.

MARILOU WAS SIXTY-EIGHT and had recently been diagnosed with breast cancer. Her husband, Ned, sixty-seven, had retired from running a local bookstore, which he'd heroically sustained until it was cannibalized by the internet. With his grizzled white beard and work clothes, he looked entirely at home puttering in their junk-festooned bungalow, Marilou had a down-to-earth, no-frills energy, close-cropped gray hair, and a raspy voice. Looking ahead to her treatments, and back at their thirty-five-year marriage, they were feeling renewed love and attraction for each other.

"When we were younger and had troubles, we'd fly apart," said Marilou. "At our lowest point, we both had sex with other people. Who knows why? Hurt, anger, revenge. Drinking, of course. But, it turns out, you can't get rid of love by having sex with other people." She laughed. "It's still there, as mysterious as ever. We're not a match made in heaven, but at some point, you learn to respect love. You're not always happy, but belonging to each other means more than anything else."

"When things were rough, what helped us more than anything was our friends," said Ned. "We called them 'the tribe.' They could see good in both of us, even when we couldn't. They helped us not let our grudges swamp the good.

"With my first wife, there was always a crisis. I tried to take care of them all. I wore myself out. It killed me to think of leaving, but it was killing me to stay. I found a therapist and she saved my life. I started to learn what a healthy relationship felt like. When I met Marilou, she had her crises. But she didn't act like they were all my fault. She was difficult sometimes—"

"Was I ever," she said.

"But at least we talked about it."

"Sometimes. We *learned* how to talk. Bit by bit, brick by brick."

"Yeah, but I wouldn't have figured out how if you weren't willing to listen," he said.

"I wanted to learn how to listen."

A smile passed between them.

"It would be simplistic to say things get easier or smooth out," Ned said. "The same stuff comes up again and again. If there's a change, it's feeling that there are better things to do than have the same old battles."

"We still have important conversations, though. They're conversations that could have happened a long time ago, but now they feel less risky."

"It's true. And if things go south, I quote my favorite line from *The Aeneid*: 'A joy it will be one day, perhaps, to remember even this.'"

"Here I am, almost seventy," sighed Marilou, "and I've realized it takes so long to grow up. It takes a while to accept that you spend your whole life learning. We're the grown-ups now, we get to figure it out for ourselves. Feeling good with each other, being good to each other—that's all that really counts."

Are we all good at couple conversation? Not necessarily, and that's okay. In midlife, one barrier to change is that people think they should already know what they are doing. In fact, being open to not knowing what you are doing is the first step to learning something new. We don't have to be experts. We've never been here before. What counts is our intention to engage. And that intention will be realized if we keep trying to have three kinds of conversations, until the day we die.

1. Keep having the hard (and easy) conversations with each other.

The easy conversations are a source of domestic joy—the humor, the familiar routines, the shared moments with the kids, the checking in, the private languages, the playful sexual proposals, the loving words. Never let up on the easy conversations, and don't hold pleasurable moments hostage to the problem of the day. Marriage juxtaposes minor irritations with intimate sex with boring chores with exciting adventures with painful disconnection with warm affection. Even when it's good, that's what marriage *is*. Try to ride the wave.

Hard conversations are easier in a climate of trust and safety; but regardless, they pretty much always take guts. At first, it may feel as if you are hacking away with blunt tools at the teeming undergrowth in the Amazonian rain forest. But it's better to start hacking away *now* since hard conversations rarely get easier. If you are married to an avoider, don't give up trying to connect, even if you tinker with your strategy. Those of you who are married to emoters, stay compassionate and firm: "I'll be able to listen better and respond if you take it down a couple notches." What if you can barely remember what it felt like to be close? Start a conversation about *that*. An honest conversation about how alienated you feel can allow you to view your problem as shared. It could bring you closer or at least help you find a path forward.

Gestures count too. Don't sniff at a hug or a trip to the hardware store as a means of communication. Verbal conversation is required to hash out complex emotions, but not to express affection. It's a trap to require the exact right words (or the exact right gesture) as the proof of devotion. For Jane, staying in conversation didn't involve a lot of measured talk. It meant staying engaged with her husband and seeing through a very difficult forty-year marriage—in her words, "staying in the saddle." Her husband had recently died when we spoke. She told me about their messy beginnings, their dramatic fights, his intermittent gambling and impossible approach to money. Did she ever feel it would have been healthier to leave? "I couldn't have done that to the kids. That was sometimes all I had to hang on to. There were times when I hated him. But through it all, there was a lot of love there. It was a 'What God hath joined together, let no man put asunder' kind of thing. He was a tortured man in some ways, and he could torture me at times, but I loved him. Now that he's gone, I'm proud of what we did. We kept coming back and working it out. We had backbone. If you'd caught me at many points in those forty years, you might have thought, 'Why is she staying with that guy?' I might have been thinking that too! But I'm stubborn." She smiled. "I read about some actress who said she didn't want plastic surgery because she was too interested in what she'd look like when she was old. My marriage was like that for me. I never stopped being interested in where we were headed."

2. Keep having conversations with yourself.

For relationships to stay alive, the individuals within them have to stay alive. Our freedom-seeking core is precious—not freedom *from* others, but the freedom *to* discover our own emotional life. Sometimes only in midlife do we begin to befriend this part of ourselves. Imagination, fantasy, creativity, pleasure in aesthetic and intellectual pursuits, social action, are all facets of your individuality, and they deserve attention and celebration. The last thing you want is a marriage that takes over your mind.

Don't underestimate the value of solitude. Kendall was fifty and had been with her partner, Liza, for seventeen years. "Two years ago, I lost a good friend," Kendall told me. "I got it in my head to go on a pilgrimage along the Way of St. James to Santiago de Compostela. I saved up money and vacation time and walked for five weeks. I wanted to do it by myself. I wanted time alone. I wanted to slow down life. Being able to be apart, without fear, is so important. When I was alone, I could contemplate whether I am right with myself. The ways I negatively treat Liza are the ways I negatively treat myself. To figure out how to relate to her, I'd better figure out how to relate to me.

"Walking day after day, mile after mile, gave me solitude, and it ultimately brought me close to people. I walked with a retired couple I met on the way and got to know them in a way I might not have had Liza been there. Now they've become our friends. Through being alone, I brought new people and interests into our relationship."

3. Keep having conversations with the culture.

In our individualistic culture, where feelings of community have widely deteriorated, couple relationships may seem like life rafts in a sea of disconnection. But couple relationships thrive best in a supportive community. Community is where we express our common humanity and nurture each other in our need. It's not incidental that communities so often have an implicit or explicit spiritual core. They create an atmosphere of plenty and gratitude that extends into, and beyond, our familial realms. They help us connect with people who are wiser than we are about relationships. A friend who married at twenty-one and divorced at thirty-five said, "Elders have wisdom. They can be mentors and even judges when we need emotional strength or have weak egos." Ideally, communities become places where we share our burdens, giving and receiving support.

We also need to talk back to the culture. Its myths about love, marriage, and family life can be phony and exhausting. When we buy into cultural myths, we sometimes lord them over the real people we're supposed to actually love. Advertising harasses us with commercialized simulations of love and domestic comfort—the juxtaposition of swiping credit cards and sexual ecstasy, the holiday commercials with the fake snow and the bundled-up nuclear family with their overly white teeth. An endless stream of technological distractions disrupt conversation, fragment our consciousness, and worm their way into our dreams. Worst of all, work has been transformed into a 24-7 enterprise in the digital age, and its threatened stranglehold on family life and insidious invasion of the bedroom require ongoing vigilance.

We're also surrounded by suspect pop-psychological ideas with considerable currency—about men and women, but also about marriage and sex. One-on-one conversation can free you from the "have sex this way" or "do love that way" formulas that parade themselves as scientific truth. The beauty of marriage is that it's between just two people; you and your partner get to figure out for *yourselves* what makes you feel satisfied. Despite the noisy doomsday headlines, plenty of couples quietly go along engaging in fun sex and treating each other affectionately for decades. They can do this because they've mastered, through some of the means we've explored in these pages, the art of living together.

Talking back to the culture also means trusting personal experience over social norms, which may include arranging your marriage in a nonconventional way, or deciding to divorce. George spoke with me over coffee one day, a year after his divorce papers were final. "It's taken me a while to realize this," he said, "but once Tricia and I weren't trying so hard to stay together, we figured out a new way to talk to each other. We started paying attention to how we really felt and were more interested in what the other person was going through.

"We didn't give the kids a living example of a loving marriage, and I'll always be sad about that. On the other hand, we've managed to be so much less bitter than my parents were when they divorced. We disagree sometimes, and it can get heated, but we don't boil over like we did when we were married, and I believe that's better for the kids. It lets them do what they are supposed to do—pay attention to their own lives and not get all wrapped up in us."

George regretted that he hadn't realized his dream of an intact family for his children. But he had the courage to face his fear of stigma and sense of failure, and make what he believed was the right choice. The security he and Tricia had promoted through respectful and honest conversation represented an achievement of which they were justly proud. A good divorce can be more of a "marriage" than some marriages are. "Even though we no longer live together," George said, "we're true partners in raising our kids."

It's through conversation that we learn the essential truth of relationships: I can try to understand what you think and feel, without its taking away from the reality of my own experience. Conversations take time, and patience, and they unfold through the ongoing attempt to let things settle, to tolerate confusion, and to remain receptive. They flourish when we can trust that our story won't be swept away, and we'll be seen and recognized by the other person. The engine of couple happiness is to engage early and often. Deepen inward by investing in your we story. Expand outward by nurturing friendships and cultivating your interests. Go to church if you seek community and spiritual sustenance. Go to therapy if you can't find a way to talk. If you ever loved your partner, do everything you can to uncover the embers of warmth and fan them. Do not lull yourself into a dysfunctional narrative that, like a sleepwalker, you can't snap out of—that no marriage is happy, or the kids don't notice the fighting, or the only solution is to escape through drink or screens or work. These self-anesthetizing strategies disconnect you from your life and your partner. You only have one of each.

AT THEIR BEST, marriages are living, breathing creations between two people. If you are ready to have a continuing conversation, a lot is possible. You listen, you explore, you innovate, you jointly write your script. You arrive at your own agreements. Any path, conventional or not, involves gains and losses. No choice offers nirvana. Time apart, separate vacations, agreed-upon domains of privacy—any possibility is fair game. You learn as you go, about yourselves and your marriage. There's good news here: the clearer you become about what you want as a couple, the freer you are to enjoy yourself. Whatever shape a relationship takes, one definition of love might be this: "I want to know you. I care what happens next between us." The road may not be marked, but being open to discovery can lead us back to a truer, deeper sense of home.

If there's a gift on the other side of the rough patch, it's emerging with a life that feels enlarged and enlightened. When we've figured out how to be who we are, while staying in loving connection with others, we've arrived at the harmonic balance of intimacy and exploration, commitment and freedom. We've put our hearts into it, and now, astonishingly, all that work, all those hard conversations, pay off. We go out and live, with our whole spirit and our whole self. Love is a conversation—with a partner, certainly, but with all the other people and things that matter to us too. There's always a different angle, a new way to listen. You don't know what's next. You *can't* know. The world is still new.

Acknowledgments

I owe my deepest thanks to the many people who have placed their trust in me as their therapist. It takes courage to look at oneself, and to change, and I have been honored to listen to your stories and help you make new ones. Many people agreed to be interviewed for this book and confided their personal experiences to me in hopes of helping others. I am grateful to all of them for their generosity and candor.

My therapist colleagues have been ongoing source of intellectual stimulation and challenge as I've wrestled with the clinical complexities of the rough patch. A huge thank-you to the members of my writing group, for their thoughtful comments and lively interest: Richard Almond, Joseph Caston, Marilyn Caston, Dianne Elise, Sam Gerson, Peter Goldberg, Erik Hesse, Mary Main, Deborah Melman, Shelley Nathans, Harvey Peskin, Tsipora Peskin, Carolyn Wilson, Mitchell Wilson, and the late Robert and Judith Wallerstein. For our mutual trust and care, I sincerely thank my fellow clinicians David Frankel and Dawn Smith.

I am also grateful to the many colleagues, scholars, and professionals in various fields who gave of their time and expertise: Joe Astrachan, Mike Austin, Ellyn Bader, David Blacker, Louann Brizendine, Stephanie Brown, Chris Cole, Lucy Collier, Tom Connelly, Carolyn Cowan, Philip Cowan, Colette de Marneffe, Peter de Marneffe, Bill Donaldson, Diane Donnelly, Julie Friend, Harville Hendrix, Stephen Hinshaw,

Celeste Hirschman, Helen LaKelly Hunt, Meg Jay, Sam Jinich, Ian Kerner, Brenda Kinsel, Ruth Krumbhaar, Robert Levenson, Barry McCarthy, Sarah McNeil, Karly Mitchell, Deborah Price, Stephen Purcell, Owen Renik, Alan Rubenstein, Lia Rudnick, Marc Schulz, Kanade Shinkai, Karen Skerrett, Renee Spencer, Mary Target, Meridel Tobias, Robert Weiss, and Joe Zarate-Sanderlin. For their research assistance, I thank Henri Garrison-Desany, Alexandra McKim Kelly, Michelle Sullivan, and especially Adrianne Lange for her knowledge of infant development and her careful reading of several chapters.

This book would not exist without the loyalty, inspiration, and vision of my agent, Tina Bennett. I know I am not alone in regarding Tina as one of the best people in my life. She is a remarkable model of generativity, and I deeply appreciate her fierce devotion to the ideas she champions, including my own. Her verve, integrity, and sheer, sparkling brilliance are the best medicine for writerly rough patches and pretty much everything else. It has also been my great good fortune to work with my editor, Colin Harrison. Colin is a true editor, and his humanity, insight, and aesthetics are felt on every page. As he is fond of saying, a book is a process, and I am profoundly thankful to him for making the process enjoyable and collaborative, as well as intermittently hilarious. My gratitude also goes to Svetlana Katz of WME and to all the superb professionals at Scribner, including Susan Moldow, Nan Graham, Roz Lippel, Jaya Miceli, Brian Belfiglio, Dan Cuddy, Steve Boldt, and Sarah Goldberg.

For their steadfast support and friendship, my heartfelt thanks go to Debra Fine, Susan Morrison, Maureen Katz, Sue Warhaftig, Dawn Smith, Kira Keane, Amy Kaufman Burk, Arietta Slade, Jeanne Leary, Jessica Marshall, Wendy Stern, and Mary Margaret McClure. I can't imagine my life without my brother Peter and sister Colette, my enduring conversational partners, on whose sensitivity and perceptiveness I continue to rely. I am grateful to the extended Becker and de Marneffe families for their unfailing generosity and thoughtfulness, and especially to my parents, Nancy Ferranti and Francis de Marneffe, for their abiding love. Though their early divorce spurred my interest in the question of what makes marriages work, their long second marriages to my devoted stepparents helped to provide some valuable answers.

My greatest love and thanks go to my husband and our children. To Sophie, Alex, and Nicholas, thank you for your affection, wit, sweetness, and good character, and for all the joy and meaning you bring to our lives. It has been my great privilege to nurture you and watch you grow. It's now an extraordinary gift to relate to you as young adults. I hope that perhaps in some small way this book will aid you in the journey ahead.

To Terry, thank you for everything you've shared with me—the pleasure, the humor, the encouragement, the kindness, the children, and the love. For decades now, you've been my special friend. I married you for about twelve reasons and it's grown to twelve hundred. I don't know if I'll ever be able to express them all, but as a believer in conversation, I'll never stop trying.

Notes

Chapter 1—The Rough Patch: An Introduction

1 **people are happier at sixty-five than forty-five:** D. Blanchower and A. Oswald, "Is well-being U-shaped over the life cycle?," *National Bureau of Economic Research*, Working Paper 12935 (2007), http://www.nber.org/papers/w12935.

7 **"An open secret in our world":** S. Cavell, *The Pursuits of Happiness* (Cambridge, MA: Harvard University Press, 1981), 141.

7 **hold stunningly inconsistent romantic narratives:** A. J. Cherlin, *The Marriage-Go-Round* (New York: Vintage, 2009), 32; E. Illouz, *Consuming the Romantic Utopia* (Berkeley: University of California Press, 1997), chap. 5, esp. 179–80.

7 **Not many rules are left:** See S. Coontz, *Marriage, a History* (New York: Penguin, 2006), 282.

7 **the religious right divorce *more* often than other people:** J. Glass and P. Levchak, "Red states, blue states, and divorce: Understanding the impact of conservative Protestantism on regional variation in divorce rates," *American Journal of Sociology* 119, no. 4 (2014): 1002–46; Cherlin, *Marriage-Go-Round*, 135.

8 **Demographic research over the past two decades:** A. J. Cherlin, "Demographic trends in the United States: A review of the research in the 2000s," *Journal of Marriage and Family* 72, no. 3 (2010): 403–19; R. D. Putnam, *Our Kids: The American Dream in Crisis* (New York: Simon & Schuster, 2015), chaps. 1 and 2.

8 **goal of being a good parent:** National Marriage Project, *State of Our Unions, 2010* (Charlottesville: University of Virginia), www.stateofourunions.org; K. S. Hymowitz, *Marriage and Caste in America* (Chicago: Ivan R. Dee, 2006).

8 **"to take the place of parents who love each other":** W. Bion, *Learning from Experience* (New York: Rowman and Littlefield, 1983), 128.

10 **the marriage of true minds:** W. Shakespeare, sonnet 116.

11 **Our emotions form the core of our sense of meaning:** D. Meltzer, "The Kleinian expansion of Freud's metapsychology," *International Journal of Psychoanalysis* 62 (1981): 182.

11 **self is grounded in emotions, and emotions happen within a body:** See, for example, A. Damasio, *Self Comes to Mind: Constructing the Conscious Brain* (New York: Pantheon, 2010); J. Panksepp, *Affective Neuroscience: The Foundations of Human and Animal Emotions* (New York: Oxford University Press, 2005); W. Porges, *The Polyvagal Theory: Neurophysiological Foundations of Emotions, Attachment, Communication, and Self-Regulation* (New York: Norton, 2011).

11 **that allows the dove to fly:** My thanks to Alessandra Lemma for this allusion. See P. W. Bruno, *Kant's Concept of Genius: Its Origin and Function in the Third Critique* (New York: Bloomsbury, 2010), 126.

11 **our minds are formed in relationships:** See, for example, D. Siegel, *The Developing Mind*, 2nd ed. (New York: Guilford, 2012); P. Fonagy, H. Steele, M. Steele, G. S. Moran, and A. C. Higgitt, "The capacity for understanding mental states: The reflective self in parent and child and its significance for security of attachment," *Infant Mental Health Journal* 12, no. 3 (1991): 201–18.; J. Holmes and A. Slade, *Attachment for Therapists: From Science to Practice*, (Thousand Oaks, CA: Sage Publications, 2017), 34.

11 **Psychology has made huge strides:** To name just a few important sources: J. J. Gross (ed.), *Handbook of Emotion Regulation*, 2nd ed. (New York: Guilford, 2014); Siegel, *Developing Mind*; L. Bloch, C. M. Haase, and R. W. Levenson, "Emotion regulation predicts marital satisfaction: More than a wives' tale," *Emotion* 14, no. 1 (2014): 130–44; A. N. Schore, *Affect Regulation and the Repair of the Self* (New York: Norton, 2003); P. Fonagy, G. Gergely, E. L. Jurist, and M. Target, *Affect Regulation, Mentalization, and the Development of the Self* (New York: Other Press, 2002); M. Mikulincer and P. Shaver, *Attachment in Adulthood: Structure, Dynamics, and Change*, 2nd ed. (New York: Guilford, 2016).

12 **our emotions signal what's important:** J. J. Campos, E. A. Walle, A. Dahl, and A. Main, "Reconceptualizing emotion regulation," *Emotion Review* 3 (2011): 26–35.

13 **short shrift in writings on couples:** Exceptions include the work of Ellyn Bader and Peter Pearson, www.couplesinstitute.com; M. Schulz, M. K. Pruett, P. K. Kerig, and R. D. Parke, *Strengthening Couple Relationships for Optimal Child Development* (Washington, DC: American Psychological Association Press, 2010).

15 **one of their proudest accomplishments is their marriage:** L. L. Carstensen, *A Long Bright Future* (New York: Broadway Books, 2009), 120.

16 **fatally flawed marriages:** This term was coined by the psychologist and sex therapist Barry McCarthy. B. McCarthy, interview, September 19, 2016.

Chapter 2—A Brief History of the Midlife Crisis

19 **invention of "childhood" in the 1600s and "adolescence" in the early 1900s:** W. Kesson, "The American child and other cultural inventions," *American Psychologist* 34, no. 10 (1979): 815–20; J. J. Arnett, "Adolescent storm and stress, reconsidered," *American Psychologist* 54, no. 5 (1999): 317–26.

19 **White men's life expectancy:** https://www.cdc.gov/nchs/data/hus/2010/022 .pdf.

19 **a series of adult stages:** E. Erikson, *Childhood and Society* (New York: Norton, 1950).

19 **In a 1965 article cheerfully entitled "Death and the Midlife Crisis":** E. Jaques, "Death and the midlife crisis," *International Journal of Psycho-Analysis* 46 (1965): 502–14.

19 **George Vaillant, Roger Gould, and Daniel Levinson:** G. E. Vaillant, *Adaptation to Life* (Boston: Little, Brown, 1977); R. L. Gould, *Transformations: Growth and Change in Adult Life* (New York: Simon and Schuster, 1978); D. J. Levinson, *The Seasons of a Man's Life* (New York: Ballantine, 1978); G. Sheehy, *Passages* (New York: Dutton, 1976).

20 **Between 1966 and 1979, the American divorce rate doubled:** Coontz, *Marriage, a History*, 261.

20 **"a slob, and a poor housekeeper":** Levinson, *Seasons of a Man's Life*, 117–18.

20 **"a special woman who would help him pull his life together":** Ibid., 169.

21 **change from an "attractive twenty-eight-year-old newlywed":** Ibid., 310–11.

21 **"undermine[s] his formerly idealized view of her"**: Ibid., 308.
21 **Tracy began doing things [Joan's] way, restricting his life to please her**: Ibid., 311.
22 **the romantic genre of adult development**: See K. Murray, "Literary pathfinding: The work of popular life constructors," in *Narrative Psychology: The Storied Nature of Human Conduct*, ed. T. Sarbin (New York: Praeger, 1986), 276–92.
22 **"whatever counterfeit safety"**: G. Sheehy, *Passages* (New York: Dutton, 1976), 251.
22 **demanding husband or time-intensive children**: G. Sheehy, *Sex and the Seasoned Woman* (New York: Random House, 2006), 194.
22 **"romantic, excited, eager"**: S. Shellenbarger, *The Breaking Point* (New York: Henry Holt, 2005), 37.
23 **"from euphoria to black despair"**: Ibid., 38.
23 **"Old values and standards of behavior began falling away"**: Ibid., 9.
23 **"jettison her hard-won career of thirty years"**: Ibid., 9–10.
24 **"activist stance in expressing personal frustration"**: Ibid., 13.
24 **posed as a hero's quest**: The "hero's journey" derives from J. Campbell, *The Hero with a Thousand Faces* (Novato, CA: New World Library, 2008).
24 **"to rekindle her inner passions"**: Shellenbarger, *Breaking Point*, 46.
25 **the costs of workplace bias**: See, for example, J. C. Williams, *Reshaping the Work-Family Debate* (Cambridge, MA: Harvard University Press, 2010).
25 **clarifying what matters to us**: See, for example, R. Josselson, *Revising Herself: The Story of Women's Identity from College to Midlife* (New York: Oxford University Press, 1996).
25 **over a third cite emotional abuse**: Austin Institute for the Study of Family and Culture, "Relationships in America" (2014), http://relationshipsinamerica.com/marriage-and-divorce/what-reasons-do-divorcees-offer-for-leaving.
25 **"prophets of personal reinvention"**: N. Gibbs, "Midlife Crisis? Bring It On!" *Time*, May 16, 2005, 53.
25 **"de-repression of emotions"**: G. Labouvie-Vief and M. R. DeVoe "Emotion regulation in adulthood and later life: A developmental view," in *Annual Review of Gerontology and Geriatrics: Focus on Emotion and Adult Development*, series ed. M. P. Lawton and volume ed. K. W. Schaie (New York: Springer, 1991), 17: 181.
26 **"many opposing affects in sometimes tragic fashion"**: G. Labouvie-Vief, L. M. Chiodo, L. A. Goguen, M. Diehl, and L. Orwoll, "Representations of the self across the lifespan," *Psychology and Aging* 10 (1995): 405.
26 **"inner states, in which conflicting feelings may war with one another"**: C. Magai and B. Halpern, "Emotional development during the middle years," in *Handbook of Midlife Development*, ed. M. E. Lachman (John Wiley, 2001), 315. Italics in original.
26 **the midlife journey should cause "a minimum of human damage"**: G. Sheehy, *Pathfinders* (New York: William Morrow, 1981), 41.
26 **the psychologist Dan McAdams**: D. McAdams, *The Redemptive Self: Stories Americans Live By* (New York: Oxford University Press, 2006).
32 **a psychological response that put her in contact with a state of profound security and safety**: C. Cole, interview, August 17, 2016.
34 **Research is unequivocal**: See, for instance, C. P. Cowan and P. A. Cowan, *When Partners Become Parents* (New York: Basic Books, 1992); E. Lawrence, A. D. Rothman, C. J. Cobb, M. T. Rothman, and T. N. Bradbury, "Marital satisfaction across the transition to parenthood," *Journal of Family Psychology* 22 (2008): 41–50.
35 **In a research study entitled "The Rested Relationship"**: H. M. Maranges, and J. K. McNulty, "The rested relationship: Sleep benefits marital evaluations," *Journal of Family Psychology* 31, no. 1 (2017): 117–22.

36 **Turning toward each other:** J. M. Gottman and N. Silver, *The Seven Principles for Making Marriage Work* (New York: Three Rivers Press, 1999), chap. 5.

38 **curious durability of the "midlife crisis":** See, for instance, J. Heckhausen, "Adaptation and resilience in midlife," *Handbook of Midlife Development*, ed. Lachman, 345–94.

39 **"but you will, and must, move on":** Cherlin, *Marriage-Go-Round*, 31–32.

39 **"individualistic marriage," "consumer marriage," or "expressive divorce":** These terms are drawn, respectively, from Cherlin, *Marriage-Go-Round*; W. Doherty, *Take Back Your Marriage*, 2nd ed. (New York: Guilford, 2013); and B. D. Whitehead, *The Divorce Culture* (New York: Vintage, 1998).

40 **not best managed by simple suppression:** See, for example, E. A. Impett, A. Kogan, T. English, O. John, C. Oveis, A. M. Gordon, and D. Keltner, "Suppression sours sacrifice: Emotional and relational costs of suppressing emotions in romantic relationships," *Personality and Social Psychology Bulletin* 38, no. 6 (2012): 707–20.

40 **the longest-running study of men's adult development:** The Harvard Study of Adult Development, or the Grant Study, has been the basis of several books by George E. Vaillant, including *Triumphs of Experience* (Cambridge, MA: Harvard University Press, 2012); see also R. Waldinger, "What makes a good life? Lessons from the longest study on happiness," https://www.ted.com/talks/robert_waldinger_what _makes_a_good_life_lessons_from_the_longest_study_on_happiness?language=en.

40 **Recent data analyses show:** R. J. Waldinger and M. S. Schulz, "The long reach of nurturing family environments: Links with midlife emotion-regulatory styles and late-life security in intimate relationships," *Psychological Science* 27, no. 11 (2016): 1443–50.

Chapter 3—Feeling Close, in Love and Sex

44 **It is unhealthy to be in such a relationship:** See, for example, J. K. Kiecolt-Glaser and T. L. Newton, "Marriage and health: His and hers," *Psychological Bulletin* 127, no. 4 (2001): 472–503.

45 **dutifully read the popular sex experts:** See, for example, E. Perel, *Mating in Captivity* (New York: HarperCollins, 2005).

46 **"A great number of both men and women":** H. V. Dicks, *Marital Tensions: Clinical Studies Toward a Psychological Theory of Interaction* (New York: Basic Books, 1967), 36.

48 **our partner steps in and helps "co-regulate" us:** J. A. Coan, H. S. Schaefer, and R. J. Davidson, "Lending a hand: Social regulation of the neural response to threat," *Psychological Science* 17 (2006): 1032–39.

50 **either too *absorbed* in the child's emotional experience, or too *distant* from it:** Fonagy et al., *Affect Regulation*, 38; B. Beebe and E. McCrorie, "The optimum midrange: Infant research, literature, and romantic attachment," *Attachment: New Directions in Relational Psychoanalysis and Psychotherapy* 4, no. 1 (2010): 39–58.

50 **Having a benign and thoughtful adult:** Fonagy et al., *Affect Regulation*, 4.

50 **this activity goes by the name of *reflective functioning*:** Fonagy et al., "Capacity for understanding mental states"; A. Slade, "Parental reflective functioning: An introduction," *Attachment and Human Development* 7, no. 3 (2005): 269–81.

50 **"the non-defensive willingness to engage emotionally":** Slade, "Parental reflective functioning," 271.

50 **The "good enough" relationship:** D. Winnicott, *The Child, the Family, and the Outside World* (New York: Perseus Publishing, 1992); D. de Marneffe, *Maternal Desire: On Children, Love, and the Inner Life* (New York: Little, Brown, 2004),

81; E. Tronick, "Emotions and emotional communication in infants," *American Psychologist* 44, no. 2 (1989): 112–19.

51 **develop the same capacity within *ourselves*:** Holmes and Slade, *Attachment for Therapists*, chap. 4.

54 **"how they experience and express these emotions":** J. J. Gross, "The emerging field of emotion regulation: An integrative review," *Review of General Psychology* 2 (1998): 275, doi:10.1037/1089-2680.2.3.271.

55 **can replace the idea "I am a bad person":** This example comes from M. Main, "Metacognitive knowledge, metacognitive monitoring, and singular (coherent) vs. multiple (incoherent) model of attachment: Findings and directions for future research," in *Attachment Across the Life Cycle*, ed. C. M. Parkes, J. Stevenson-Hinde, and P. Marris (New York: Routledge, 1993), 136–37.

55 **mindfulness is a useful technique for cultivating nonjudgmental awareness:** See, for example, J. Kabat-Zinn, *Full Catastrophe Living* (New York: Bantam, 2013).

55 **Of course you can't reflect during a fight:** D. B. Wile, *After the Honeymoon: How Conflict Can Improve Your Relationship* (Oakland, CA: Collaborative Couple Therapy Books, 2008), 191–212; R. W. Levenson, interview, October 11, 2016.

56 **act as friends, we respond to each other's bids:** J. M. Gottman and N. Silver, *What Makes Love Last?* (New York: Simon & Schuster, 2012), chap. 3.

56 **become lost in absorbing negative states:** J. Gottman, *The Science of Trust: Emotional Attunement for Couples*, (New York: Norton, 2011), chaps. 2 and 3.

56 **They don't behave in their *own* best interests, either:** C. F. Camerer, *Behavioral Game Theory: Experiments in Strategic Interaction* (New York: Russell Sage, 2003), 11, quoted in Gottman, *Science of Trust*, 69–70.

56 **worth attempting a "bottom-up" rather than a "top-down" strategy:** D. Siegel, *The Neurobiology of We* (Louisville, CO: Sounds True, 2011), chap. 7.

58 **it's society's fault:** See, for example, L. Kipnis, *Against Love: A Polemic* (New York: Vintage, 2004).

58 **as sociobiologists are quick to point out:** For example, H. Fisher, *Why We Love: The Nature and Chemistry of Romantic Love* (New York: Henry Holt, 2004).

58 **"relief from the strain of psychic structure itself":** S. Mitchell, *Can Love Last? The Fate of Romance over Time* (New York: Norton, 2002), 85.

62 **it's not performance but attitude that's key:** McCarthy, interview.

62 **"the ability to 'contain hate in the framework of love'":** Dicks, *Marital Tensions*, 31.

Chapter 4—Marriage as a Story

67 **"so that it could be shaped *by* story":** J. Gottschall, *The Storytelling Animal* (New York: Houghton Mifflin, 2012), 56.

67 **Personal identity *itself* takes the form of a story:** D. P. McAdams, "The psychology of life stories," *Review of General Psychology* 5, no. 2 (2001): 101.

67 **a primary goal of young adulthood in our culture:** Erikson, *Childhood and Society*. See McAdams, *Redemptive Self*, chap. 3.

68 **Life satisfaction relates to telling a meaningful story:** D. P. McAdams, "Generativity in midlife," in *Handbook of Midlife Development*, ed. Lachman, 395–443.

68 **"the capacity to keep a particular narrative going":** A. Giddens, *Modernity and Self-Identity: Self and Society in the Late Modern Age* (Stanford, CA: Stanford University Press, 1991), 54. Quoted in McAdams, "Psychology of life stories," 112.

68 **"assumes the form of the cliché":** E. Schachtel, *Metamorphosis* (New York: Basic Books, 1959), 288. Quoted in M. Skura, "Creativity: Transgressing the limits of consciousness," *Daedalus* 109, no. 2 (1980): 128.

69 When dissatisfied partners disengage: D. Vaughn, *Uncoupling* (New York: Oxford University Press, 1986), 5; Doherty, *Take Back Your Marriage*, 120.

69 they still need a story that makes sense of it: Vaughn, *Uncoupling*, 5, 28–30.

69 mistaking slogans for personal experience: Wile, *After the Honeymoon*, chap. 12.

69 "plagiarize selectively": McAdams, "Psychology of life stories," 16.

69 contradictory story lines: Cherlin, *Marriage-Go-Round*, chap. 5, esp. 135.

69 authentic love to be found, as Søren Kierkegaard argued: M. Austin, "We get to carry each other: U2 and Kierkegaard on authentic love," *Philosophy Now* 64 (2007), https://philosophynow.org/issues/64/We_Get_To_Carry_Each_Other _U2_and_Kierkegaard_on_Authentic_Love; M. Austin, interview, May 10, 2016.

69 "persistent sisyphian attempt": Illouz, *Consuming the Romantic Utopia*, 175–76.

70 "epiphanies," discoveries, and "turning points": McAdams, "Psychology of life stories," 114.

70 Stories tend to take three basic shapes: K. J. Gergen and M. M. Gergen, "Narrative form and the construction of psychological science," in *Narrative Psychology*, ed. Sarbin, 27–28.

71 alternating periods of adventure and repose: From K. E. Scheibe, "Self-narratives and adventure," in *Narrative Psychology*, ed. Sarbin, 133.

71 Some sizable subset of long-term couples report ongoing feelings of intensity: B. P. Acevedo and A. Aron, "Does a long-term relationship kill romantic love?," *Review of General Psychology* 13, no. 1 (2009): 59–65.

72 psychologists call it a "we story": J. A. Singer and K. Skerrett, *Positive Couple Therapy: Using We-Stories to Enhance Resilience* (New York: Routledge, 2014).

73 laid down as "implicit" memories: Siegel, *Developing Mind*, 393–94.

73 our brains are "anticipation machines": Ibid., 53.

73 "We simply enter these engrained states": Ibid., 55.

73 through the emotional lens of the past: Mikulincer and Shaver, *Attachment in Adulthood*, 110–12.

74 the "narrative self," is born: D. Stern, *The Interpersonal World of the Infant* (New York: Basic Books, 2000), xxv.

74 all infant-caregiver pairs display one of four distinct patterns: See M. Main, "The organized categories of infant, child, and adult attachment: Flexible vs. inflexible attention under attachment-related stress," *Journal of the American Psychoanalytic Association* 48 (2000): 1055–95; E. Hesse and M. Main, "Disorganized infant, child, and adult attachment: Collapse in behavioral and attentional strategies," *Journal of the American Psychoanalytic Association* 48 (2000): 1097–127.

74 When a caregiver is sensitive and responsive to the child's attachment-seeking behavior: de Marneffe, *Maternal Desire*, chap. 3.

75 simultaneously frightened and frightening behavior: Hesse and Main, "Disorganized infant, child, and adult attachment," 1112–13.

75 child's developing story of self can fluidly incorporate: Mikulincer and Shaver, *Attachment in Adulthood*, 219–20.

75 in secure relating: Siegel, *Developing Mind*, 374.

75 The parent elicits and scaffolds her child's stories: D. Stern, *Diary of a Baby* (New York: Basic Books, 1992), Part V.

75 problematic models of the attachment figure and the self: Main, "Metacognitive knowledge," in *Attachment Across the Life Cycle*, ed. Parkes, Stevenson-Hinde, and Marris, 127–59.

76 Using an instrument called the Adult Attachment Interview (AAI): M. Main, N. Kaplan, and J. Cassidy, "Security in infancy, childhood, and adulthood: A move to the level of representation," in *Growing Points of Attachment Theory and Research. Monographs of the Society for Research in Child Development* 50 (1–2, serial no. 209), ed. I. Bretherton and E. Watters (University of Chicago Press, 1985), 66–104.

76 **adults who are rated as "secure-autonomous":** Main, "Organized categories of infant, child, and adult attachment," 1055–95.

77 **That's what attachment researchers call "earned" or "evolved" security:** E. Hesse, "The Adult Attachment Interview: Protocol, method of analysis, and selected empirical studies, 1985–2015," in *Handbook of Attachment: Theory, Research, and Clinical Applications*, 3rd ed., ed. J. Cassidy and P. Shaver (New York: Guilford, 2016), 553–97.

77 **Emotional support from a therapist, or some other important figure:** R. Saunders, D. Jacobvitz, M. Zaccagnino, L. M. Beverung, and N. Hazen, "Pathways to earned security: The role of alternative support figures," *Attachment and Human Development* 13, no. 4 (2011): 403–20.

77 **A study of children reared in institutions:** M. Rutter, D. Quinton, and J. Hill, "Adult outcome of institution-reared children: Males and females compared," in *Straight and Devious Pathways from Childhood to Adulthood*, ed. L. N. Robins and M. Rutter (Cambridge, UK: Cambridge University Press, 1990), 135–57.

77 **Mothers who were abused in childhood:** B. Egeland, D. Jacobvitz, and L. A. Sroufe, "Breaking the cycle of abuse," *Child Development* 59, no. 4 (1988): 1080–88.

77 **Marriage and parenthood:** Mikulincer and Shaver, *Attachment in Adulthood*, 142.

77 **security between partners:** N. Mehta, P. A. Cowan, and C. P. Cowan, "Working Models of Attachment to Parents and Partners: Implications for Emotional Behavior Between Partners," *Journal of Family Psychology* 23 (2009): 895–99.

77 **The brilliance of the AAI:** Siegel, *Neurobiology of We*, chap. 3

77 **"think about feeling and feel about thinking":** Slade, "Parental reflective functioning," 271.

79 **Imagine a young woman who is torn:** I am grateful to Erik Hesse for this example.

80 **to modulate and modify our emotions:** See Siegel, *Developing Mind*, 36, 373.

80 **The sheer act of becoming aware:** See ibid.; M. Linehan, *Cognitive-Behavioral Treatment of Borderline Personality Disorder* (New York: Guilford, 1993); L. F. Barrett, J. Gross, T. C. Christensen, and M. Benvenuto, "Knowing what you're feeling and knowing what to do about it: Mapping the relation between emotion differentiation and emotional regulation," *Cognition and Emotion* 15, no. 6 (2001): 713–24; M. Jay, *Supernormal: The Untold Story of Adversity and Resilience* (New York: Twelve, 2017), 243.

81 **chaos and rigidity are signposts of emotional dysregulation:** Siegel, *Developing Mind*, 28–29, 361–64.

82 **unmet craving for love, tenderness, and affection:** S. M. Andersen, R. Miranda, and T. Edwards, "When self-enhancement knows no bounds: Are past relationships with significant others at the heart of narcissism?," *Psychological Inquiry* 12, no. 4 (2001): 198.

86 **Bearing guilt and responsibility for one's own feelings:** See H. Loewald, "The waning of the Oedipus complex," in *The Essential Loewald: Collected Papers and Monographs* (Hagerstown, MD: University Publishing Group, 2000).

87 **Psychoanalytic therapists refer to it as the third:** S. Ruszczynski, "'The marital triangle': Towards 'triangular space' in the intimate couple relationship," *Journal of the British Association of Psychotherapists* 3 (1998): 33–46; Gottman, *Science of Trust*, chap. 5.

87 **parallel monologue:** H. Hendrix, *Getting the Love You Want* (New York: St. Martin's Griffin, 2008), 146.

88 **To navigate a couple conversation successfully:** The best book on couple conversation is Wile, *After the Honeymoon*.

91 **"an enormously welcome relief":** J. Gottman, *Science of Trust*, 65.

91 **"To tell a story is inescapably to take a moral stance":** J. Bruner, *Acts of Meaning* (Cambridge, MA: Harvard University Press, 1990), 51.

91 **possibilities rather than certainties:** J. Bruner, *Actual Minds, Possible Worlds* (Cambridge, MA: Harvard University Press, 1987), 26.

Chapter 5—Affairs, Flirting, and Fantasy: They're Never about Nothing

97 **Affairs are about so many things for the hurt partner:** The terms *hurt partner* and *unfaithful partner* are from J. A. Spring, *After the Affair* (New York: William Morrow, 2012).

97 **tries to absorb the traumatic impact:** D. H. Baucom, D. K. Snyder, and K. C. Gordon, *Helping Couples Get Past the Affair* (New York: Guilford, 2009).

97 **"affirmation of the other's identity as a *lovable person*":** Dicks, *Marital Tensions*, 36.

98 **affairs themselves often occur on the heels of loss:** See, for example, S. Nathans, "Infidelity as a manic defense," *Couple and Family Psychoanalysis* 2 (2012): 165–80.

98 **to withstand the impulse to come apart:** See M. Cohen, *Sent Before My Time: A Child Psychotherapist's View of Life on the Neonatal Intensive Care Unit.* (London: Karnac, 2003), 69.

99 **addressed in the work of the late therapist Shirley Glass:** S. Glass, *Not "Just Friends"* (New York: Free Press, 2003).

101 **don't end up marrying the person they left the marriage for:** E. M. Hetherington and J. Kelly, *For Better or Worse: Divorce Reconsidered* (New York: Norton, 2002), 3.

104 **limerence or NRE (new-relationship energy):** D. Tennov, *Love and Limerence: The Experience of Being in Love*, 2nd ed. (Chelsea, MI: Scarborough House, 1998).

107 **"might be suitable for a Polyamorous relationship or Relationship Anarchy":** Y. Alkan, personal communication, July 17, 2016.

107 **Like many female swingers, she was bisexual:** E. M. Fernandes; "The swinging paradigm: An evaluation of the marital and sexual satisfaction of swingers," *Dissertation Abstracts International* (2009), DAI-B 70/05.

108 **"attraction + obstacles = excitement":** J. Morin, *The Erotic Mind* (New York: HarperCollins, 1995), 72.

108 **My only abiding worry had to do with the children:** For a perspective from social science, see E. Sheff, "Strategies in polyamorous parenting," in *Understanding Non-Monogamies*, ed. M. J. Barker and D. Landridge (New York: Routledge, 2010), 169–81.

110 **routinely integrate their sexual thoughts into a shared experience:** See, for instance, M. E. Metz and B. McCarthy, *Enduring Desire* (New York: Routledge, 2011), 107; Morin, *Erotic Mind*; I. Kerner, interview, July 19, 2016.

110 **about everything from sex, to food, to sleep:** T. D. Fisher, Z. T. Moore, and M. Pittenger, "Sex on the brain? An examination of frequency of sexual cognitions as a function of gender, erotophilia, and social desirability," *Journal of Sex Research* 29 (2012): 69–77, doi:10.1080/00224499.2011.565429.

110 **to "enchant" reality:** S. Mitchell, *Relationality: From Attachment to Intersubjectivity* (New York: Routledge, 2003), 24.

111 **Virtually all the sex experts agree:** See, for example, B. Zilbergeld, *The New Male Sexuality*, rev. ed. (New York: Bantam, 1999); L. Barbach, *For Yourself: The Fulfillment of Female Sexuality* (New York: Signet, 2000); E. Nagoski, *Come as You Are* (New York: Simon & Schuster, 2015).

111 **people's typical styles of desire vary:** Nagoski, *Come as You Are*, chap. 7.

111 **"neurochemical cocktail":** Kerner, interview, July 19, 2016.

112 **which sexual triggers *do* elicit each partner's arousal and desire:** S. J. Dawson and M. L. Chivers, "Gender differences and similarities in sexual desire," *Current Sexual Health Reports* (December 2014): doi:10.1007/s11930-014-0027-5.

112 **an "independent libidinal state":** S. Sarin, R. M. Amsel, and Y. M. Binik, "Disentangling desire and arousal: A classificatory conundrum," *Archives of Sexual Behavior* 42 (2013): 1079–100, doi:10.1007/s10508-013-0100-6.

112 **interfere with tuning in sexually:** M. Meana and S. E. Nunnink, "Gender differences in the content of cognitive distraction during sex," *Journal of Sex Research* 43, no. 1 (2006): 59–67.

115 **in the direction of less moralism and more aesthetics:** I. Z. Hoffman, "Poetic transformations of erotic experience: Commentary on paper by Jody Messler Davies," *Psychoanalytic Dialogues* 8, no. 5 (1998): 791–804.

116 **2.5 million adult sites:** O. Ogas and S. Gaddam, *A Billion Wicked Thoughts* (New York: Dutton, 2011), 8.

116 **35 percent of all web traffic:** I. Kerner, "The case for porn," *Psychotherapy Networker* (January/February 2016): 21.

116 **where on the continuum of "cheating" the consumption of pornography falls:** See, for example, R. Douthat, "Is pornography adultery?," theatlantic .com, October 2008, http://www.theatlantic.com/magazine/archive/2008/10 /is-pornography-adultery/306989/.

117 **they create the very secrecy they fear:** Morin, *Erotic Mind*, 293.

118 **"core erotic themes":** See ibid., 292–93 and chap. 5.

118 **enduring and adapting to their male partners' pornography use:** M. N. Resch and K. G. Alderson, "Female partners of men who use pornography: Are honesty and mutual use associated with relationship satisfaction?," *Journal of Sex and Marital Therapy* 40 (2014): 410–24.

118 **a climate of honesty around pornography mitigates distress:** Ibid., 420.

118 **Thirty percent of pornography users are women:** Kerner, "Case for porn," 21.

118 **more open to trying new things and talking:** J. M. Albright, "Sex in America online: An exploration of sex, marital status, and sexual identity in internet sex seeking and its impacts," *Journal of Sex Research* 45 (2008): 184.

118 **greater couple satisfaction, on average, than when one partner (usually the man) is viewing it alone:** A. M. Maddox, G. K. Rhoades, and H. J. Markman, "Viewing sexually-explicit materials alone or together: Associations with relationship quality," *Archives of Sexual Behavior* 40, no. 2 (2009): 441–48; J. C. Manning, "The impact of internet pornography on marriage and the family: A review of the research," *Sexual Addiction and Compulsivity* 13 (2006): 131–65.

118 **Kerner offers his clients "pornography tours":** Kerner, "Case for porn," 43; I. Kerner, interview, July 19, 2016, and August 1, 2016.

118 **a wider shared menu for them to choose from:** Kerner, interview, July 19, 2016.

118 **women respond more readily:** Ogas and Gaddam, *A Billion Wicked Thoughts*, 19, 255.

119 **"It's a wasteland of artifice":** Kerner, "Case for porn," 21.

119 **"43 percent more satisfied with sexuality in *Second Life*":** LMU Newsroom, "Studies: Online Relationships Better than Real Life," August 12, 2010 http:// newsroom.lmu.edu/2010/08/12/studies-online-relationships-better-than-real -life/; R. L. Gilbert, M. A. Gonzalez, and N. A. Murphy, "Sexuality in the 3D internet and its relationship to real-life sexuality," *Psychology and Sexuality* 2, no. 2 (2011): 107–22.

119 **psychically set by adolescence:** G. E. Brannon, "Paraphilic disorders clinical presentation," medscape.com, December 3, 2015, http://emedicine.medscape.com /article/291419-clinical.

120 **Yet, if the marketplace is any measure of the sexual id:** Ogas and Gaddam, *A Billion Wicked Thoughts*.

120 **limit us to certain kinds of (socially sanctioned) difference:** M-J. Barker, "What does a queer relationship look like?," rewriting-the-rules.com, accessed July 25, 2016, https://rewritingtherules.files.wordpress.com/2016/02/queerrelationshipzine .pdf.

120 **"cheerleaders with fake breasts dancing in my head":** D. Zillman and J. Bryant, "Pornography's impact on sexual satisfaction," *Journal of Applied Social Psychology* 18 (1988): 438–53; Albright, "Sex in America online," 175–86.

121 **little agreement exists on the validity of the "pornography addiction" concept:** A. Duffy, D. L. Dawson, and R. Das Nair, "Pornography addiction in adults: A systematic review of definitions and reported impact," *Journal of Sexual Medicine* 13, no. 5 (2016): 760–77.

121 **eleven hours or more of porn use a week:** A. Cooper, D. L. Delmonico, and R. Burg, "Cybersex users, abusers, and compulsives: New findings and implications," *Sexual Addiction and Compulsivity: The Journal of Treatment and Prevention* 7 (2000): 5–29.

121 **despite the accumulation of adverse consequences:** American Society of Addiction Medicine, "Public policy statement: Definition of addiction," August 15, 2011, http://www.asam.org/quality-practice/definition-of-addiction.

121 **to deal with stress and create emotional distance:** Manning, "Impact of internet pornography," 144.

121 **some of these men are attachment avoidant:** D. M. Szymanski and D. N. Stewart-Richardson, "Psychological, relational, and sexual correlates of pornography use on young adult heterosexual men in romantic relationships," *Journal of Men's Studies* 22, no. 1 (2014): 64–82.

122 **"great value to a false need and the depreciation of true ones":** G. Maté, *In the Realm of Hungry Ghosts* (Berkeley, CA: North Atlantic Books, 2010), 181.

122 **The couple therapist Terrence Real:** T. Real, *I Don't Want to Talk About It: Overcoming the Secret Legacy of Male Depression* (New York: Scribner, 1998).

122 **"Is he an addict or an asshole?":** R. Weiss, interview, April 13, 2016.

123 **Women's anger in relationships is typically activated by powerlessness, injustice, and irresponsibility:** J. Gottman, J. S. Gottman, D. Abrams, and R. C. Abrams, *The Man's Guide to Women* (New York: Rodale, 2016), 128–30.

125 **try to give the other person something he or she wants, graciously and generously:** M. E. Weiner-Davis, *The Sex-Starved Marriage* (New York: Simon & Schuster, 2004); Metz and McCarthy, *Enduring Desire*, 51.

125 **Try what some sex therapists recommend:** E. Nagoski, "Do you know when you want it?," thedirtynormal.com, accessed July 26, 2016, http://www.thedirtynormal.com/blog/2010/02/27/do-you-know-when-you-want-it/.

126 **"states of conviction and revenge" as his "preferred self-cures":** A. Phillips, *Missing Out: In Praise of the Unlived Life* (New York: Farrar, Straus and Giroux, 2012), 168.

127 **"I satisfy myself by being committed to my commitment":** Glass, *Not "Just Friends,"* 255.

Chapter 6—Alcohol and Other Attempted Escapes

131 **domestic reentry after a long day:** J. G. Grzywacz and N. F. Marks, "Family, work, work-family spillover and problem drinking during midlife," *Journal of Marriage and the Family* 62, no. 2 (2000): 336–48.

131 **Search *alcohol and marriage*:** F. A. Torvik, E. Røysamb, K. Gustavson, M. Idstad, and K. Tambs, "Discordant and concordant alcohol use in spouses as predictors of marital dissolution in the general population: Results from the Hunt Study," *Alcoholism: Clinical and Experimental Research* 37, no. 5 (2013): 877–84, doi:10.1111/acer.12029.

131 **Search *marijuana and marriage*:** P. H. Smith, G. G. Homish, R. L. Collins, G. A. Giovino, and H. R. White, "Couples' marijuana use is inversely related to their intimate partner violence over the first 9 years of marriage," *Psychology of Addictive Behaviors* 28, no. 3 (2014): 734–42, doi:10.1037/a0037302.

132 **as a *central activity*:** H. Fingarette, *Heavy Drinking* (Berkeley: University of California Press, 1988).

132 **touch the sublime:** M. Ruti, *The Singularity of Being* (New York: Fordham University Press, 2012), 26.

133 **the most common reasons people give for drinking:** M. L. Cooper, M. R. Frone,

M. Russell, and P. Mudar, "Drinking to regulate positive and negative emotions: A motivational model for alcohol use," *Journal of Personality and Social Psychology* 69 (1995): 990–1005.

133 **Substances help us lose self-consciousness:** J. G. Hull, "Self-awareness model," in *Psychological Theories of Drinking and Alcoholism*, ed. K. E. Leonard and H. T. Blane (New York: Guilford, 1987), 272–304.

134 **strongest reasons for problem drinking are for** *regulating negative emotions*: K. J. Sher and E. R. Grekin, "Alcohol and affect regulation," in *Handbook of Emotion Regulation*, 1st ed., ed. J. J. Gross (New York: Guilford, 2007), 571.

134 **Our daily stresses end up stressing our marriage:** A. A. Buck and L. A. Neff, "Stress spillover in early marriage: The role of self-regulatory depletion," *Journal of Family Psychology* 26 (2012): 698–708, doi:10.1037/a0029260.

135 **More than half of US adults:** NCAAD.org, July 25, 2015, https://www.ncadd.org/about-addiction/alcohol/facts-about-alcohol.

135 **they recruit the natural reward centers of the brain:** For a detailed discussion of these concepts, see Maté, *In the Realm of Hungry Ghosts*, pts. 4, 5.

135 **decrease our reactivity to stress:** See, for example, K. M. Grewen and K. C. Light, "Plasma oxytocin is related to lower cardiovascular and sympathetic reactivity to stress," *Biological Psychology* 87, no. 3 (2011): 340–49, doi:10.1016/j.biopsycho.2011.04.003.

135 **can be harnessed to any anticipated reward:** R. Sapolsky, "The pleasures and pains of maybe," Lecture 7, *Being Human: Lessons from the Frontiers of Science* (Chantilly, VA: Great Courses, 2011).

135 **relationships with caregivers** *are* **the child's early environment:** See P. Fonagy, G. Gergely, E.L. Jurist, and M. Target, "The behavioral geneticist's challenge to the psychosocial model of the development of mentalization," in Fonagy et al., *Affect Regulation*, 97–144; also Maté, *In the Realm of Hungry Ghosts*, pt. 4.

136 **"a situation that has been called proximate separation":** Maté, *In the Realm of Hungry Ghosts*, 252. "Proximate separation" is a concept from A. N. Schore, *Affect Regulation and the Origin of the Self* (Hillsdale, NJ: Erlbaum Associates, 1994).

136 **seeking chemical replacements later in life:** Maté, *In the Realm of Hungry Ghosts*, 164.

136 **four times the risk of having a substance use problem in adulthood:** H. Kober, "Emotion regulation in substance use disorders," in *Handbook of Emotion Regulation*, 2nd ed., ed. Gross, 432.

138 **drinking is a major culprit:** Vaillant, *Triumphs of Experience*, chap. 6.

139 **a powerful effect on his** *thinking*: See, for example, S. Brown, *Treating the Alcoholic: A Developmental Model of Recovery* (New York: Wiley, 1985), 96–98.

140 **"wants to overcome its own dysfunction":** Maté, *In the Realm of Hungry Ghosts*, 155.

140 **more differentiation, more individuation, and more autonomy:** For the general model of couple and individual growth I am presenting, see S. Brown and V. Lewis, *The Alcoholic Family in Recovery* (New York: Guilford, 1999).

141 **"a personal accounting system":** Brown, *Treating the Alcoholic*, 79–80.

141 **That's when the dopamine release kicks in:** Maté, *In the Realm of Hungry Ghosts*, 169.

142 **substance use disorders are "primary":** R. D. Margolis and J. E. Zweben, *Treating Patients with Alcohol and Other Drug Problems: An Integrated Approach*, 2nd ed. (Washington, DC: American Psychological Association, 2011), 54; Brown and Lewis, *Alcoholic Family in Recovery*, 44.

145 **I played the role of witness, coach, support, and sounding board:** Brown and Lewis, *Alcoholic Family in Recovery*, 27, 185, 222.

145 **They had entered what addiction specialists call transition:** Ibid., esp. chaps. 6 and 9.

145 "Defective relations with other human beings": *Twelve Steps and Twelve Traditions* (New York: Alcoholics Anonymous World Services, 1981), 80.

146 which created a challenge as parents: Brown and Lewis, *Alcoholic Family in Recovery*, esp. pt. 4.

149 "resentment that they are not different": Maté, *In the Realm of Hungry Ghosts*, 401.

152 "Alcohol is special to the alcoholic": Brown, *Treating the Alcoholic*, 78.

152 "to ward off conscious and unconscious anxieties": W. Colman, "Marriage as a psychological container," in *Psychotherapy with Couples*, ed. S. Ruszczynski (London: Karnac, 1993), 93–94.

152 his own problem with codependency: See, for example, P. Mellody, A. W. Miller, and J. K. Miller, *Facing Codependence* (New York: Harper and Row, 2003).

153 Traumatic events lead to dissociation: B. van der Kolk, *The Body Keeps the Score: Brain, Mind, and Body in the Healing of Trauma* (New York: Viking, 2014), 180.

155 "painful messages from your emotional brain": Ibid., 211.

155 "evoke negative attachment models from the past": S. M. Johnson, *Emotionally Focused Couple Therapy with Trauma Survivors* (New York: Guilford, 2002), 43.

156 "Would our help, good looks, higher income, or cleaner house": Al-Anon Family Groups, *How Al-Anon Works for Families and Friends of Alcoholics* (Audiobooks, Virginia Beach, VA: Al-Anon Family Group Headquarters, 2013), chap. 5.

157 One of *Saturday Night Live*'s most popular skits: "Xanax for Gay Summer Weddings," *Saturday Night Live*, nbc.com, accessed August 12, 2016, http://www .nbc.com/saturday-night-live/video/new-xanax/n37070.

157 growing cultural acceptance of gay marriage: D. Masci and S. Motel, "5 facts about same-sex marriage," Pew Research Center, June 26, 2015, http://www .pewresearch.org/fact-tank/2015/06/26/same-sex-marriage/.

158 "stressful to the self-image of girls and women": K. McMillan, "The truth about prescription pills: One writer's story of anxiety and addiction," vogue.com, April 25, 2014, http://www.vogue.com/865132/prescription-pill-addiction-drug-abuse/.

158 Benzodiazepine use is twice as common among women as men: M. Olfson, M. King, and M. Schoenbaum, "Benzodiazepine use in the United States," *JAMA Psychiatry* 72, no. 2 (2015): 136–42, doi:10.1001/jamapsychiatry.2014.1763.

158 pose risks of bone fractures and cognitive decline: Ibid.

158 total quantity of benzodiazepine prescriptions filled tripled: M. A. Bachhuber, S. Hennessy, C. O. Cunningham, and J. L. Starrels, "Increasing benzodiazepine prescriptions and overdose mortality in the United States, 1996–2013," *American Journal of Public Health Research* 106, no. 4 (2016): 686–88, doi:10.2105 /AJPH.2016.303061.

158 discontinuation after just three or four weeks: J. Brett and B. Murion, "Management of benzodiazepine misuse and dependence," *Australian Prescriber* 38, no. 5 (2015): 152–55, doi:10.18773/austprescr.2015.055.

159 "on our way to the finish line": A. Tone, *The Age of Anxiety: A History of America's Turbulent Affair with Tranquilizers* (New York: Basic Books, 2009), 232.

161 its new Private Reserve Vintner Dinner: Accessed August 22, 2016, http://wine train.rezgo.com/details/103164/private-reserve-dinner-series-raymond-vineyards.

161 a form of emotionality called *communitas*: Illouz, *Consuming the Romantic Utopia*, 143.

Chapter 7—Money: The Knife in the Drawer

165 "There's a high percentage of people who don't deal with money": K. Mitchell, interview, August 9, 2016.

165 Bay Area "money coach": D. Price, *Money Magic* (Novato, CA: New World Library, 2003); D. Price, interview, September 8, 2016.

166 **couples that have high levels of debt:** E. Dunn and M. Norton, *Happy Money: The Science of Smarter Spending* (New York: Simon & Schuster, 2013), 95.

166 **A quarter of those seeking divorce:** Austin Institute for the Study of Family and Culture, "Relationships in America" (2014).

167 **"one house, one spouse" rule:** L. Weston, "Secrets of next-door millionaires," nerdwallet.com, August 26, 2016, https://www.nerdwallet.com/blog/investing /secrets-of-next-door-millionaires/?wpmm=1andwpisrc=nl_finance.

171 **commercial underpinnings are not entirely comfortable:** See I. Hoffman, *Ritual and Spontaneity in the Psychoanalytic Process* (New York: Routledge, 2001), xix.

171 **Marriage is an "I-Thou" relationship:** M. Buber, *I and Thou* (New York: Touchstone, 1971).

175 **to be intimate with another person:** Fisher, *Uninvited Guest,* 43.

178 **"tolerat[ing] the truth of another's experience":** Ibid., 56. Fisher refers to this as a "major developmental achievement."

179 **contribute to both lower marriage rates and higher divorce rates:** B. Stevenson and J. Wolfers, "Marriage and divorce: Changes and their driving forces," Working Paper 19244, National Bureau of Economic Research (2007), 10, http://www .nber.org/papers/w12944.

179 **Wealth inequality in the United States has skyrocketed:** E. J. Finkel, C. M. Hui, K. L. Carswell, and G. M. Larson, "The suffocation of marriage: Climbing Mount Maslow without enough oxygen," *Psychological Inquiry* 25 (2014): 35.

179 **weaken the stability and quality of marriages:** R. D. Conger, K. J. Conger, and M. J. Martin, "Socioeconomic status, family process, and individual development," *Journal of Marriage and the Family* 72, no. 3 (2010): 685–704.

179 **the white-picket-fence dream of marriage:** National Marriage Project, *State of Our Unions, 2010.*

179 **Americans from across different wealth, ethnic, and age categories continue to highly value marriage:** Finkel et al., "Suffocation of marriage," 6; G. R. Lee, *The Limits of Marriage: Why Getting Everyone Married Won't Solve Our Problems* (Lanham, MD: Lexington Books, 2015), 124–25; Coontz, *Marriage, a History,* 278.

180 **maintaining flexibility in partner arrangements:** Lee, *Limits of Marriage,* 169–70.

180 **prompts doubts and anxieties:** K. K. Charles and M. Stephens, "Disability, job displacement and divorce," *Journal of Labor Economics* 22, no. 2 (2004): 489–523.

180 **marital dissatisfaction in our era:** Finkel et al., "Suffocation of marriage."

181 **receive in another (imagined or real) relationship:** Gottman, *Science of Trust,* 337, 453.

181 **Spouses will have different bargaining positions:** See L. Cohen, "Marriage, divorce, and quasi-rents: Or, 'I gave him the best years of my life,'" *Journal of Legal Studies* 16, no. 2 (1987): 267–303.

182 **through a custody arrangement' that favors her:** M. F. Brinig and D. W. Allen, "'These boots are made for walking': Why most divorce filers are women," *American Law and Economics Review* 2, no. 1 (2000): 130.

182 **women file for divorce roughly two-thirds of the time:** Austin Institute, "Relationships in America."

182 **if they feel trust eroded early on:** Brinig and Allen, "'These boots are made for walking,'" 134.

182 **husbands' lack of full-time employment:** A. Killewald, "Money, work, and marital stability: Assessing change in gendered determinants of divorce," *American Sociological Review* 81, no. 4 (2016): 696–719, doi:10.1177/0003122416655340.

183 **sexual problems in a marriage, as well as physical violence:** Hetherington and Kelly, *For Better or Worse,* 35–36.

184 **"at the expense of family time and group needs":** A. Lareau, *Unequal Childhoods: Class, Race, and Family Life* (Berkeley: University of California Press, 2003), 39.

184 the well-known "time famine" that sociologists have long decried: See, for example, A. R. Hochschild, *The Time Bind* (New York: Holt, 1997); J. Schor, *The Overworked American* (New York: Basic Books, 1991).

185 feed into subjective feelings of marital dissatisfaction: See, for instance, Buck and Neff, "Stress spillover in early marriage."

185 "allow people of all ages more options": Carstensen, *Long Bright Future*, 68–69.

186 "to try to get the people of the world's rich countries": "How to be happy, rich, and save the world," mrmoneymustache.com, October 10, 2016, http://www.mrmoneymustache.com/2016/10/10/how-to-be-happy-rich-and-save-the-world/.

186 "the power of now": Dunn and Norton, *Happy Money*, 90.

186 "Past You gave Present You the shaft": "Are you giving the shaft to your future self?," mrmoneymustache.com, November 11, 2014, http://www.mrmoney mustache.com/2014/11/11/are-you-giving-the-shaft-to-your-future-self/.

187 "It was that dollar blown long ago": Ibid.

194 as a corrective to their own: S. I. Rick, D. A. Small, and E. J. Finkel, "Fatal (fiscal) attraction: Spendthrifts and tightwads in marriage," *Journal of Marketing Research* 48, no. 2 (2011): 228–37.

195 locate the pain of reality in the failings of a spouse: Fisher, *Uninvited Guest*, 105.

Chapter 8—Lovesickness and Longing: Putting Them to Use

199 "nature has bred philandering into our genes": J. Holland, *Moody Bitches* (New York: Penguin Press, 2015), 87.

199 "high testosterone levels": Ibid., 129.

199 the intense cravings of love and cocaine: B. P. Acevedo and A. P. Aron, "Romantic love, pair-bonding, and the dopaminergic reward system," in *Mechanisms of Social Connection: From Brain to Group*, ed. M. Mikulincer and P. R. Shaver (Washington, DC: American Psychological Association, 2014).

199 to fall in love again every four years: Fisher, *Why We Love*, 134–35.

199 garner resources by confusing men about their paternity: H. Fisher, *Anatomy of Love* (New York: Fawcett, 1992), 91–93.

200 focused on partners who couldn't love them back: P. Mellody, *Facing Love Addiction* (New York: Harper Collins, 2003).

201 "people's diminished capacity to regulate their thoughts, feelings, and actions": R. F. Baumeister and J. Tierney, *Willpower* (New York: Penguin, 2011), 28.

201 "how one thinks about the problem at hand or distracting oneself": Ibid., 130–31.

203 dangers and allures of romantic passion: R. May, *Love and Will* (New York: Norton, 1969), 146; D. de Rougemont, *Love in the Western World* (Princeton, NJ: Princeton University Press, 1940).

203 "with the doctor who is analysing her": S. Freud, "Observations on Transference-Love" (1915), in *The Standard Edition of the Complete Psychological Works of Sigmund Freud*, ed. J. Strachey (London: Hogarth Press, 1962), 12:159.

203 "what is essential about being in love": Ibid., 12:168–69.

204 Love relationships enable the imaginative reorganization of self: My description is indebted to Hans Loewald and Jonathan Lear, specifically H. Loewald, "Transference and love," in "Psychoanalysis and the history of the individual," in *Essential Loewald*, 562; and J. Lear, *Therapeutic Action* (New York: Other Press, 2003), 168.

205 weaving a new story feels like growth and personal evolution: R. Stein, "The otherness of sexuality: Excess," *Journal of the American Psychoanalytic Association* 56 (2008): 57.

205 accepting chaos while not being broken by it: See Ruti, *Singularity of Being*, 35.

205 an article by the French Canadian psychoanalyst Allannah Furlong: A. Furlong, "Meditation of lovesickness, loss, and temporality," *Journal of the American Psychoanalytic Association* 75 (2009): 1072.

206 "inordinate arousal that makes one feel it cannot be encompassed": Stein, "Otherness of sexuality," 44.

206 "grasp the elusive, ineffable quality of the sexual other": Ibid., 45.

206 our sexuality is built up through our "translating" these not-wholly-translatable messages: The view of Jean Laplanche, as discussed in R. Stein, "The enigmatic dimension of sexual experience: The 'otherness' of sexuality and primal seduction," *Psychoanalytic Quarterly* 67 (1998): 594–625.

207 validate each other's excitement: Stein, "Otherness of sexuality," 65.

207 how our states of physiological arousal: For a classic study, see D. G. Dutton and A. P. Aron, "Some evidence for heightened sexual attraction under conditions of high anxiety," *Journal of Personality and Social Psychology* 30 (1974): 510–17.

207 over the subsequent hours and days: J. Bowers and H. Sivers, "Cognitive impact of traumatic events," *Development and Psychopathology* 10 (1998): 625–54. Quoted in Siegel, *Developing Mind*, 75.

211 "Gerber folding knife and several other items": https://en.wikipedia.org/wiki/Lisa_Nowak.

211 "do severe bodily harm or death": "Astronaut charged with attempted murder," *New York Times*, February 6, 2007, http://nyti.ms/1OYQJmu.

211 "absolute fabrication": "Lawyer: Ex-astronaut didn't wear diaper," accessed July 18, 2016, http://www.nbcnews.com/id/19508417/#.V40OMVc0mCQ.

213 it is a *real* pressure, exerted through genuine, if subtle, interactions: T. Ogden, "On projective identification," *International Journal of Psychoanalysis* 60 (1979): 359.

Chapter 9—Body, Health, and Age: The Stakes Only Get Higher

227 "a vague eeriness": J. Choo and G. O'Daniel, "The uncanny valley: Implications for facial plastic surgery," *Aesthetic Surgery Journal* 36, no. 1 (2016): NP28–NP29, doi.org/10.1093/asj/sjv179.

227 an "operated-on" look: Ibid.

227 facial changes make for category "uncertainty": J. Choo and G. O'Daniel, "Sensitivity to the uncanny valley in facial plastic surgery," *Interaction Studies* 16, no. 2 (2015): 215–18.

227 share emotion through micromimicking: D. T. Neal and T. L. Chartrand, "Embodied emotion perception: Amplifying and dampening facial feedback modulates emotion perception accuracy," *Social Psychological and Personality Science* 2, no. 6 (2011): 673–78.

228 "I don't want to do them without knowing why": K. Shinkai, interview, November 15, 2015.

228 "'I feel young but I look old' is the chronic lament": V. L. Blum, *Flesh Wounds* (Berkeley: University of California Press, 2003), 162.

228 we regard ourselves as never changing: A. Balfour, "Growing old together in mind and body," *fort da* 21, no. 2 (2015): 53–76.

231 As Mitch's sexual responsiveness slowed: J. H. J. Bancroft, "Sex and aging," *New England Journal of Medicine* 357 (2007): 820–22; S. B. Levine, *Sexuality in Mid-Life* (New York: Plenum Press, 1998), chap. 6.

231 even at risk of giving up on it: Metz and McCarthy, *Enduring Desire*, 202.

231 "ideal" model of heterosexual sex: A. C. Lodge and D. Umberson, "All shook up: Sexuality of mid- to later-life married couples," *Journal of Marriage and Family* 74, no. 3 (2012): 428–43, doi:10.1111/j.1741-3737.2012.00969.x.

232 more pronounced in the forties and fifties: Ibid.

232 sex continues to be an important part of relationship satisfaction: J. R. Heiman,

J. S. Long, S. N. Smith, W. A. Fisher, M. S. Sand, and R. C. Rosen, "Sexual satisfaction and relationship happiness in midlife and older couples in five countries," *Archives of Sexual Behavior* 40 (2011): 741–53, doi:10.1007/s10508-101-9703-3.

232 **80 percent of men and 75 percent of women consider sex important:** O. Kontula and E. Haavio-Mannila, "The impact of aging on human sexual activity and sexual desire," *Journal of Sex Research* 46, no. 1 (2009): 46–56.

232 **The frequency of sex decreases with age:** Ibid., 46.

232 **satisfaction with their sexual relationship tends to lead couples to be happy in their marriage:** H.-C. Yeh, F. O. Lorenz, K. A. S. Wickrama, R. D. Conger, and G. H. Elder, "Relationships among sexual satisfaction, marital quality, and marital instability at midlife," *Journal of Family Psychology* 20, no. 2 (2006): 339–43.

233 **When partners operate as an intimate team:** McCarthy, interview.

233 **get aroused in three ways:** Metz and McCarthy, *Enduring Desire*, esp. chap. 10.

233 **14 million yoga practitioners over the age of fifty:** 2016 Yoga in America Study, https://www.yogaalliance.org/Portals/0/2016%20Yoga%20in%20America%20Study%20RESULTS.pdf

237 **the effect of "the change" on women's psyches:** See, for example, C. Northrup, *The Wisdom of Menopause* (New York: Bantam, 2012).

237 **"tend and befriend" hormones:** S. E. Taylor, "Tend and befriend theory," in *Handbook of Theories of Social Psychology*, ed. P. A. M. Van Lange, A. W. Kruglanski, and E. T. Higgins (Thousand Oaks, CA: Sage, 2011), 32–49; Holland, *Moody Bitches*, 21–22.

238 **"What is it about my life that isn't working?":** L. Brizendine, *The Female Brain* (New York: Morgan Road Books, 2006), 136.

239 **"moody bitch":** Holland, *Moody Bitches*.

240 **can aim for a pragmatic compromise:** L. Brizendine, interview, December 28, 2015.

240 **"You'll have to ask someone else, I'm only sixty":** Quoted in J. Mitchell, "The difference between gender and sexual difference," in ed. I Matthis, *Dialogues on Sexuality, Gender, and Psychoanalysis* (London: Karnac, 2004), 74.

240 **"There's just enough time to have one more baby":** Holland, *Moody Bitches*, 174.

241 **resulting in weeks of the menstrual cycle when hormone levels surge:** Brizendine, interview.

243 **high cholesterol and insulin resistance:** C. Bouchez, "Better sex: What's weight got to do with it?," webmd.com, accessed February 22, 2017, http://www.webmd.com/sex-relationships/features/sex-and-weight?

243 **help them chart a course for dealing with their sexual issues:** M. E. Metz and B. McCarthy, *Coping with Erectile Dysfunction* (Oakland, CA: New Harbinger, 2004); B. McCarthy and E. McCarthy, *Sexual Awareness* (New York: Routledge, 2012).

246 **declarations that they *just aren't attracted anymore*:** See, for example, "If my wife won't lose weight, am I justified in leaving her?," goodtherapy.org, accessed October 31, 2016, http://www.goodtherapy.org/blog/dear-gt/if-my-wife-wont-lose-weight-am-i-justified-in-leaving-her?replytocom=389522#respondForm; E. North, "I'm not attracted to my wife anymore. And I'm ashamed of the reason," mamamia.com, August 14, 2015, http://www.mamamia.com.au/not-attracted-to-wife/.

246 **The "lack of respect" model conveys real pain:** See, for example, E. Redding, "18 people talk about what it's like when your spouse gets fat but you don't," thoughtcatalog.com, July 1, 2015, http://tcat.tc/1RSTcfJ.

246 **"no matter how much he complained or shared his feelings with Jeana":** C. Turner, *Gain Weight, Lose Your Mate* (Bloomington, IN: Xlibris, 2011), 26.

246 **the empirical evidence that self-help is often insufficient:** G. Kolata, "Many wrong on causes of obesity, study finds," *New York Times*, November 1, 2016, A12, A14.

253 **"third person in the marriage—one with demands, desires, and a disposition all its own":** A. Paturel, "Sex, love, and multiple sclerosis," *Neurology Now* 3, no. 3 (2007): 34–37, http://patients.aan.com/resources/neurologynow/?event=home .showArticleandid=ovid.com:/bib/ovftdb/01222928-200703030-00024.

253 **"They are people you'd want to marry":** Wile, *After the Honeymoon*, 65.

254 **"its exquisite individuality, character, and beauty":** P. A. Levine, *Waking the Tiger—Healing Trauma* (Berkeley, CA: North Atlantic Books, 1997), 33.

254 **"even if it's only now and again?":** N. Hornby, "Rock of Ages," *New York Times*, May 21, 2004, http://nyti.ms/1IK4aWd.

Chapter 10—The Empty Nest: Children, Parents, and the Turning of the Generations

260 *Gray divorce* **refers to the trend of people over fifty leaving their marriages:** S. L. Brown and I.-F. Lin, "The gray divorce revolution: Rising divorce among middle-aged and older adults, 1990–2010," *Journals of Gerontology, Series B: Psychological Sciences and Social Sciences* 67, no. 6 (2012): 731–41.

262 **"to creative scientific work":** D. W. Winnicott, "Transitional objects and transitional phenomena," in *Playing and Reality* (New York: Tavistock, 1971), 14.

262 **reliably** *present* **in the background:** Winnicott, "Playing: A theoretical statement," in ibid., 47–48.

263 **sense of guilt arose from their** *subjective worry*: M. E. Nagy and J. A. Theiss, "Applying the relational turbulence model to the empty-nest transition: Sources of relationship change, relational uncertainty, and interference from partners," *Journal of Family Communications* 13 (2013): 296.

264 **more privacy, more freedom, and more fun:** Ibid., 288.

264 **involve risk-taking and self-disclosure:** A.A. Aron, C.C. Norman, E.N. Aron, C. McKenna, and R.E. Heyman, "Couples' shared participation in novel and arousing activities and experienced relationship quality," *Journal of Personality and Social Psychology* 78, no. 2 (2000): 282.

265 **"alone is in itself an experience of health":** D. W. Winnicott, "The capacity to be alone," *International Journal of Psychoanalysis* 39 (1958): 417.

265 **being together in a state of trust is possible:** Ibid., 417. See also E. H. Schein, *Helping* (San Francisco: Berrett-Koehler, 2009).

266 **"great predicaments":** Gottschall, *Storytelling Animal*, 55.

266 **They can leave things unsaid:** J. Friend, "Love as Creative Illusion and Its Place in Psychoanalytic Couple Therapy," *Couple and Family Psychoanalysis* 31 (2013): 13.

266 **Karen Skerrett and I talked about this issue:** K. Skerrett, interview, January 5, 2016.

269 **Research suggests that people recover best from the death of a parent:** D. Umberson, *Death of a Parent: Transition to a New Adult Identity* (Cambridge, UK: Cambridge University Press, 2003).

272 **but appears to relate to greater health and longer life:** T. L. Gruenwald, D. H. Liao, and T. E. Seeman, "Contributing to others, contributing to oneself: Perceptions of generativity and health in later life," *Journals of Gerontology, Series B: Psychological Sciences and Social Sciences* 67, no. 6 (2012): 660–65.

274 **"lights go out":** Levenson, interview.

274 **skill of reducing their negative interactions:** J. C. Yuan, M. McCarthy, S. R. Holley, and R. W. Levenson, "Physiological down-regulation and positive emotion in marital interaction," *Emotion* 10, no. 4 (2010): 467–74.

275 **psychological research has helped shift our paradigm of later life:** L. L. Carstensen, B. Turan, S. Scheibe, N. Ram, H. Ersner-Hershfield, G. R. Samanez-Larkin, K. P. Brooks, and J. R. Nesselroade, "Emotional experience improves with age: Evidence based on over 10 years of experience sampling," *Psychology and Aging* 26, no. 1 (2011): 21–33.

275 "joyous and never-ending design project of building your way forward": B. Burnett and D. Evans, *Designing Your Life* (New York: Knopf, 2016), 219.

Chapter 11—Staying or Leaving

278 fails to respond to the other at a critical moment of vulnerability or need: J. A. Makinen and S. M. Johnson, "Resolving attachment injuries in couples using Emotionally-Focused Therapy: Steps toward forgiveness and reconciliation," *Journal of Consulting and Clinical Psychology* 74, no. 6 (2006): 1055–64.

278 a common point of impasse: B. Bradley and J. L. Furrow, "Toward a mini-theory of the blamer softening event: Tracking down moment-by-moment process," *Journal of Marital and Family Therapy* 30, no. 2 (2004): 234.

280 his heartfelt distress were a dart of criticism aimed at her: See, for instance, S. D. Jayamaha, Y. U. Girme, and N. C. Overall, "When attachment anxiety impedes support provision: The role of feeling unvalued and unappreciated," *Journal of Family Psychology* 31, no. 2 (2017): 181.

282 score lower on a number of measures of behavior . . . continuing conflict between parents: P. R. Amato, "Research on divorce: Continuing trends and new developments," *Journal of Marriage and Family* 72 (2010): 650–66.

282 "such as weddings and graduations": Ibid., 656.

282 biggest worry about divorce is not seeing their children: X. P. Montenegro, *The Divorce Experience: A Study of Divorce at Midlife and Beyond* (Washington, DC: AARP, 2004), 24.

283 how divorce affects children has become more nuanced over the years: Amato, "Research on divorce," 653–58.

283 less informative to look at *average* differences between children: Ibid., 661.

283 chronic negativity and conflict contribute the most to poor child outcomes: E. M. Hetherington, M. Bridges, and G. M. Insabella, "What matters? What does not? Five perspectives on the association between marital transitions and children's adjustment," *American Psychologist* 53 (1998): 167–84.

283 higher rates of depression, antisocial behavior, addiction: Ibid., 170.

283 marital conflict has more bearing on children's behavior: E. M. Cummings and P. Davies, *Children and Marital Conflict* (New York: Guilford Press, 1994), 9.

283 how anger is handled: Ibid., chap. 7; J. H. Grych and F. D. Fincham, "Marital conflict and children's adjustment: A cognitive-contextual framework," *Psychological Bulletin* 108, no. 2 (1990): 267–90; R. E. Emergy, *Marriage, Divorce, and Children's Adjustment* (Newbury Park, CA: Sage, 1988).

283 "almost like emotional Geiger counters," and they are exquisitely sensitive: Cummings and Davies, *Children and Marital Conflict*, 134.

284 the difference between destructive and constructive conflict: E. M. Cummings and P. S. Keller, "Marital discord and children's emotional self-regulation," in *Emotion Regulation in Couples and Families: Pathways to Dysfunction and Health*, ed. D. K. Snyder, J. Simpson, and J. N. Hughes (Washington, DC: APA Press, 2006), 163–82.

284 conflict tactics such as calm discussion, affection, and support: E. M. Cummings, M. C. Goeke-Morey, and L. M. Papp, "Children's responses to everyday marital conflict tactics in the home," *Child Development* 74, no. 6 (2003): 1918–29.

284 strategies to regulate their emotions: P. T. Davies, D. Cicchetti, and M. J. Martin, "Toward greater specificity in identifying associations among interparental aggression, child emotional reactivity to conflict, and child problems," *Child Development* 83, no. 5 (2012): 1789–1804.

284 Some become appeasing, some aggressive: P. Davies and M. Martin, "Children's coping and adjustment in high-conflict homes: The reformulation of emotional security theory," *Child Development Perspectives* 8, no. 4 (2014): 242–49.

284 **their uppermost goal at all times is** *security*: E. M. Cummings and P. Davies, *Marital Conflict and Children: An Emotional Security Perspective* (New York: Guilford, 2010).

284 **Breakdown of parents' attentive caregiving:** B. C. Feeney and J. K. Monin, "Divorce through the lens of attachment theory," in *Handbook of Attachment*, 3rd ed., ed. Cassidy and Shaver, 954–55.

284 **to recover quickly from conflict or to let issues go:** M. M. McGinn, P. T. McFarland, and A. Christensen, "Antecedents and consequences of demand/withdraw," *Journal of Family Psychology* 23, no. 5 (2009): 750.

285 **"resolution appears to act as a 'wonder drug'":** Cummings and Davies, *Children and Marital Conflict*, 144–47.

285 **withdrawal and ongoing nonverbal hostility:** Cummings, Goeke-Morey, and Papp, "Children's responses to everyday marital conflict," 1923.

285 **parents sometimes assume they are protecting their children:** Cummings and Keller, "Marital discord and children's emotional self-regulation," 169.

285 **model for their children an unhealthy strategy for coping with feelings:** Cummings and Davies, *Children and Marital Conflict*, 142–43.

285 **when their parents' interactions were** *low* **conflict, rather than high conflict, prior to divorce:** S. R. Braithwaite, R. A. Doxey, K. K. Dowdle, and F. D. Fincham, "The unique influences of parental divorce and parental conflict on emerging adult relationships," *Journal of Adult Development* 23 (2016): 214–25.

285 **Young adults whose parents** *stayed* **in high-conflict marriages expressed** *lower* **commitment:** P. R. Amato and D. D. DeBoer, "The transmission of marital instability across generations: Relationship skills or commitment to marriage?," *Journal of Marriage and Family* 63, no. 4 (2001): 1038–51.

292 **A third of divorcing women in their fifties say:** Montenegro, *Divorce Experience*.

293 **women are more likely to blame:** Ibid.

297 **the first year after a separation:** Hetherington and Kelly, *For Better or Worse*, chap. 3.

298 **your most thoughtful and compassionate approach:** A good resource is J. S. Wallerstein and S. Blakeslee, *What About the Kids? Raising Your Children Before, During, and After Divorce* (New York: Hyperion, 2003).

298 **hellish, protracted custody wars:** M. B. Donner, "Tearing the child apart: The contribution of narcissism, envy, and perverse modes of thought to child custody wars," *Psychoanalytic Psychology* 23 (2006): 542–53.

298 **Constance Ahrons, the author of** *The Good Divorce,* **says yes:** C. Ahrons, *The Good Divorce* (New York: Quill, 1994).

299 **most marital conflicts ended up "unresolved":** McGinn, McFarland, Christensen, "Antecedents and consequences of demand/withdraw," 756.

Chapter 12—Love Is a Conversation

304 **An honest conversation about how alienated you feel:** Wile, *After the Honeymoon*, esp. chap. 2.

308 **A good divorce can be more of a "marriage":** Fisher, *Uninvited Guest*, 2.

Index